D1057844

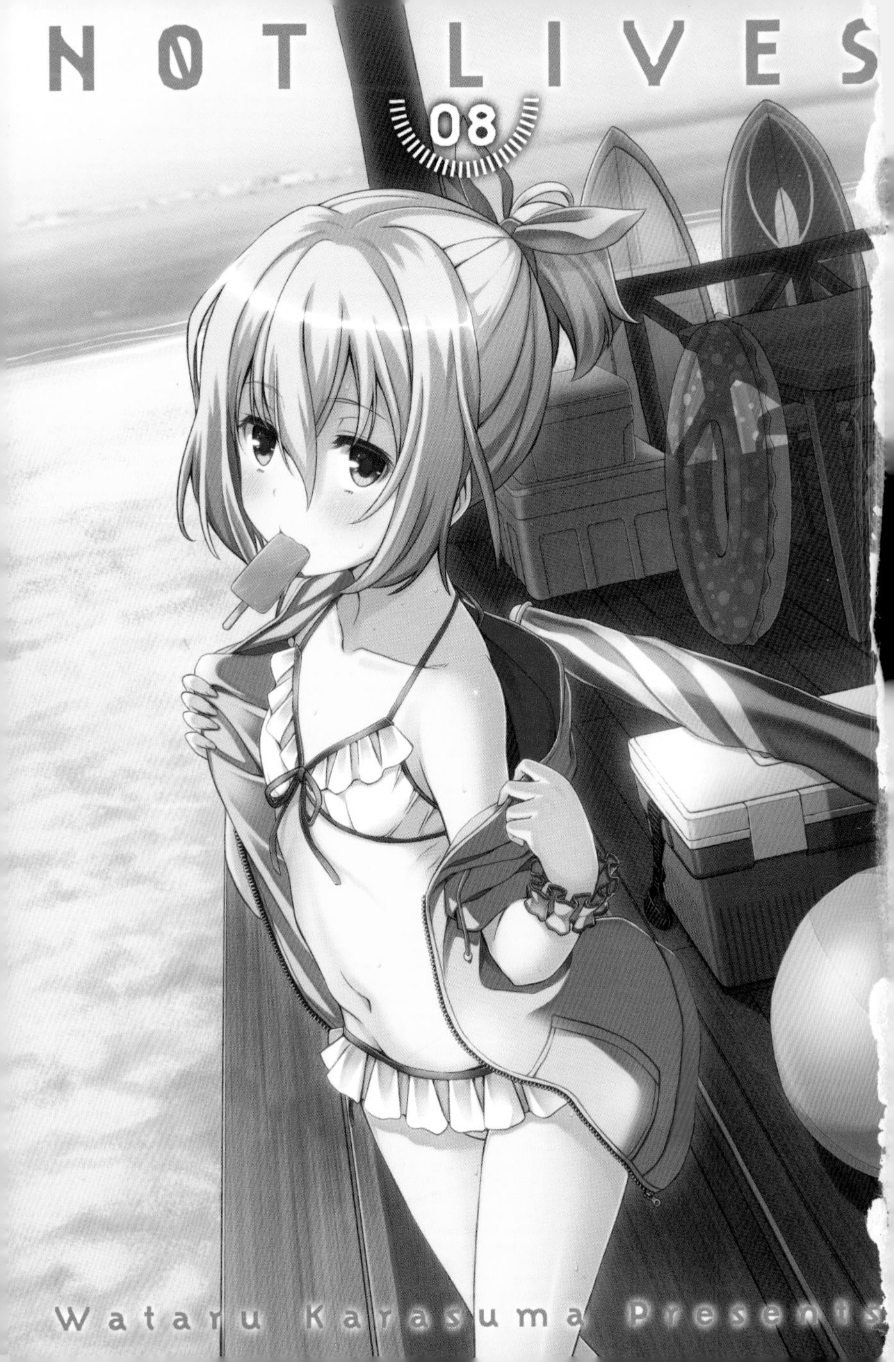
N0T LIVES
08
Wataru Karasuma Presents

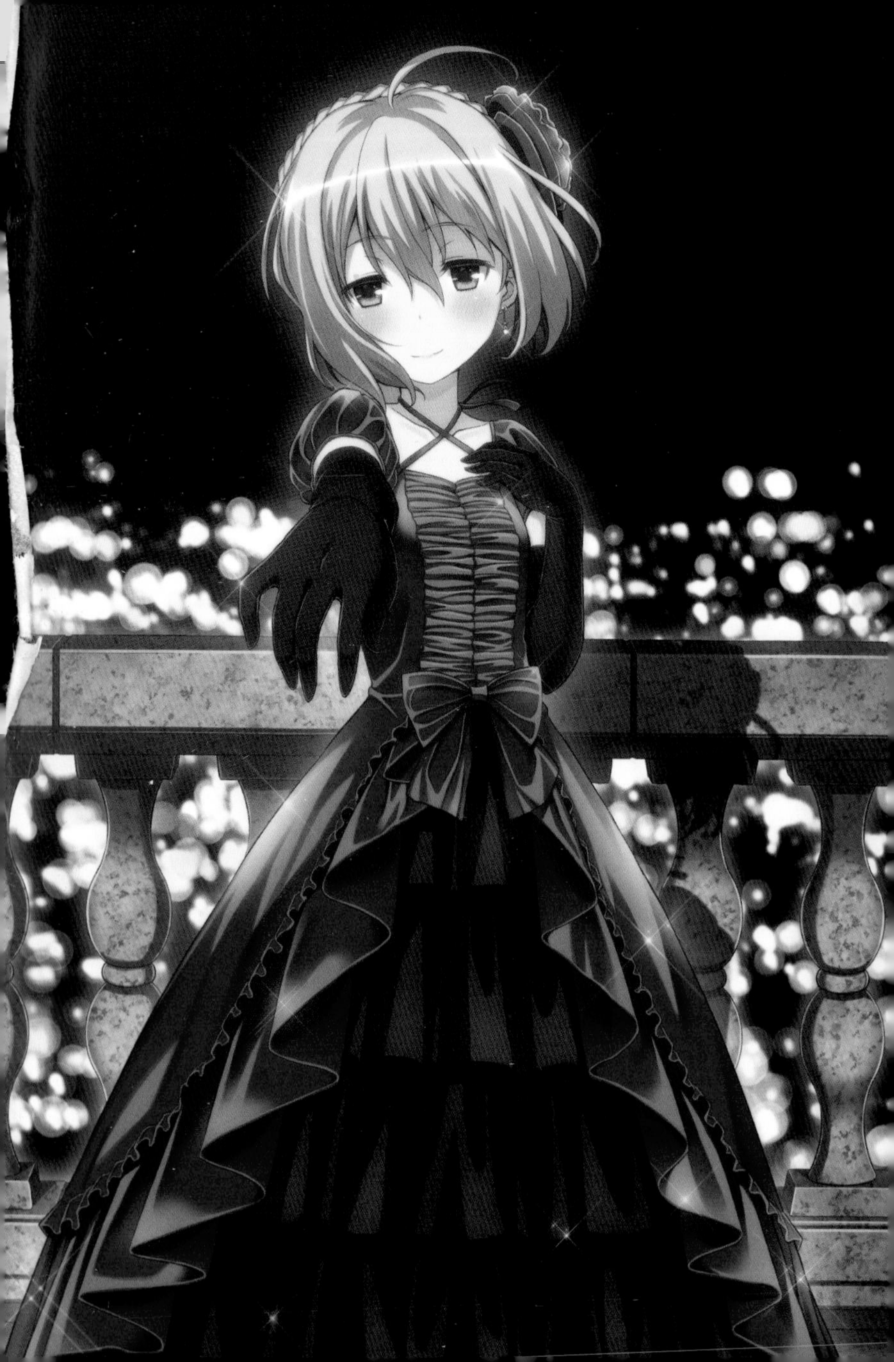

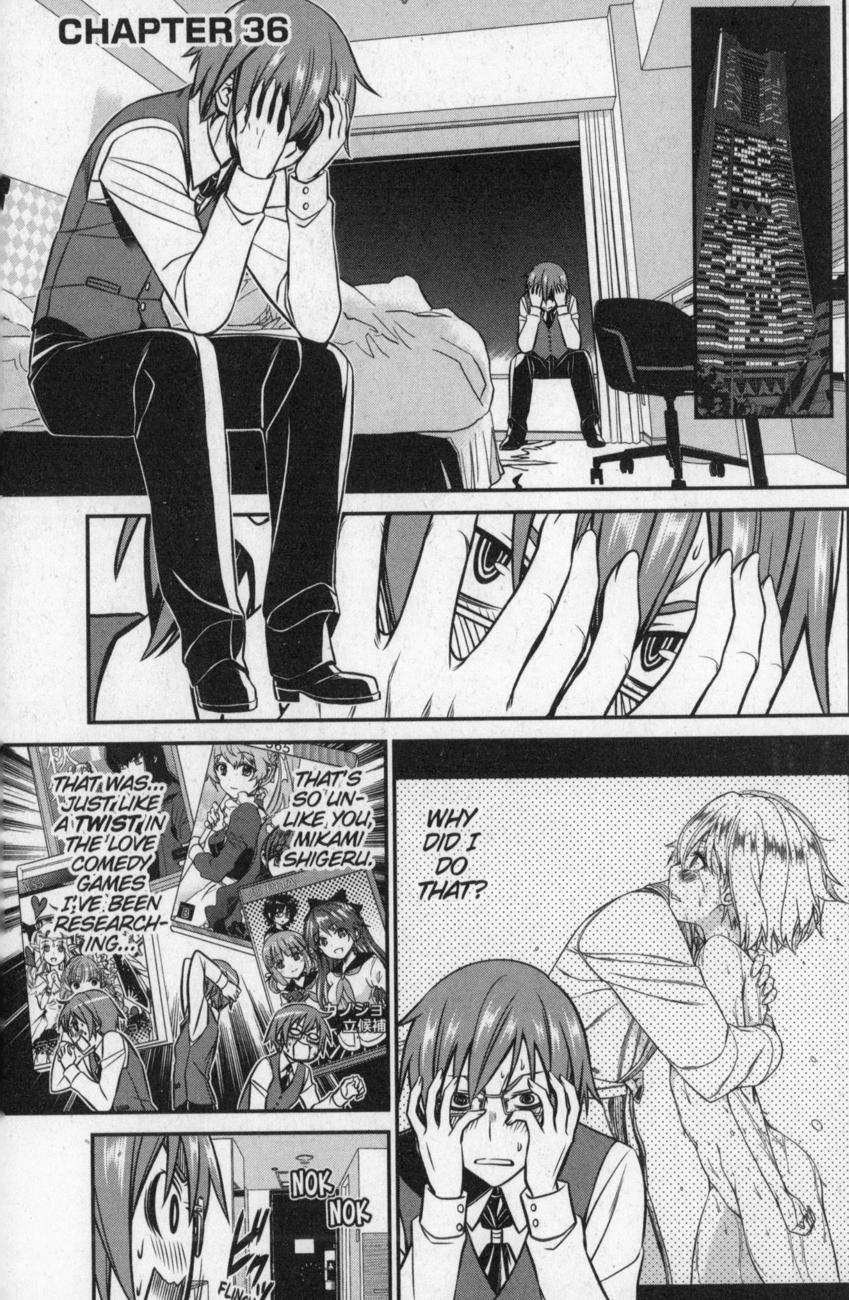
CHAPTER 36
WHY DID I DO THAT?
THAT'S SO UN-LIKE YOU, MIKAMI SHIGERU.
THAT WAS... JUST LIKE A TWIST IN THE LOVE COMEDY GAMES I'VE BEEN RESEARCH-ING...
NOK NOK
FLINCH

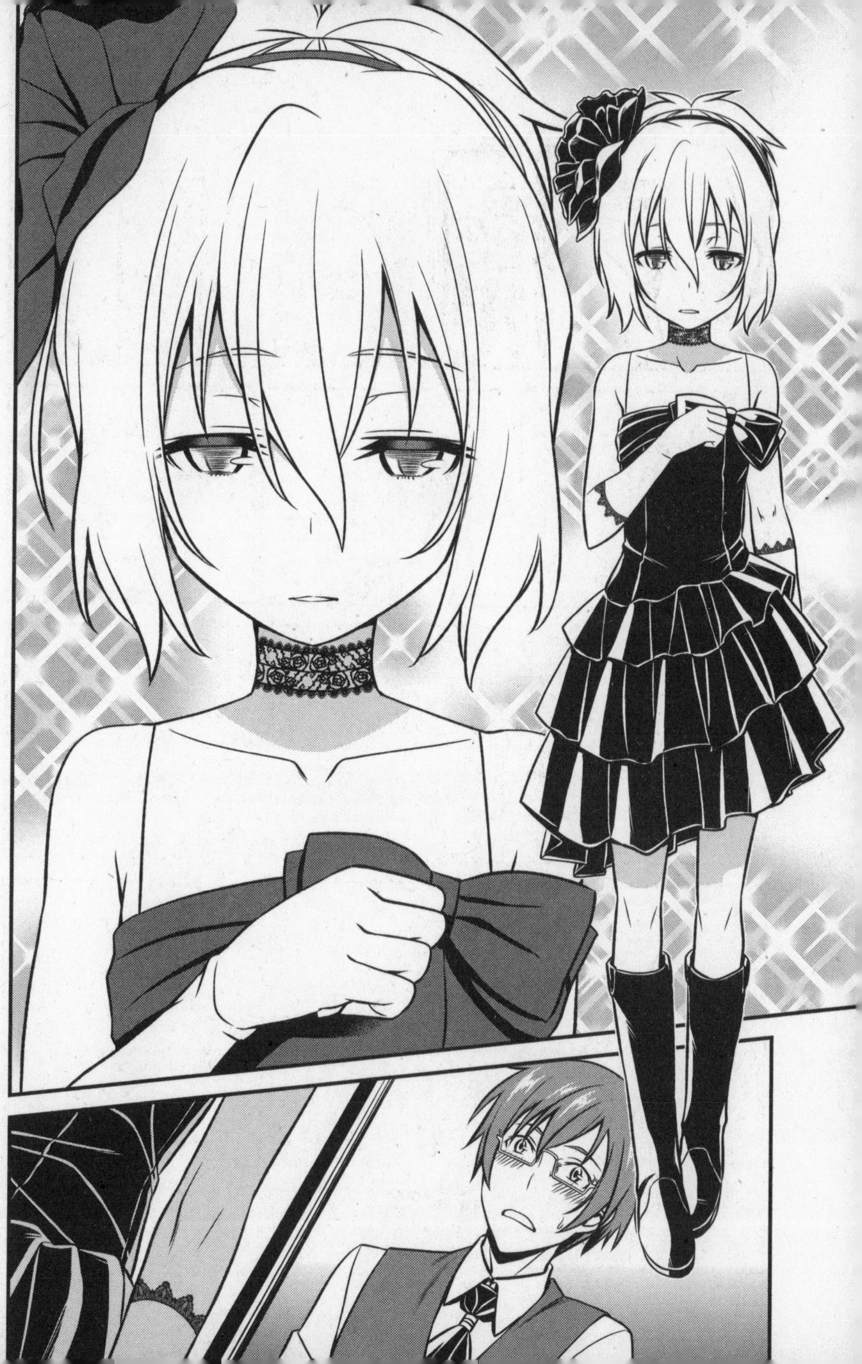

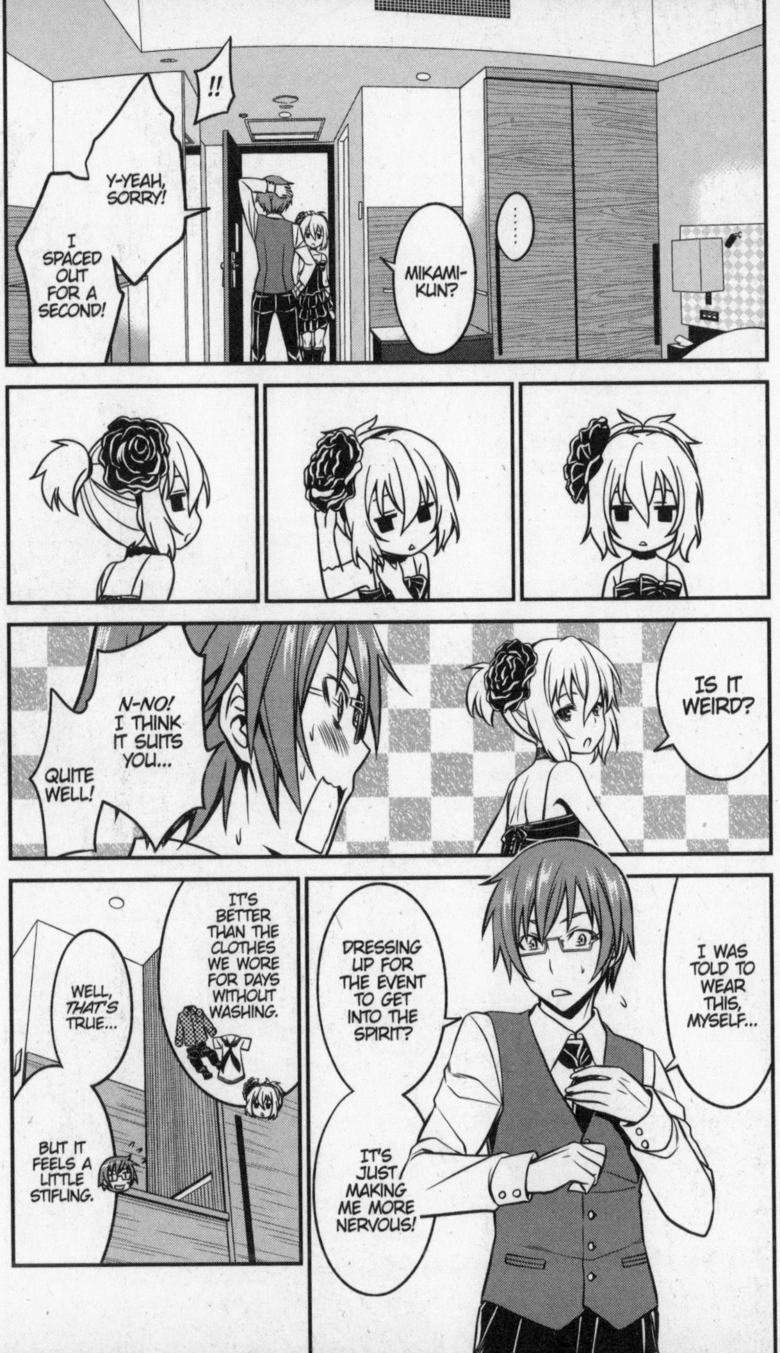
MIKAMI-KUN?
......
!!
Y-YEAH, SORRY!
I SPACED OUT FOR A SECOND!
IS IT WEIRD?
N-NO! I THINK IT SUITS YOU...
QUITE WELL!
I WAS TOLD TO WEAR THIS, MYSELF...
DRESSING UP FOR THE EVENT TO GET INTO THE SPIRIT?
IT'S JUST MAKING ME MORE NERVOUS!
IT'S BETTER THAN THE CLOTHES WE WORE FOR DAYS WITHOUT WASHING.
WELL, *THAT'S* TRUE...
BUT IT FEELS A LITTLE STIFLING.

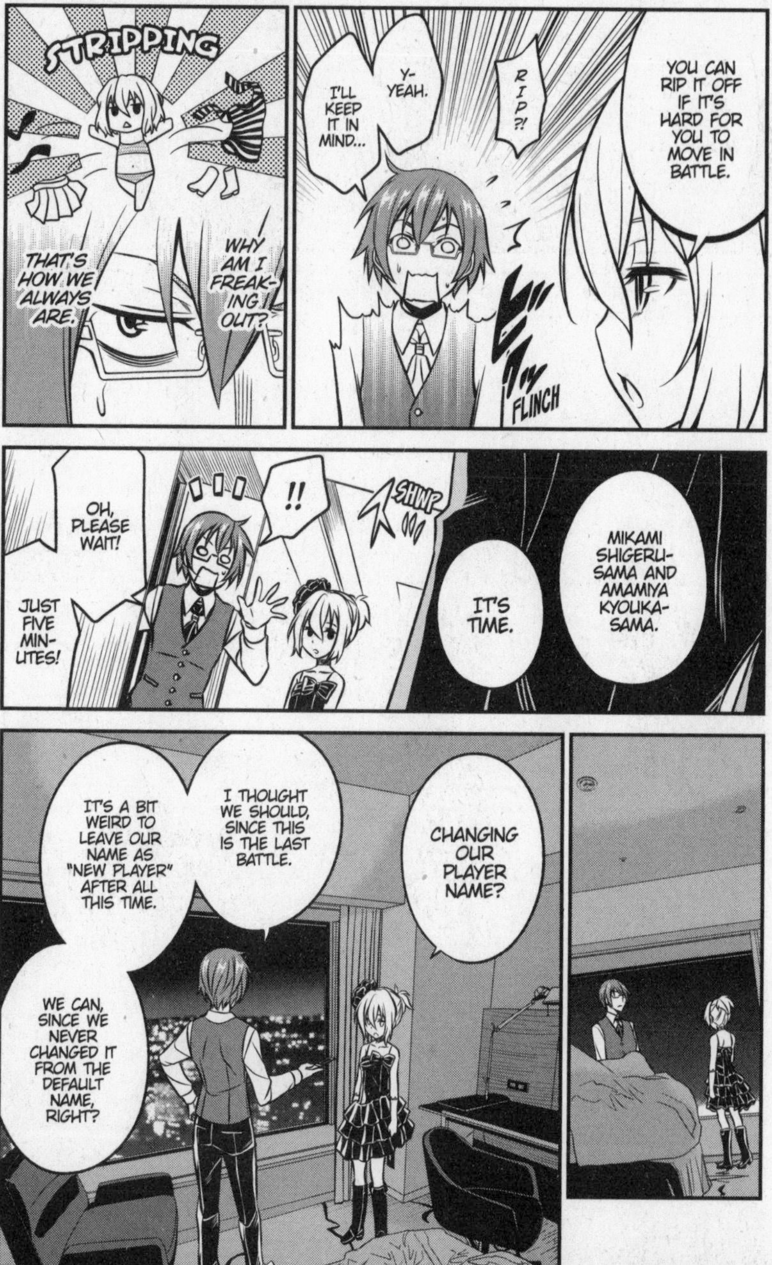
YOU CAN RIP IT OFF IF IT'S HARD FOR YOU TO MOVE IN BATTLE.
FLINCH
RIP?!
Y-YEAH.
I'LL KEEP IT IN MIND...
WHY AM I FREAKING OUT?
THAT'S HOW WE ALWAYS ARE.
STRIPPING
MIKAMI SHIGERU-SAMA AND AMAMIYA KYOUKA-SAMA.
IT'S TIME.
SHWP
!!
OH, PLEASE WAIT!
JUST FIVE MINUTES!
CHANGING OUR PLAYER NAME?
I THOUGHT WE SHOULD, SINCE THIS IS THE LAST BATTLE.
IT'S A BIT WEIRD TO LEAVE OUR NAME AS "NEW PLAYER" AFTER ALL THIS TIME.
WE CAN, SINCE WE NEVER CHANGED IT FROM THE DEFAULT NAME, RIGHT?

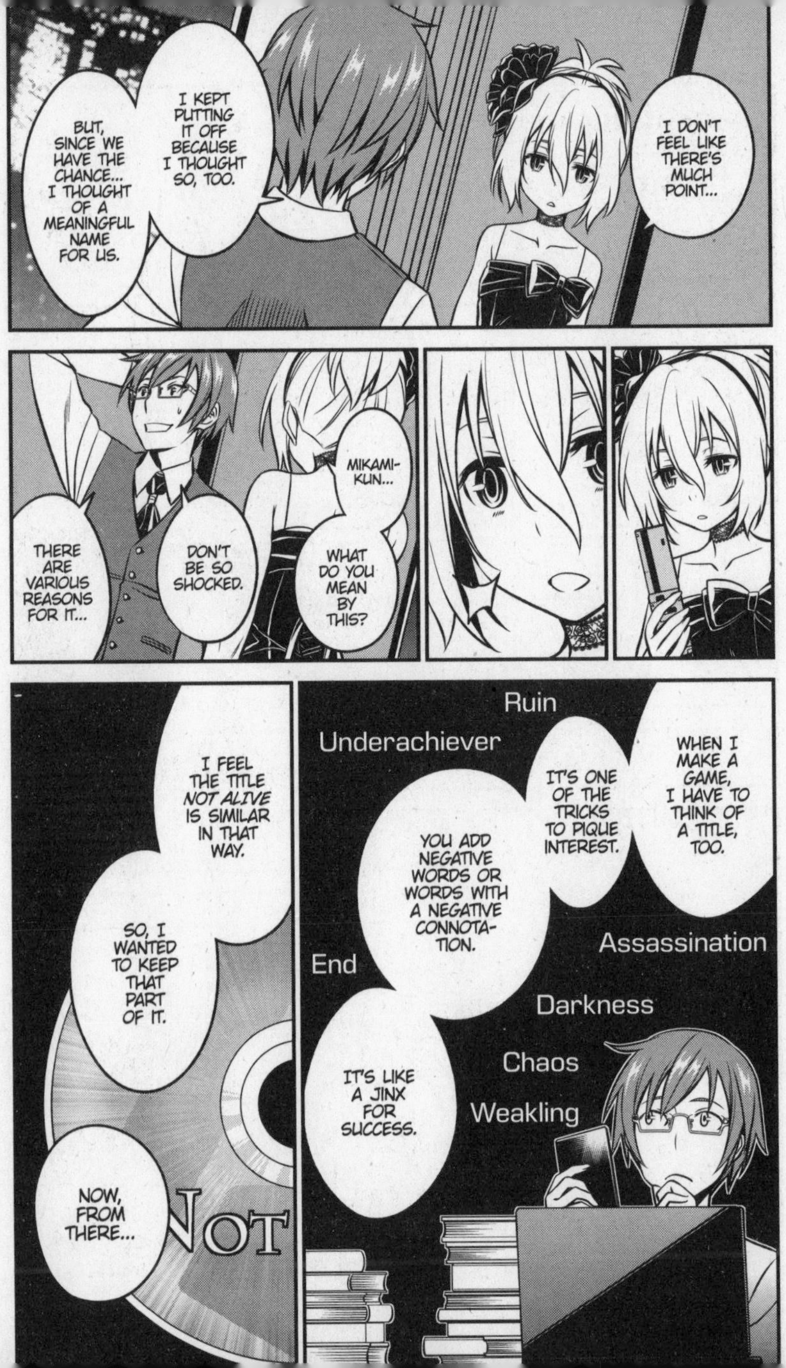
I DON'T FEEL LIKE THERE'S MUCH POINT...
I KEPT PUTTING IT OFF BECAUSE I THOUGHT SO, TOO.
BUT, SINCE WE HAVE THE CHANCE... I THOUGHT OF A MEANINGFUL NAME FOR US.
MIKAMI-KUN...
WHAT DO YOU MEAN BY THIS?
DON'T BE SO SHOCKED.
THERE ARE VARIOUS REASONS FOR IT...
WHEN I MAKE A GAME, I HAVE TO THINK OF A TITLE, TOO.
IT'S ONE OF THE TRICKS TO PIQUE INTEREST.
Ruin
Underachiever
YOU ADD NEGATIVE WORDS OR WORDS WITH A NEGATIVE CONNOTATION.
Assassination
End
Darkness
Chaos
Weakling
IT'S LIKE A JINX FOR SUCCESS.
I FEEL THE TITLE NOT ALIVE IS SIMILAR IN THAT WAY.
SO, I WANTED TO KEEP THAT PART OF IT.
NOT
NOW, FROM THERE...

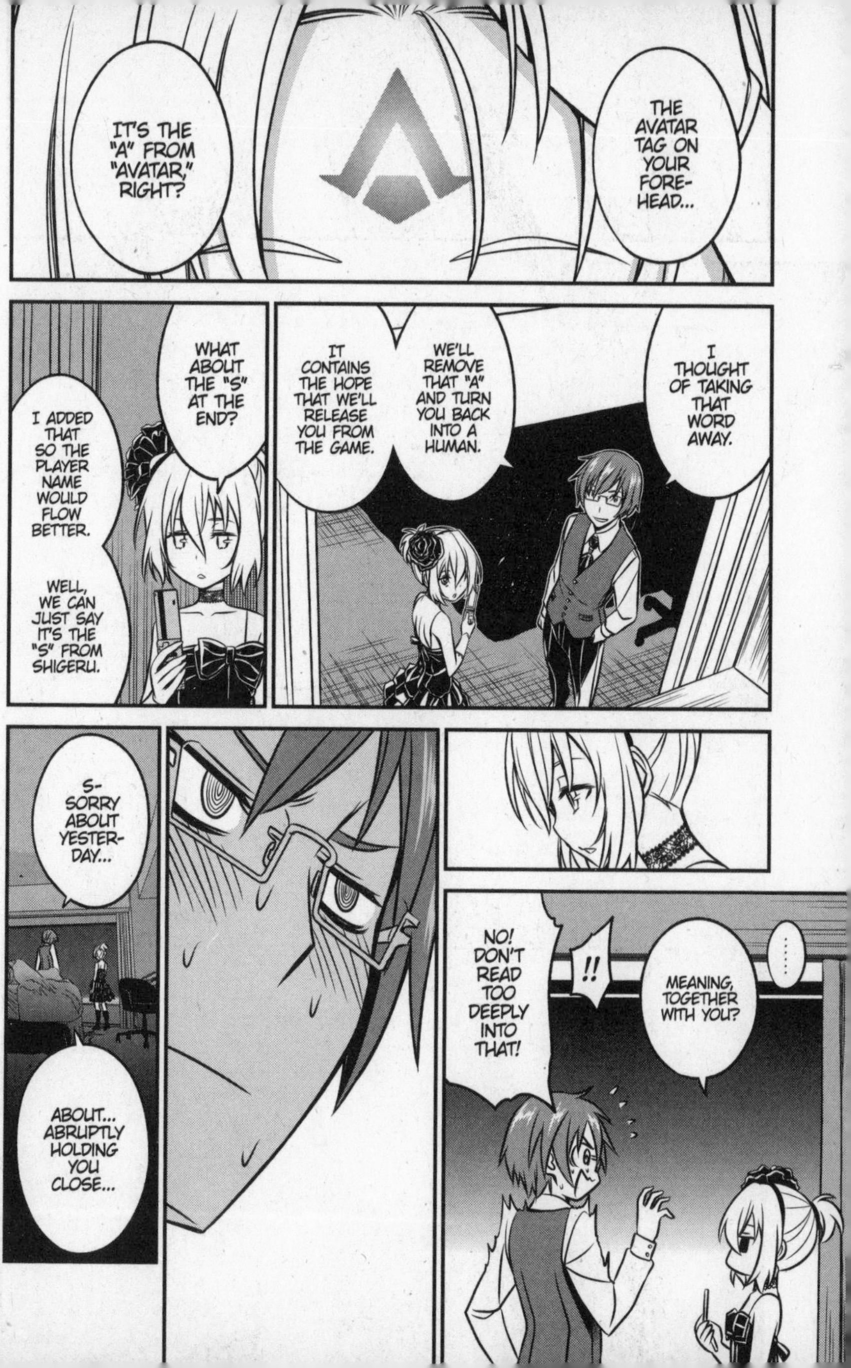
THE AVATAR TAG ON YOUR FORE-HEAD...
IT'S THE "A" FROM "AVATAR," RIGHT?
I THOUGHT OF TAKING THAT WORD AWAY.
WE'LL REMOVE THAT "A" AND TURN YOU BACK INTO A HUMAN.
IT CONTAINS THE HOPE THAT WE'LL RELEASE YOU FROM THE GAME.
WHAT ABOUT THE "S" AT THE END?
I ADDED THAT SO THE PLAYER NAME WOULD FLOW BETTER.
WELL, WE CAN JUST SAY IT'S THE "S" FROM SHIGERU.
......
MEANING, TOGETHER WITH YOU?
!!
NO! DON'T READ TOO DEEPLY INTO THAT!
S-SORRY ABOUT YESTER-DAY...
ABOUT... ABRUPTLY HOLDING YOU CLOSE...

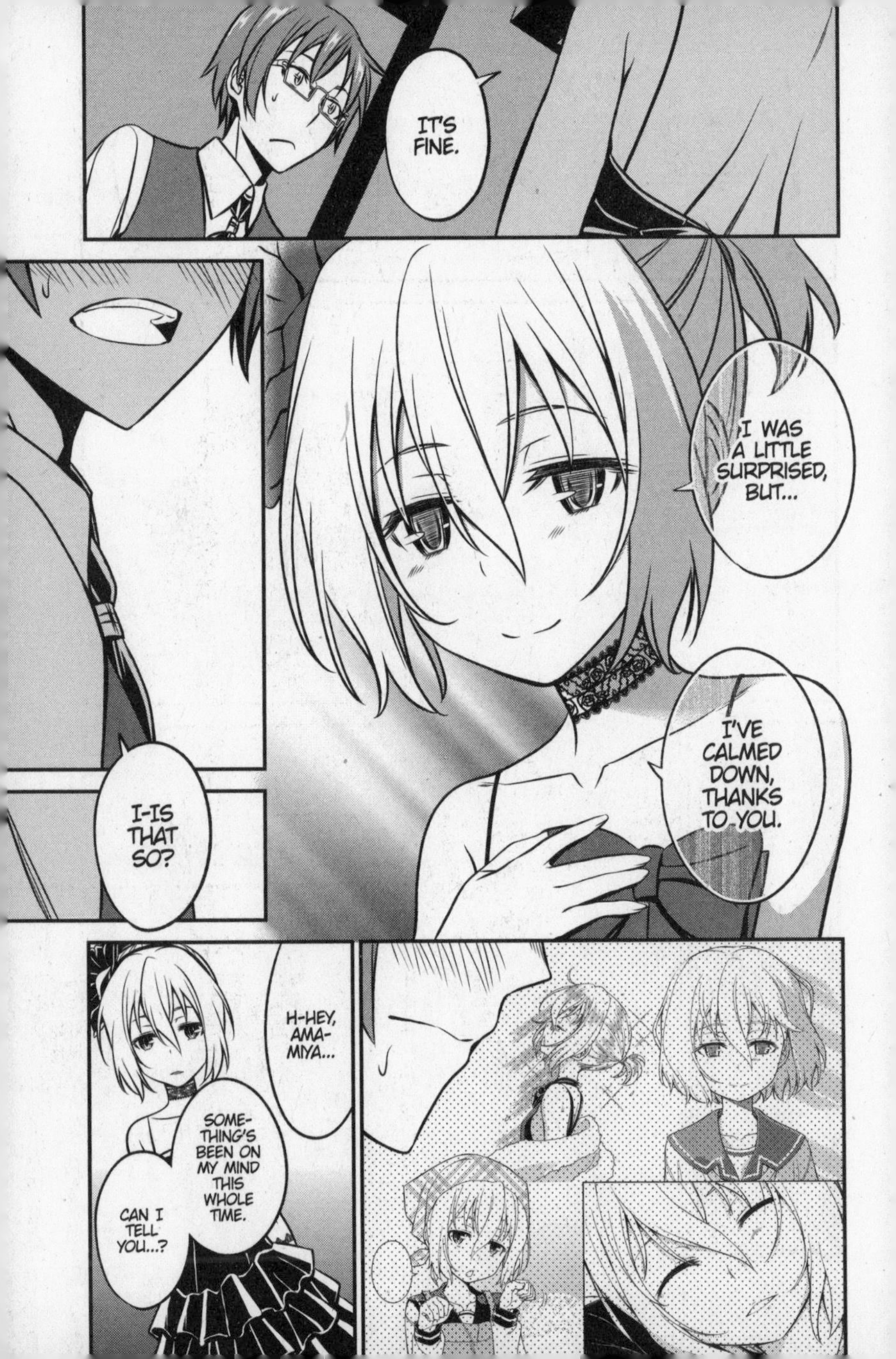
IT'S FINE.
I WAS A LITTLE SURPRISED, BUT...
I'VE CALMED DOWN, THANKS TO YOU.
I-IS THAT SO?
H-HEY, AMA-MIYA...
SOME-THING'S BEEN ON MY MIND THIS WHOLE TIME.
CAN I TELL YOU...?

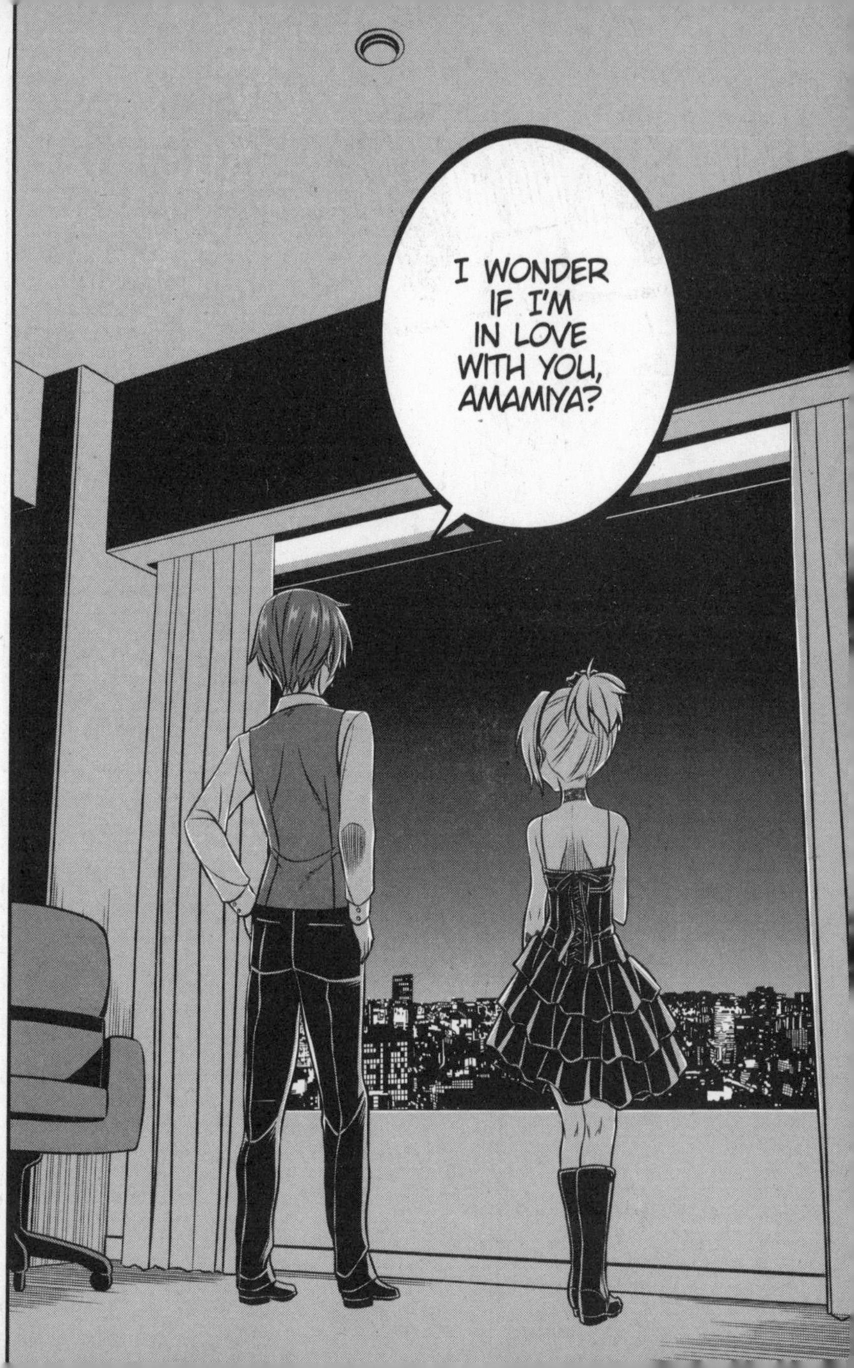
I WONDER IF I'M IN LOVE WITH YOU, AMAMIYA?

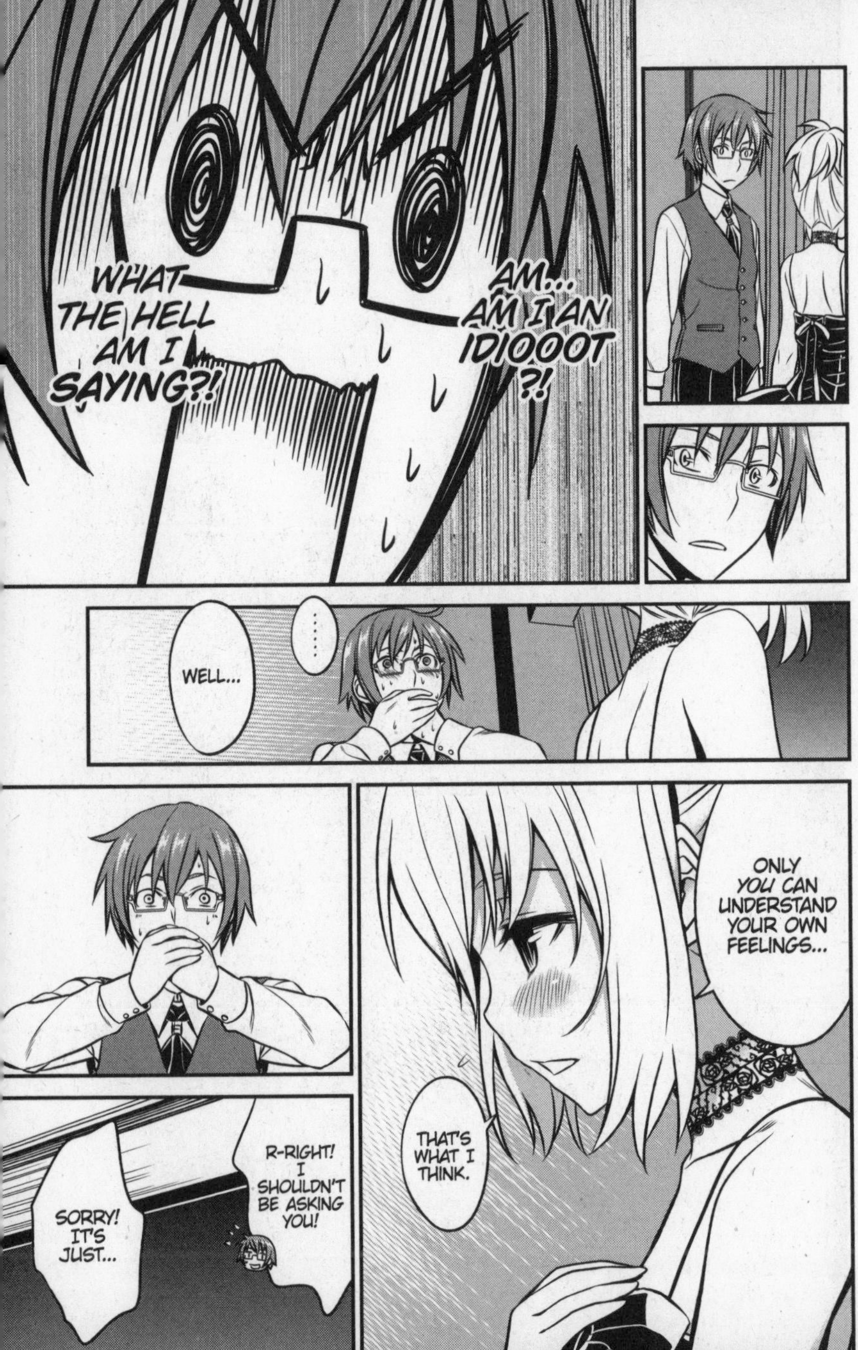
AM... AM I AN IDIOOOT ?!
WHAT THE HELL AM I SAYING?!
......
WELL...
ONLY YOU CAN UNDERSTAND YOUR OWN FEELINGS...
THAT'S WHAT I THINK.
R-RIGHT! I SHOULDN'T BE ASKING YOU!
SORRY! IT'S JUST...

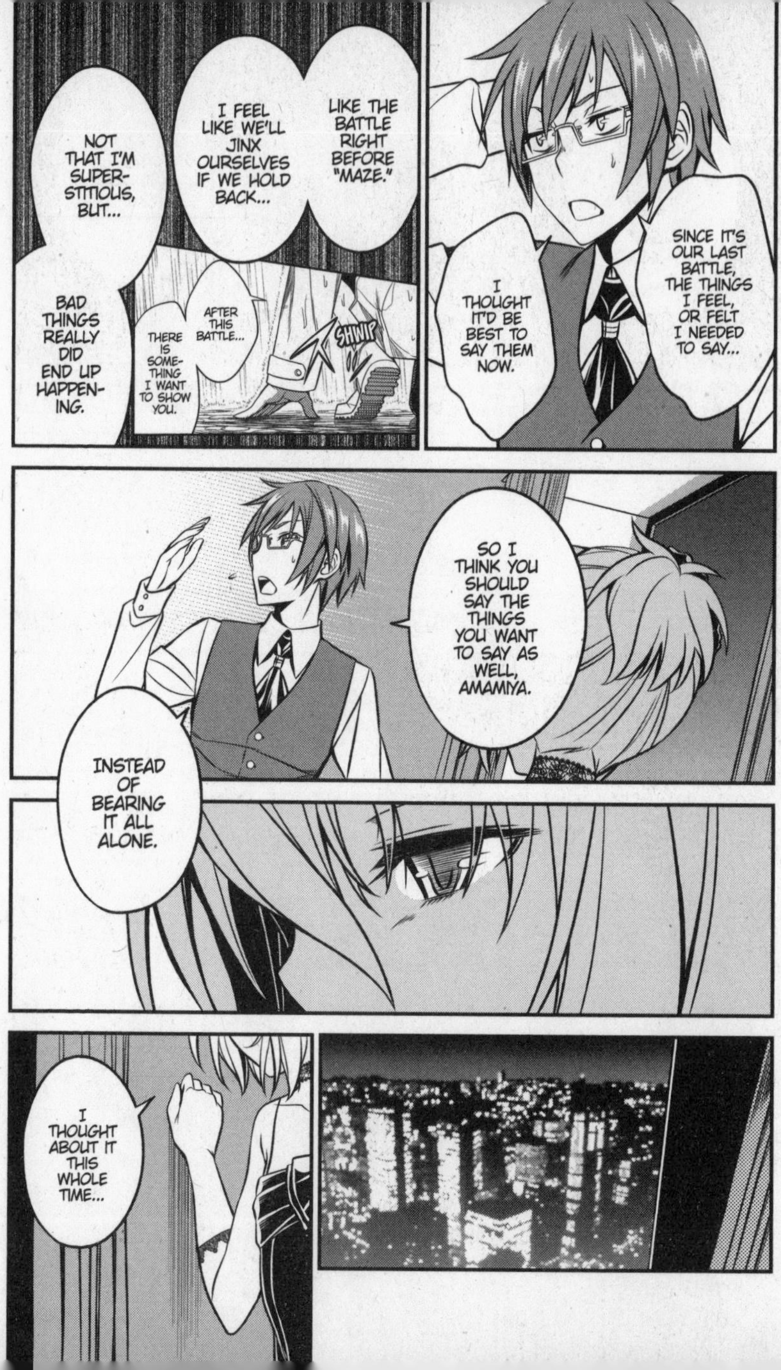
SINCE IT'S OUR LAST BATTLE, THE THINGS I FEEL, OR FELT I NEEDED TO SAY...
I THOUGHT IT'D BE BEST TO SAY THEM NOW.
LIKE THE BATTLE RIGHT BEFORE "MAZE."
I FEEL LIKE WE'LL JINX OURSELVES IF WE HOLD BACK...
NOT THAT I'M SUPER-STITIOUS, BUT...
AFTER THIS BATTLE...
THERE IS SOME-THING I WANT TO SHOW YOU.
SHWIP
BAD THINGS REALLY DID END UP HAPPEN-ING.
SO I THINK YOU SHOULD SAY THE THINGS YOU WANT TO SAY AS WELL, AMAMIYA.
INSTEAD OF BEARING IT ALL ALONE.
I THOUGHT ABOUT IT THIS WHOLE TIME...

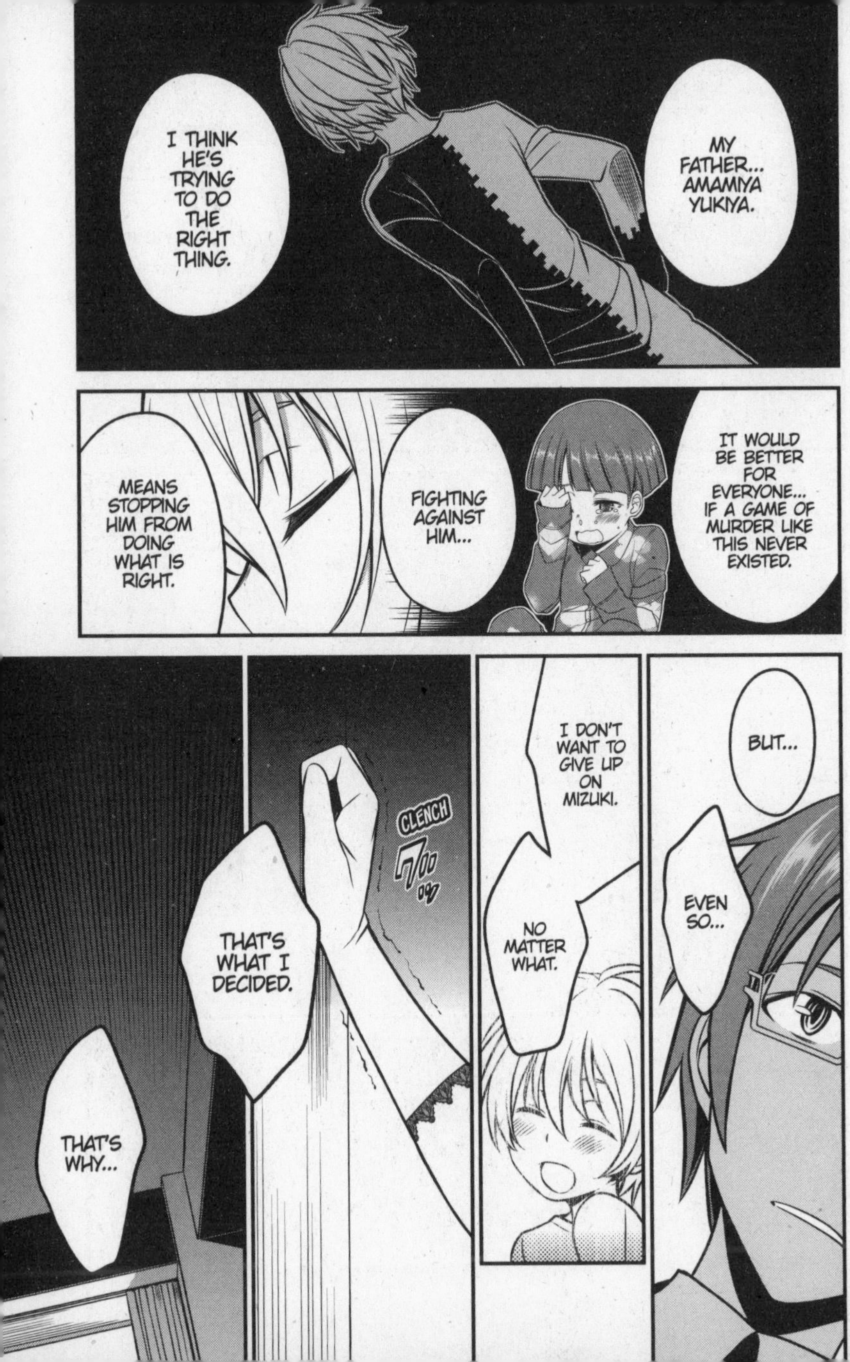
MY FATHER... AMAMIYA YUKIYA.
I THINK HE'S TRYING TO DO THE RIGHT THING.
IT WOULD BE BETTER FOR EVERYONE... IF A GAME OF MURDER LIKE THIS NEVER EXISTED.
FIGHTING AGAINST HIM...
MEANS STOPPING HIM FROM DOING WHAT IS RIGHT.
BUT...
EVEN SO...
I DON'T WANT TO GIVE UP ON MIZUKI.
NO MATTER WHAT.
CLENCH
THAT'S WHAT I DECIDED.
THAT'S WHY...

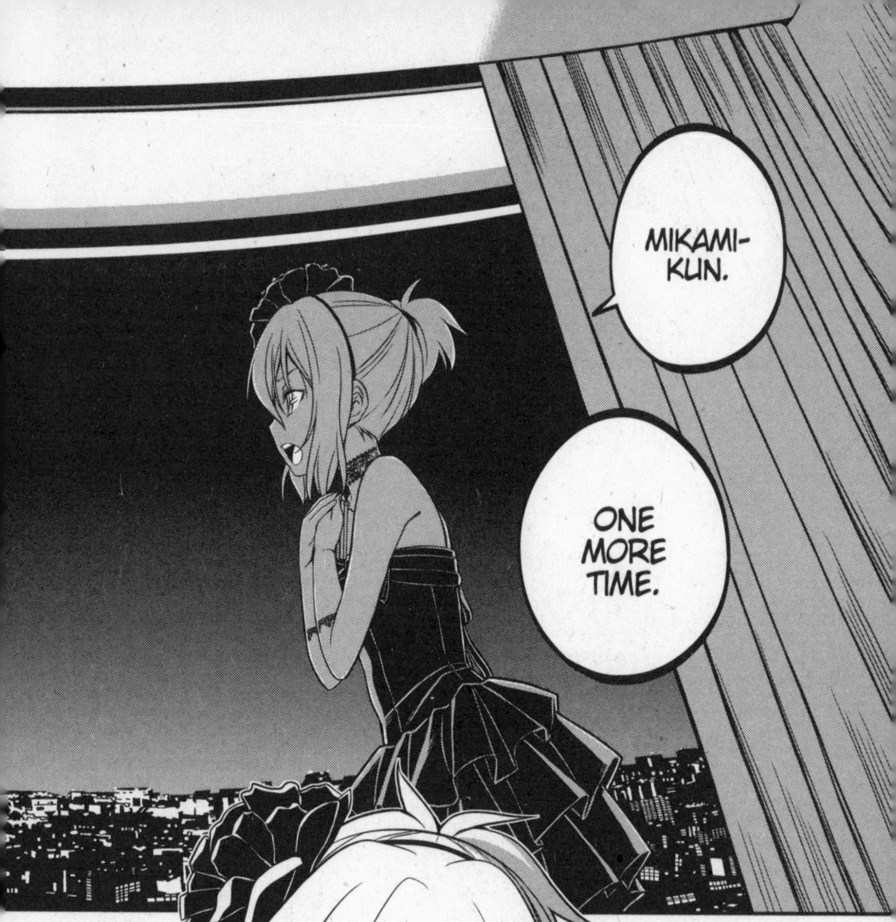
MIKAMI-KUN.
ONE MORE TIME.
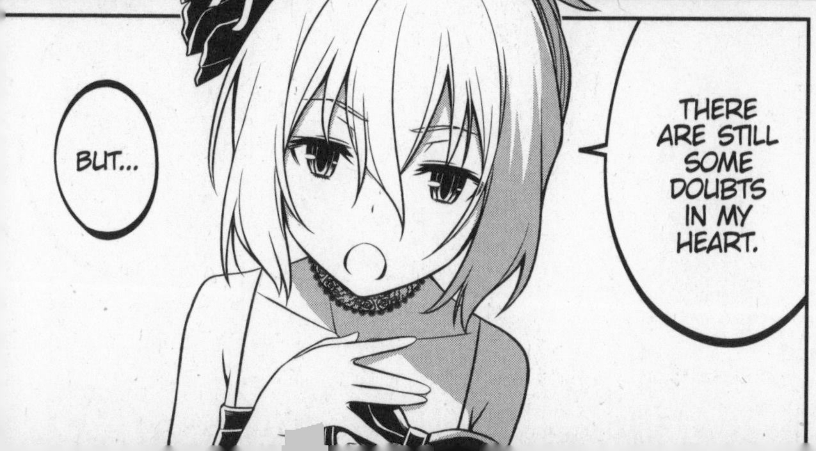
THERE ARE STILL SOME DOUBTS IN MY HEART.
BUT...

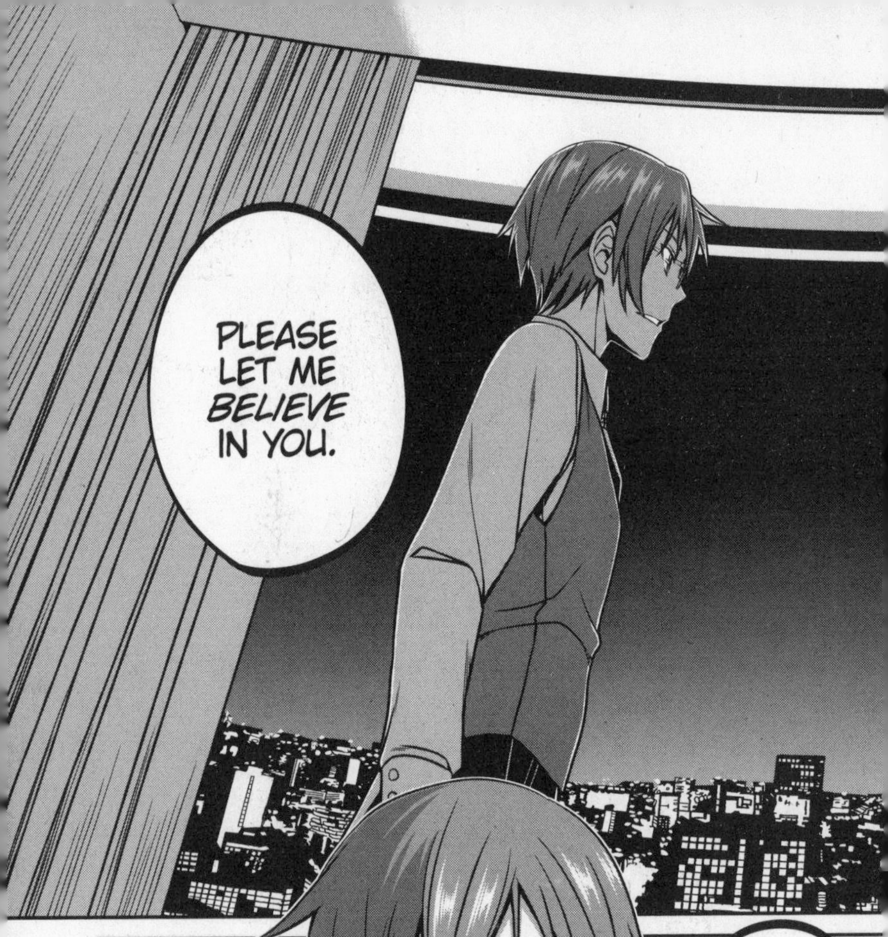
PLEASE LET ME BELIEVE IN YOU.
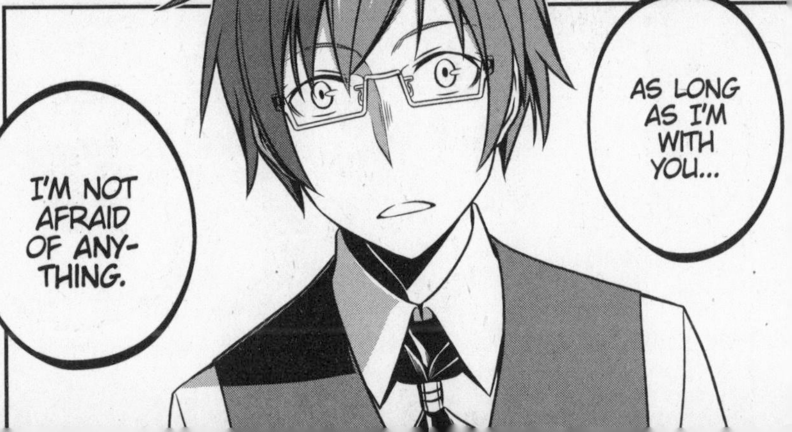
AS LONG AS I'M WITH YOU...
I'M NOT AFRAID OF ANY-THING.

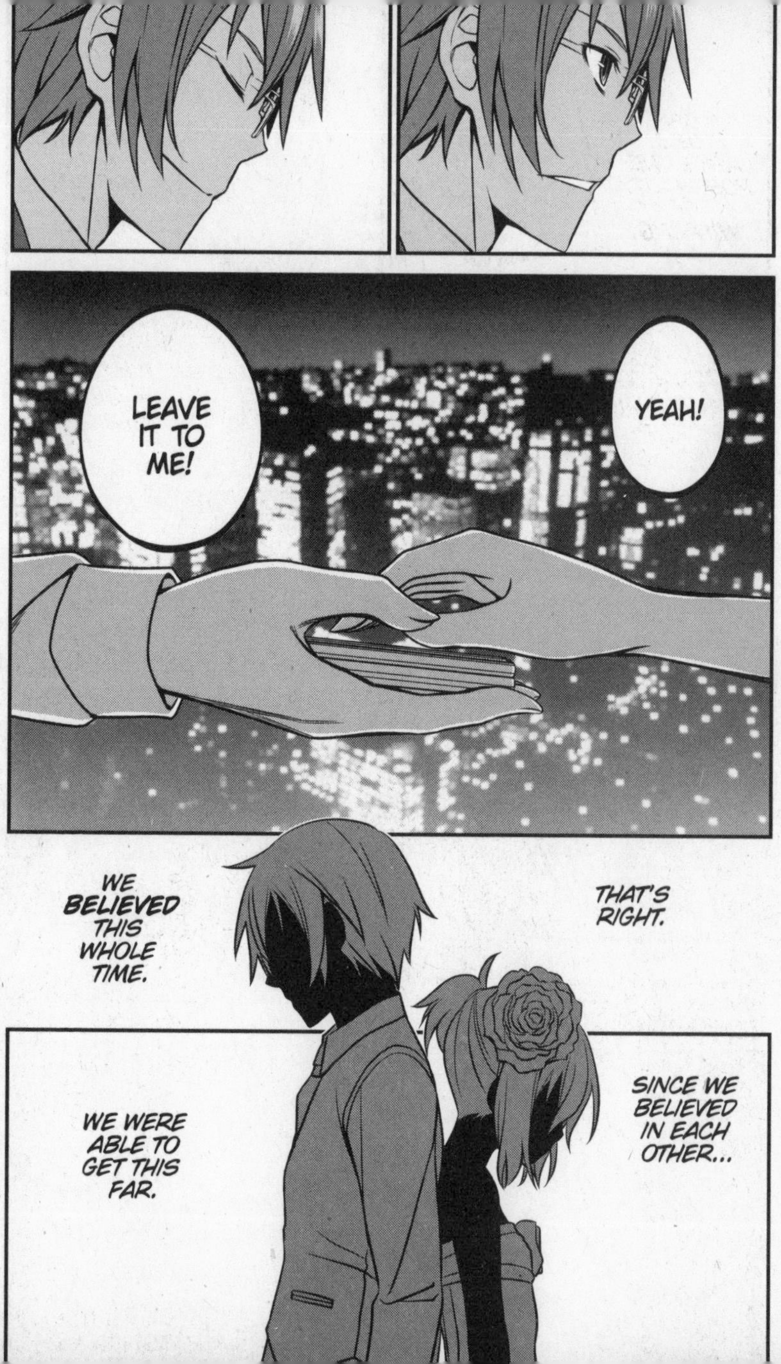
YEAH!
LEAVE IT TO ME!
THAT'S RIGHT.
WE BELIEVED THIS WHOLE TIME.
SINCE WE BELIEVED IN EACH OTHER...
WE WERE ABLE TO GET THIS FAR.

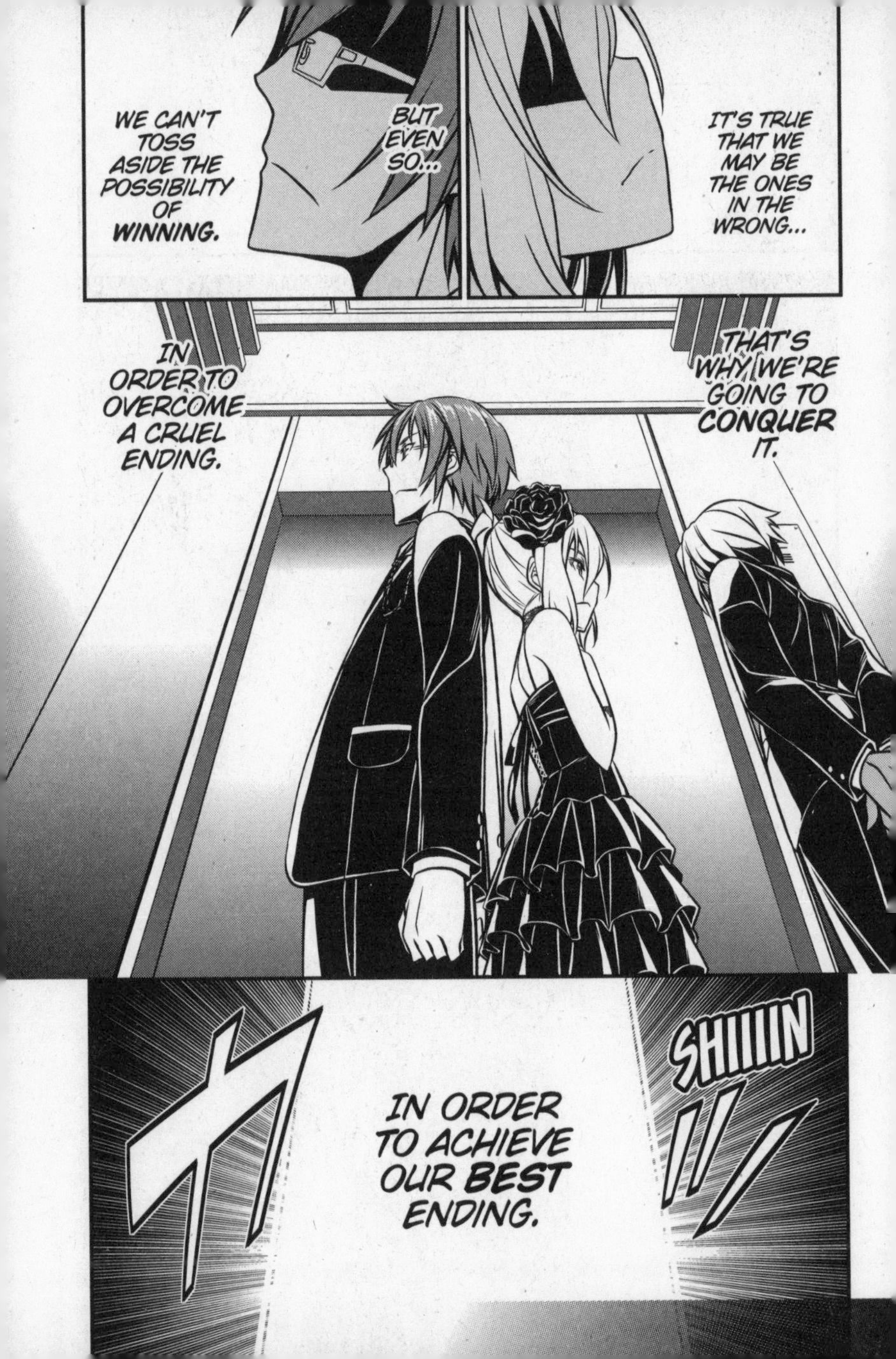
IT'S TRUE THAT WE MAY BE THE ONES IN THE WRONG...
BUT EVEN SO...
WE CAN'T TOSS ASIDE THE POSSIBILITY OF WINNING.
THAT'S WHY WE'RE GOING TO CONQUER IT.
IN ORDER TO OVERCOME A CRUEL ENDING.
SHIIIIN
IN ORDER TO ACHIEVE OUR BEST ENDING.

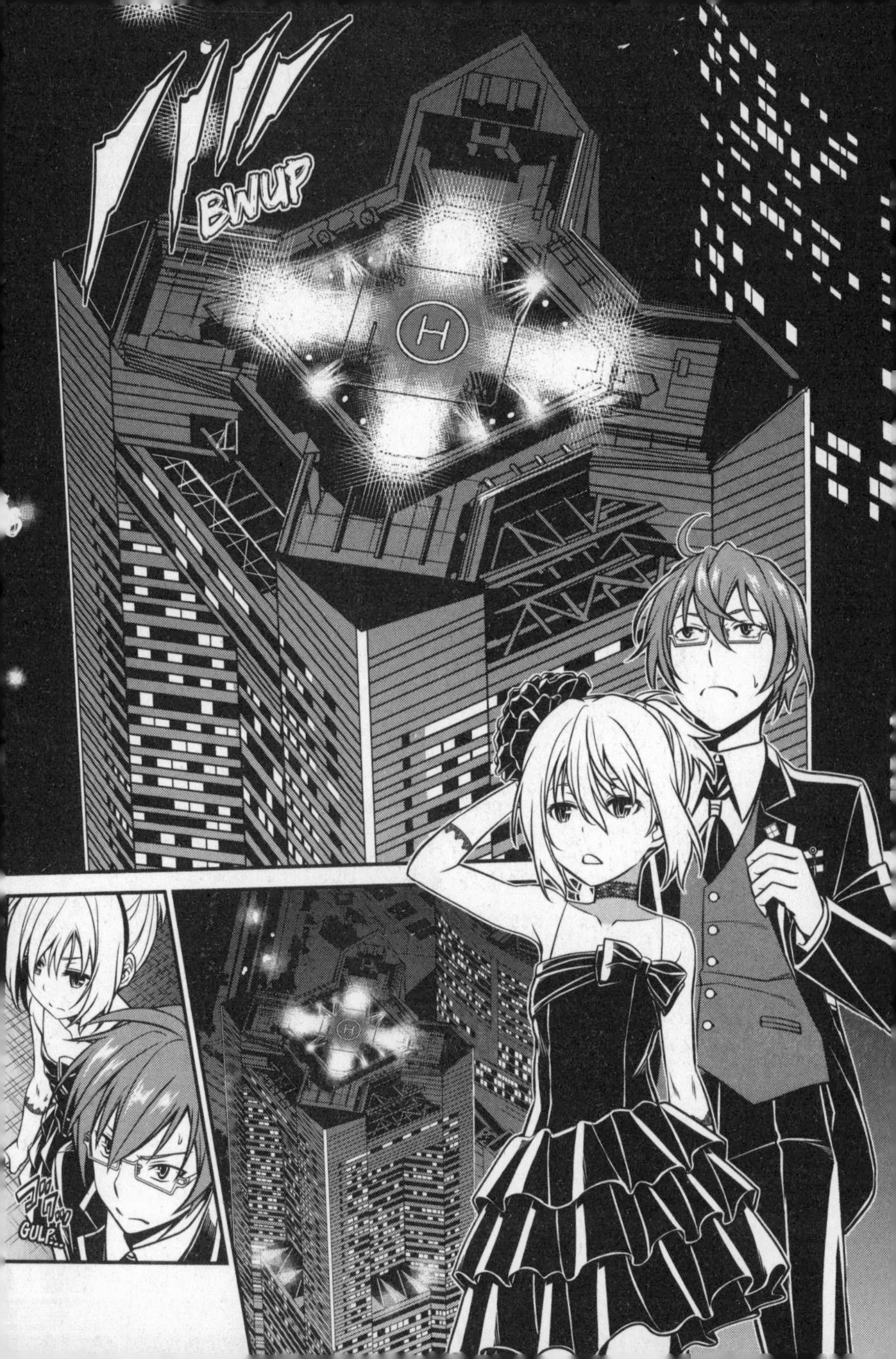
BWUP
GULP...

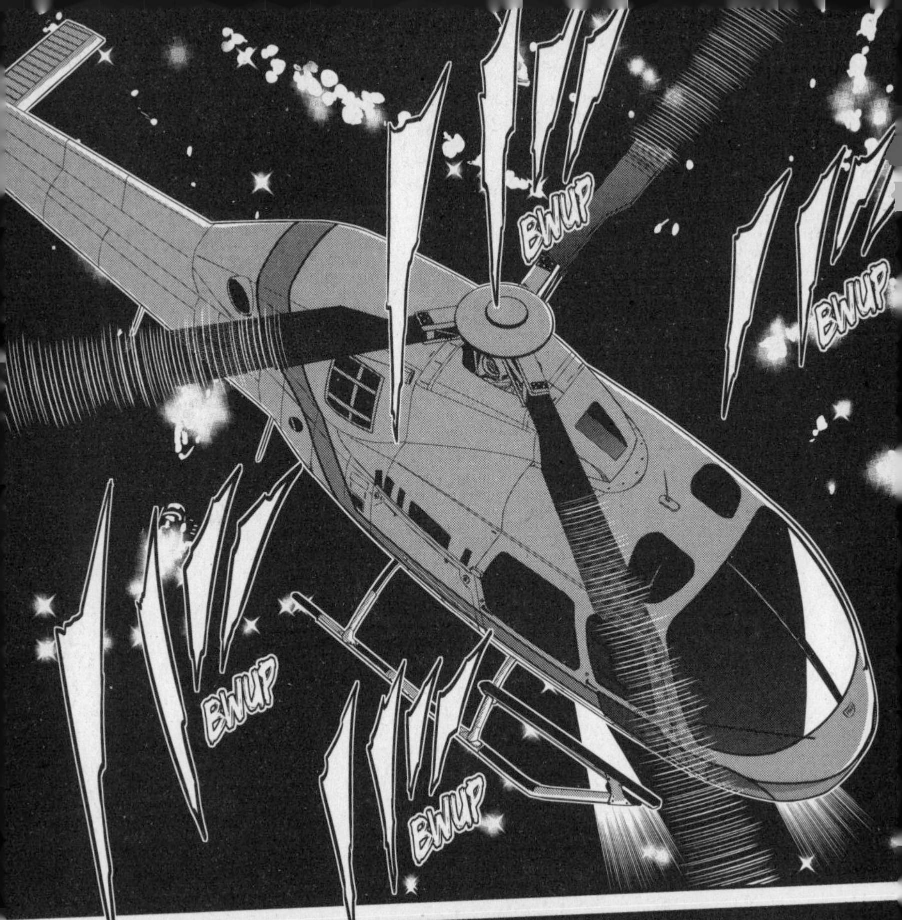
BWUP
BWUP
BWUP
BWUP
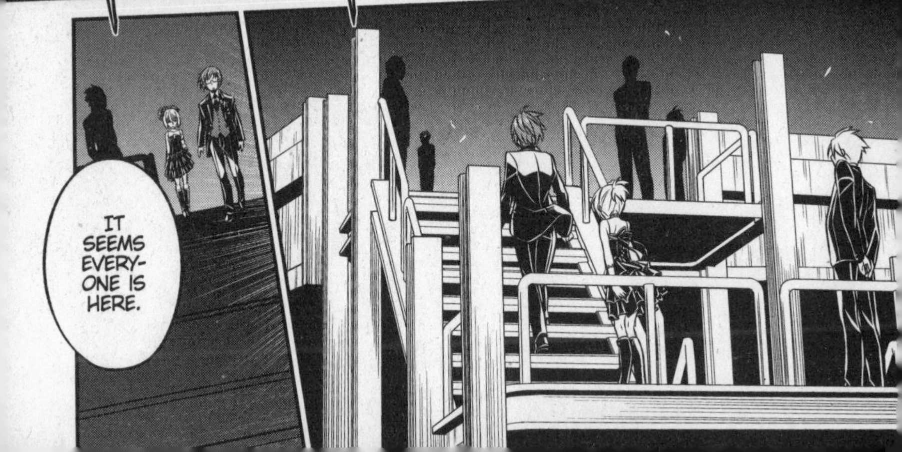
IT SEEMS EVERY-ONE IS HERE.

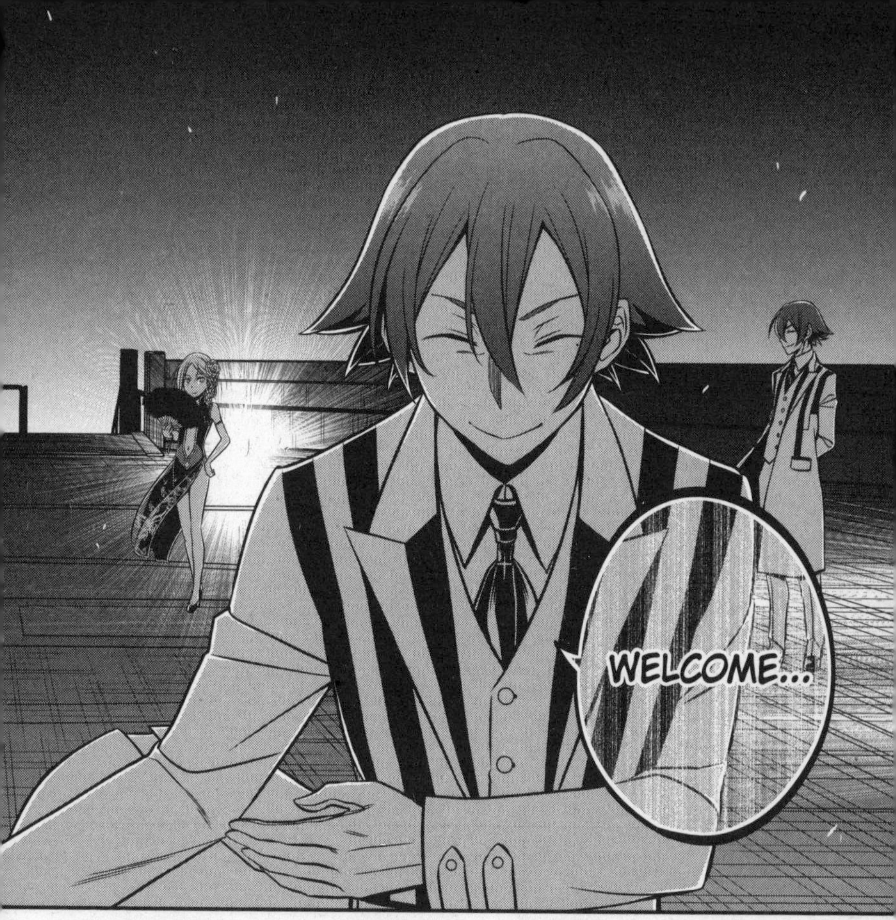
WELCOME...
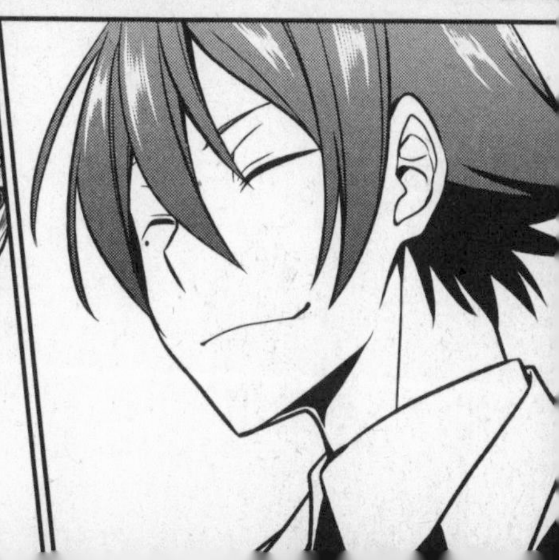
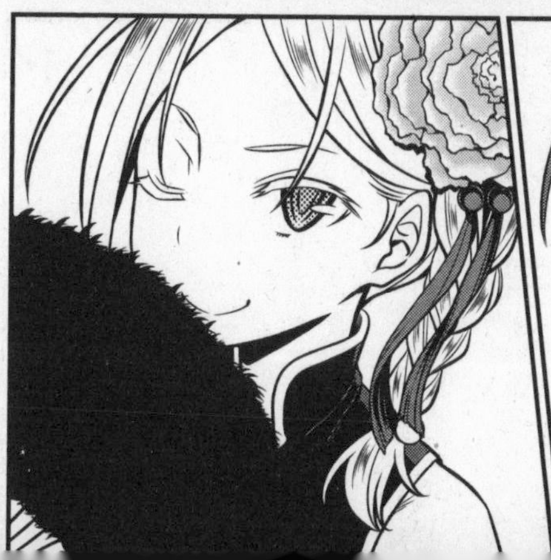

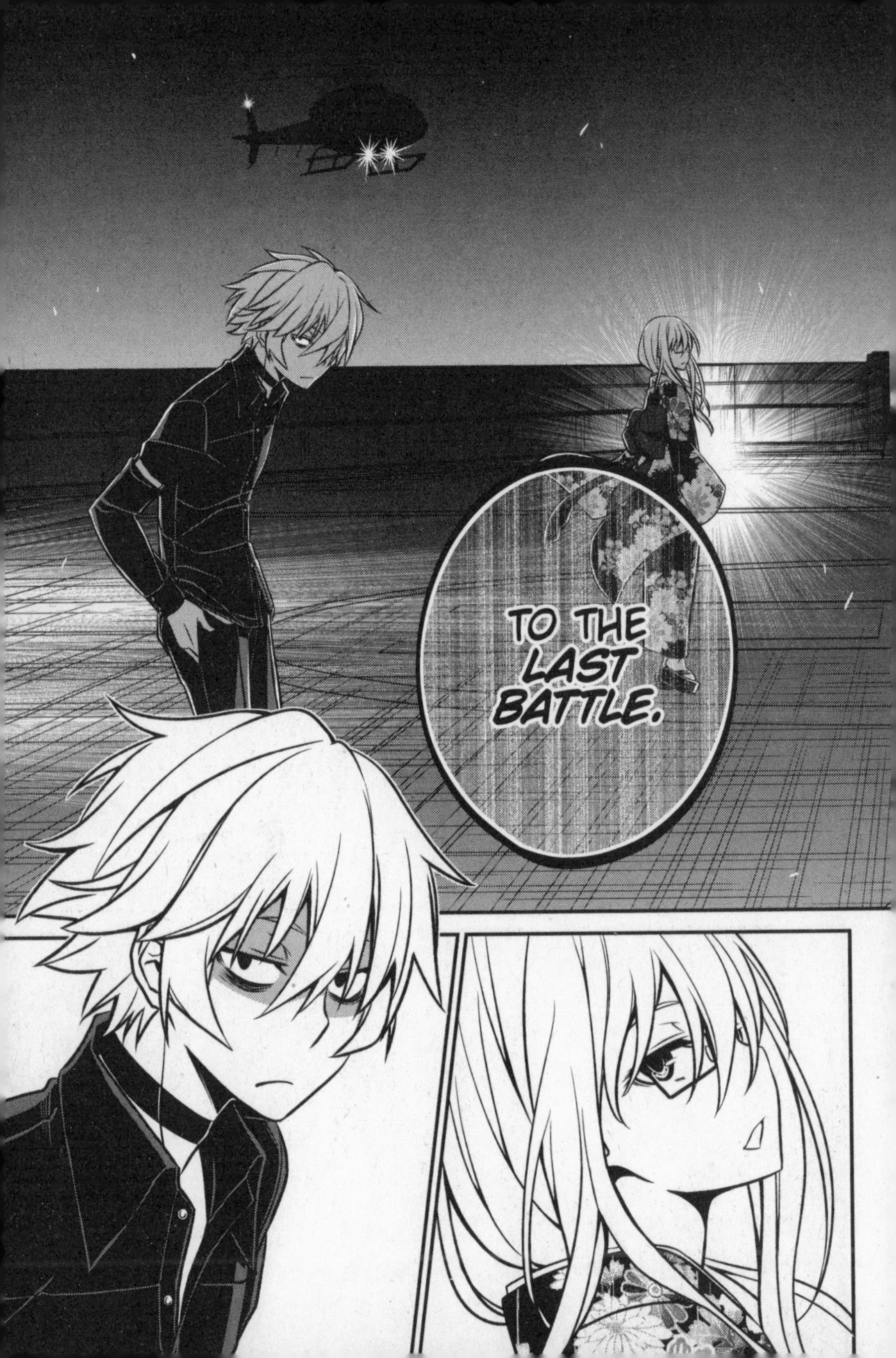
TO THE LAST BATTLE.

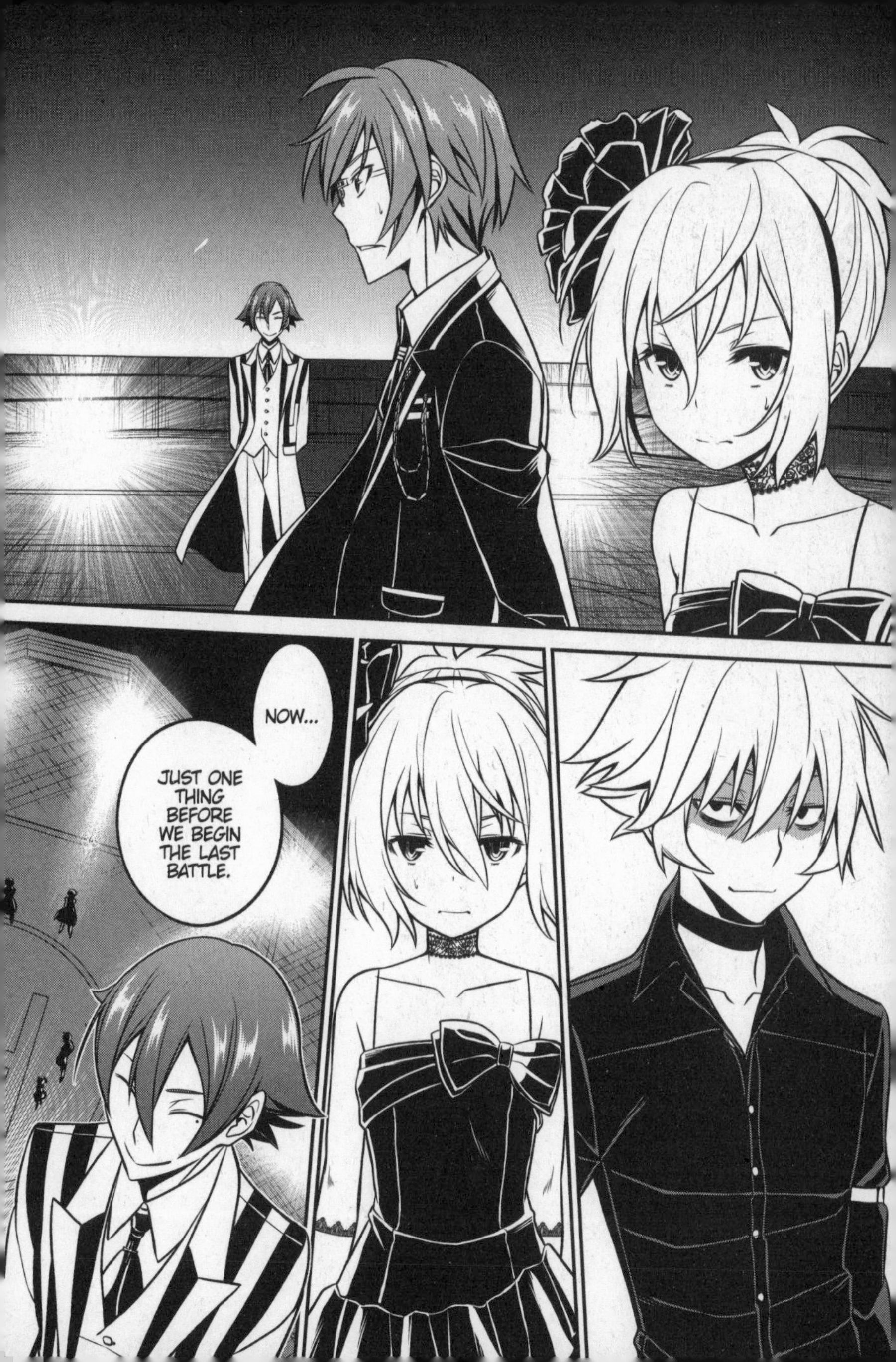
NOW...
JUST ONE THING BEFORE WE BEGIN THE LAST BATTLE.

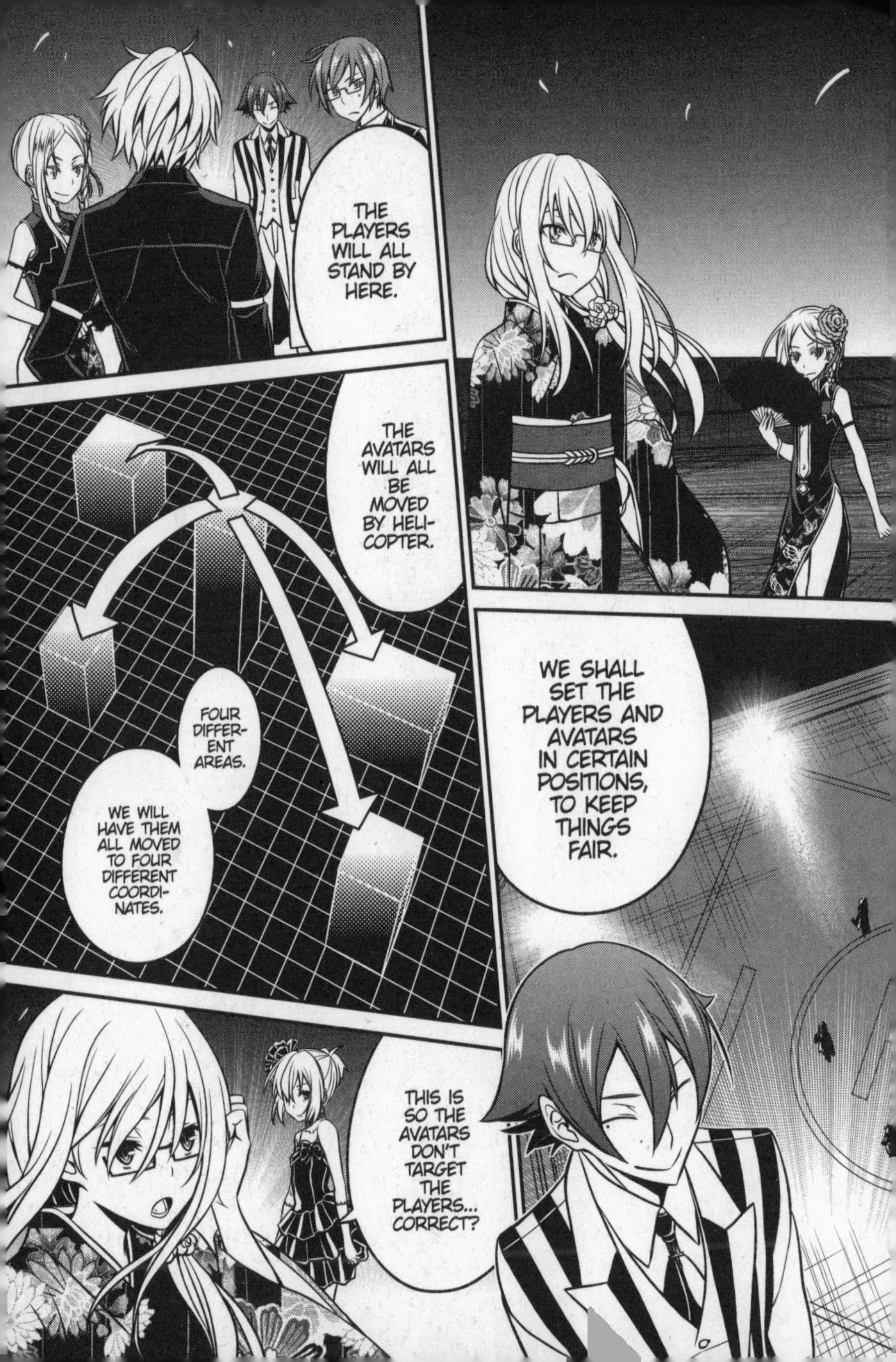
WE SHALL SET THE PLAYERS AND AVATARS IN CERTAIN POSITIONS, TO KEEP THINGS FAIR.
THE PLAYERS WILL ALL STAND BY HERE.
THE AVATARS WILL ALL BE MOVED BY HELI-COPTER.
WE WILL HAVE THEM ALL MOVED TO FOUR DIFFERENT COORDI-NATES.
FOUR DIFFER-ENT AREAS.
THIS IS SO THE AVATARS DON'T TARGET THE PLAYERS... CORRECT?

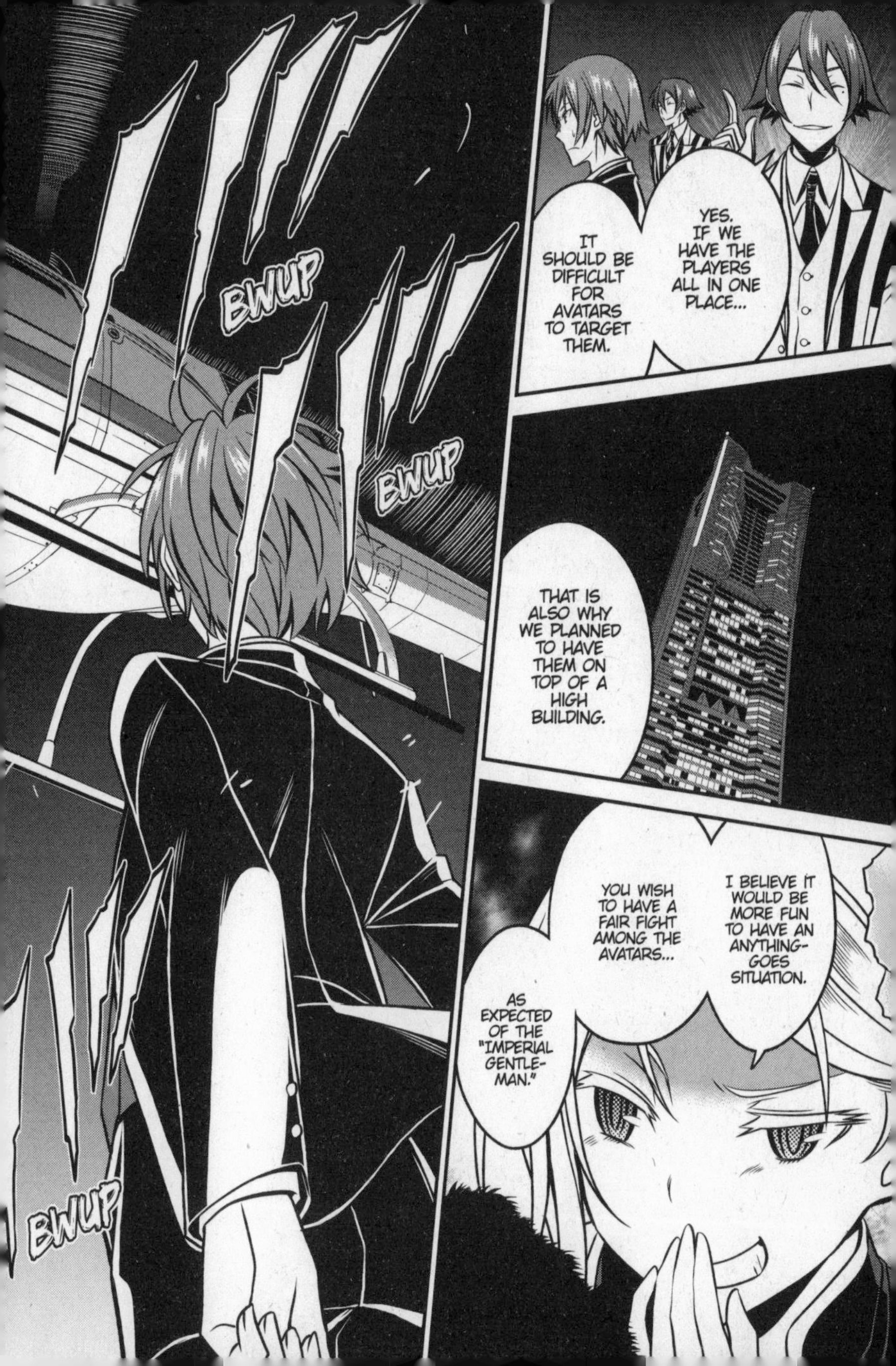
YES. IF WE HAVE THE PLAYERS ALL IN ONE PLACE...
IT SHOULD BE DIFFICULT FOR AVATARS TO TARGET THEM.
THAT IS ALSO WHY WE PLANNED TO HAVE THEM ON TOP OF A HIGH BUILDING.
I BELIEVE IT WOULD BE MORE FUN TO HAVE AN ANYTHING-GOES SITUATION.
YOU WISH TO HAVE A FAIR FIGHT AMONG THE AVATARS...
AS EXPECTED OF THE "IMPERIAL GENTLE-MAN."
BWUP
BWUP
BWUP

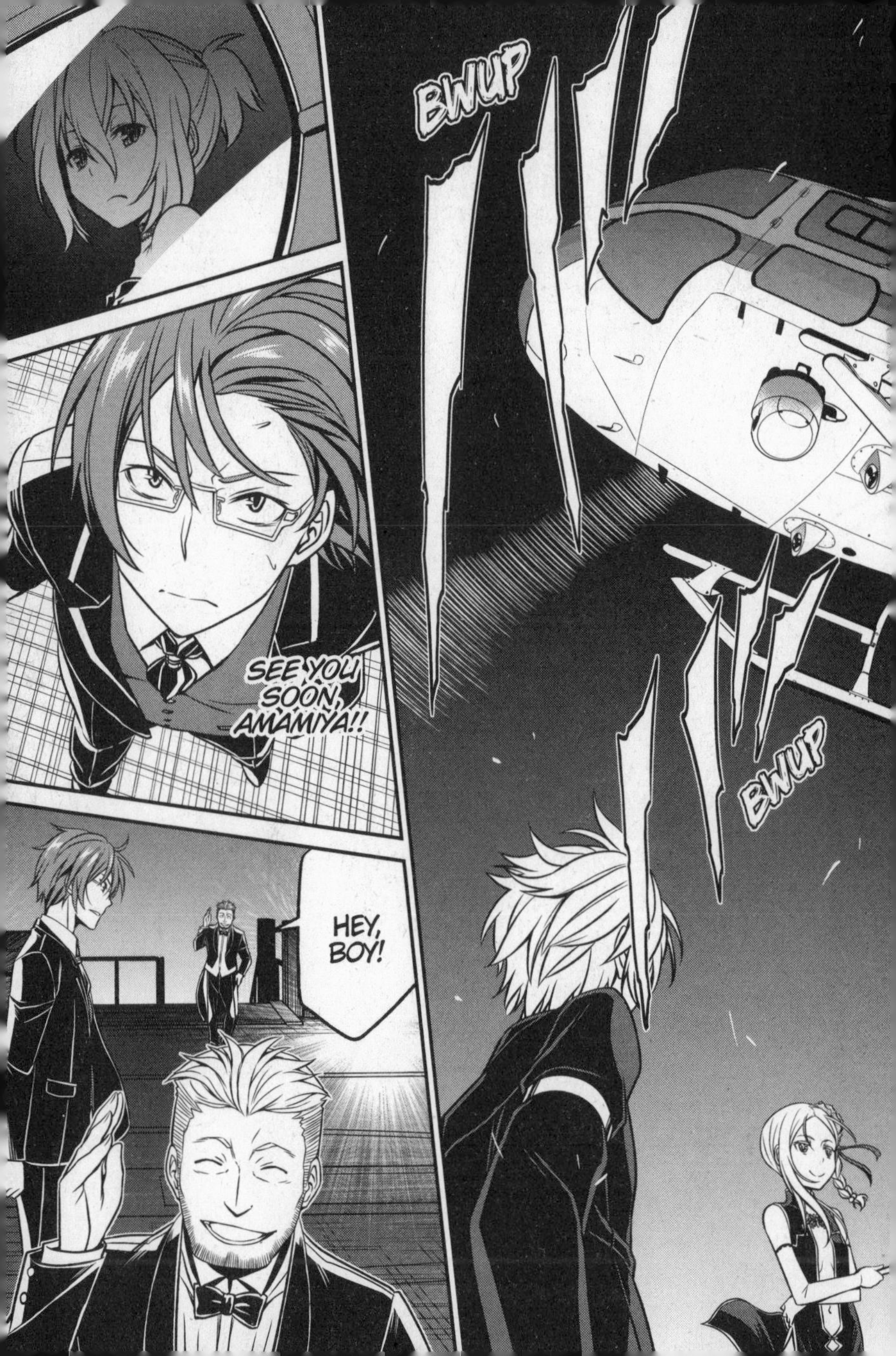
BWUP
BWUP
SEE YOU SOON, AMAMIYA!!
HEY, BOY!

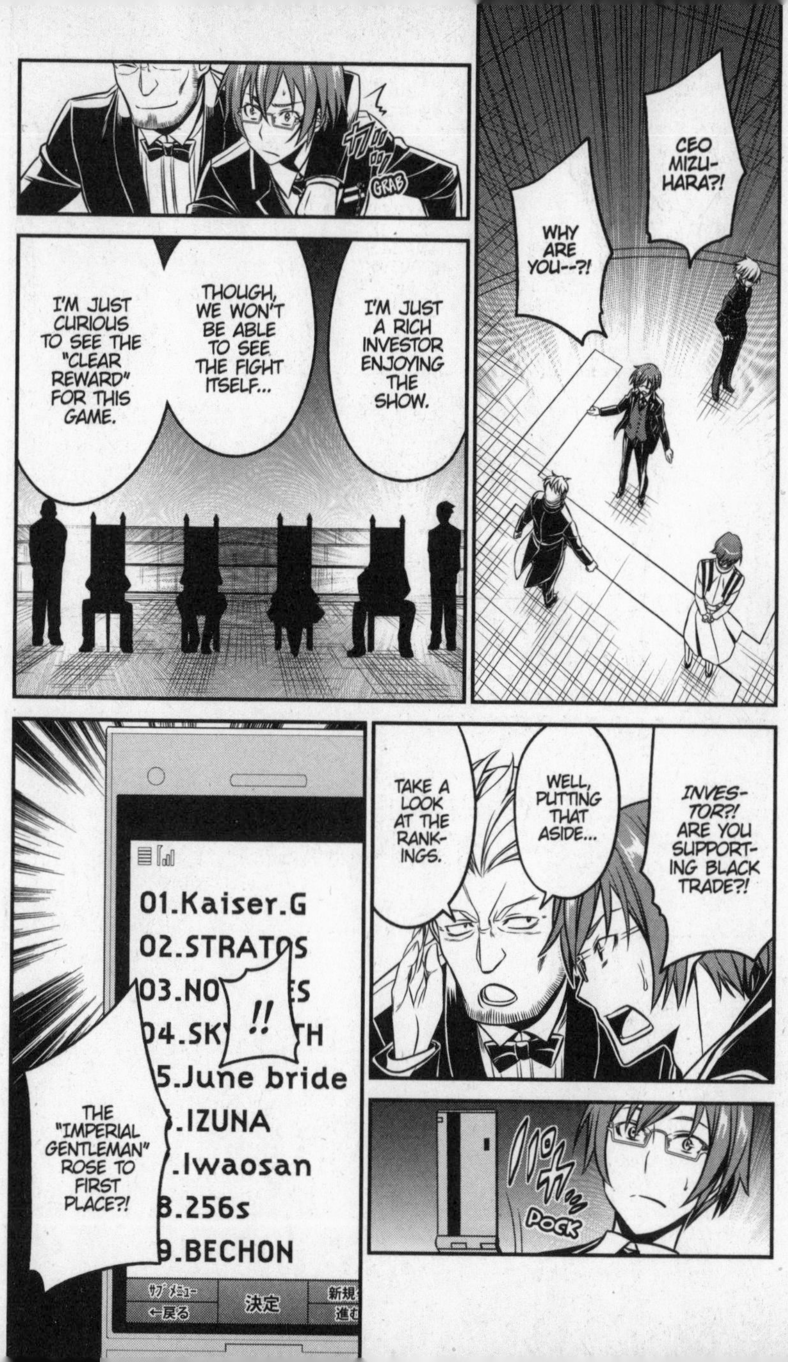
CEO MIZU-HARA?!
WHY ARE YOU--?!
GRAB
I'M JUST A RICH INVESTOR ENJOYING THE SHOW.
THOUGH, WE WON'T BE ABLE TO SEE THE FIGHT ITSELF...
I'M JUST CURIOUS TO SEE THE "CLEAR REWARD" FOR THIS GAME.
INVES-TOR?! ARE YOU SUPPORT-ING BLACK TRADE?!
WELL, PUTTING THAT ASIDE...
TAKE A LOOK AT THE RANK-INGS.
POCK
01.Kaiser.G
02.STRATOS
5.June bride
.IZUNA
.Iwaosan
8.256s
9.BECHON
サブメニュー
←戻る
決定
!!
THE "IMPERIAL GENTLEMAN" ROSE TO FIRST PLACE?!

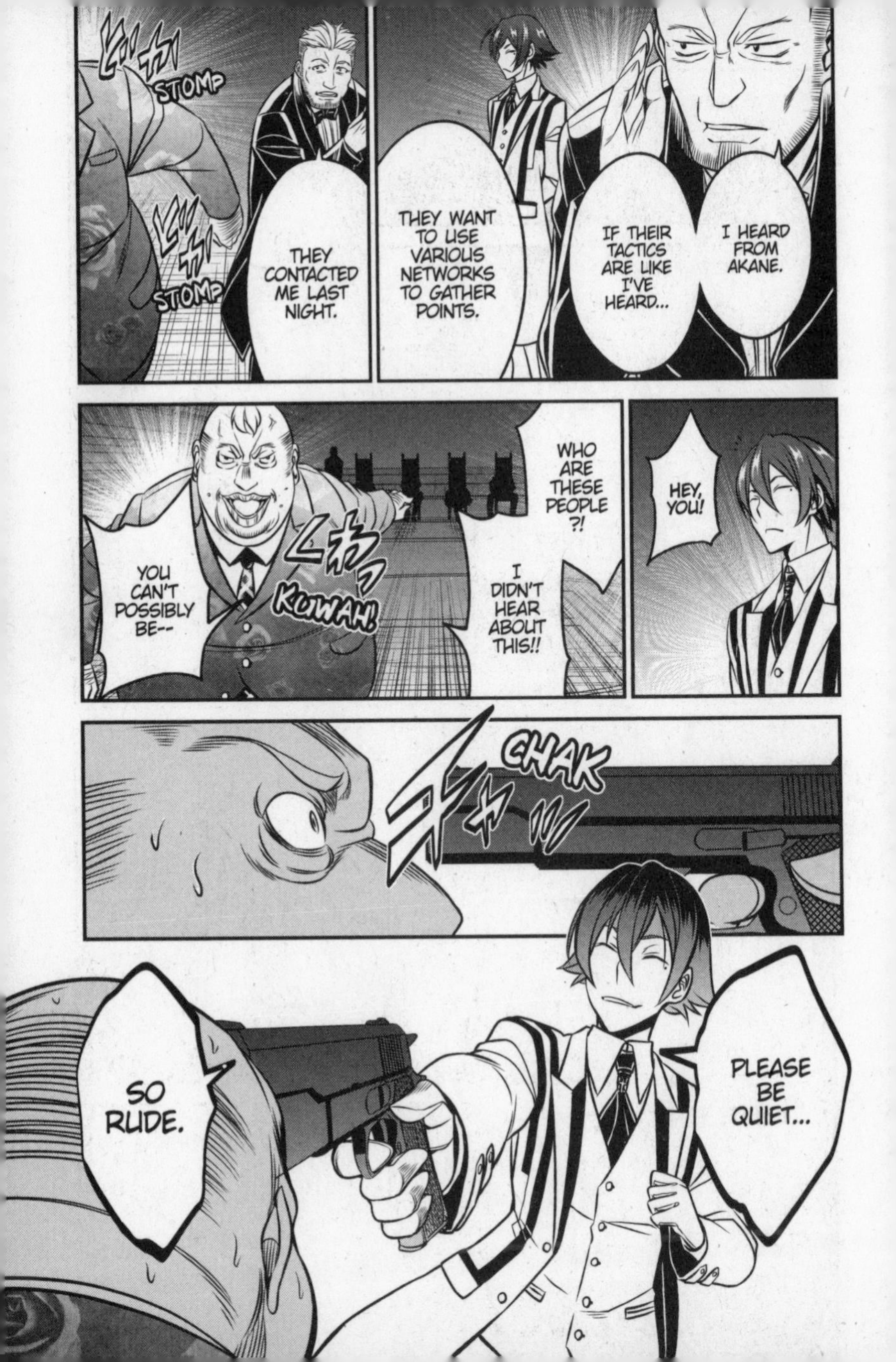
I HEARD FROM AKANE.
IF THEIR TACTICS ARE LIKE I'VE HEARD...
THEY WANT TO USE VARIOUS NETWORKS TO GATHER POINTS.
THEY CONTACTED ME LAST NIGHT.
STOMP
STOMP
HEY, YOU!
WHO ARE THESE PEOPLE ?!
I DIDN'T HEAR ABOUT THIS!!
KUWAH!
YOU CAN'T POSSIBLY BE--
CHAK
PLEASE BE QUIET...
SO RUDE.

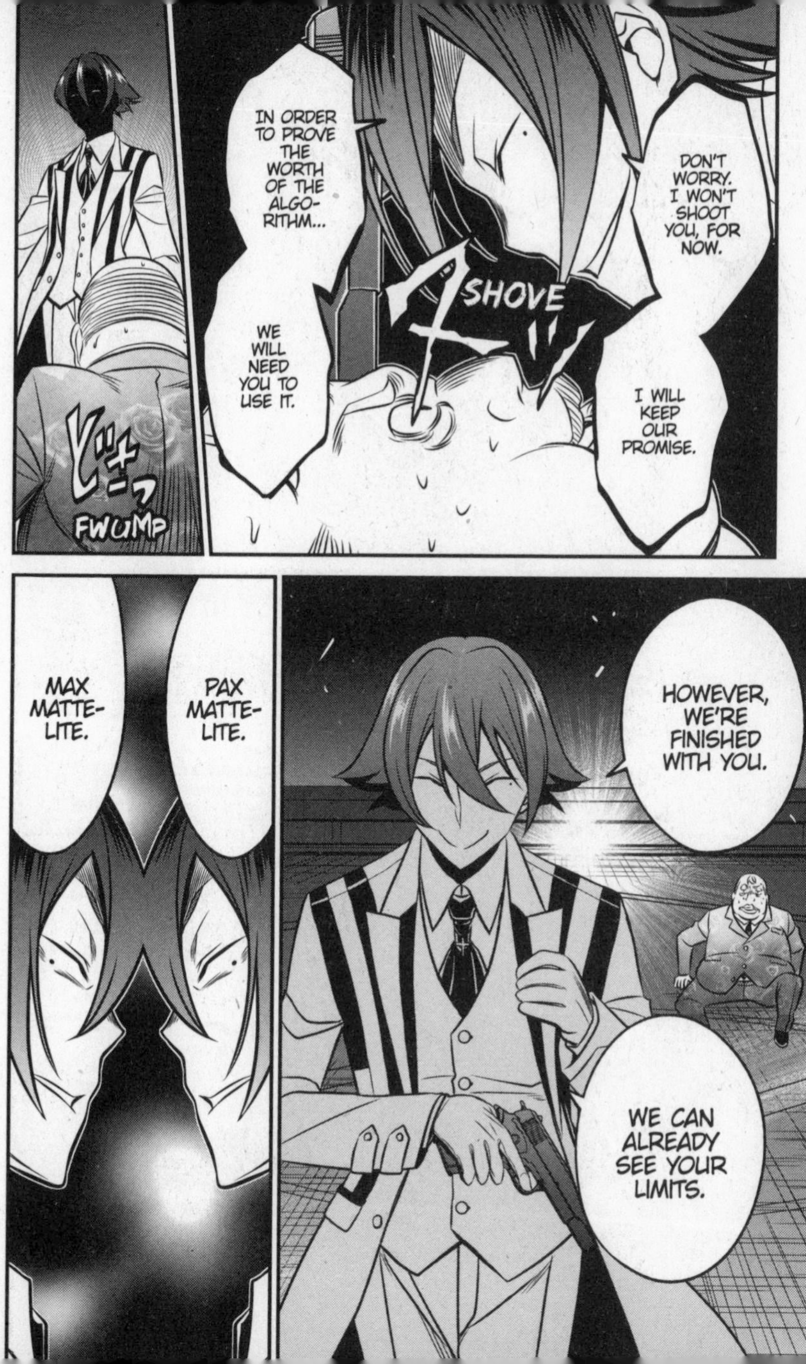
DON'T WORRY. I WON'T SHOOT YOU, FOR NOW.
SHOVE
I WILL KEEP OUR PROMISE.
IN ORDER TO PROVE THE WORTH OF THE ALGO-RITHM...
WE WILL NEED YOU TO USE IT.
FWUMP
HOWEVER, WE'RE FINISHED WITH YOU.
WE CAN ALREADY SEE YOUR LIMITS.
PAX MATTE-LITE.
MAX MATTE-LITE.

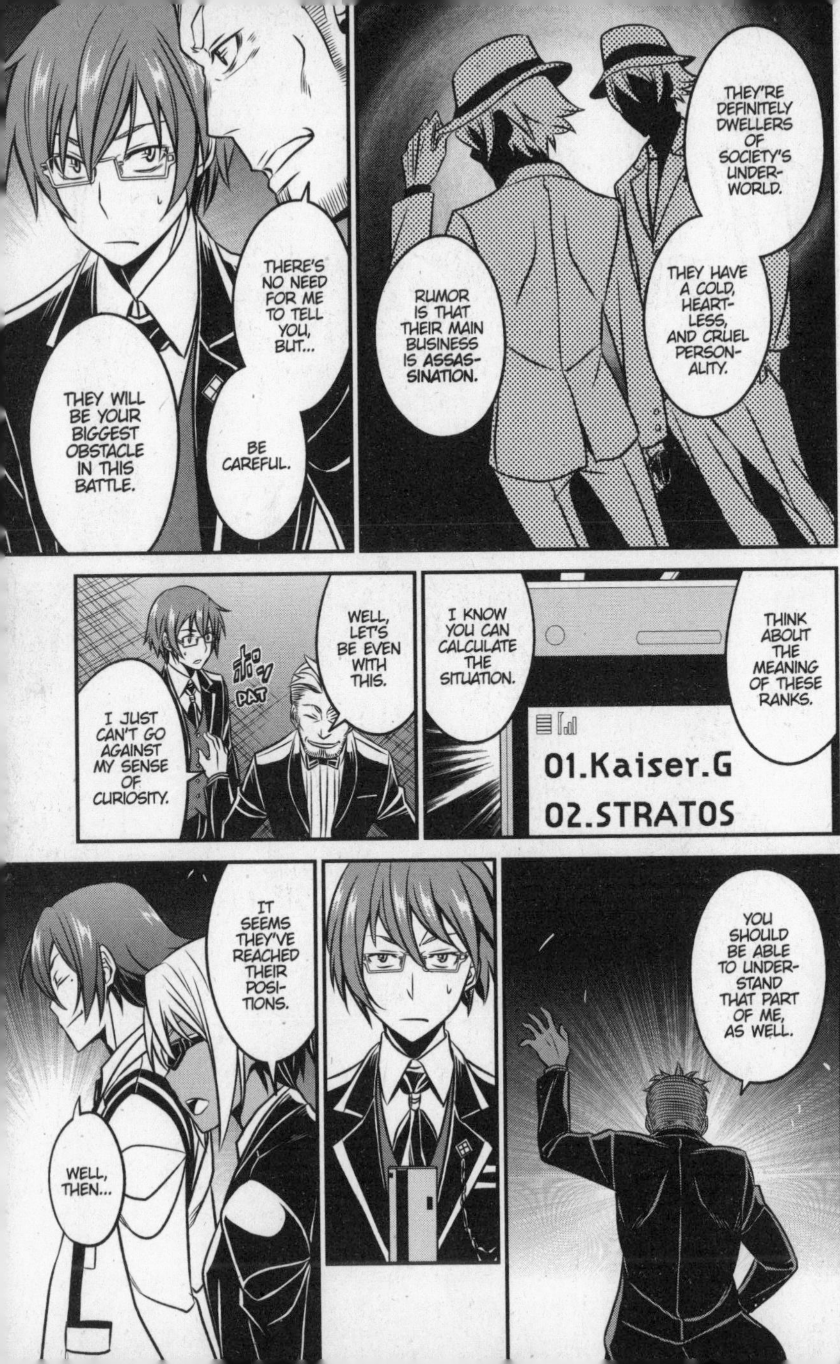
THEY'RE DEFINITELY DWELLERS OF SOCIETY'S UNDER-WORLD.
THEY HAVE A COLD, HEART-LESS, AND CRUEL PERSON-ALITY.
RUMOR IS THAT THEIR MAIN BUSINESS IS ASSAS-SINATION.
THERE'S NO NEED FOR ME TO TELL YOU, BUT...
BE CAREFUL.
THEY WILL BE YOUR BIGGEST OBSTACLE IN THIS BATTLE.
THINK ABOUT THE MEANING OF THESE RANKS.
01.Kaiser.G
02.STRATOS
I KNOW YOU CAN CALCULATE THE SITUATION.
WELL, LET'S BE EVEN WITH THIS.
PAT
I JUST CAN'T GO AGAINST MY SENSE OF CURIOSITY.
YOU SHOULD BE ABLE TO UNDER-STAND THAT PART OF ME, AS WELL.
IT SEEMS THEY'VE REACHED THEIR POSI-TIONS.
WELL, THEN...

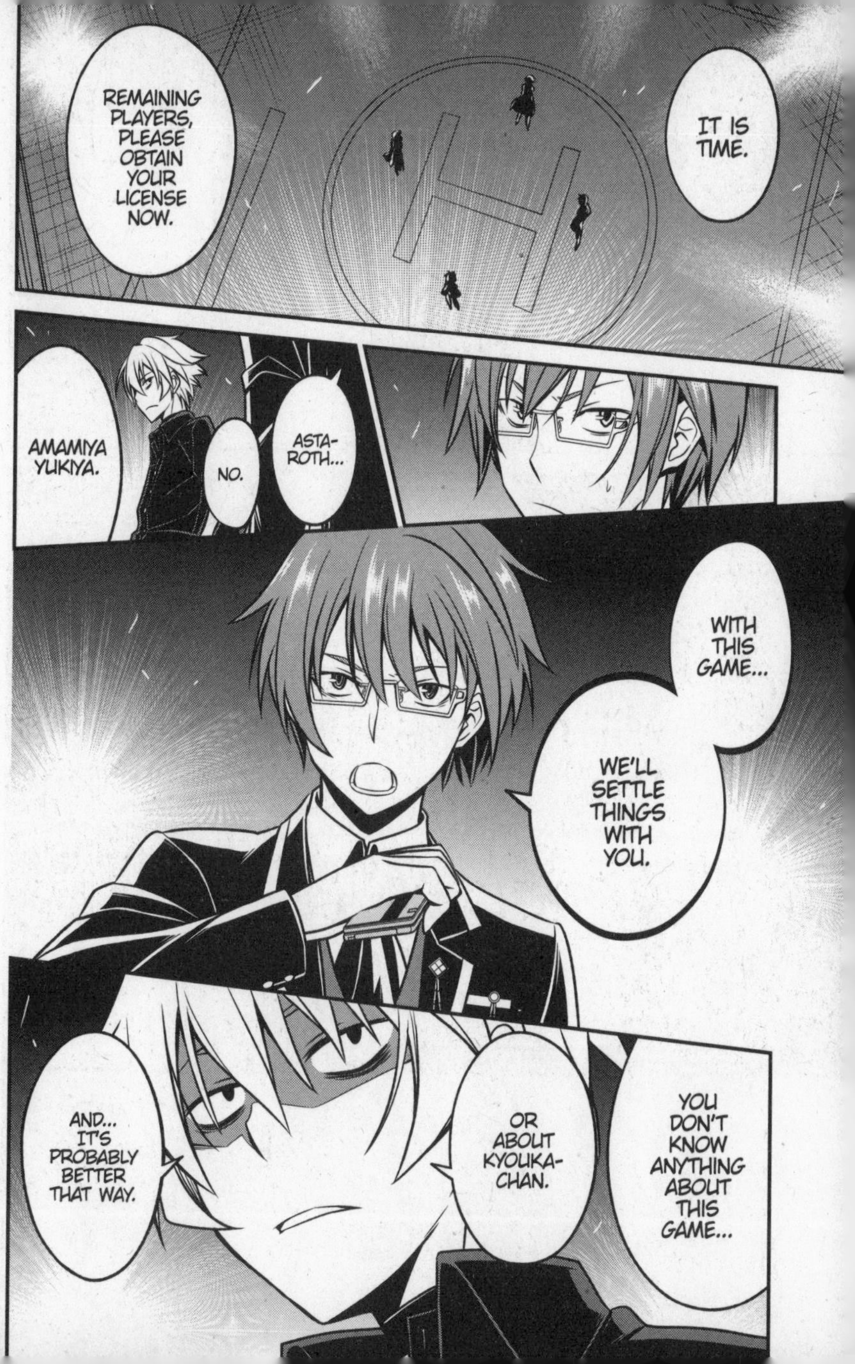
IT IS TIME.
REMAINING PLAYERS, PLEASE OBTAIN YOUR LICENSE NOW.
ASTA-ROTH...
NO.
AMAMIYA YUKIYA.
WITH THIS GAME...
WE'LL SETTLE THINGS WITH YOU.
YOU DON'T KNOW ANYTHING ABOUT THIS GAME...
OR ABOUT KYOUKA-CHAN.
AND... IT'S PROBABLY BETTER THAT WAY.

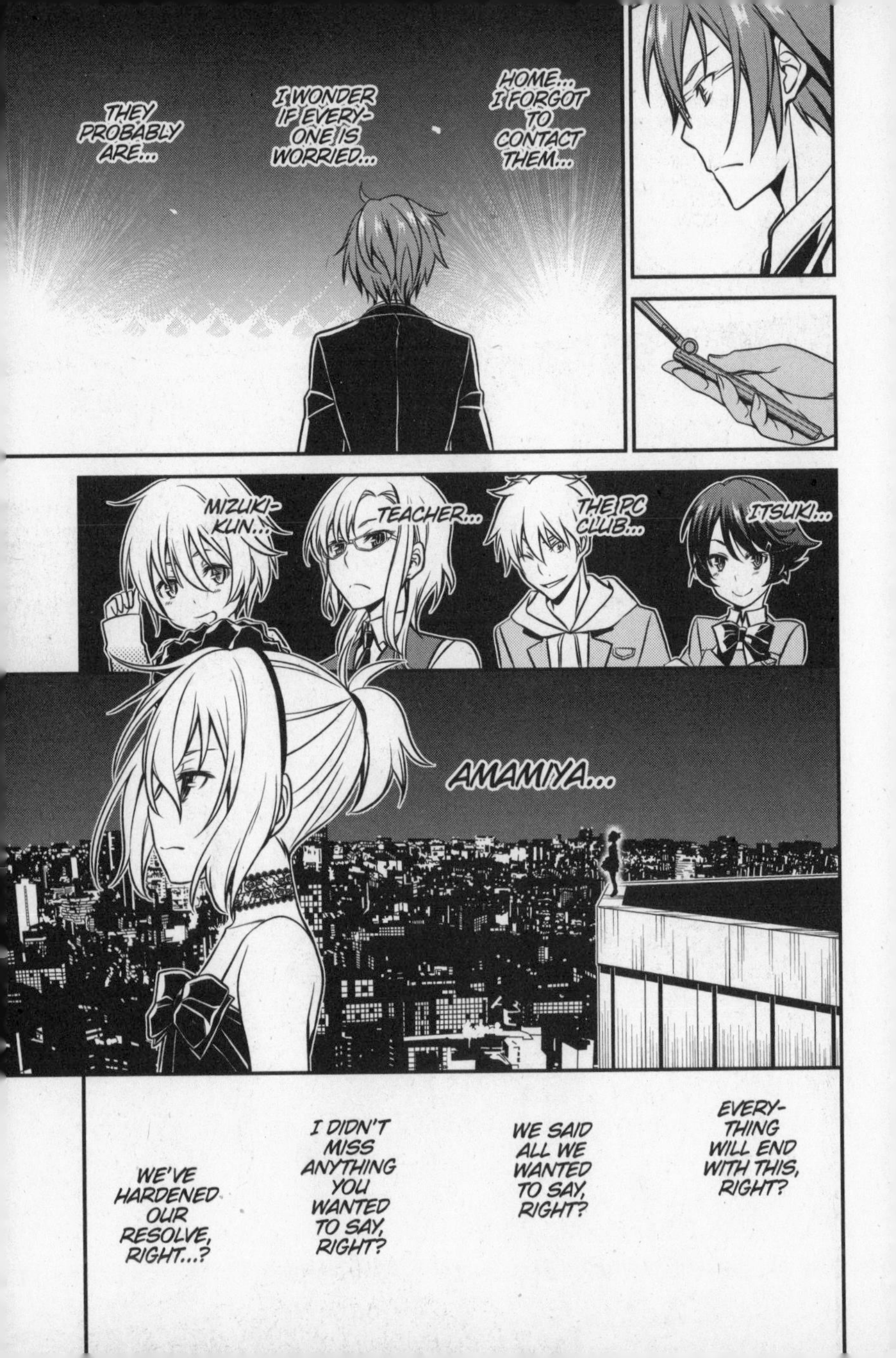
HOME... I FORGOT TO CONTACT THEM...
I WONDER IF EVERY-ONE IS WORRIED...
THEY PROBABLY ARE...
ITSUKI...
THE PC CLUB...
TEACHER...
MIZUKI-KUN...
AMAMIYA...
EVERY-THING WILL END WITH THIS, RIGHT?
WE SAID ALL WE WANTED TO SAY, RIGHT?
I DIDN'T MISS ANYTHING YOU WANTED TO SAY, RIGHT?
WE'VE HARDENED OUR RESOLVE, RIGHT...?

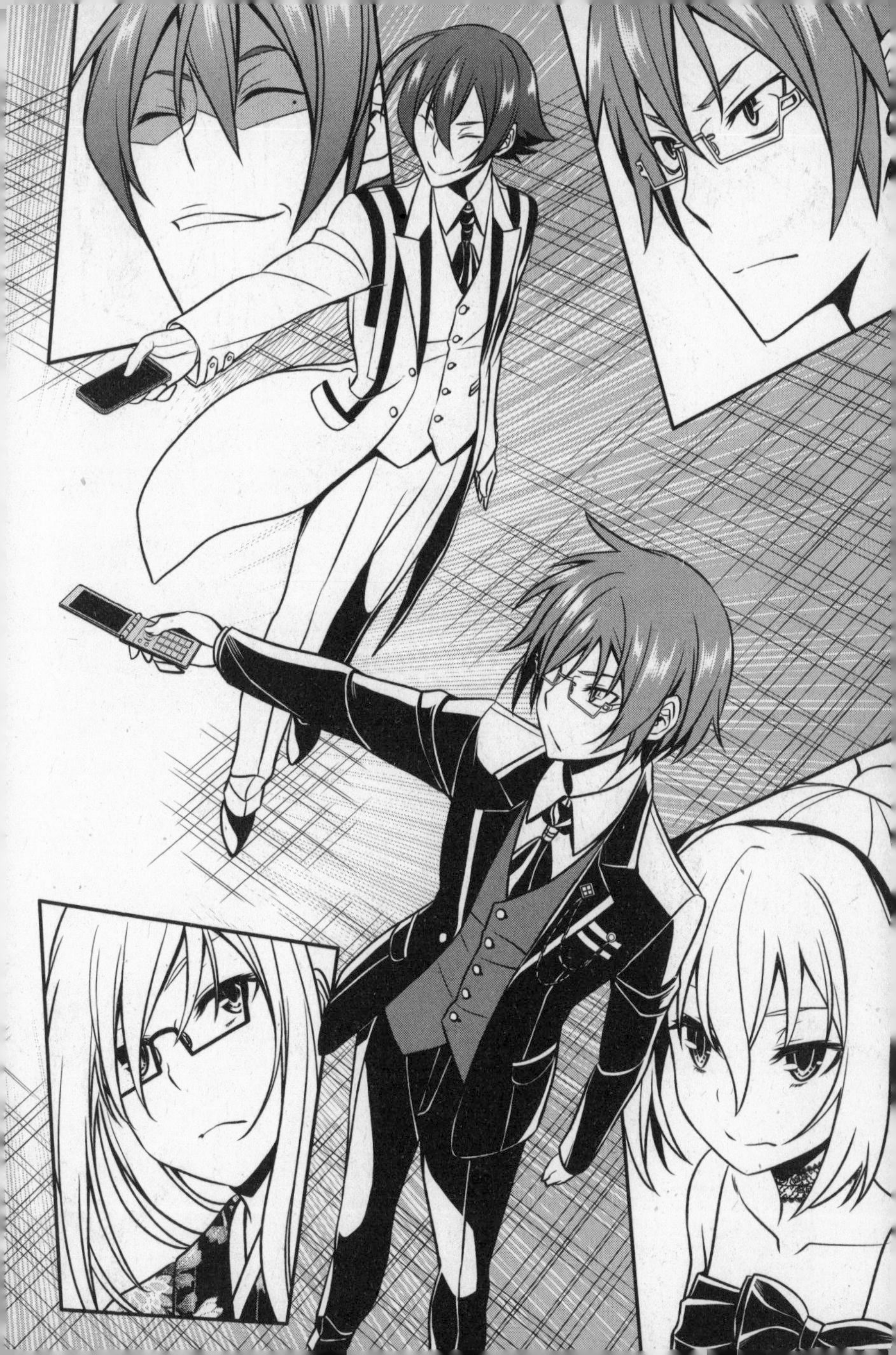

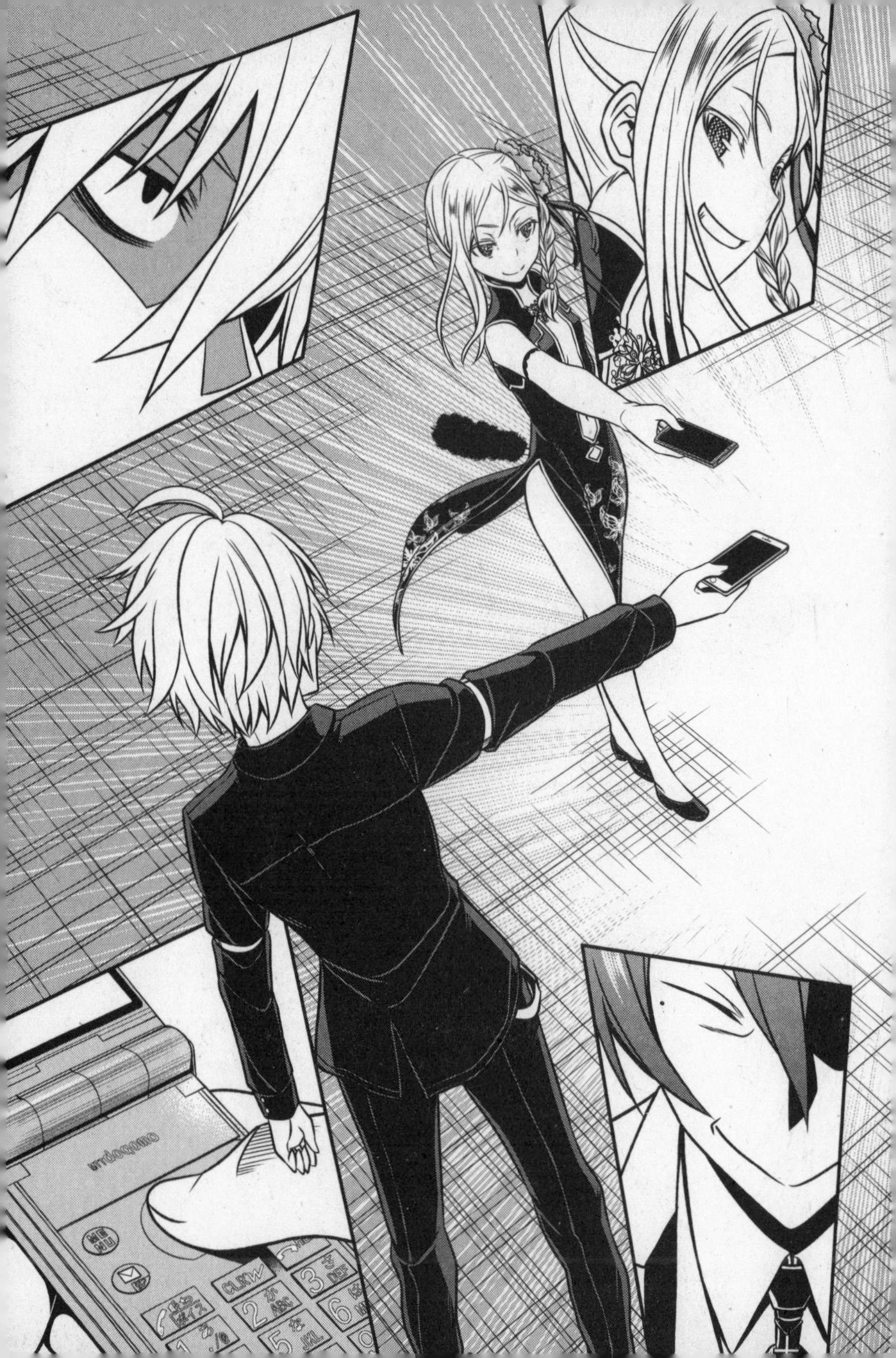

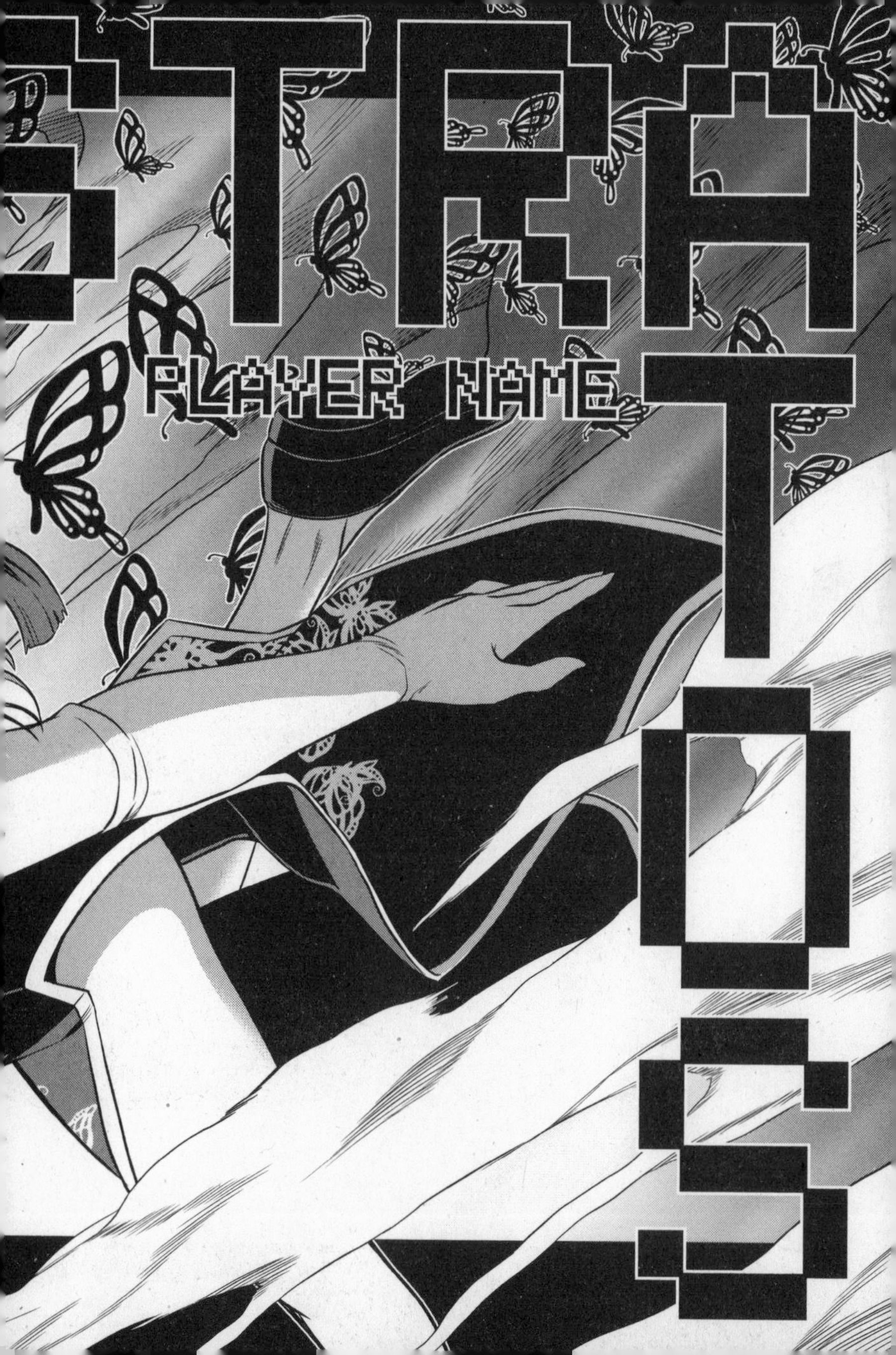
PLAYER NAME

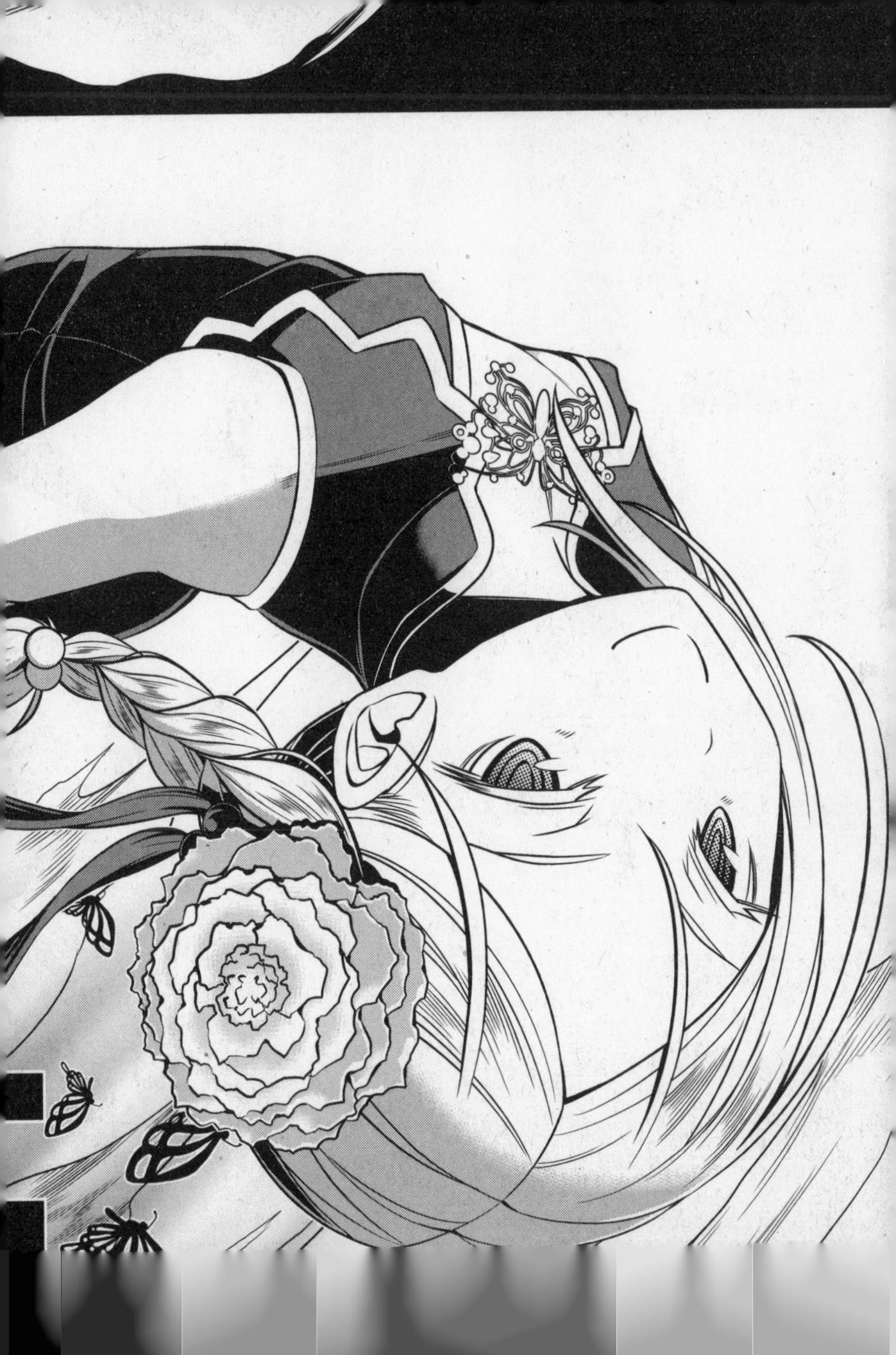

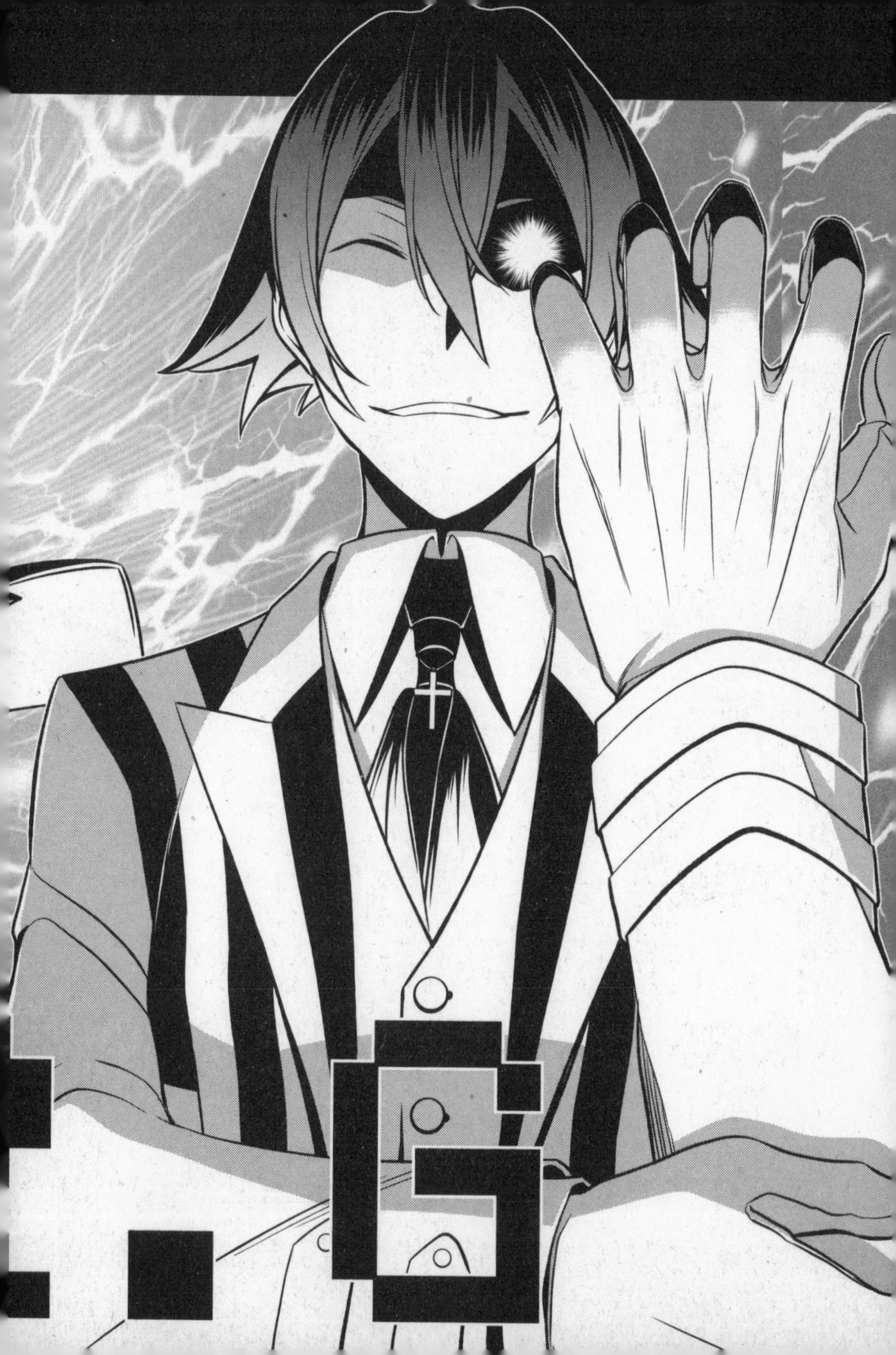

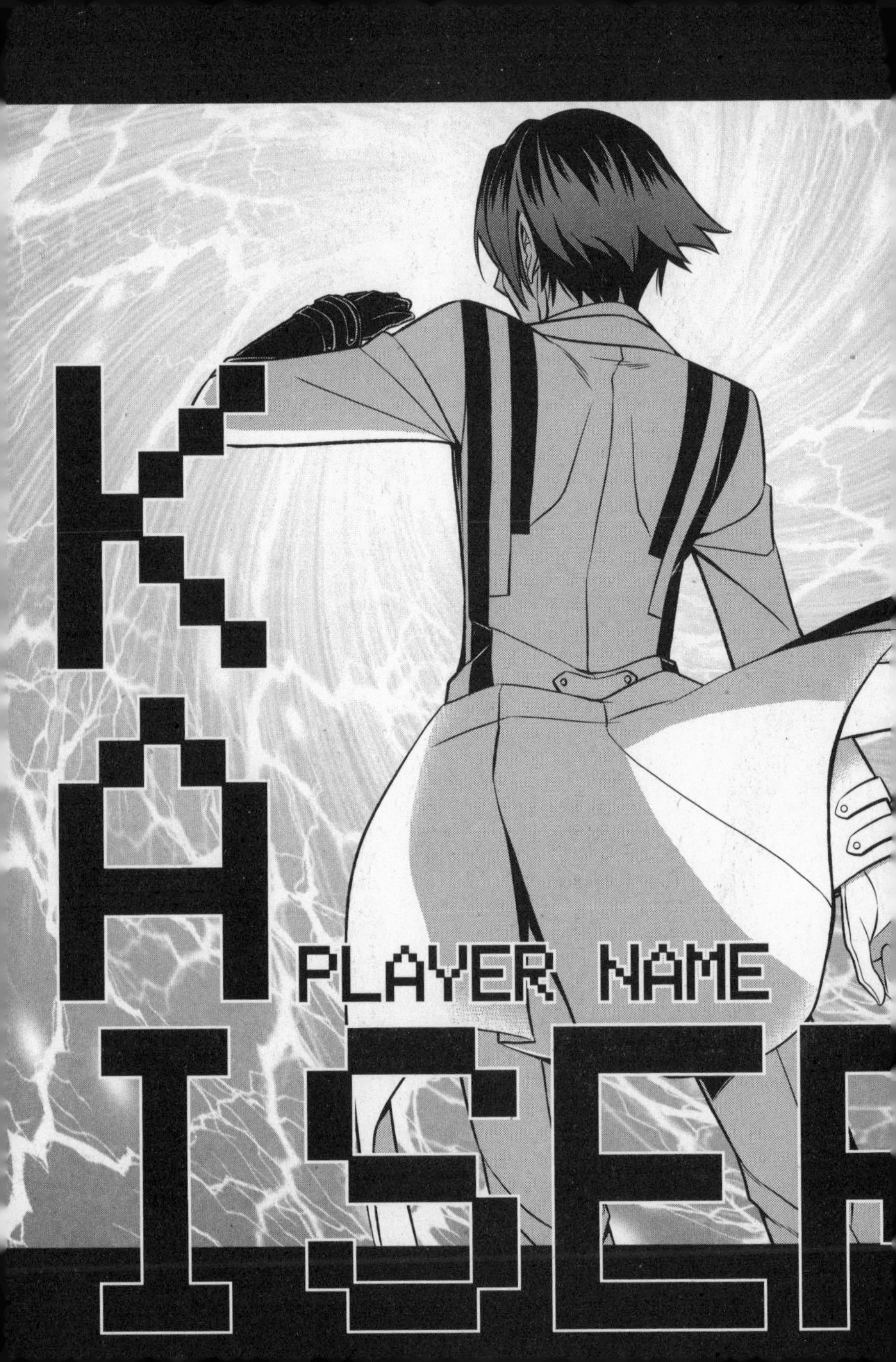
PLAYER NAME
KAISER

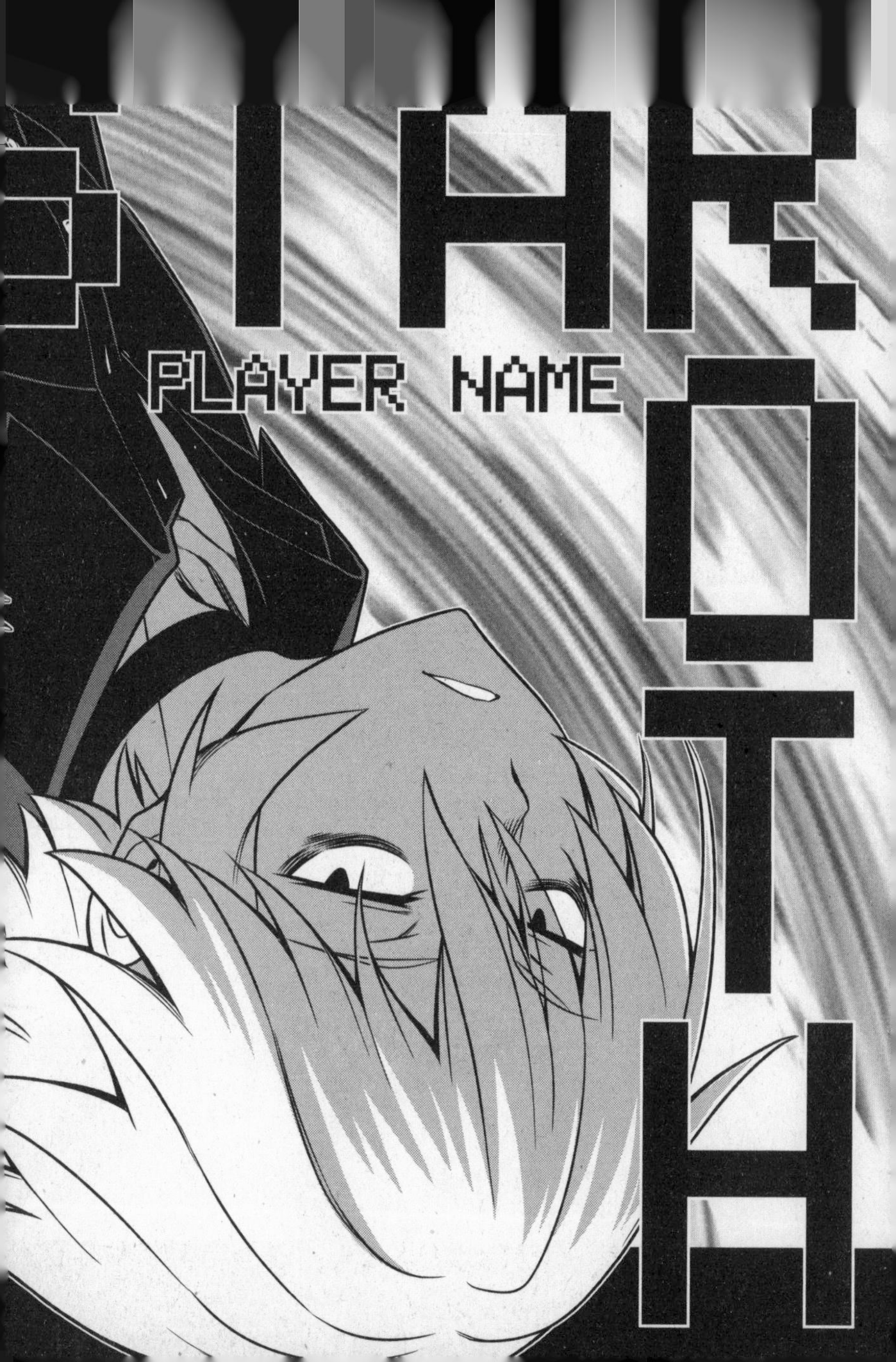
PLAYER NAME

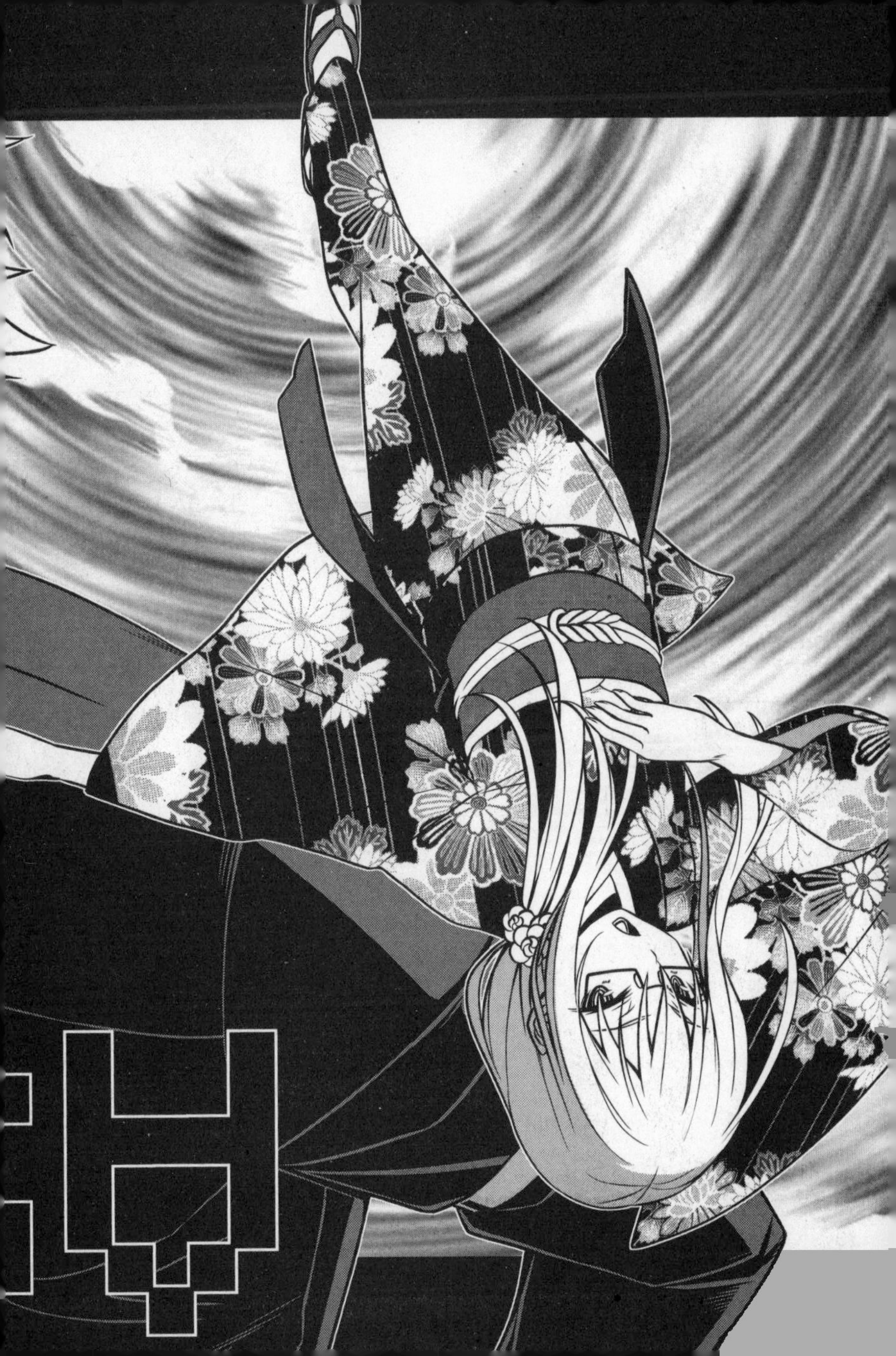

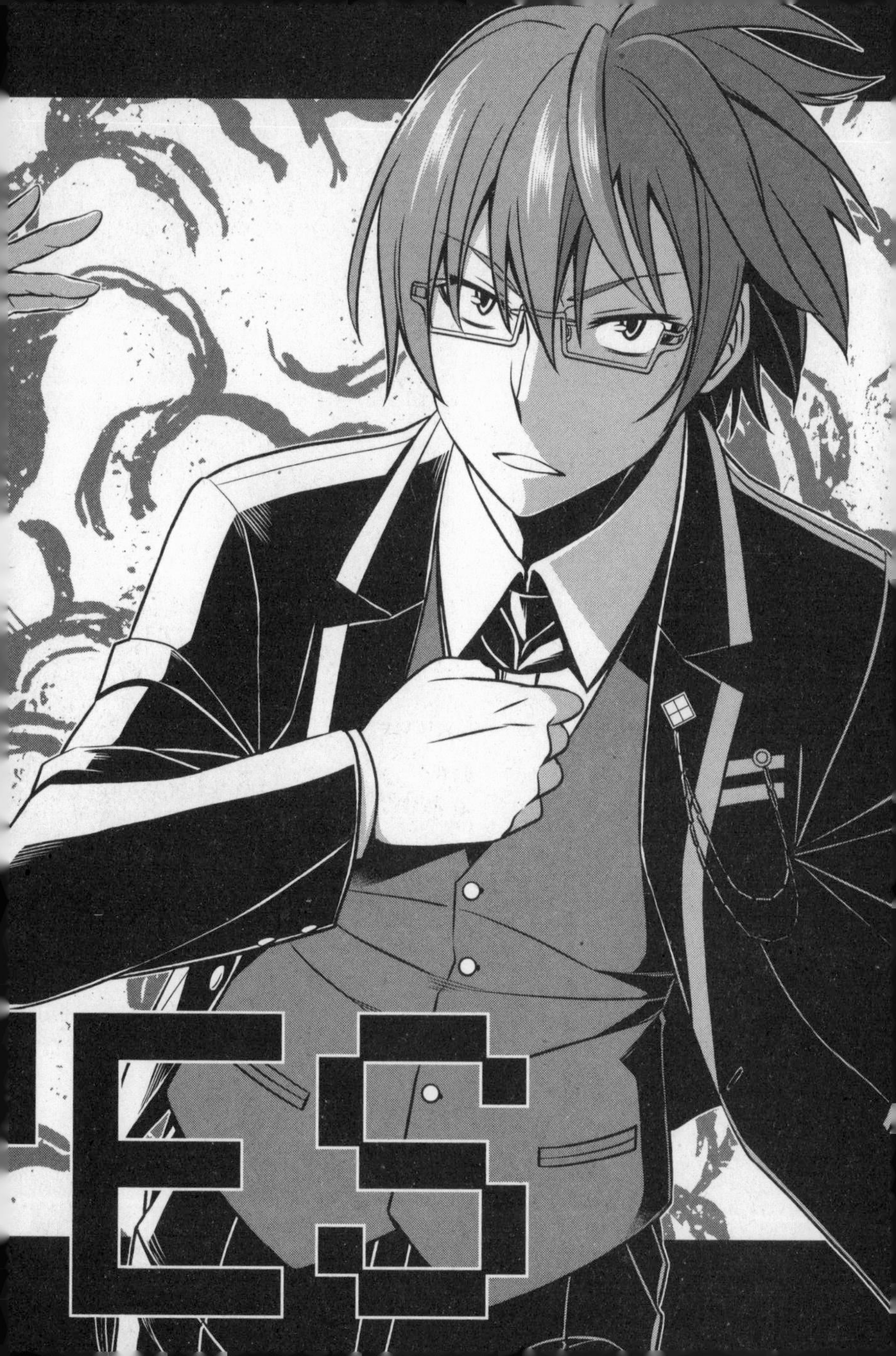
ES

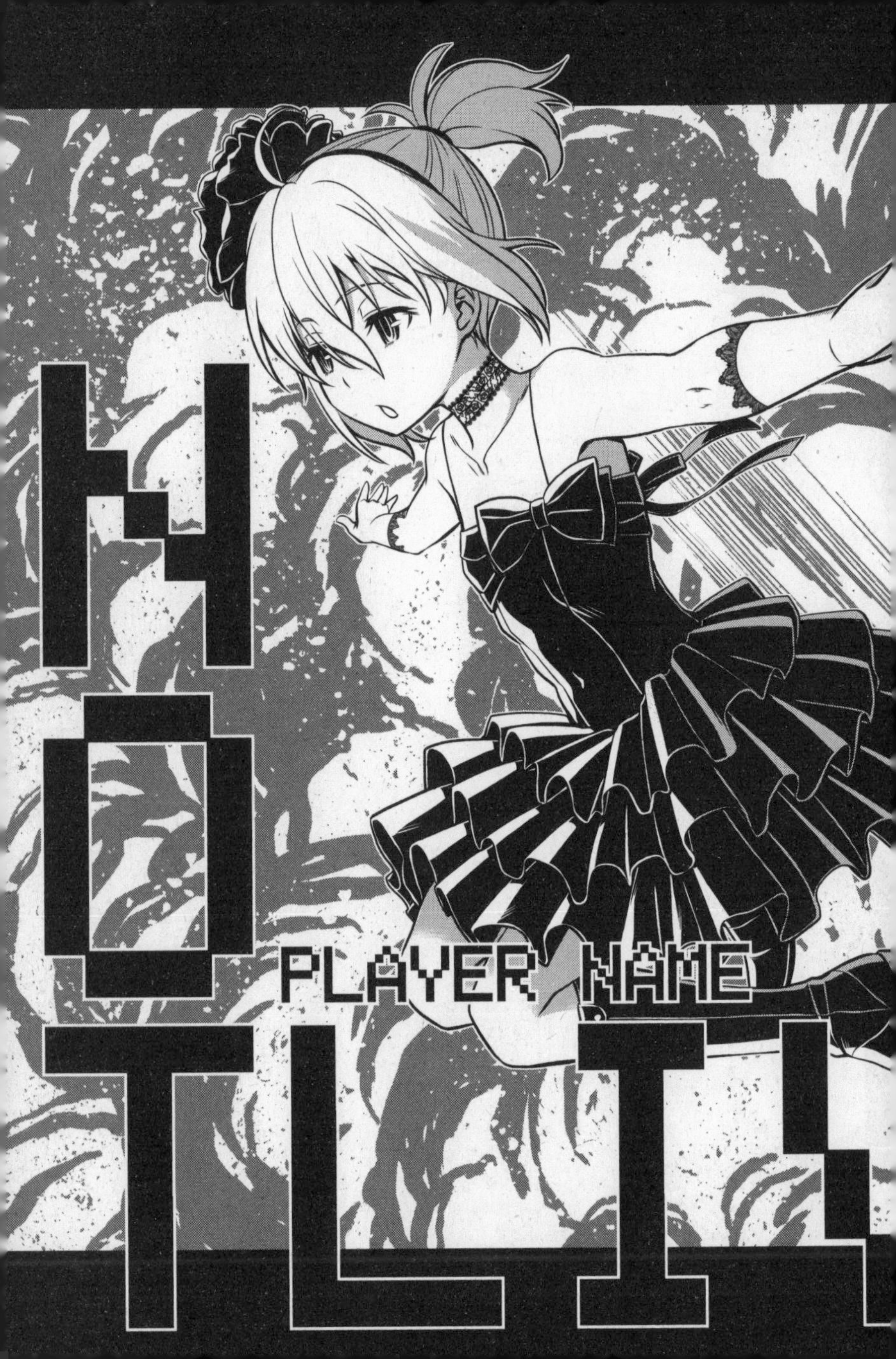
PLAYER NAME

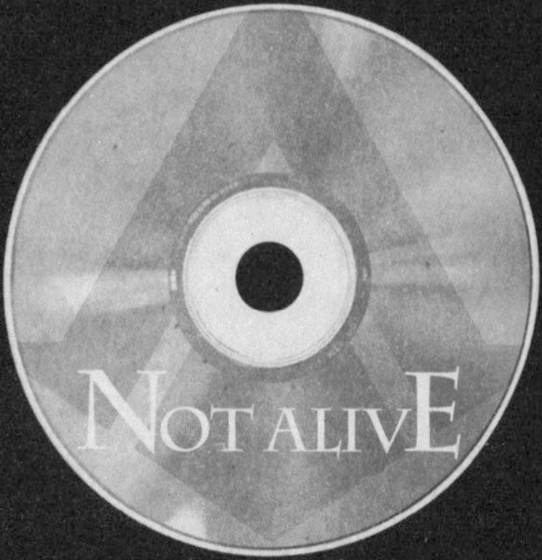
NOT ALIVE

CHAPTER 37

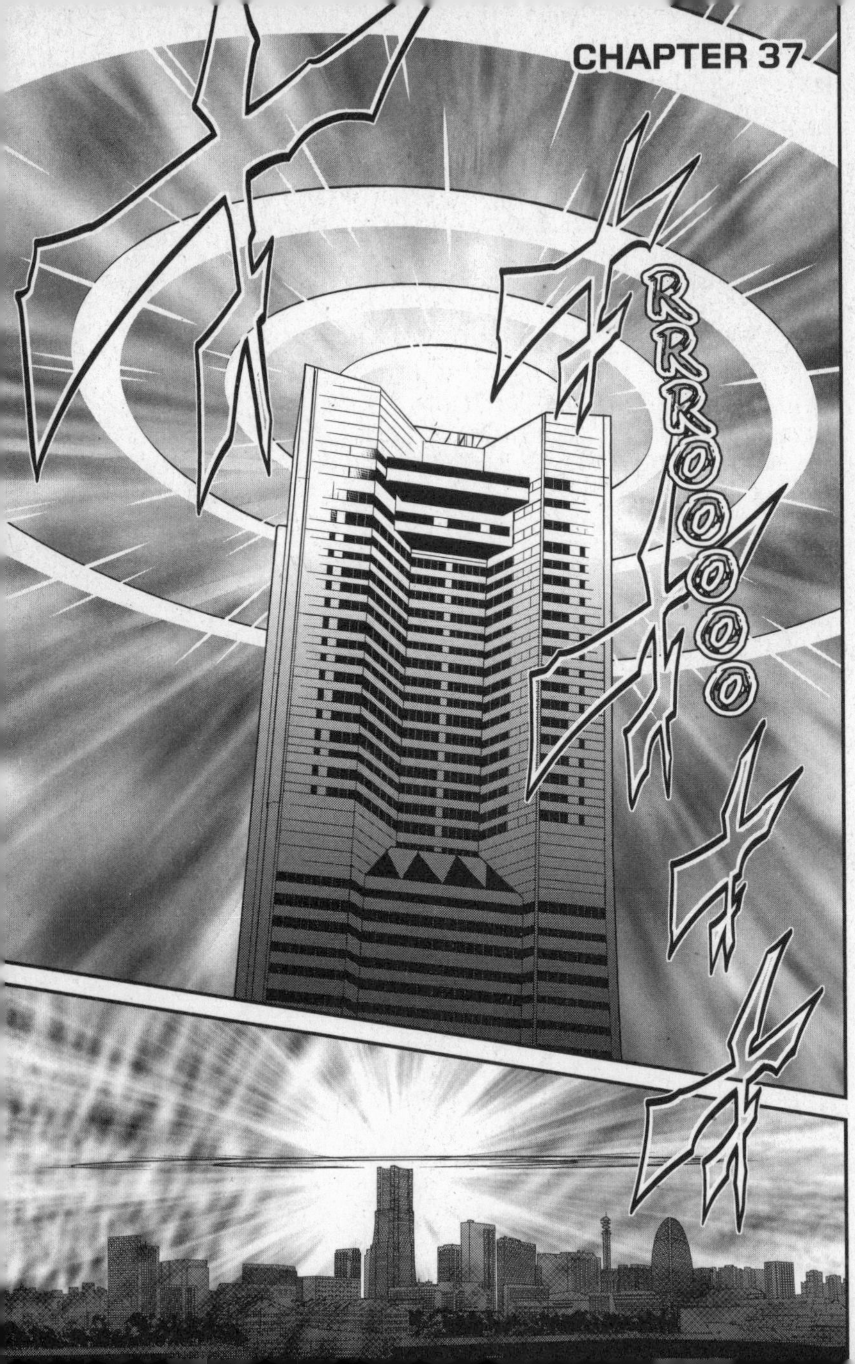
RRROOOOOO

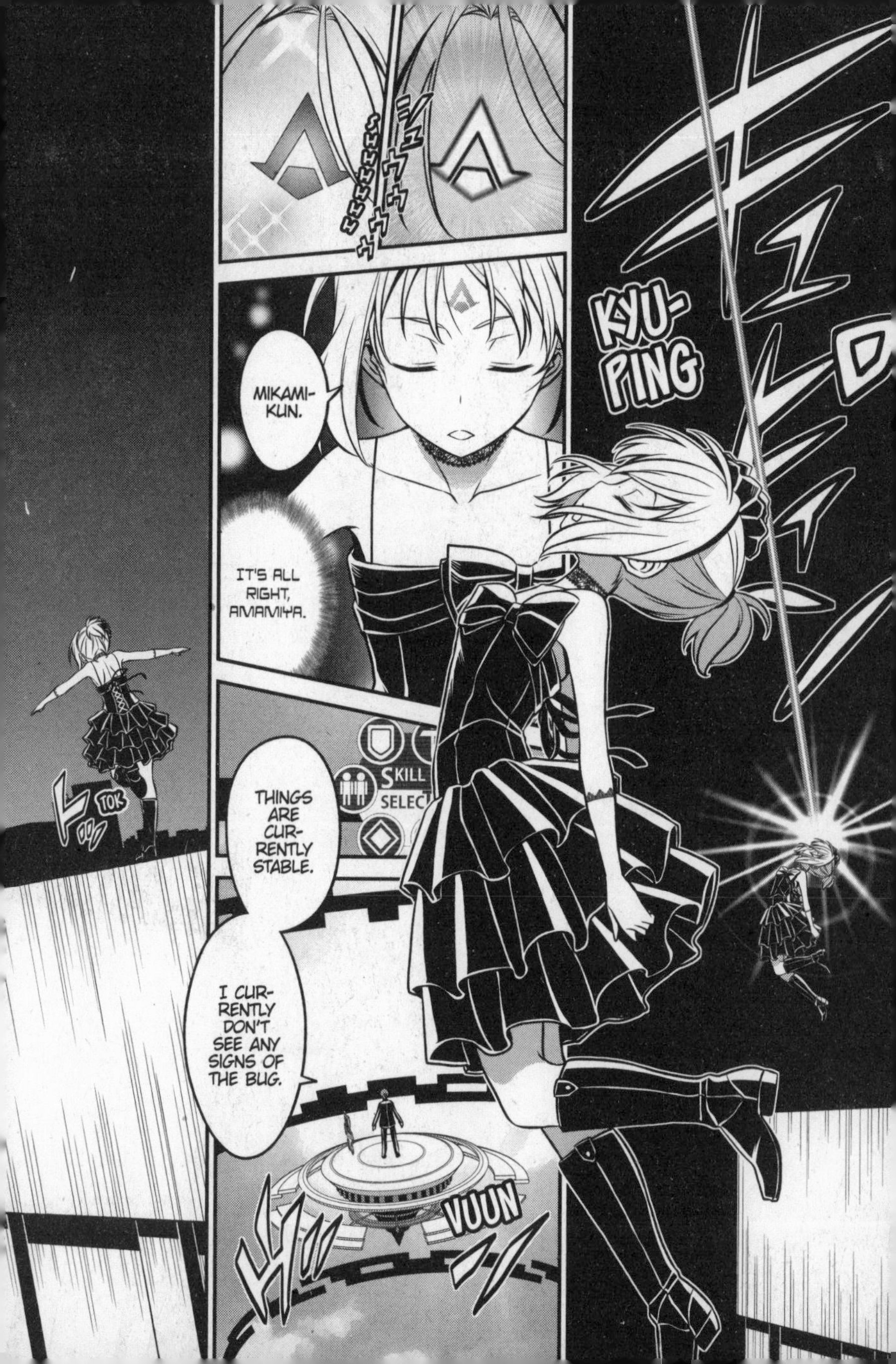
KYU-PING
MIKAMI-KUN.
IT'S ALL RIGHT, AMAMIYA.
THINGS ARE CUR-RENTLY STABLE.
I CUR-RENTLY DON'T SEE ANY SIGNS OF THE BUG.
VUUN
TOK

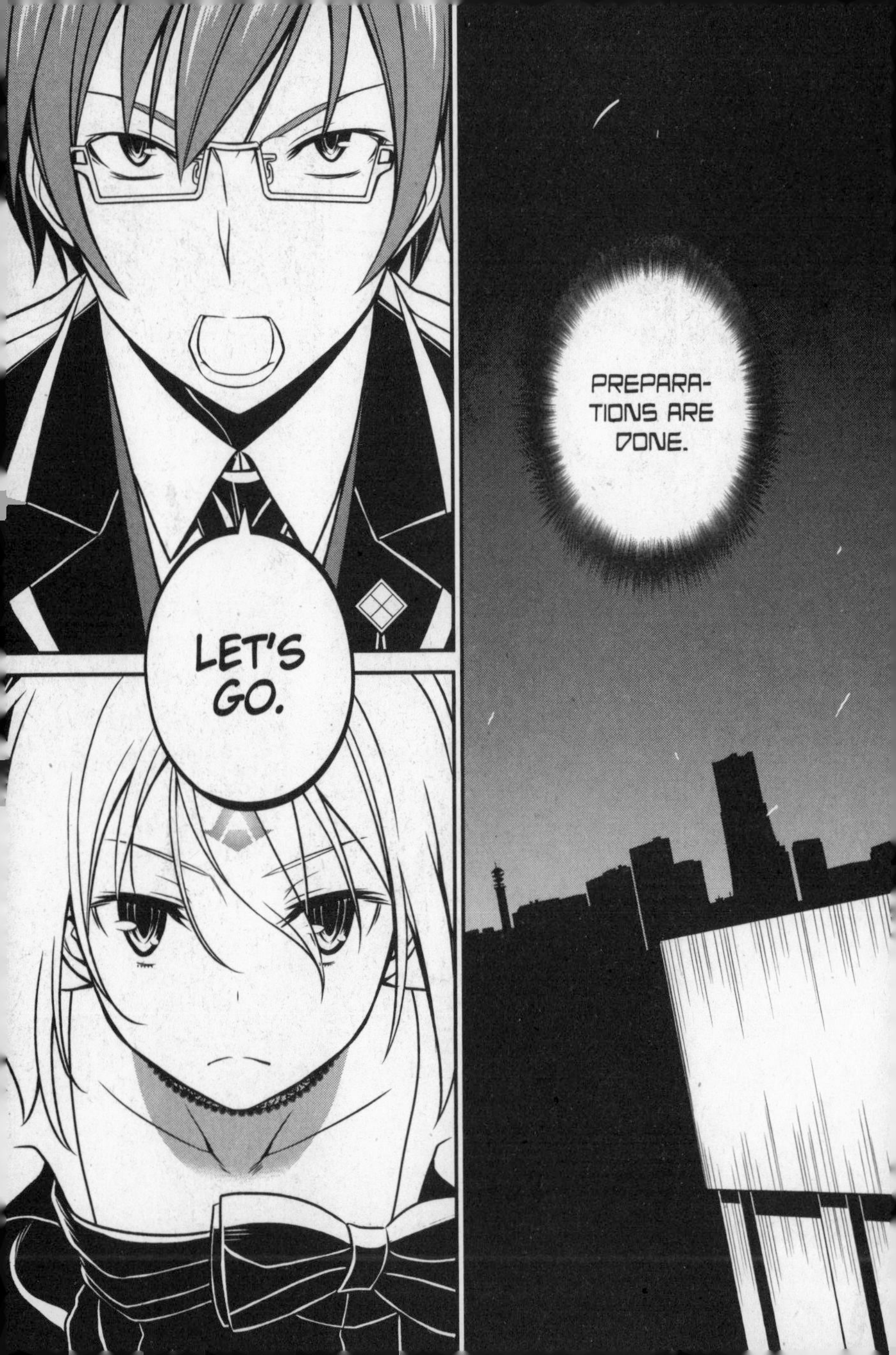
PREPARA-
TIONS ARE
DONE.
LET'S
GO.

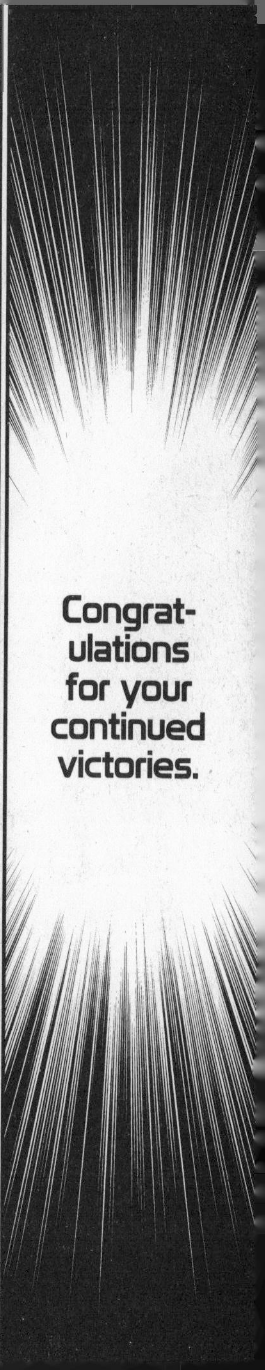
Congrat-
ulations
for your
continued
victories.
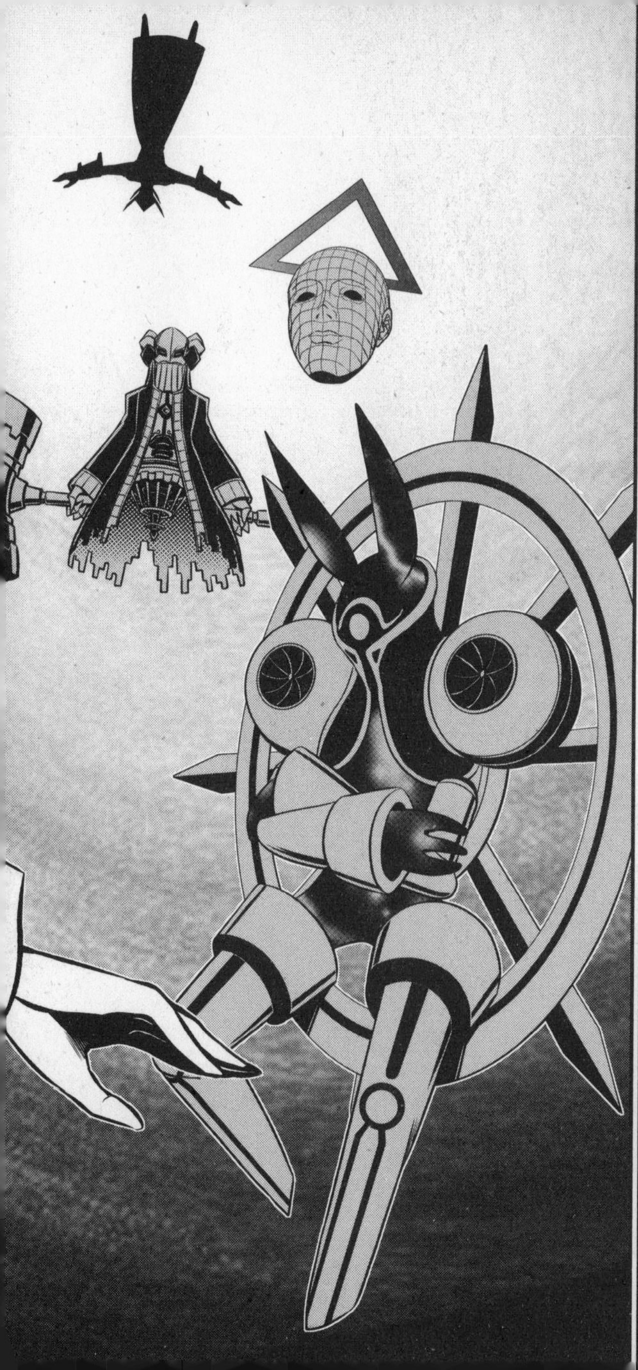

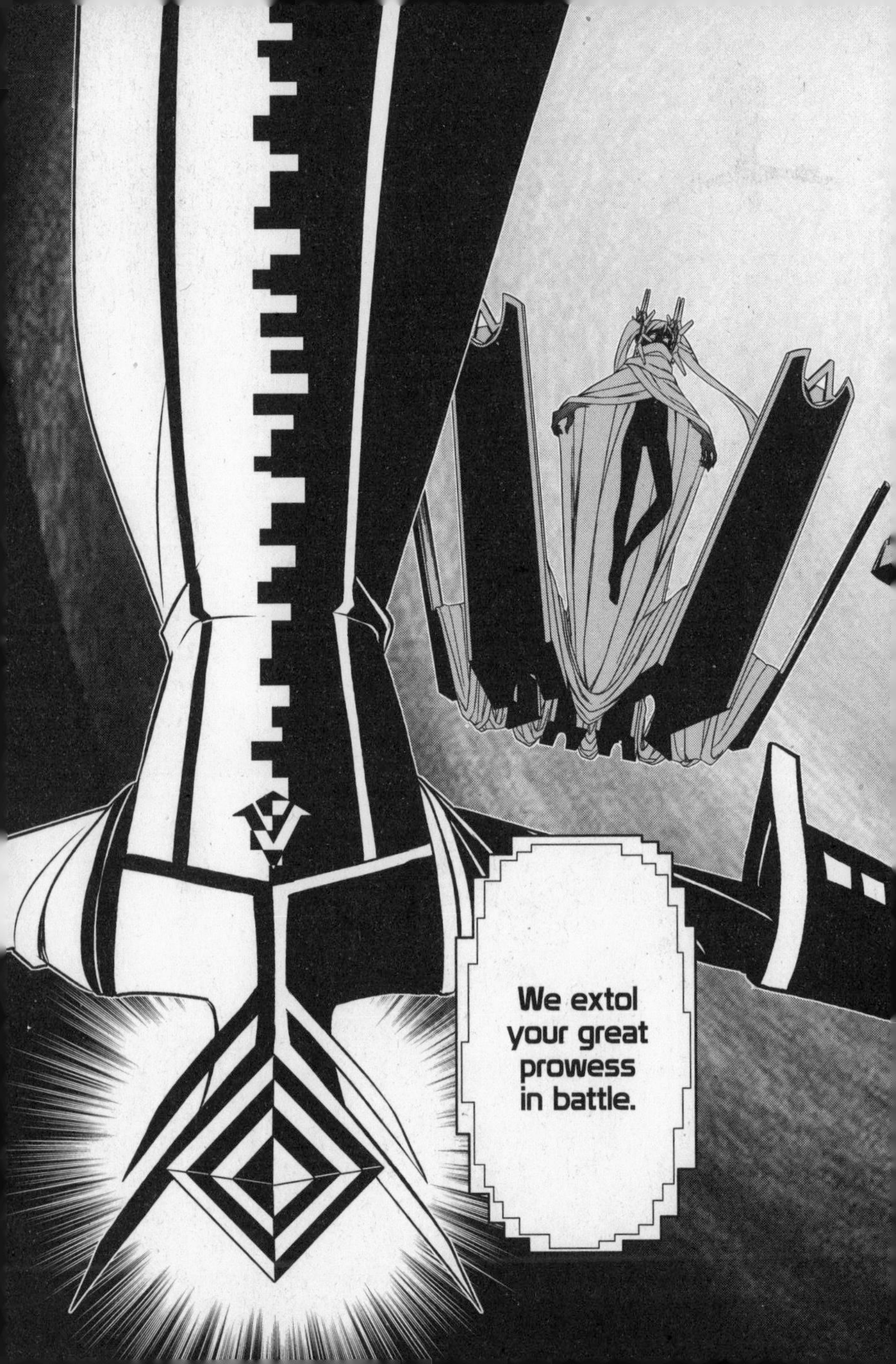
We extol your great prowess in battle.

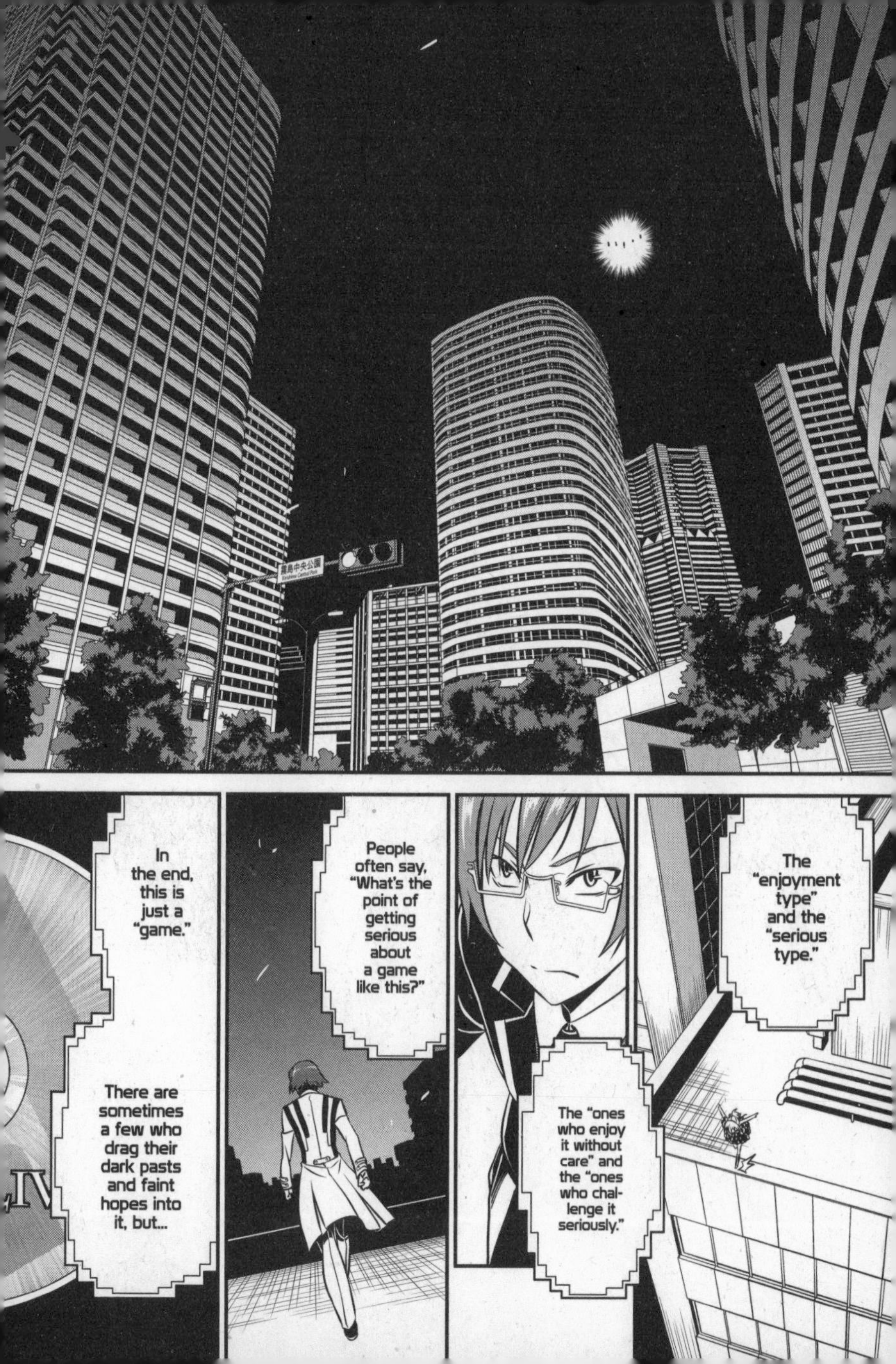
In the end, this is just a "game."
There are sometimes a few who drag their dark pasts and faint hopes into it, but...
People often say, "What's the point of getting serious about a game like this?"
The "ones who enjoy it without care" and the "ones who challenge it seriously."
The "enjoyment type" and the "serious type."

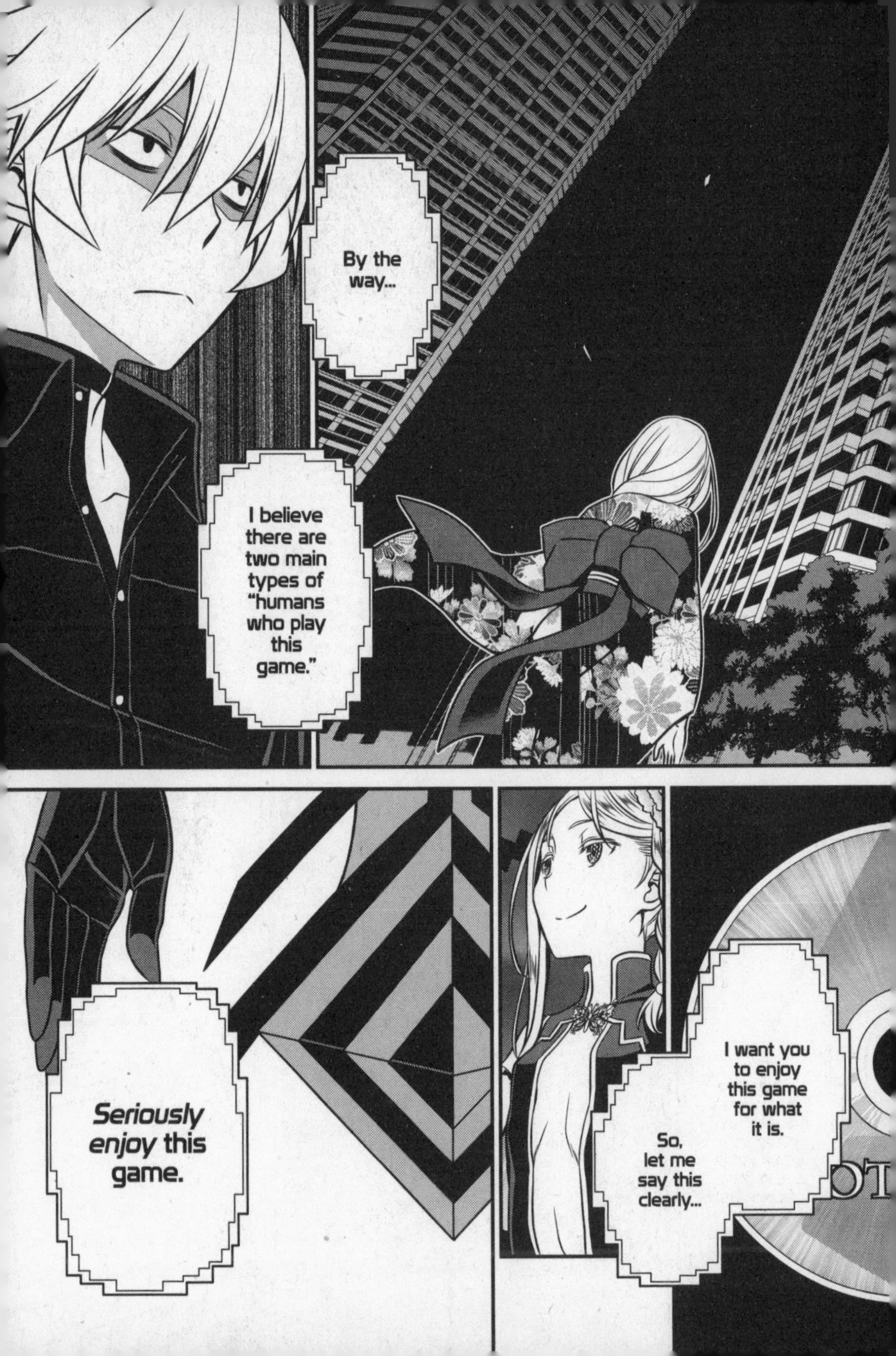
By the way...
I believe there are two main types of "humans who play this game."
I want you to enjoy this game for what it is.
So, let me say this clearly...
Seriously enjoy this game.

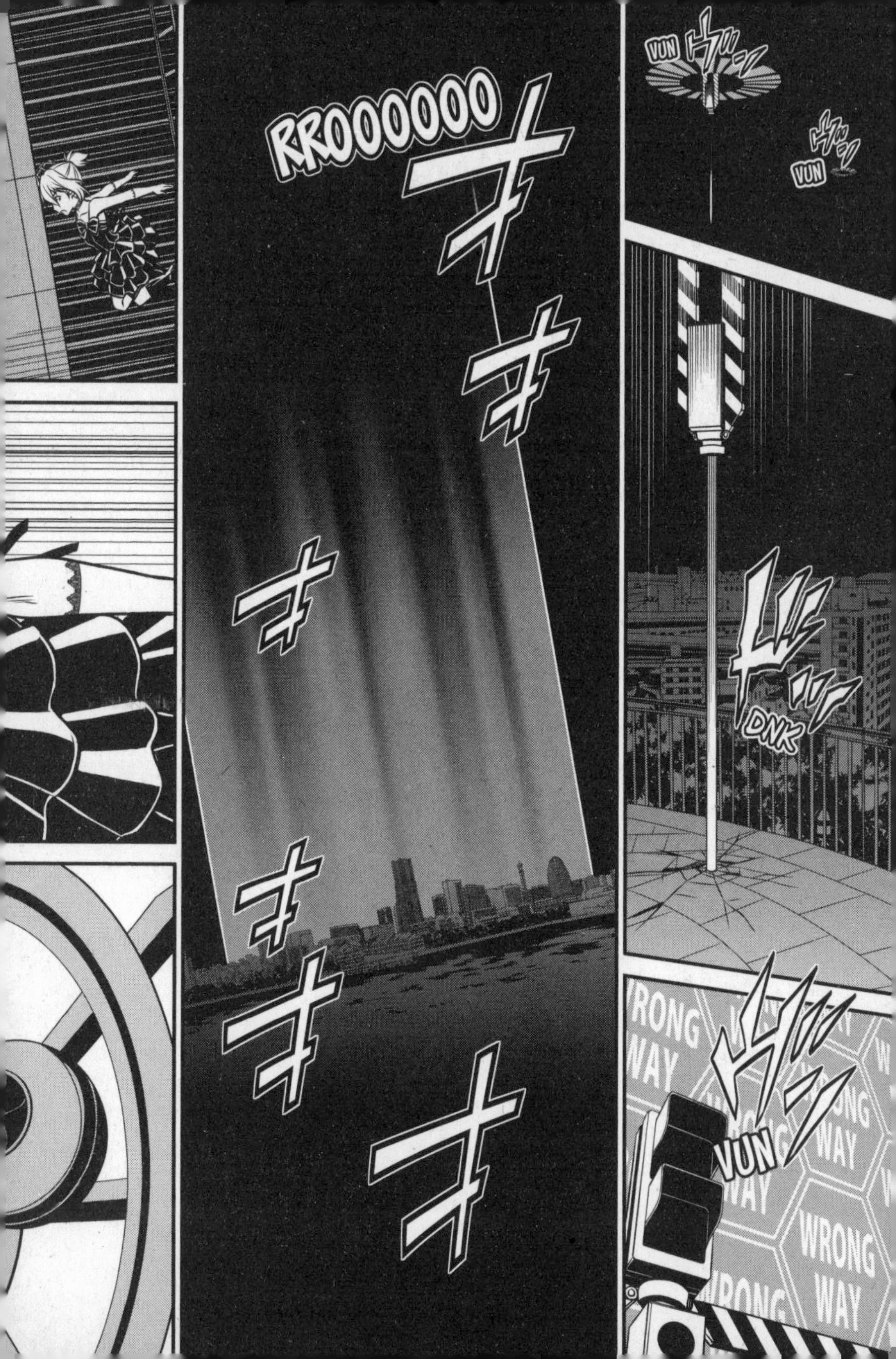
VUN
VUN
DNK
WRONG WAY
VUN
RROOOOOO

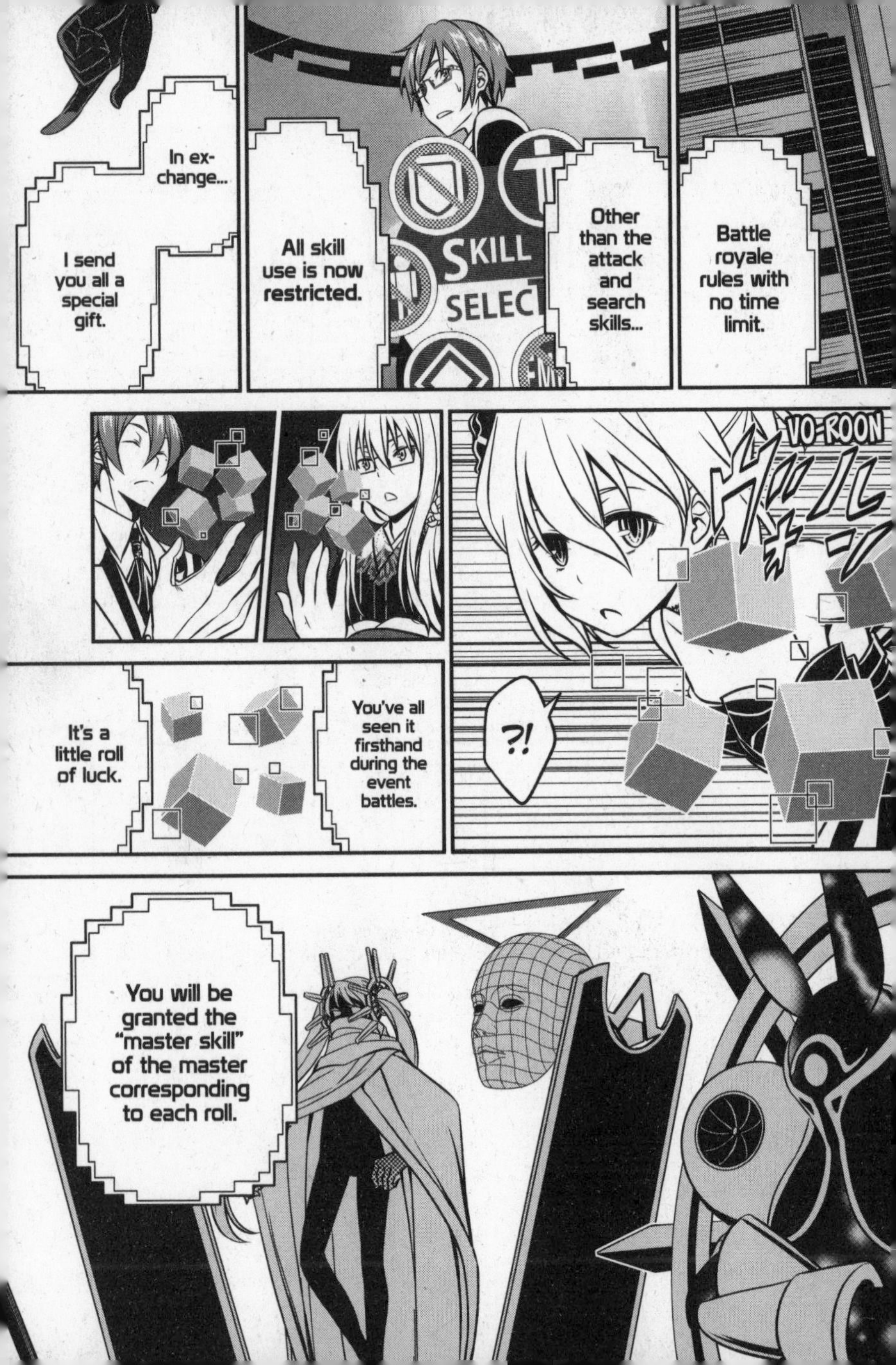
Battle royale rules with no time limit.
Other than the attack and search skills...
SKILL SELECT
All skill use is now restricted.
In ex-change...
I send you all a special gift.
VO-ROON
?!
You've all seen it firsthand during the event battles.
It's a little roll of luck.
You will be granted the "master skill" of the master corresponding to each roll.

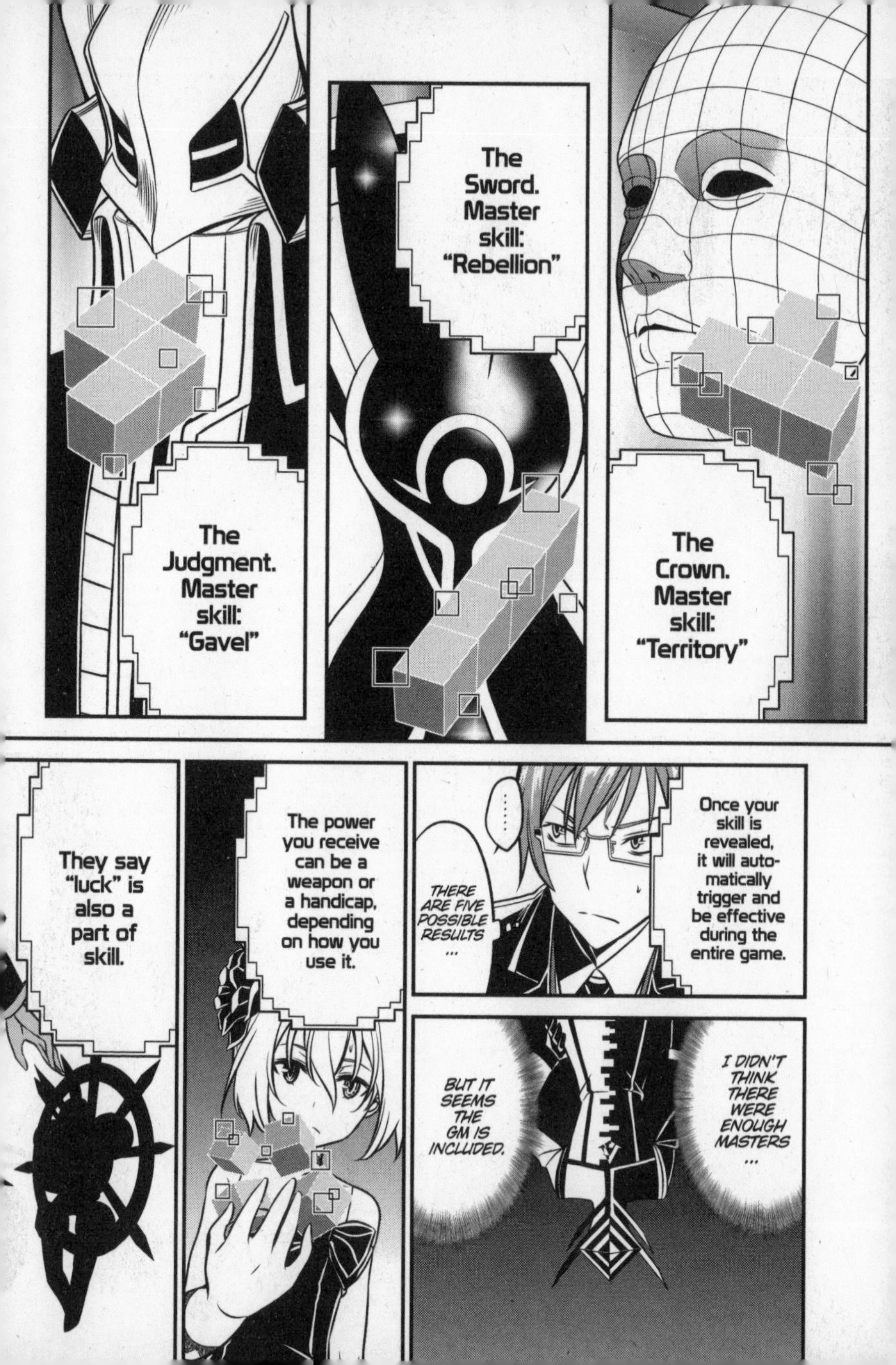
The Crown. Master skill: "Territory"
The Sword. Master skill: "Rebellion"
The Judgment. Master skill: "Gavel"
Once your skill is revealed, it will automatically trigger and be effective during the entire game.
......
THERE ARE FIVE POSSIBLE RESULTS ...
I DIDN'T THINK THERE WERE ENOUGH MASTERS ...
BUT IT SEEMS THE GM IS INCLUDED.
The power you receive can be a weapon or a handicap, depending on how you use it.
They say "luck" is also a part of skill.

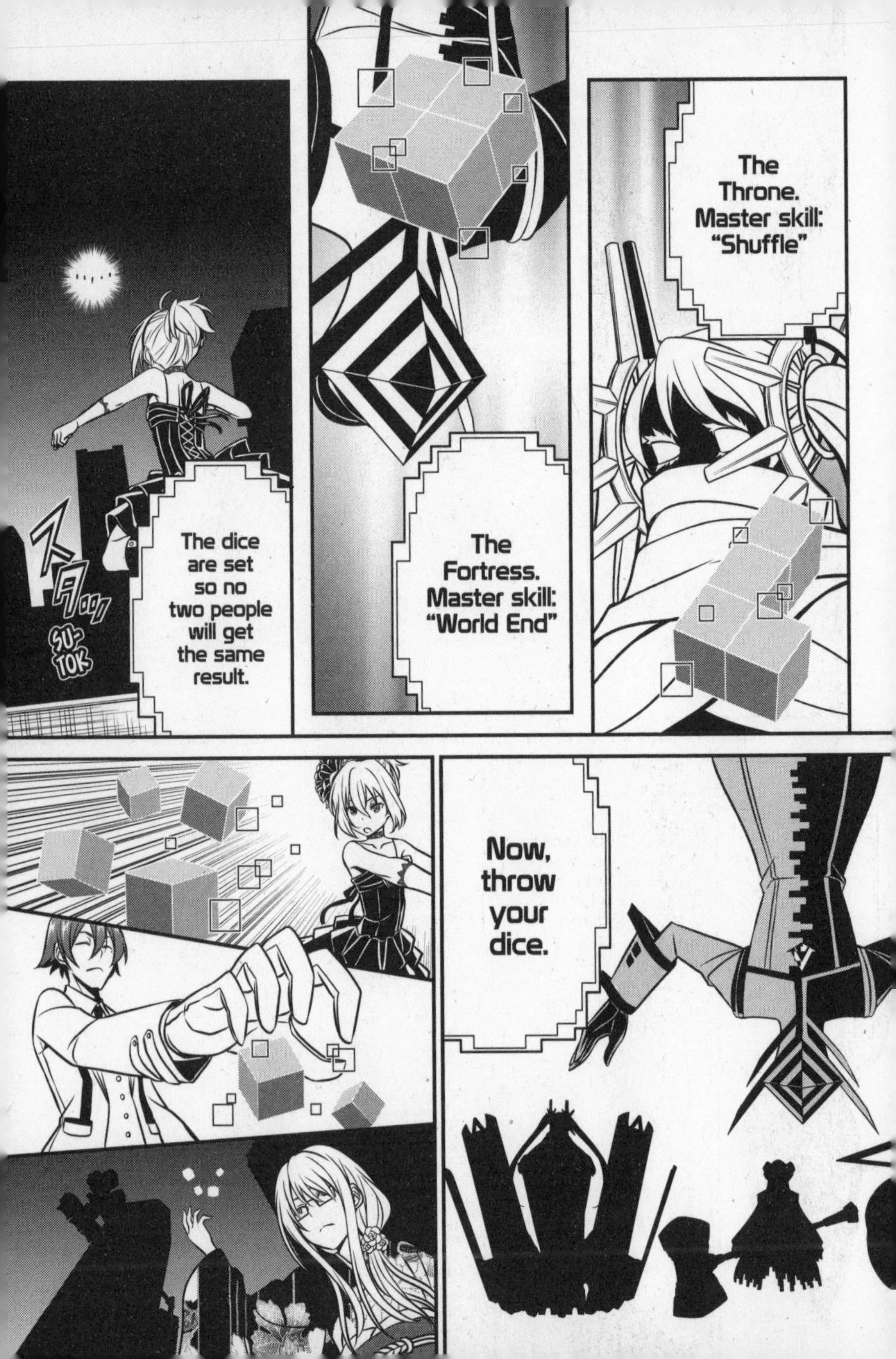
The Throne. Master skill: "Shuffle"
The Fortress. Master skill: "World End"
.....
The dice are set so no two people will get the same result.
SU-TOK
Now, throw your dice.

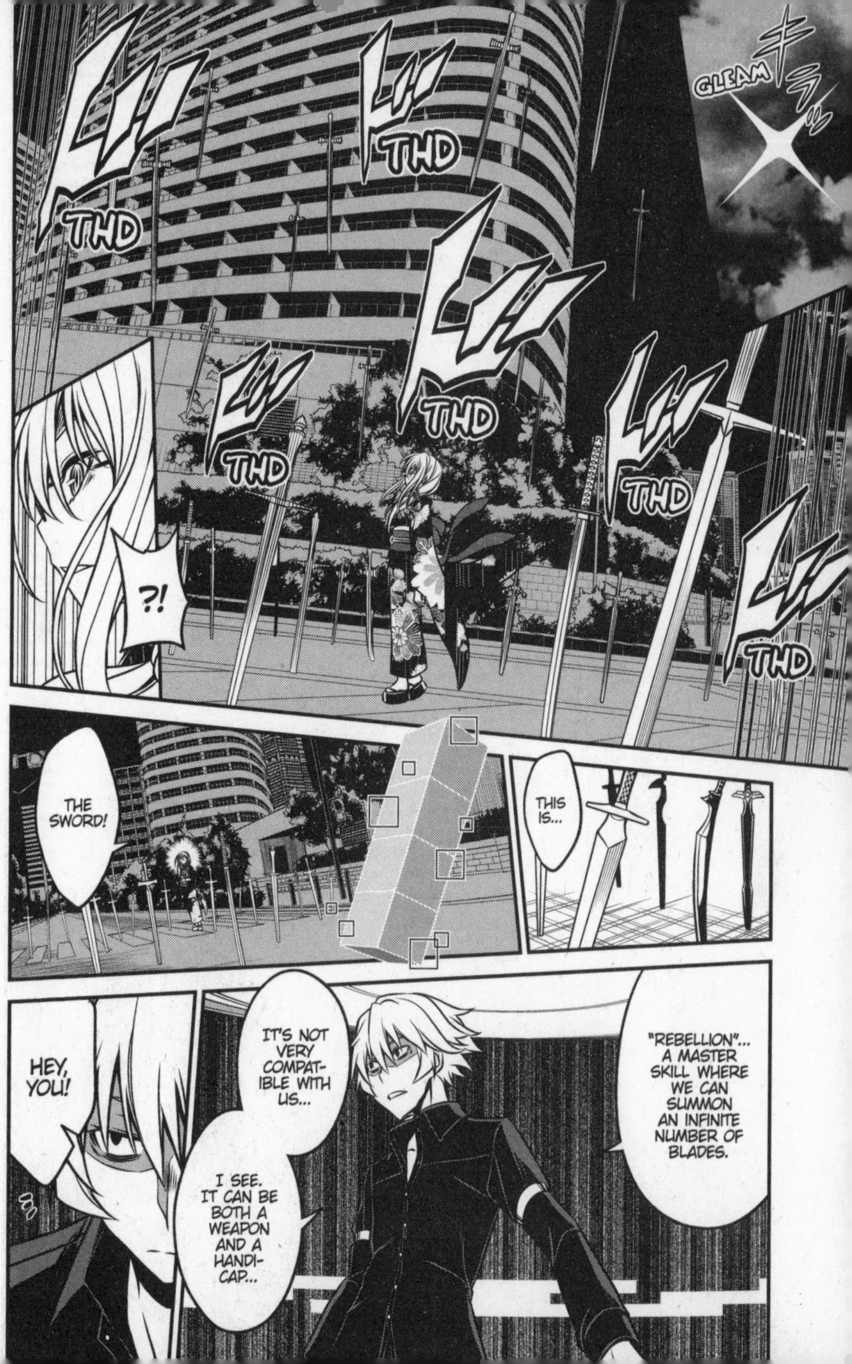
GLEAM
THD
THD
THD
THD
THD
THD
?!
THIS IS...
THE SWORD!
"REBELLION"... A MASTER SKILL WHERE WE CAN SUMMON AN INFINITE NUMBER OF BLADES.
IT'S NOT VERY COMPAT-IBLE WITH US...
I SEE. IT CAN BE BOTH A WEAPON AND A HANDI-CAP...
HEY, YOU!

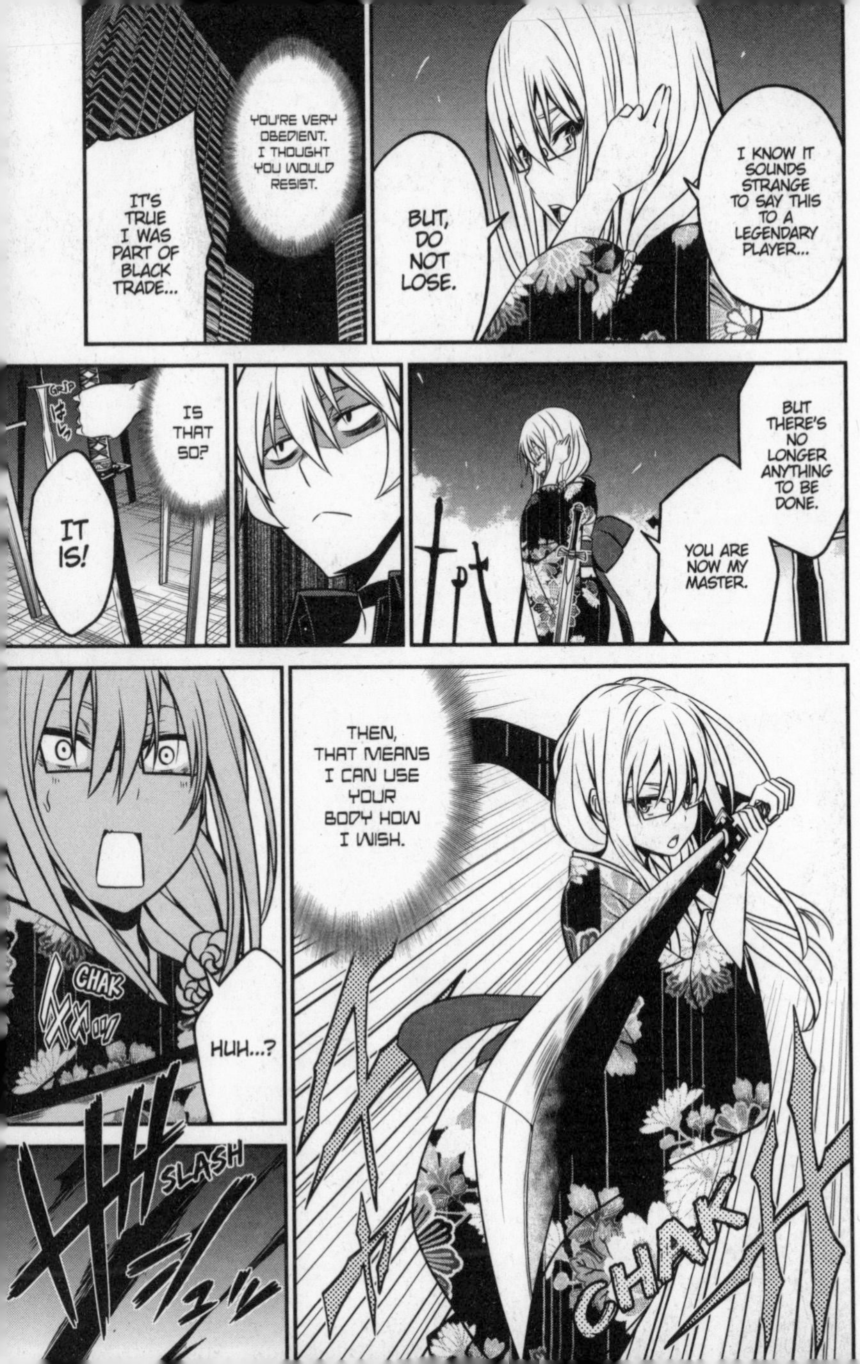
I KNOW IT SOUNDS STRANGE TO SAY THIS TO A LEGENDARY PLAYER...
BUT, DO NOT LOSE.
YOU'RE VERY OBEDIENT. I THOUGHT YOU WOULD RESIST.
IT'S TRUE I WAS PART OF BLACK TRADE...
BUT THERE'S NO LONGER ANYTHING TO BE DONE.
YOU ARE NOW MY MASTER.
IS THAT SO?
GRIP
IT IS!
THEN, THAT MEANS I CAN USE YOUR BODY HOW I WISH.
CHAK
HUH...?
CHAK
SLASH

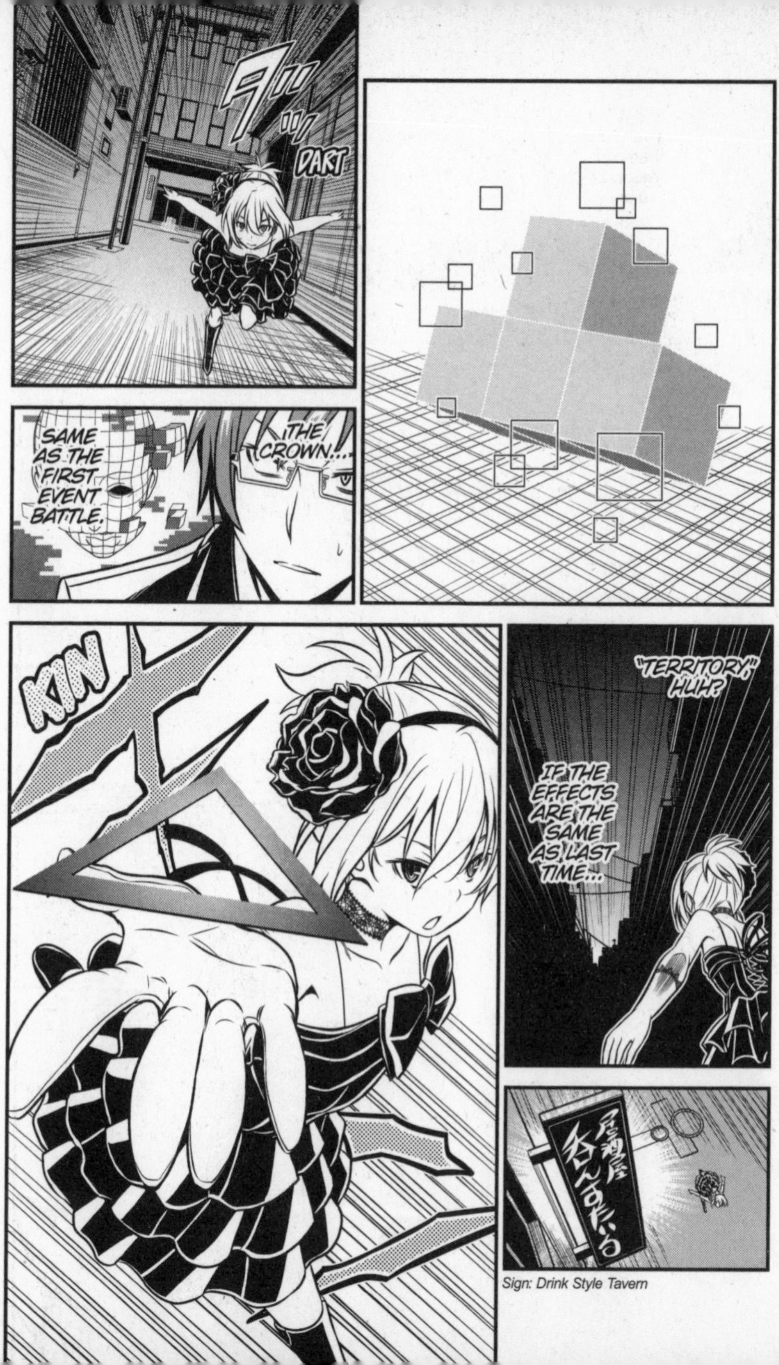
DART
...THE CROWN...
SAME AS THE FIRST EVENT BATTLE.
"TERRITORY," HUH?
IF THE EFFECTS ARE THE SAME AS LAST TIME...
KIN

Sign: Drink Style Tavern

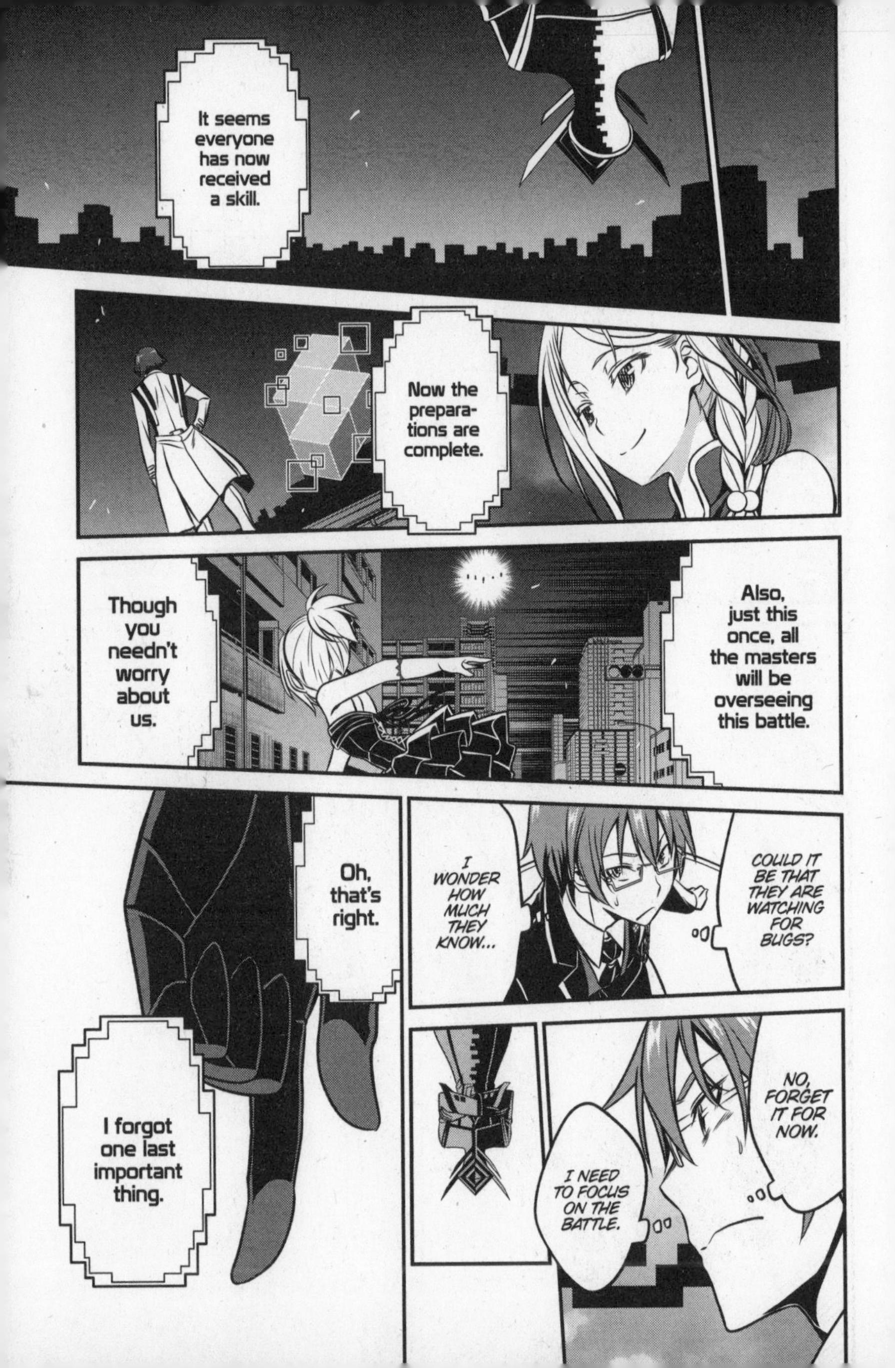
It seems everyone has now received a skill.
Now the prepara-tions are complete.
Also, just this once, all the masters will be overseeing this battle.
Though you needn't worry about us.
COULD IT BE THAT THEY ARE WATCHING FOR BUGS?
I WONDER HOW MUCH THEY KNOW...
NO, FORGET IT FOR NOW.
I NEED TO FOCUS ON THE BATTLE.
Oh, that's right.
I forgot one last important thing.

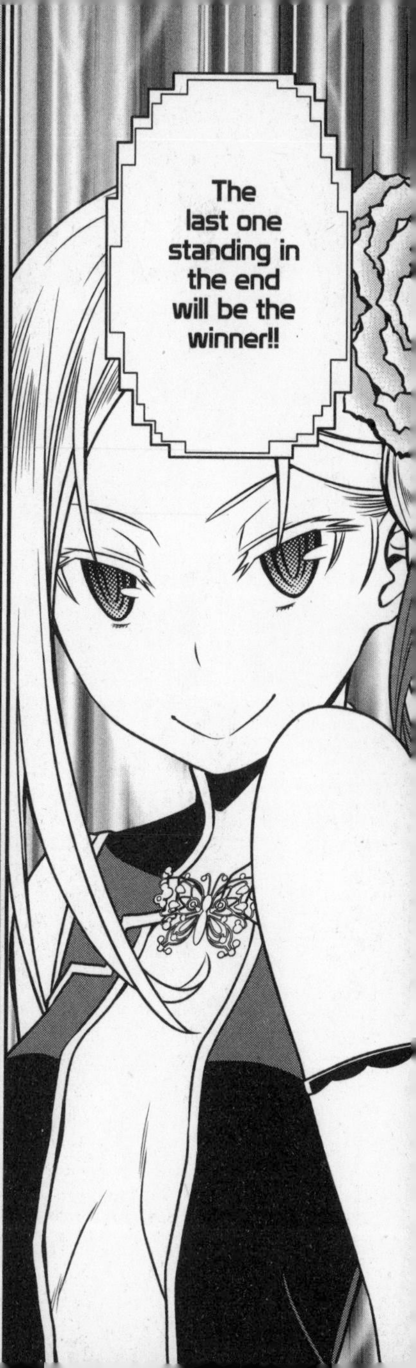
The last one standing in the end will be the winner!!
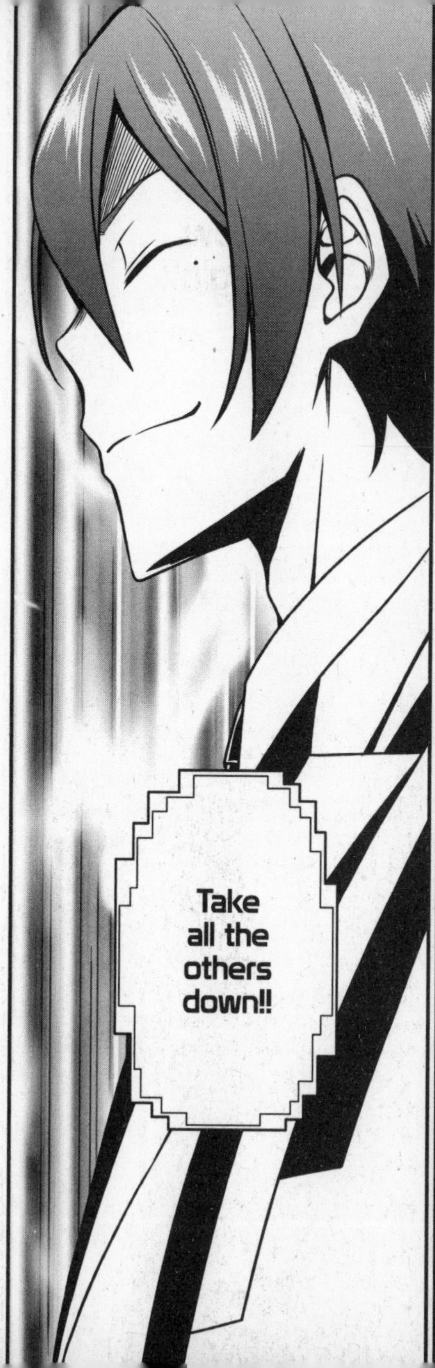
Take all the others down!!

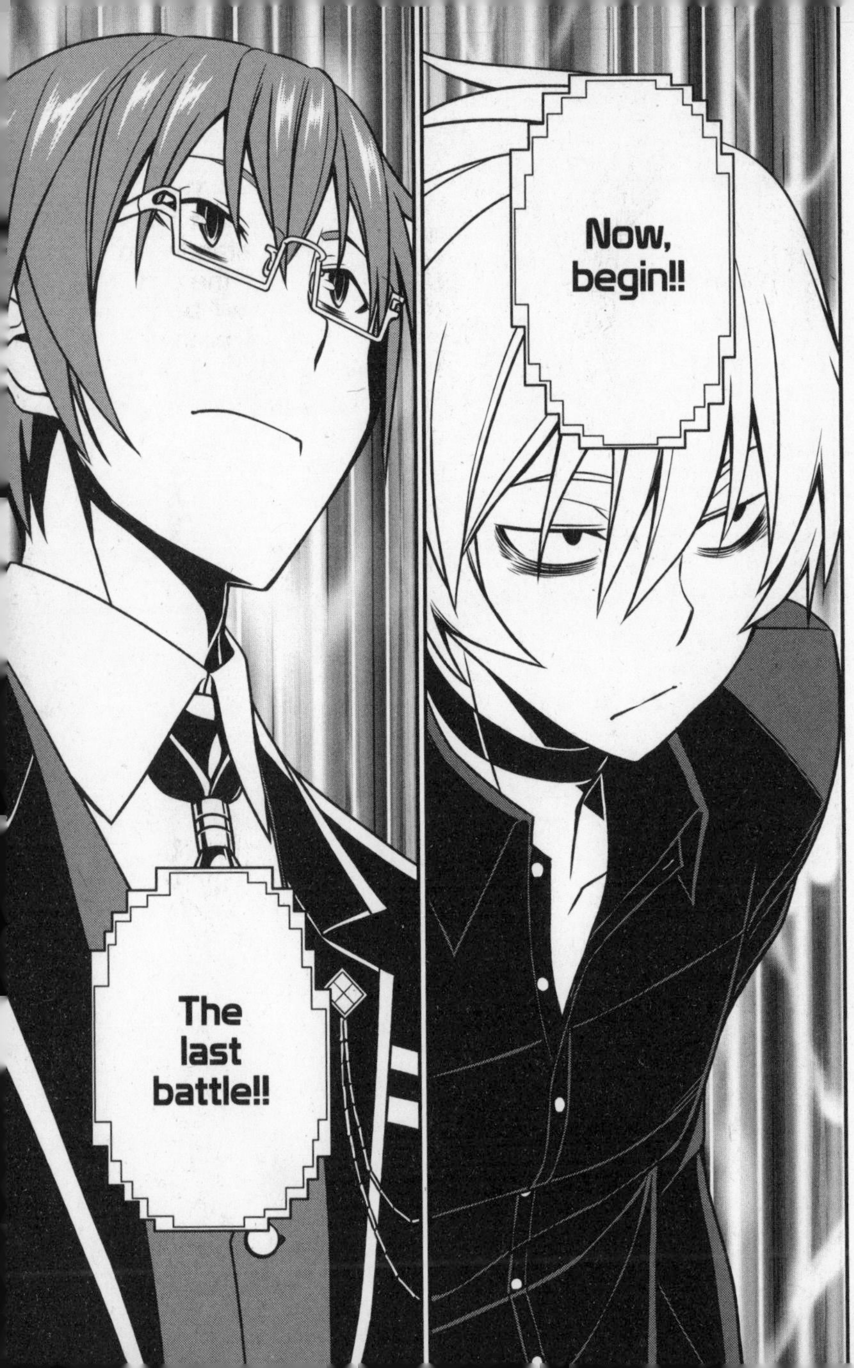
Now, begin!!
The last battle!!

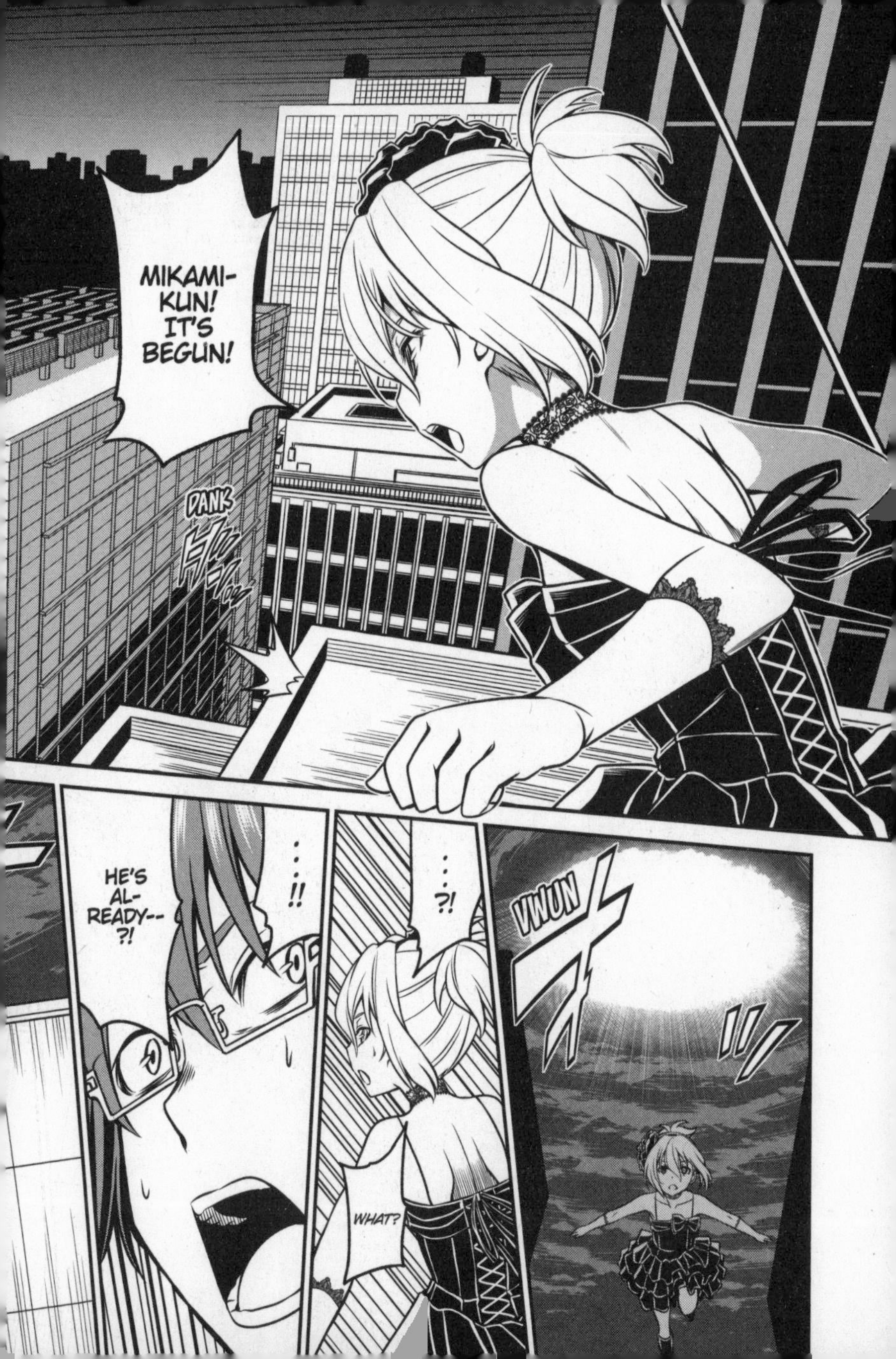
MIKAMI-KUN! IT'S BEGUN!
DANK
VWUN
...?!
WHAT?
...!!
HE'S AL-READY--?!

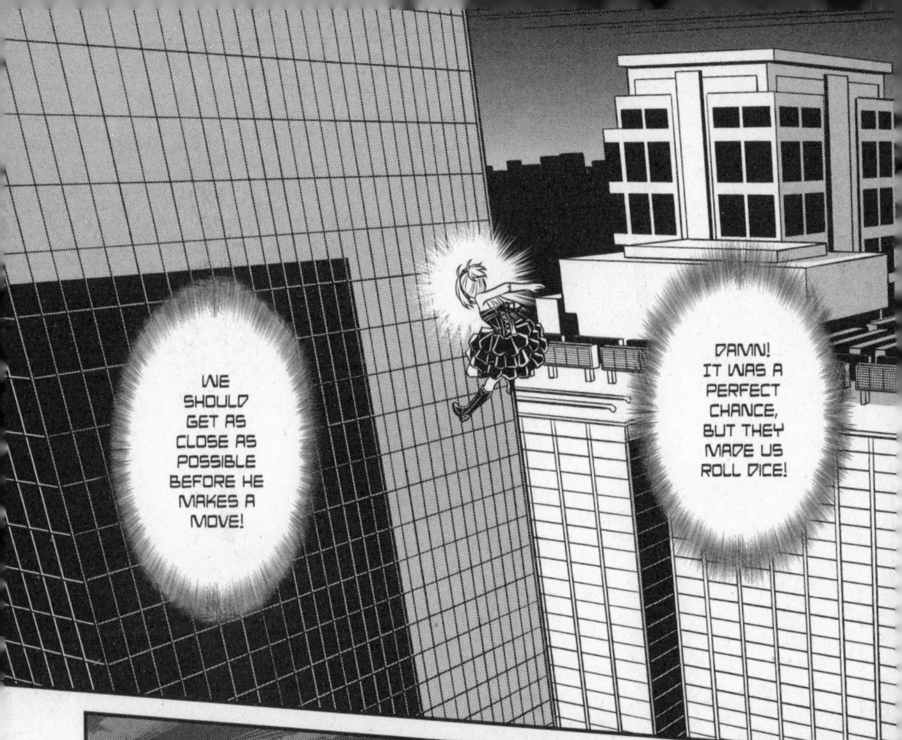
DAMN! IT WAS A PERFECT CHANCE, BUT THEY MADE US ROLL DICE!
WE SHOULD GET AS CLOSE AS POSSIBLE BEFORE HE MAKES A MOVE!
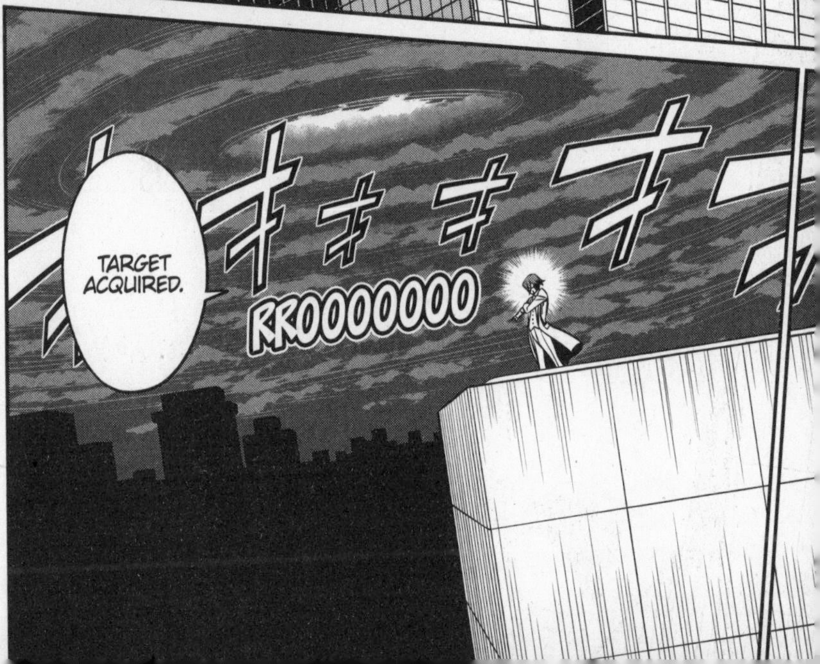
RROOOOOOO
TARGET ACQUIRED.

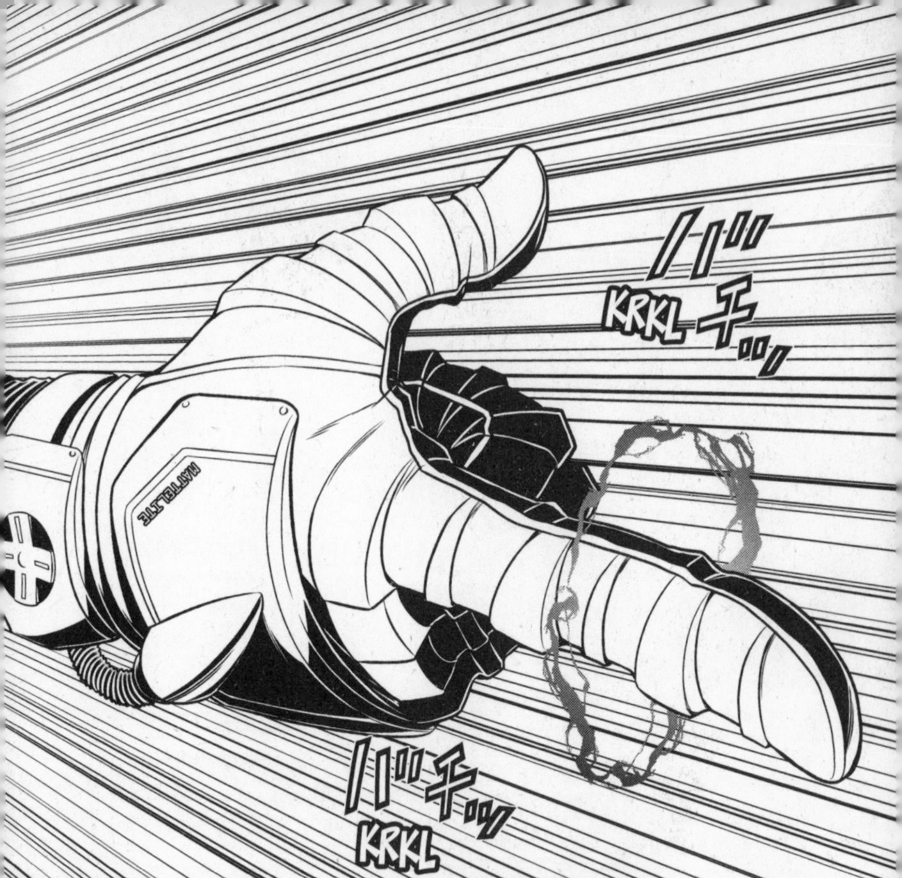
KRKL
KRKL
MATTELITE

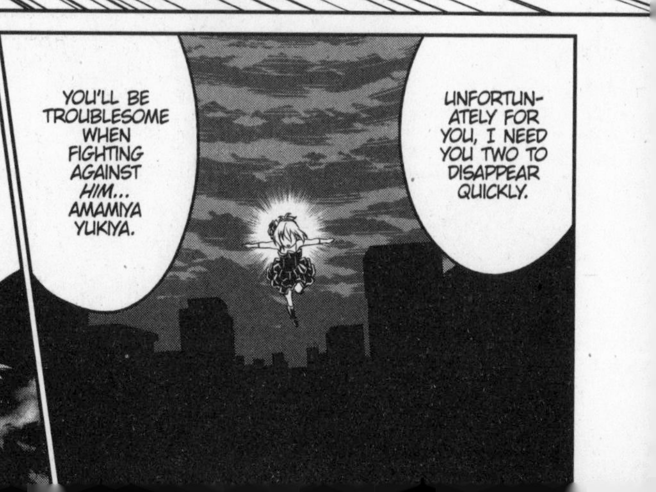
UNFORTUN-ATELY FOR YOU, I NEED YOU TWO TO DISAPPEAR QUICKLY.
YOU'LL BE TROUBLESOME WHEN FIGHTING AGAINST HIM... AMAMIYA YUKIYA.

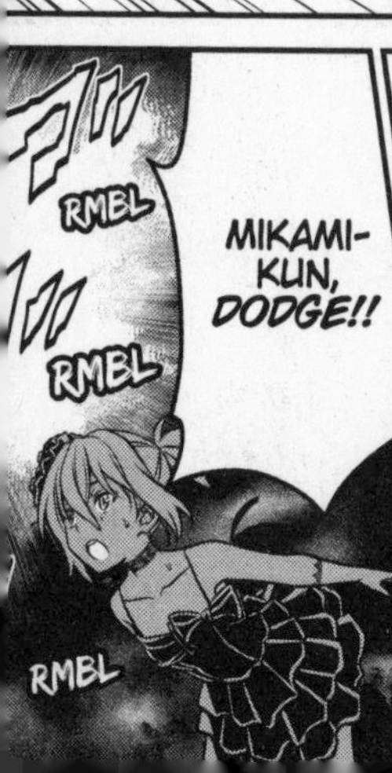
RMBL
RMBL
MIKAMI-KUN, DODGE!!
RMBL

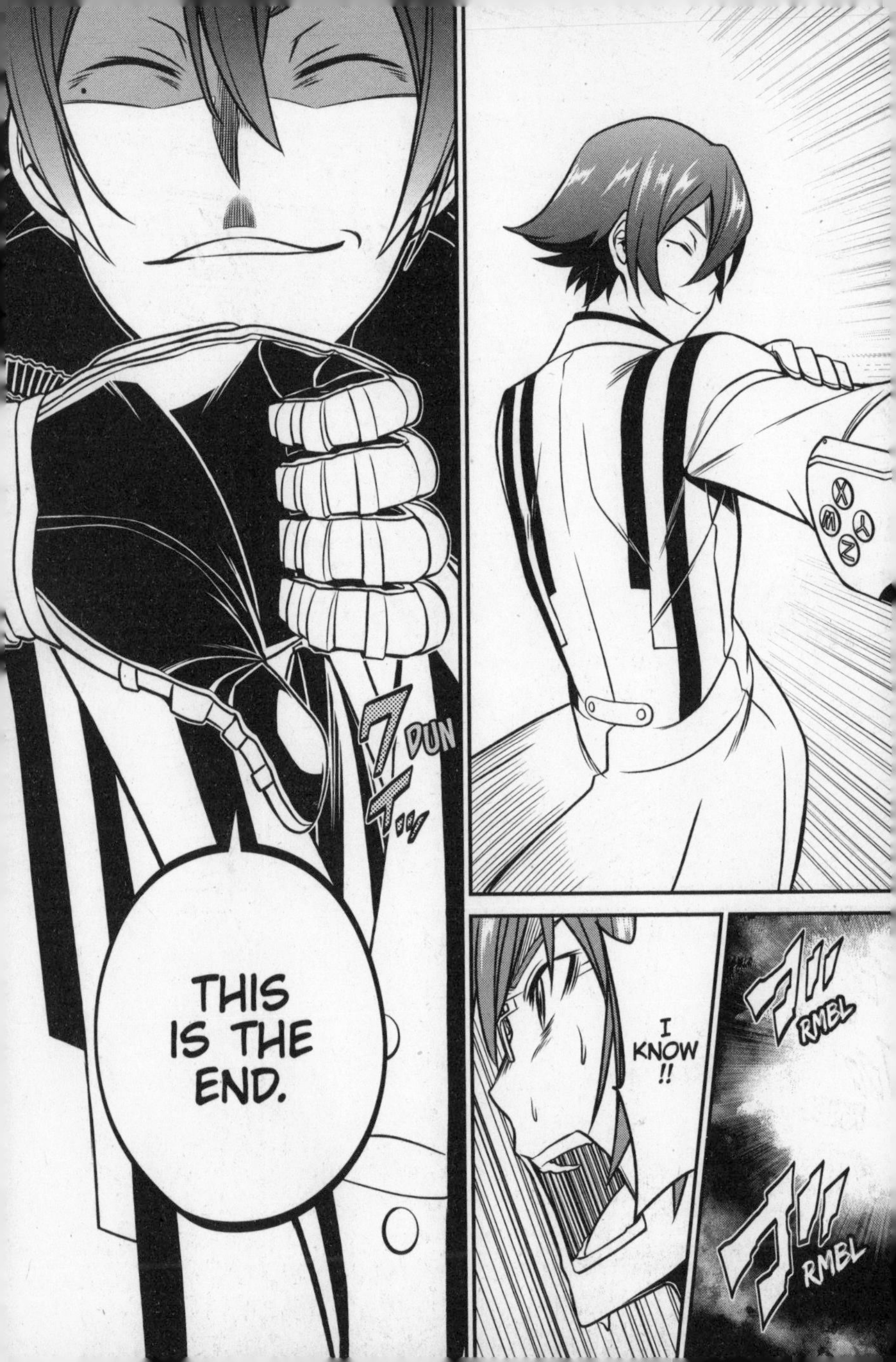
I KNOW!!
RMBL
RMBL
DUN
THIS IS THE END.

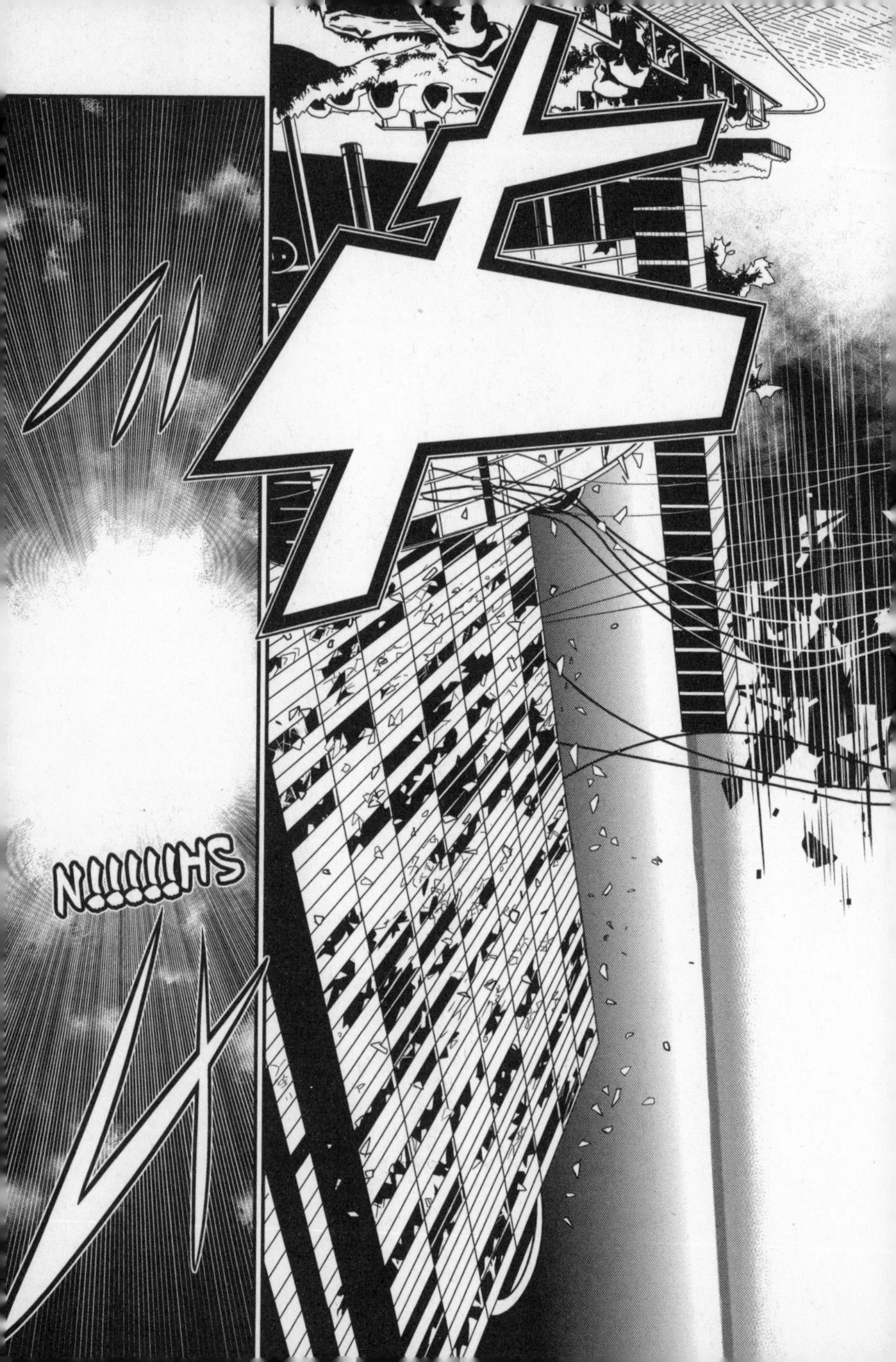
N!!!!!!HS

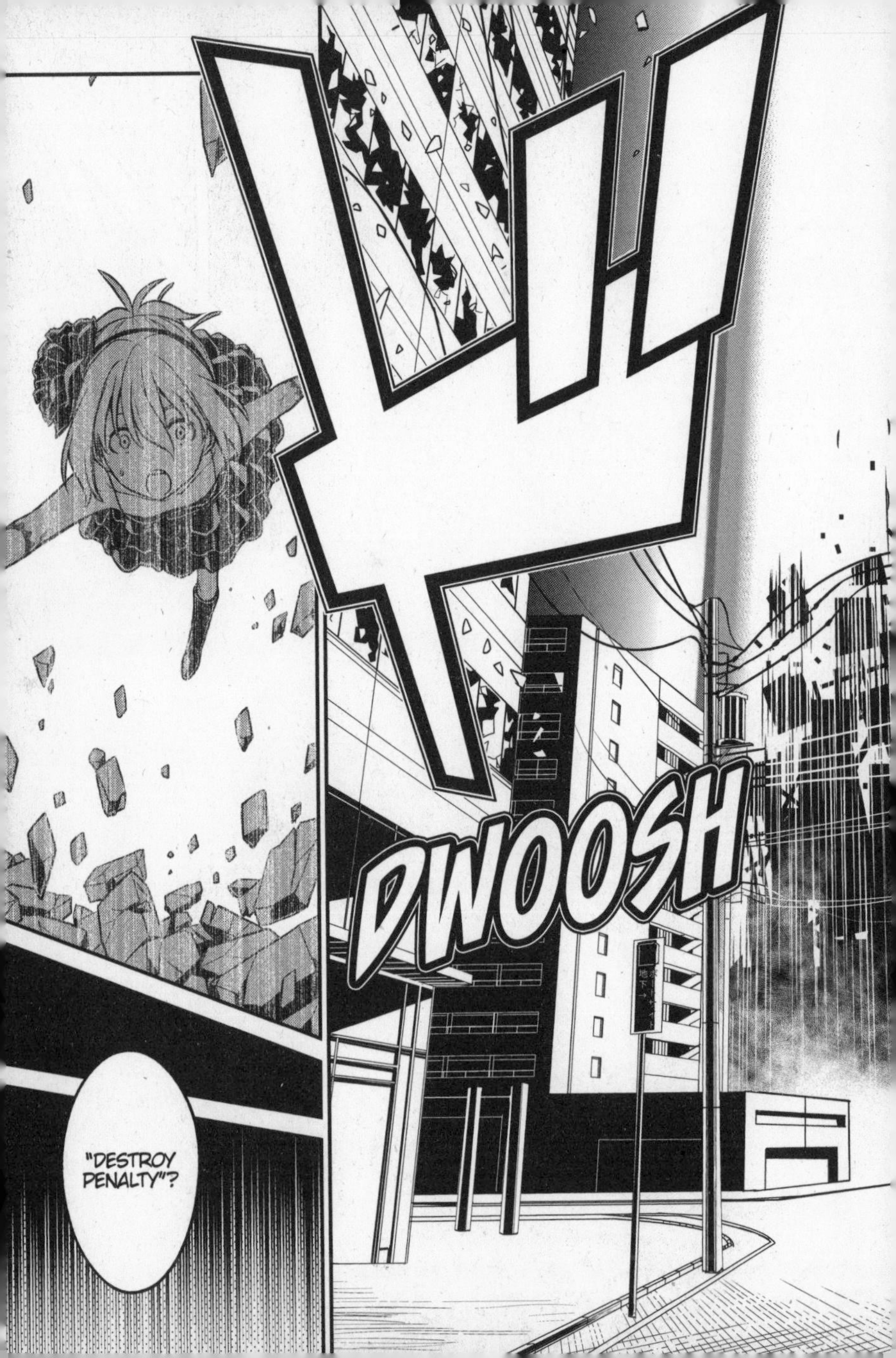
DWOOSH
"DESTROY PENALTY"?

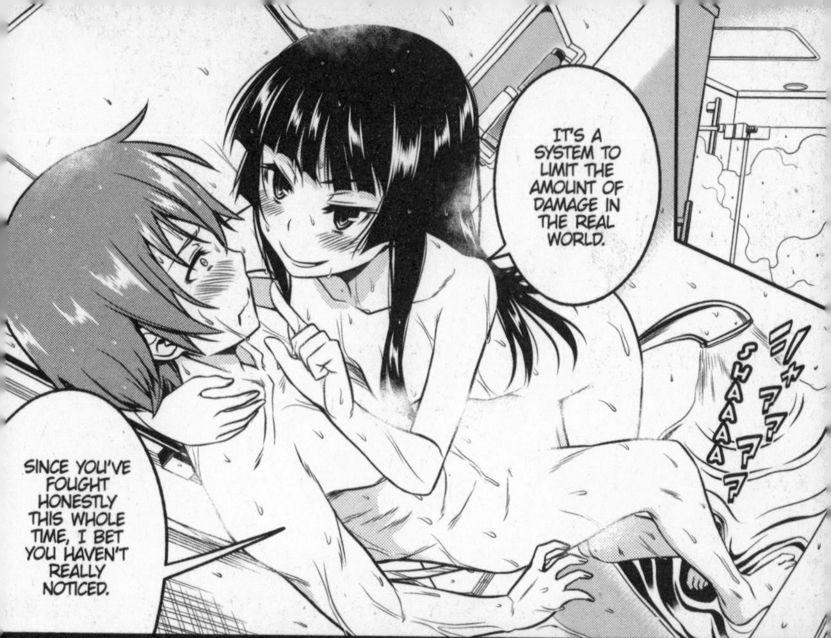
IT'S A SYSTEM TO LIMIT THE AMOUNT OF DAMAGE IN THE REAL WORLD.
SHAAAAAAA
SINCE YOU'VE FOUGHT HONESTLY THIS WHOLE TIME, I BET YOU HAVEN'T REALLY NOTICED.
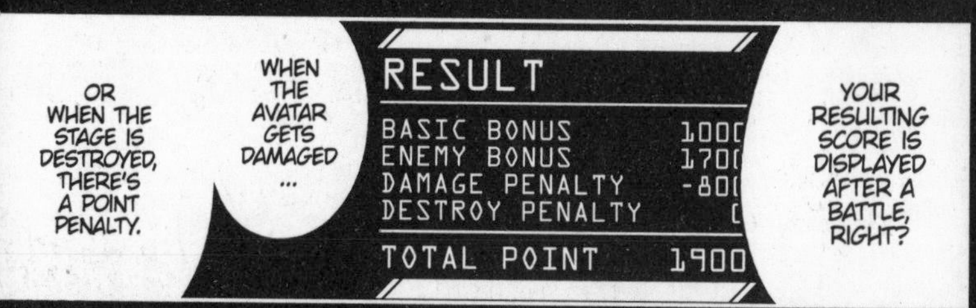
YOUR RESULTING SCORE IS DISPLAYED AFTER A BATTLE, RIGHT?
RESULT
BASIC BONUS 1000
ENEMY BONUS 1700
DAMAGE PENALTY -800
DESTROY PENALTY 0
TOTAL POINT 1900
WHEN THE AVATAR GETS DAMAGED...
OR WHEN THE STAGE IS DESTROYED, THERE'S A POINT PENALTY.
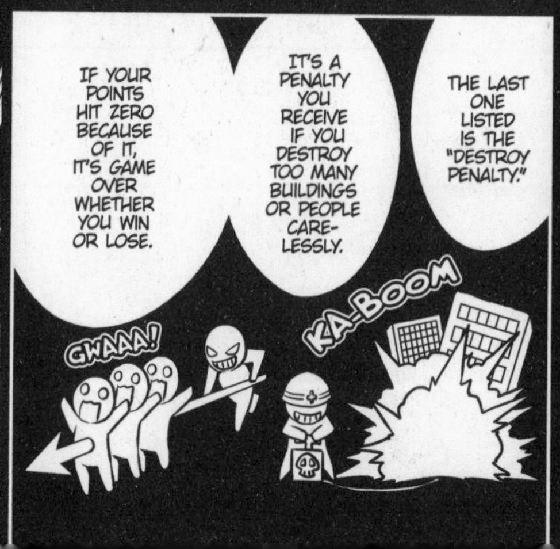
THE LAST ONE LISTED IS THE "DESTROY PENALTY."
IT'S A PENALTY YOU RECEIVE IF YOU DESTROY TOO MANY BUILDINGS OR PEOPLE CARE-LESSLY.
IF YOUR POINTS HIT ZERO BECAUSE OF IT, IT'S GAME OVER WHETHER YOU WIN OR LOSE.
KA-BOOM
GWAAA!
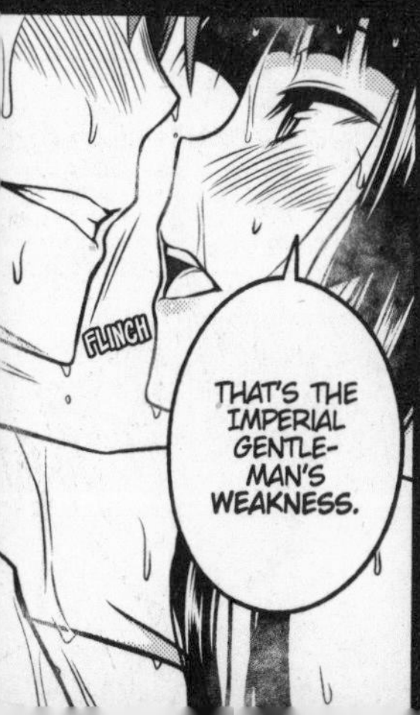
FLINCH
THAT'S THE IMPERIAL GENTLE-MAN'S WEAKNESS.

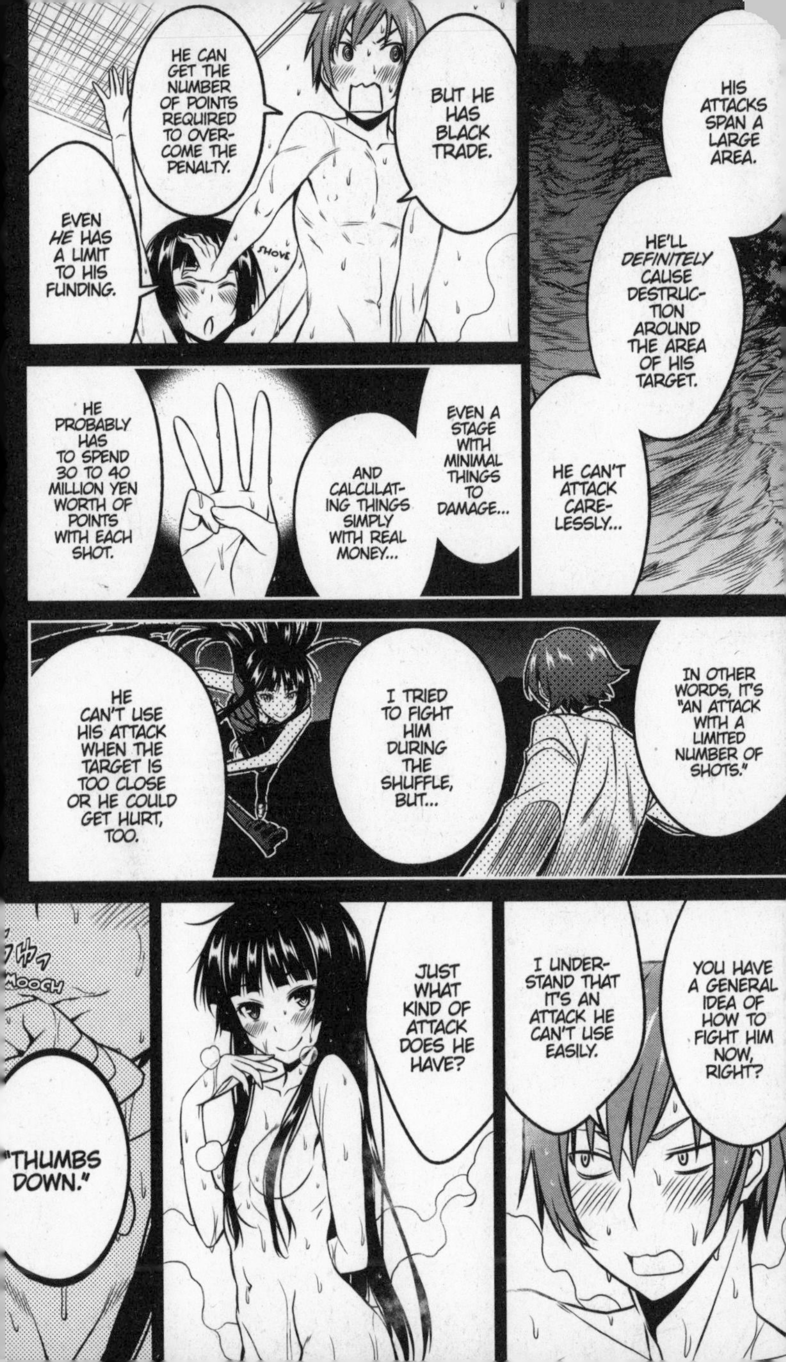
HIS ATTACKS SPAN A LARGE AREA.
HE'LL DEFINITELY CAUSE DESTRUCTION AROUND THE AREA OF HIS TARGET.
HE CAN'T ATTACK CARELESSLY...
HE CAN GET THE NUMBER OF POINTS REQUIRED TO OVERCOME THE PENALTY.
BUT HE HAS BLACK TRADE.
SHOVE
EVEN HE HAS A LIMIT TO HIS FUNDING.
EVEN A STAGE WITH MINIMAL THINGS TO DAMAGE...
AND CALCULATING THINGS SIMPLY WITH REAL MONEY...
HE PROBABLY HAS TO SPEND 30 TO 40 MILLION YEN WORTH OF POINTS WITH EACH SHOT.
IN OTHER WORDS, IT'S "AN ATTACK WITH A LIMITED NUMBER OF SHOTS."
I TRIED TO FIGHT HIM DURING THE SHUFFLE, BUT...
HE CAN'T USE HIS ATTACK WHEN THE TARGET IS TOO CLOSE OR HE COULD GET HURT, TOO.
YOU HAVE A GENERAL IDEA OF HOW TO FIGHT HIM NOW, RIGHT?
I UNDERSTAND THAT IT'S AN ATTACK HE CAN'T USE EASILY.
JUST WHAT KIND OF ATTACK DOES HE HAVE?
SMOOCH
"THUMBS DOWN."

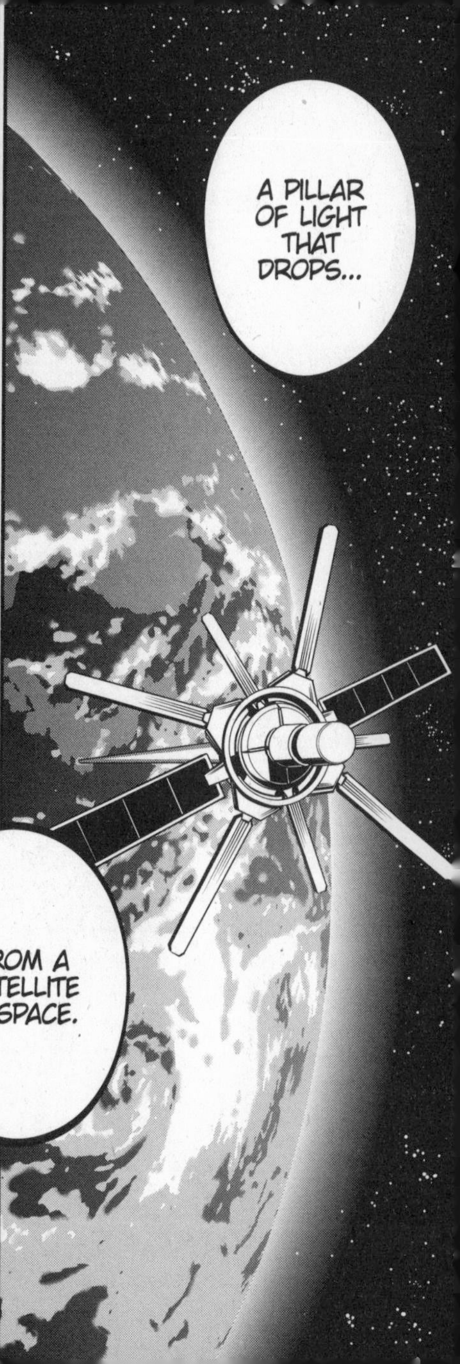
A PILLAR OF LIGHT THAT DROPS...
FROM A SATELLITE IN SPACE.
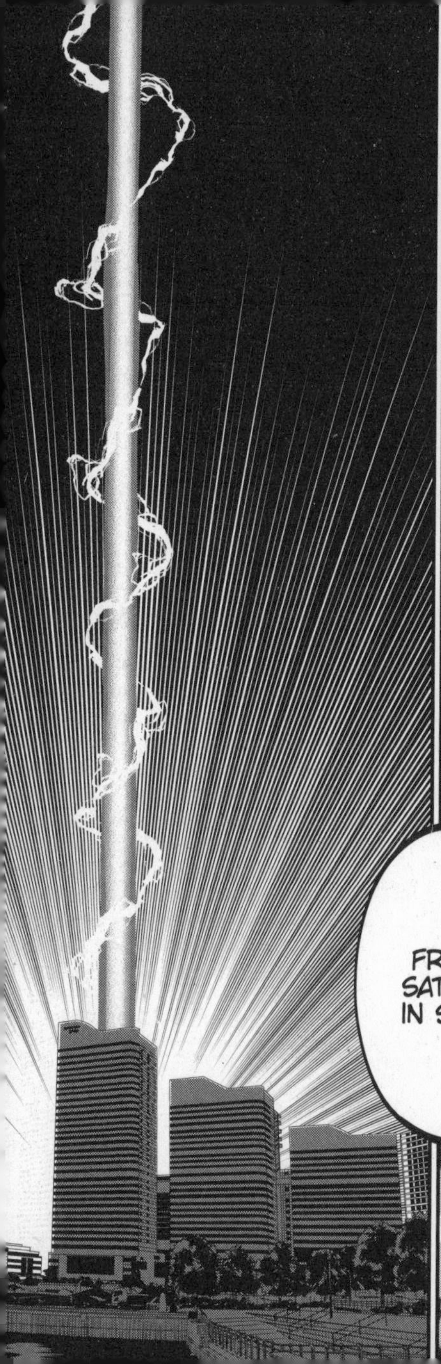

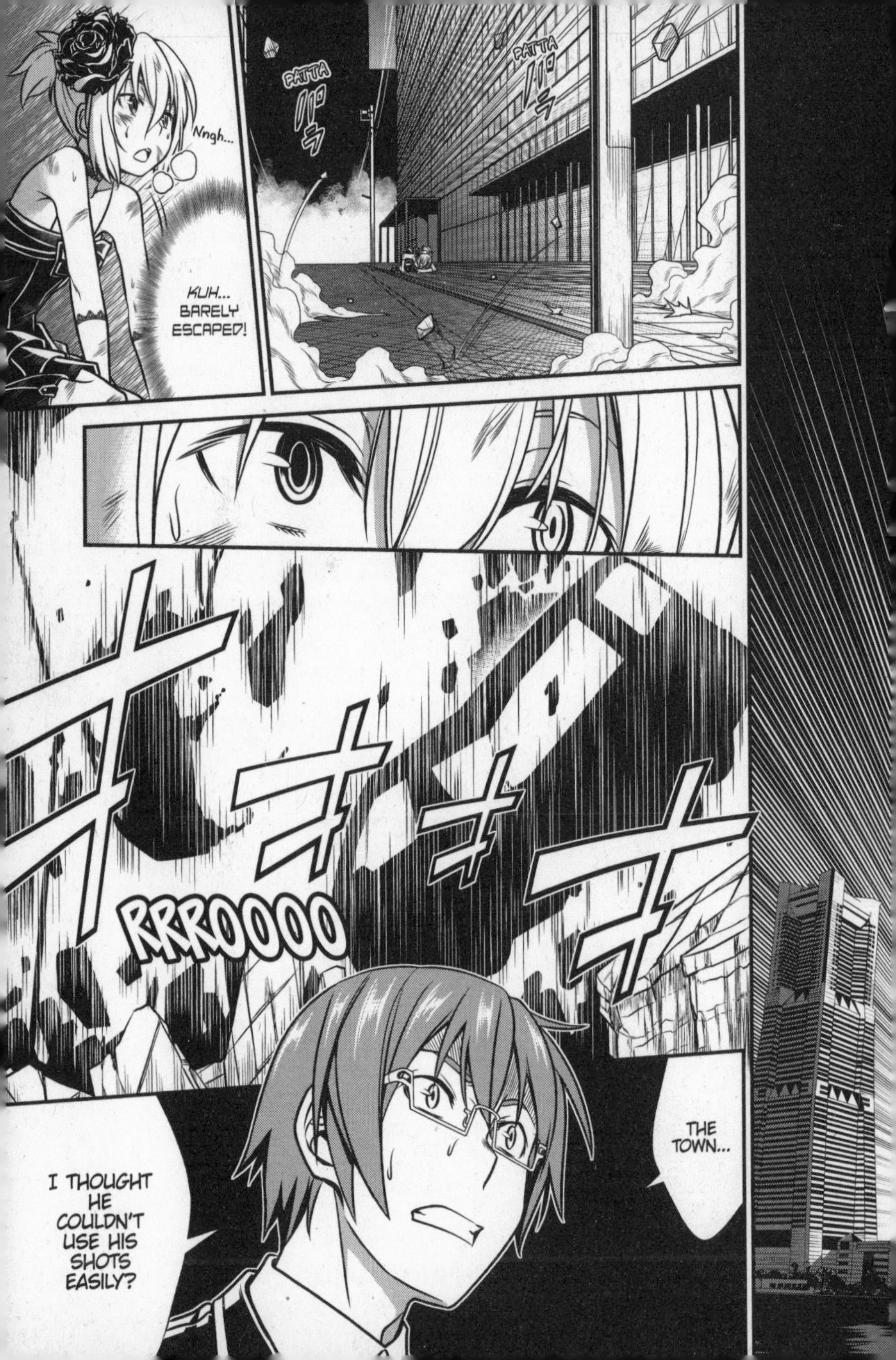
PATTA
PATTA
Nngh...
KUH... BARELY ESCAPED!
RRROOOO
THE TOWN...
I THOUGHT HE COULDN'T USE HIS SHOTS EASILY?

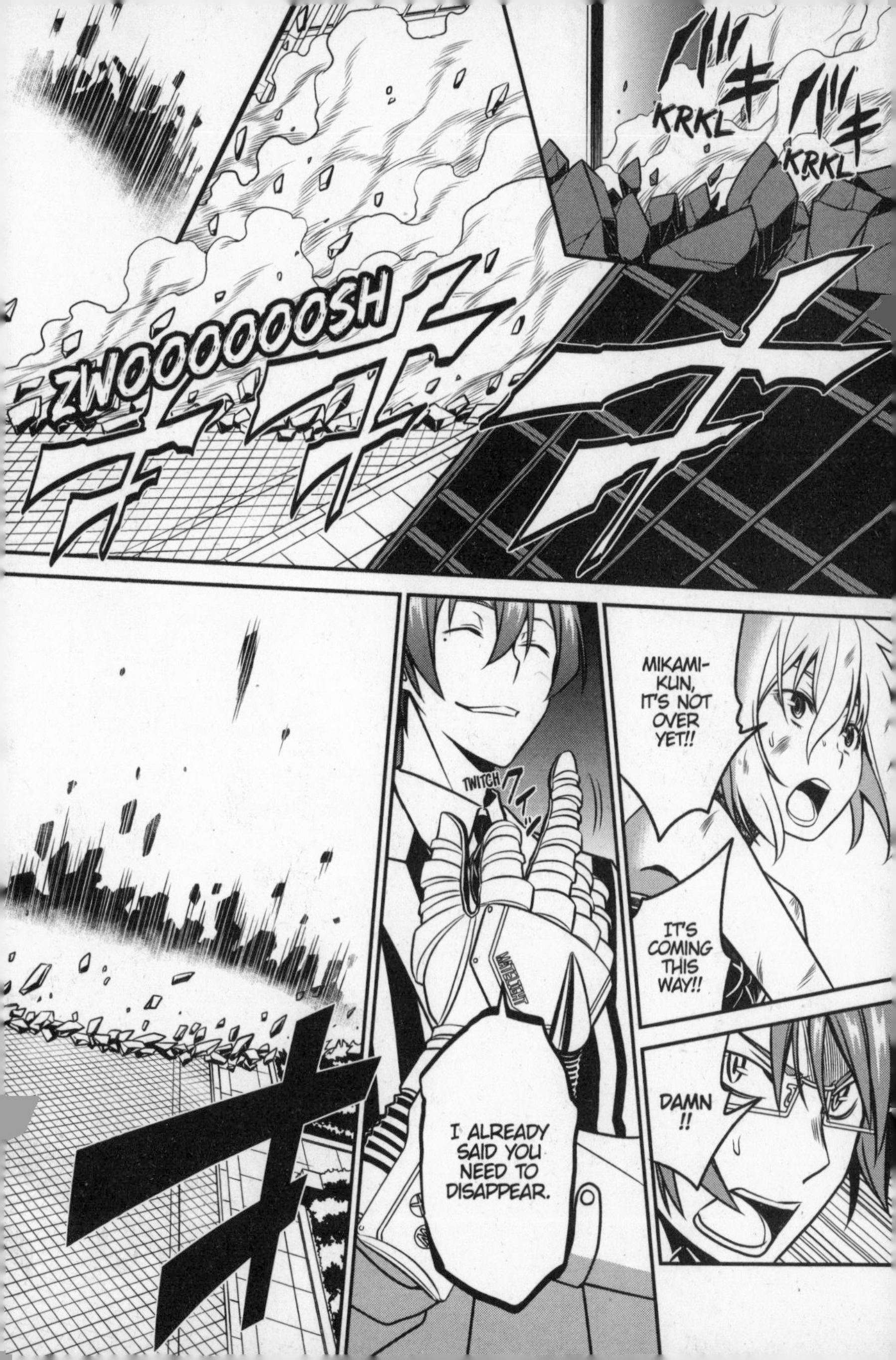
KRKL
KRKL
ZWOOOOOOOSH
MIKAMI-KUN, IT'S NOT OVER YET!!
IT'S COMING THIS WAY!!
DAMN!!
TWITCH
I ALREADY SAID YOU NEED TO DISAPPEAR.

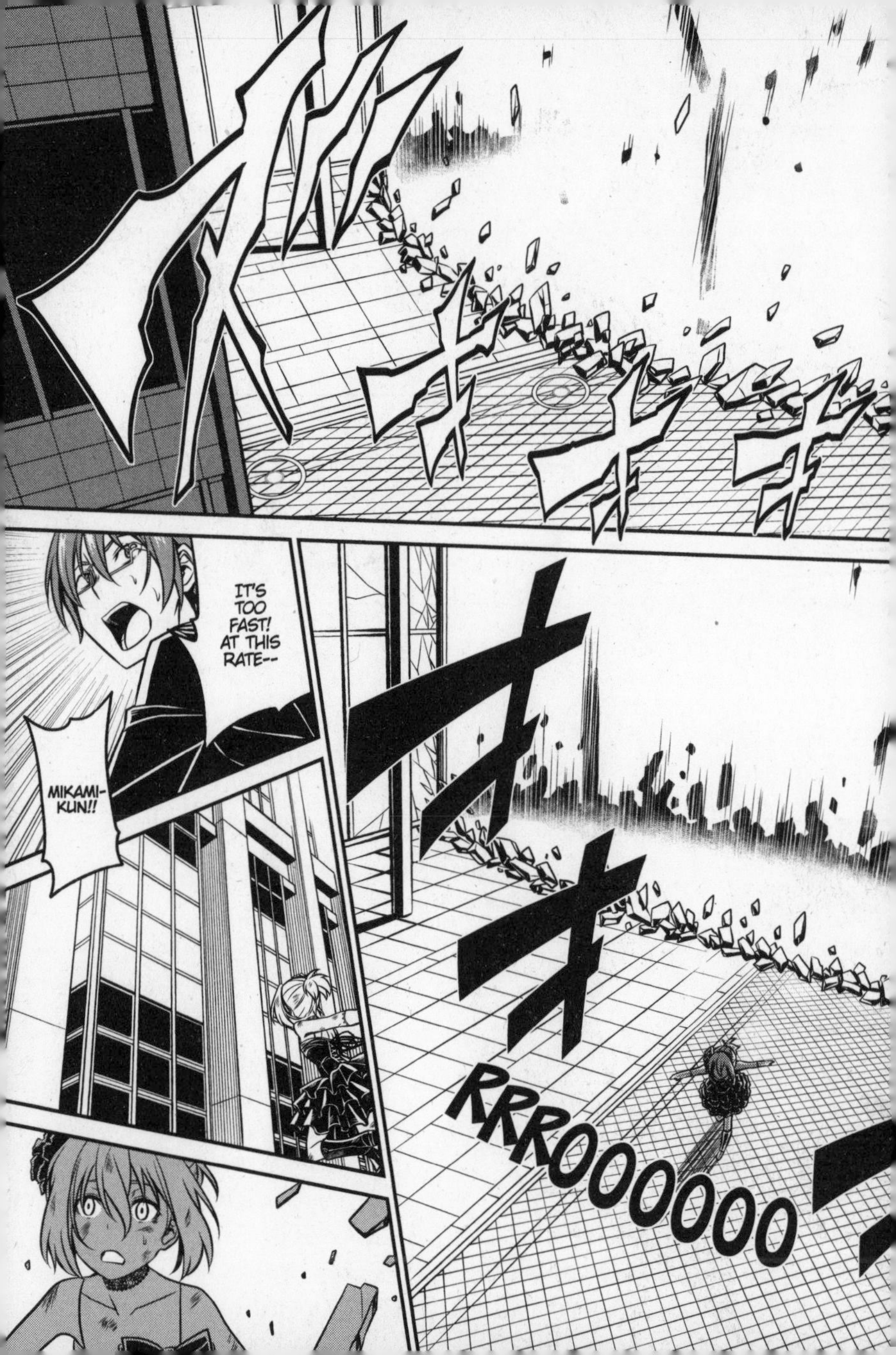
IT'S TOO FAST! AT THIS RATE--
MIKAMI-KUN!!
RRROOOOOOO

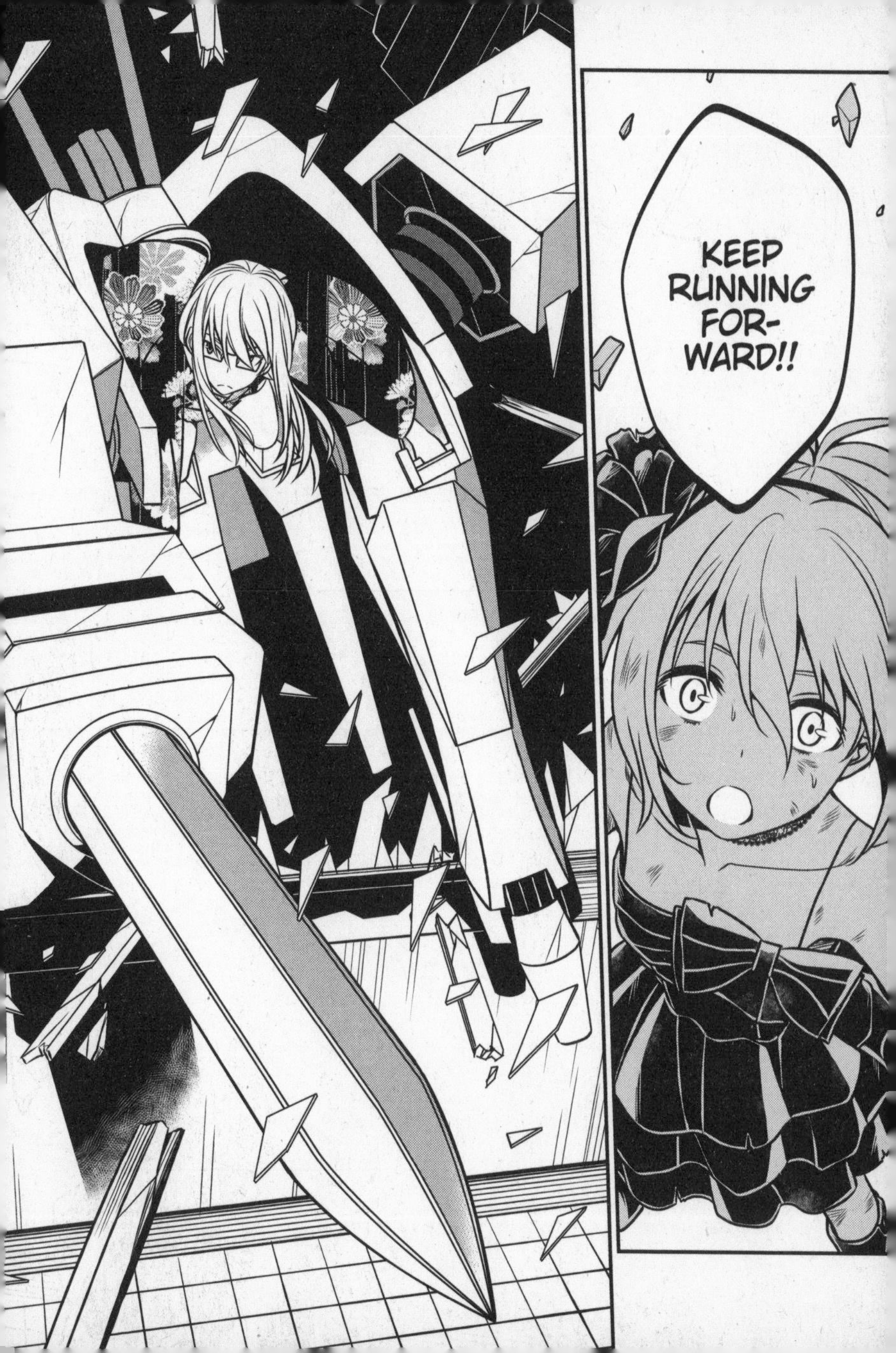
KEEP RUNNING FOR-WARD!!

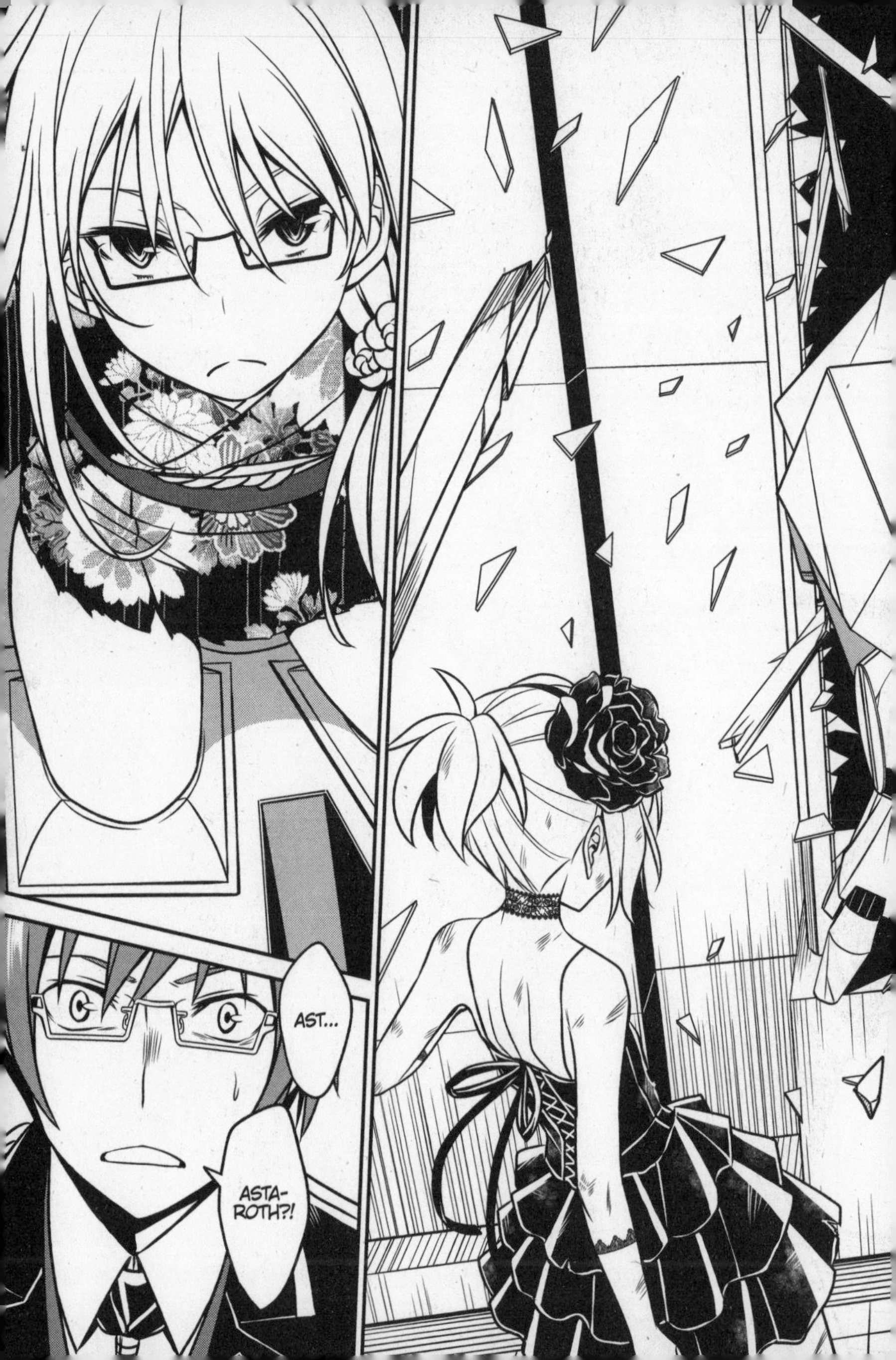
AST...
ASTA-ROTH?!

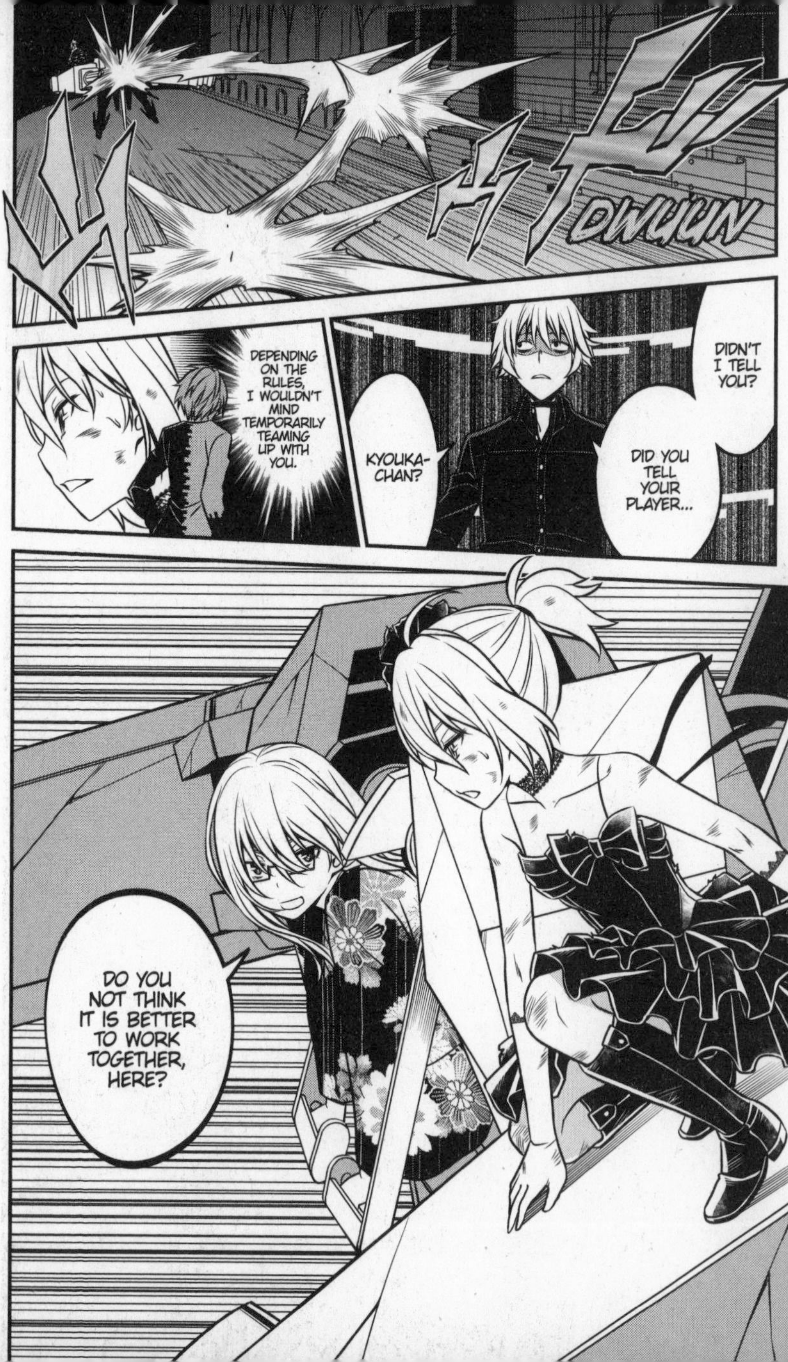
DWUUN
DIDN'T I TELL YOU?
DID YOU TELL YOUR PLAYER...
KYOUKA-CHAN?
DEPENDING ON THE RULES, I WOULDN'T MIND TEMPORARILY TEAMING UP WITH YOU.
DO YOU NOT THINK IT IS BETTER TO WORK TOGETHER, HERE?

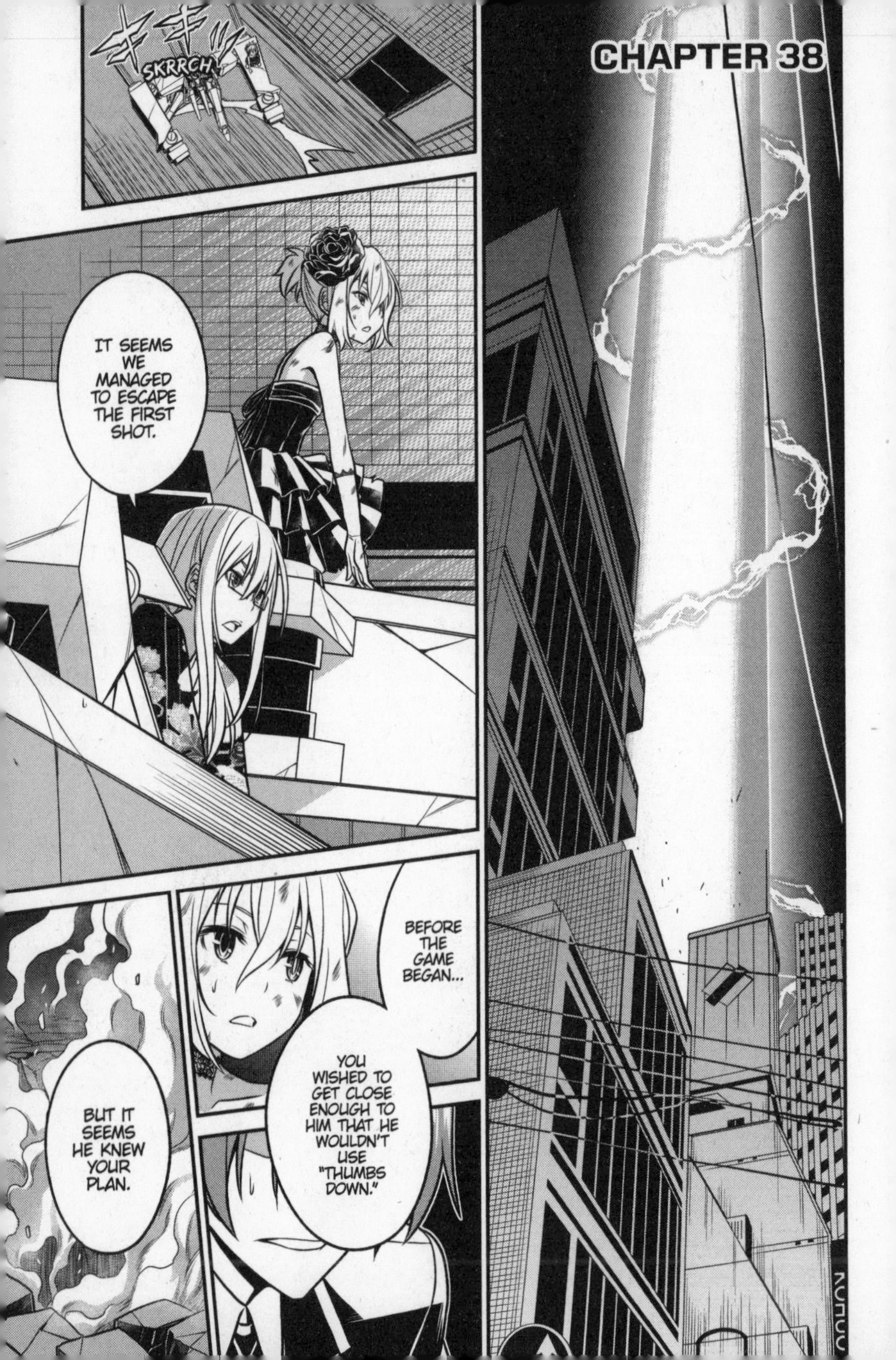
CHAPTER 38
SKRRCH
IT SEEMS WE MANAGED TO ESCAPE THE FIRST SHOT.
BEFORE THE GAME BEGAN...
YOU WISHED TO GET CLOSE ENOUGH TO HIM THAT HE WOULDN'T USE "THUMBS DOWN."
BUT IT SEEMS HE KNEW YOUR PLAN.

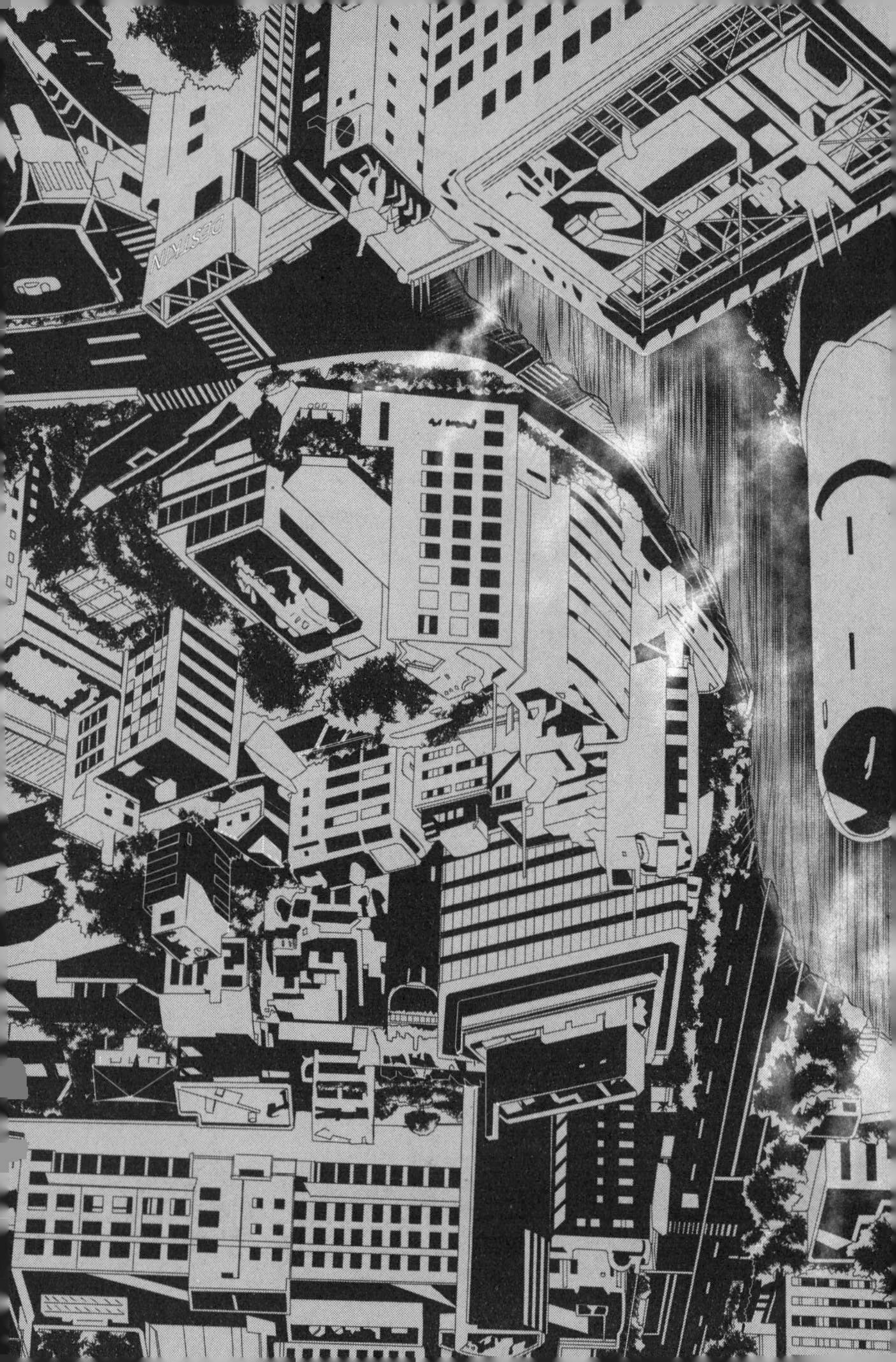

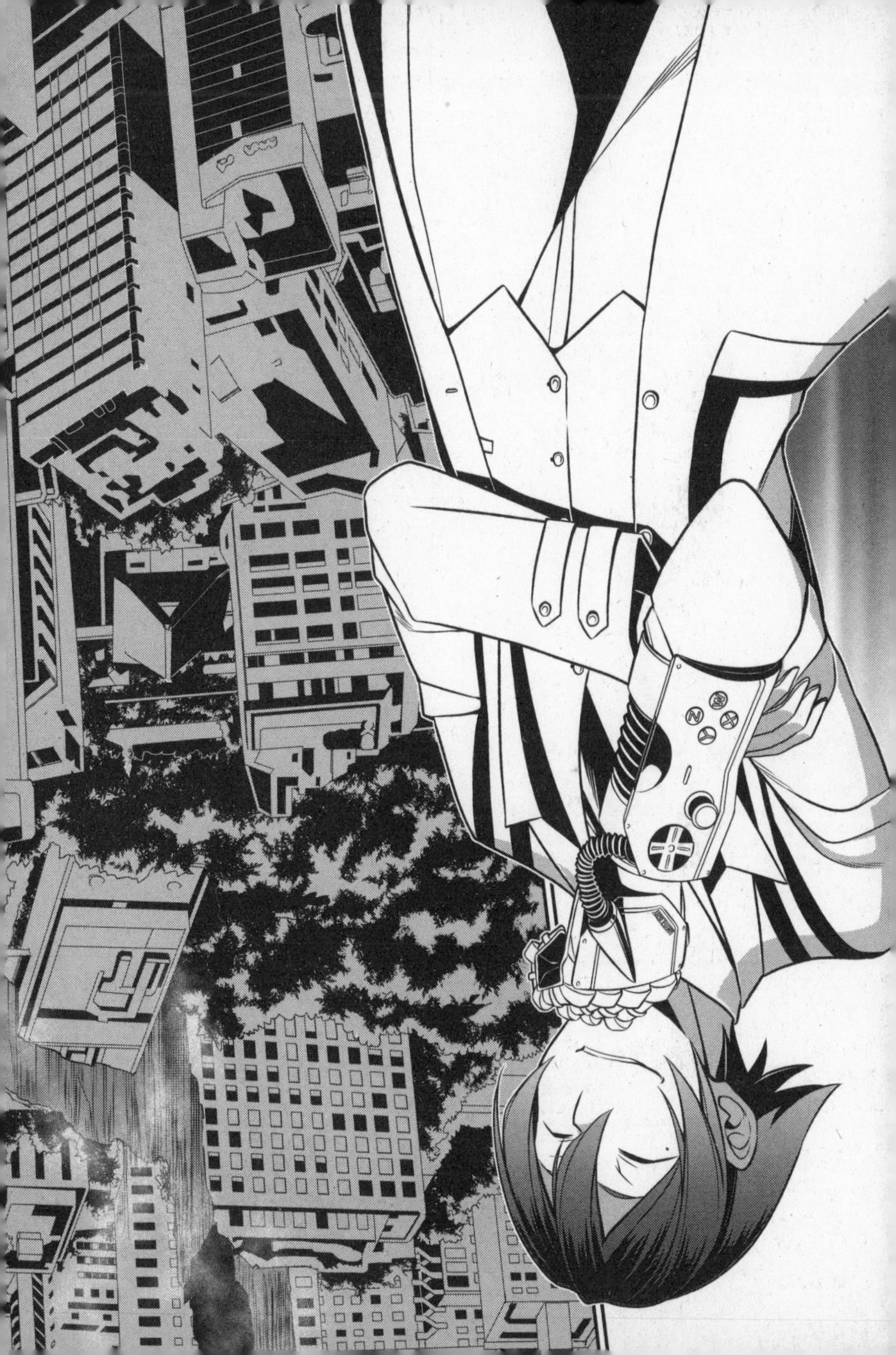

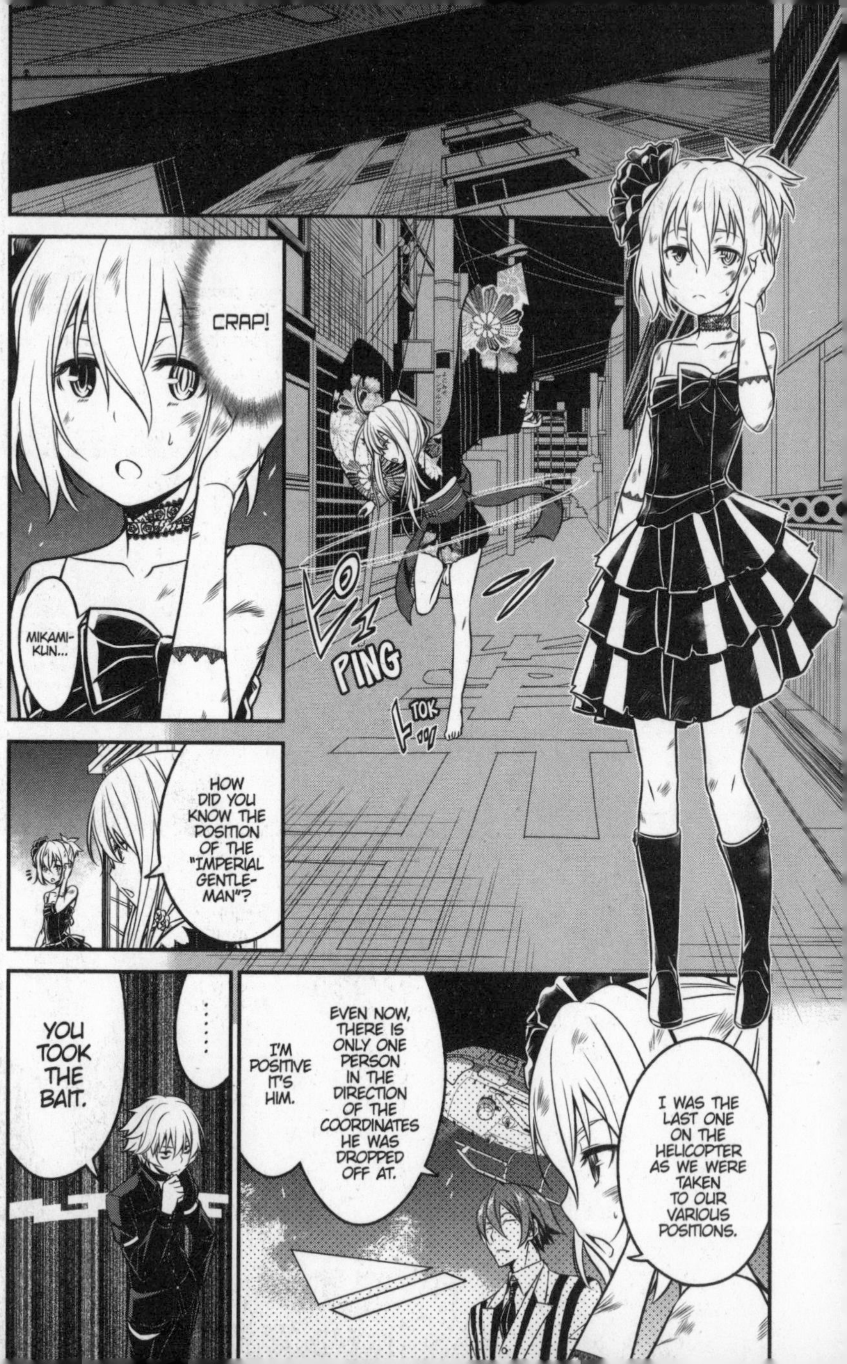
PING
TOK
CRAP!
MIKAMI-KUN...
HOW DID YOU KNOW THE POSITION OF THE "IMPERIAL GENTLEMAN"?
I WAS THE LAST ONE ON THE HELICOPTER AS WE WERE TAKEN TO OUR VARIOUS POSITIONS.
EVEN NOW, THERE IS ONLY ONE PERSON IN THE DIRECTION OF THE COORDINATES HE WAS DROPPED OFF AT.
I'M POSITIVE IT'S HIM.
......
YOU TOOK THE BAIT.

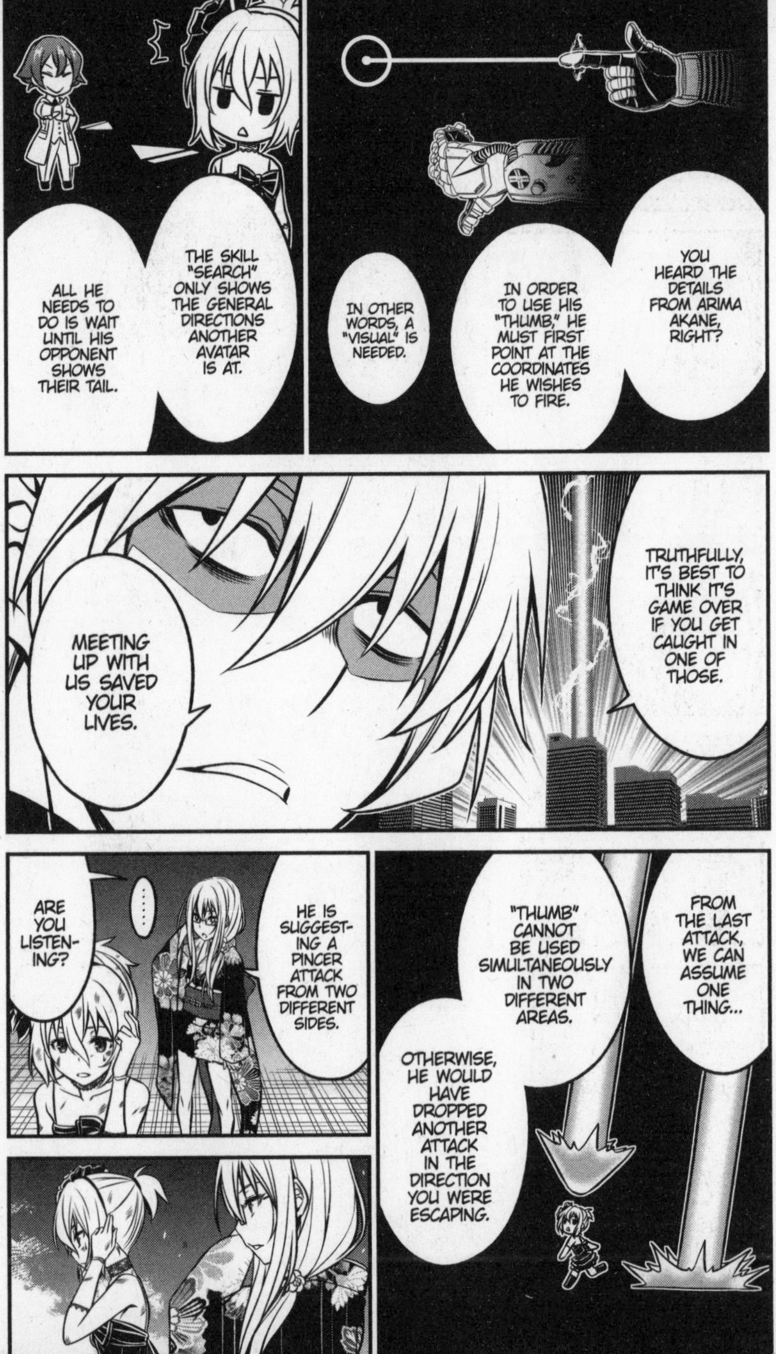
YOU HEARD THE DETAILS FROM ARIMA AKANE, RIGHT?
IN ORDER TO USE HIS "THUMB," HE MUST FIRST POINT AT THE COORDINATES HE WISHES TO FIRE.
IN OTHER WORDS, A "VISUAL" IS NEEDED.
THE SKILL "SEARCH" ONLY SHOWS THE GENERAL DIRECTIONS ANOTHER AVATAR IS AT.
ALL HE NEEDS TO DO IS WAIT UNTIL HIS OPPONENT SHOWS THEIR TAIL.
TRUTHFULLY, IT'S BEST TO THINK IT'S GAME OVER IF YOU GET CAUGHT IN ONE OF THOSE.
MEETING UP WITH US SAVED YOUR LIVES.
FROM THE LAST ATTACK, WE CAN ASSUME ONE THING...
"THUMB" CANNOT BE USED SIMULTANEOUSLY IN TWO DIFFERENT AREAS.
OTHERWISE, HE WOULD HAVE DROPPED ANOTHER ATTACK IN THE DIRECTION YOU WERE ESCAPING.
HE IS SUGGEST-ING A PINCER ATTACK FROM TWO DIFFERENT SIDES.
......
ARE YOU LISTEN-ING?

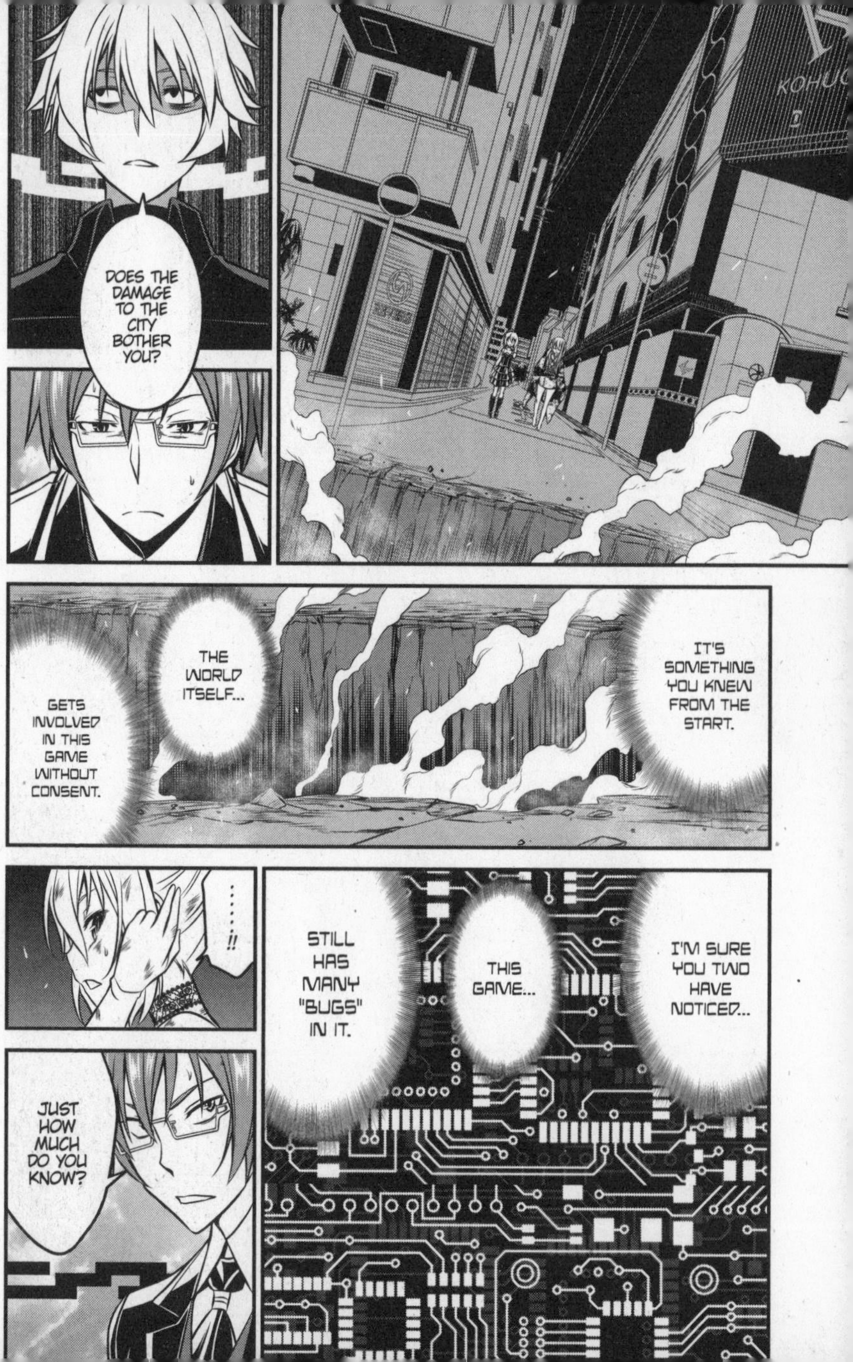
DOES THE DAMAGE TO THE CITY BOTHER YOU?
IT'S SOMETHING YOU KNEW FROM THE START.
THE WORLD ITSELF...
GETS INVOLVED IN THIS GAME WITHOUT CONSENT.
I'M SURE YOU TWO HAVE NOTICED...
THIS GAME...
STILL HAS MANY "BUGS" IN IT.
......!!
JUST HOW MUCH DO YOU KNOW?

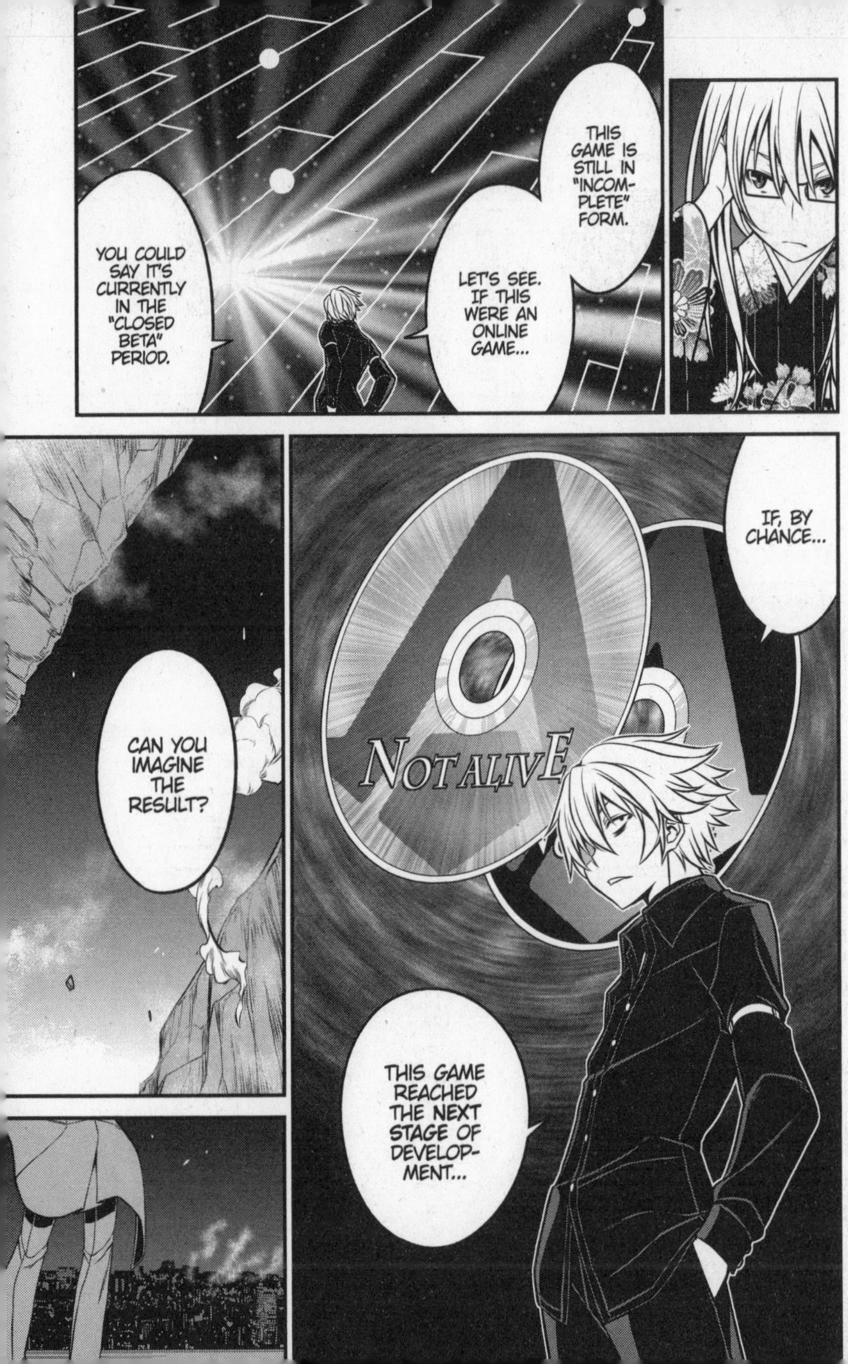
THIS GAME IS STILL IN "INCOMPLETE" FORM.
LET'S SEE. IF THIS WERE AN ONLINE GAME...
YOU COULD SAY IT'S CURRENTLY IN THE "CLOSED BETA" PERIOD.
IF, BY CHANCE...
NOT ALIVE
THIS GAME REACHED THE NEXT STAGE OF DEVELOPMENT...
CAN YOU IMAGINE THE RESULT?

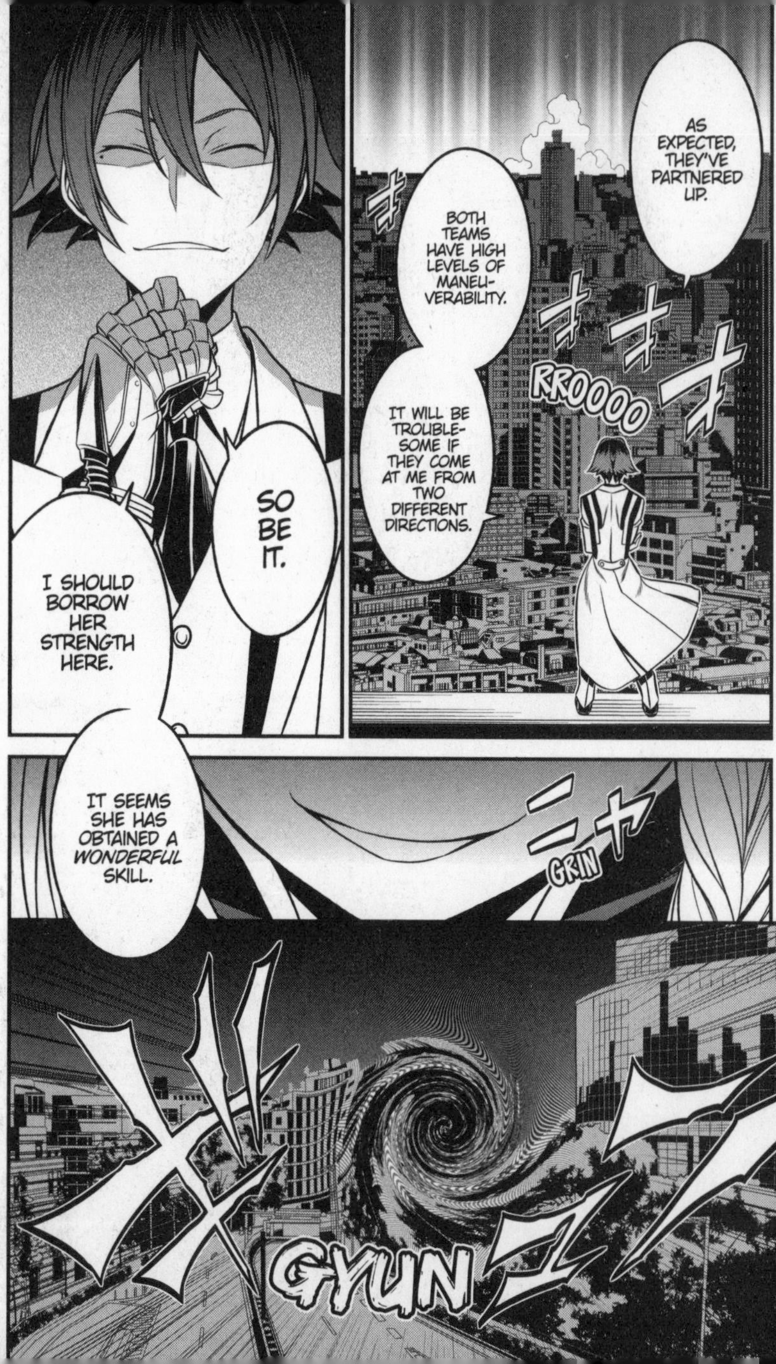
AS EXPECTED, THEY'VE PARTNERED UP.
RROOOO
BOTH TEAMS HAVE HIGH LEVELS OF MANEU-VERABILITY.
IT WILL BE TROUBLE-SOME IF THEY COME AT ME FROM TWO DIFFERENT DIRECTIONS.
SO BE IT.
I SHOULD BORROW HER STRENGTH HERE.
GRIN
IT SEEMS SHE HAS OBTAINED A *WONDERFUL* SKILL.
GYUN

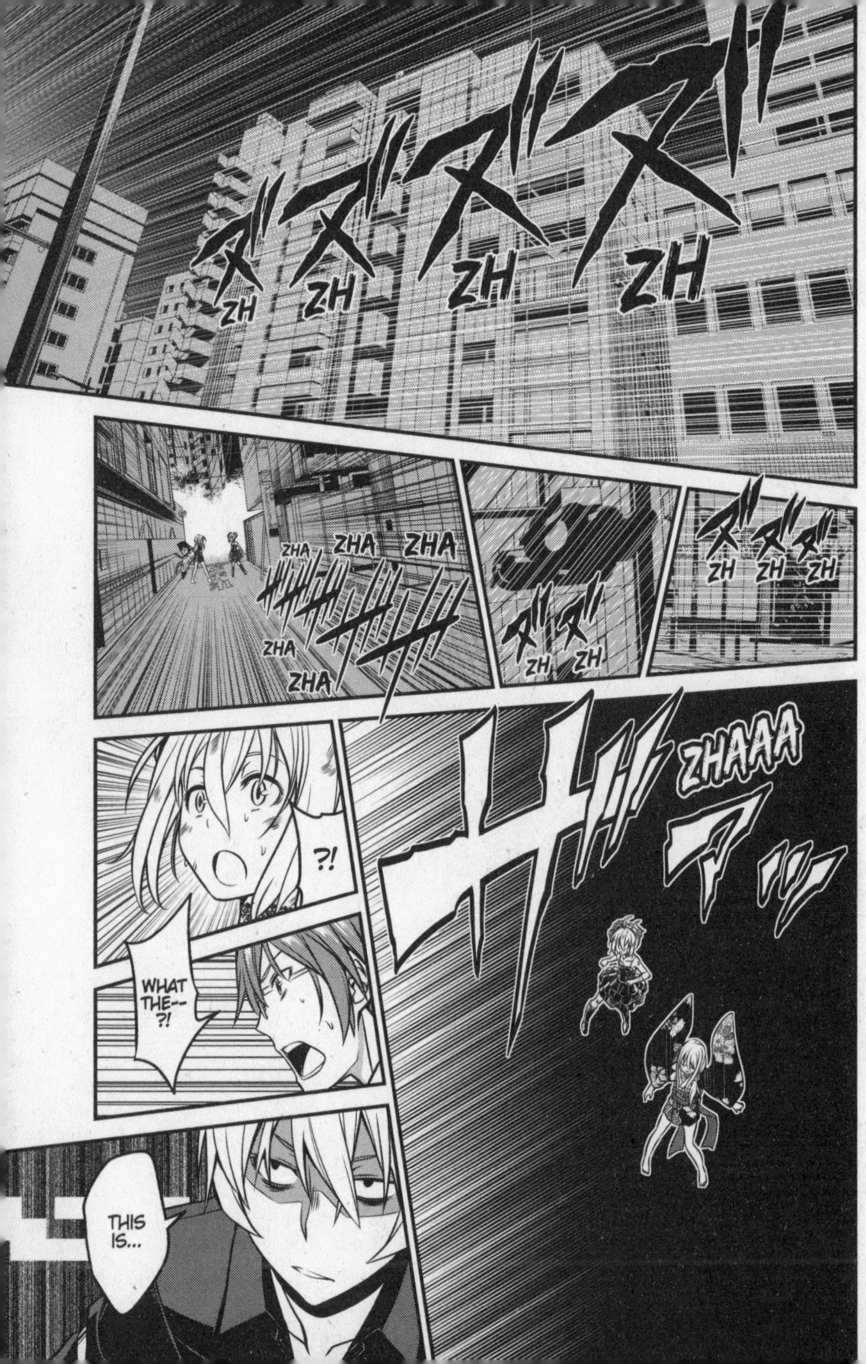
ZH ZH ZH ZH
ZH ZH ZH
ZH ZH
ZHA ZHA ZHA ZHA ZHA ZHA
ZHAAA
?!
WHAT THE-- ?!
THIS IS...

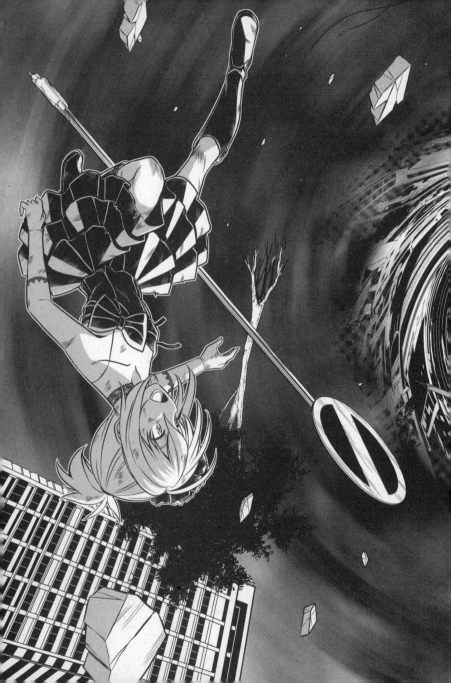

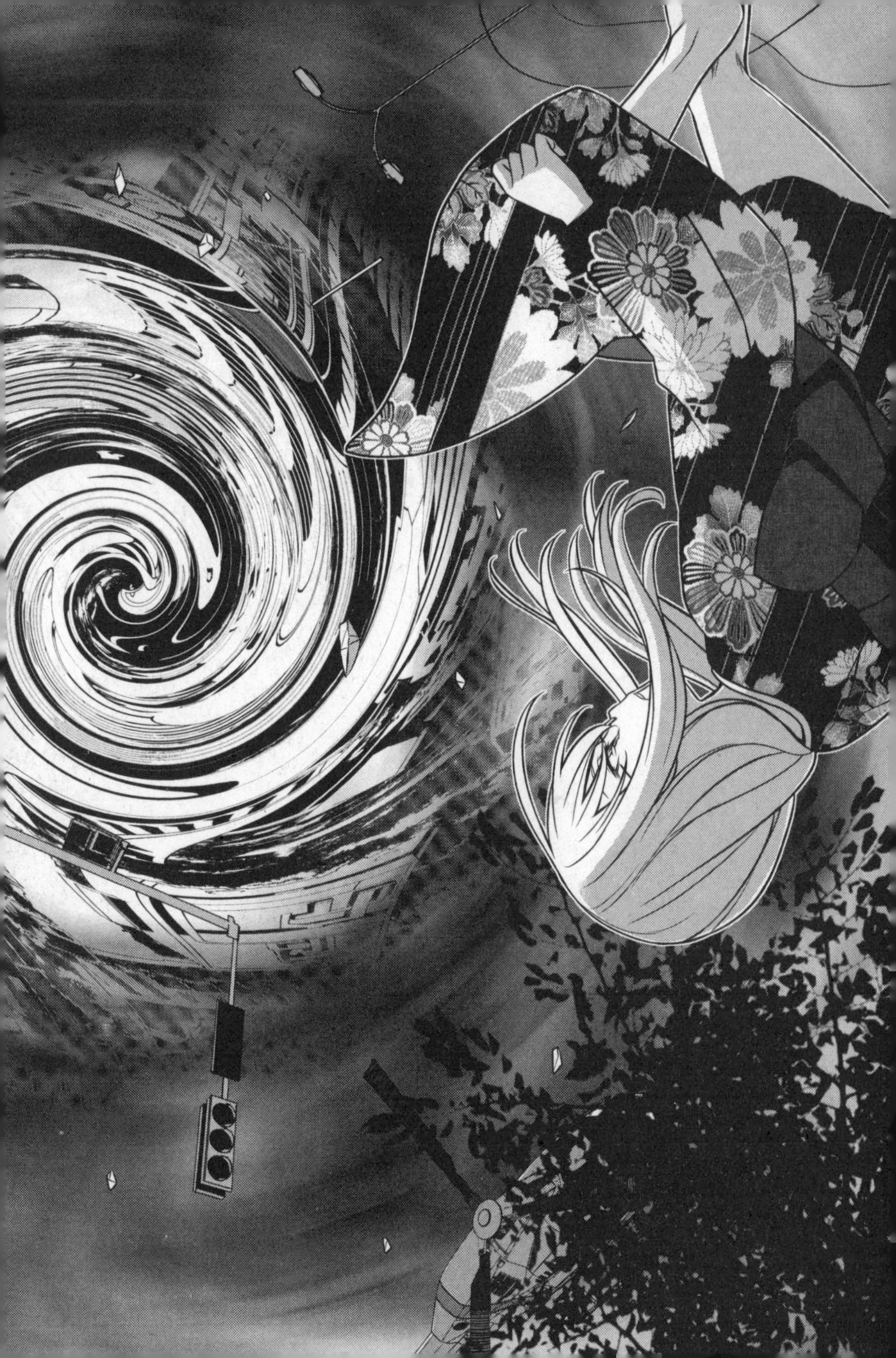

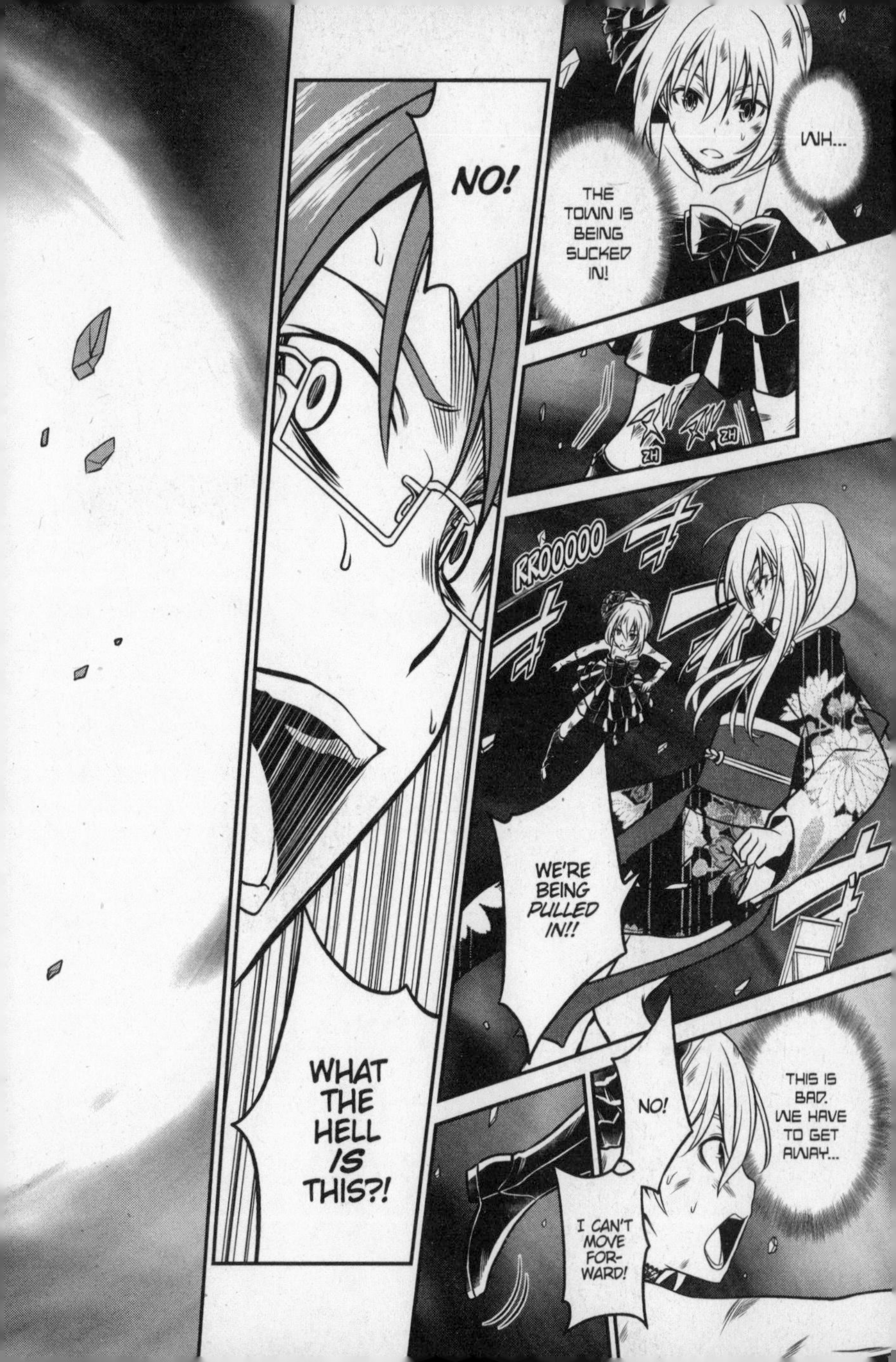
WH...
THE TOWN IS BEING SUCKED IN!
ZH ZH
RROOOOO
WE'RE BEING PULLED IN!!
THIS IS BAD. WE HAVE TO GET AWAY...
NO!
I CAN'T MOVE FOR-WARD!
NO!
WHAT THE HELL IS THIS?!

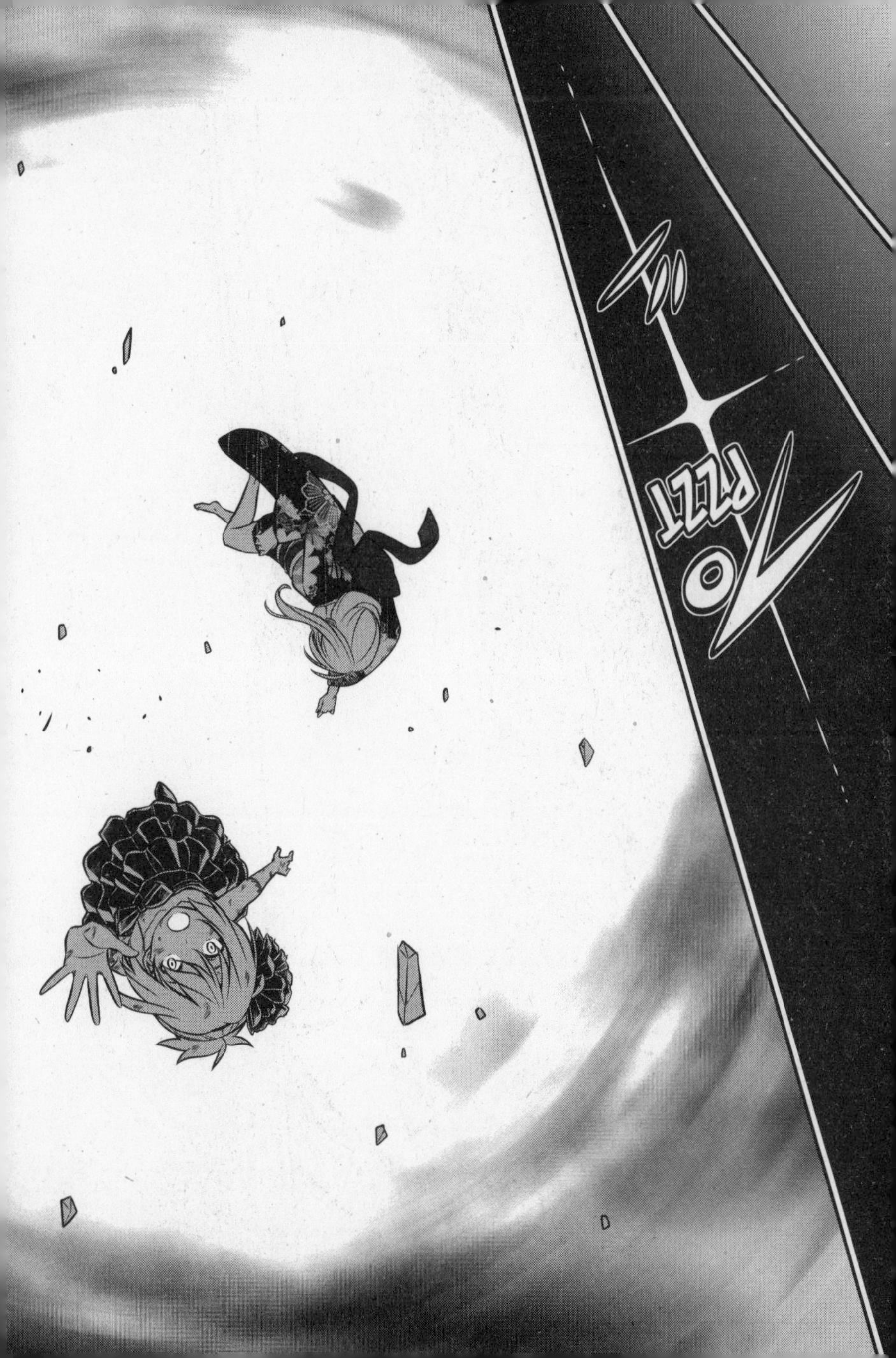
PZZT

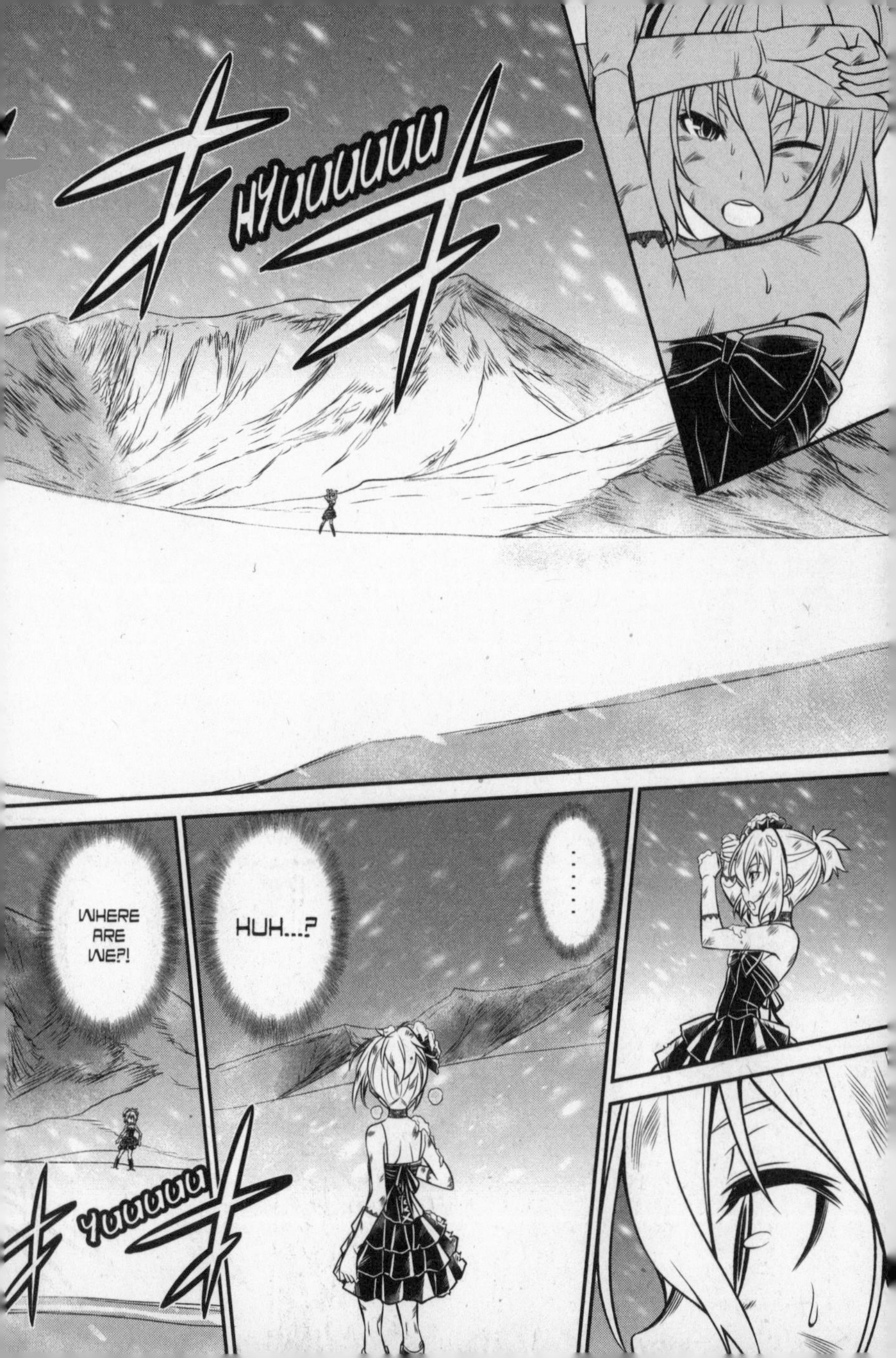
HYUUUUUUU
......
HUH...?
WHERE ARE WE?!
YUUUUUU

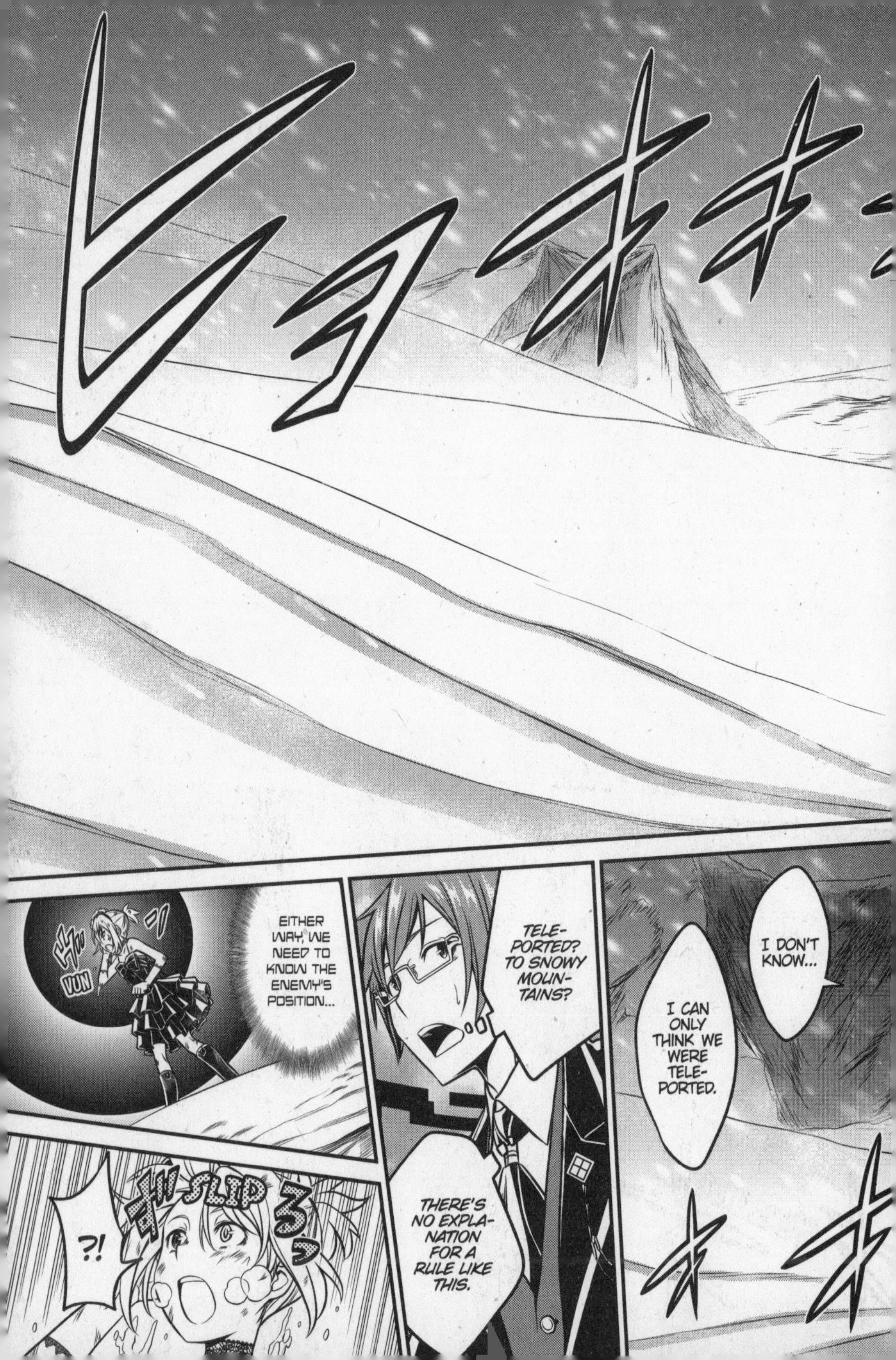
ヒョオオ
I DON'T KNOW...
I CAN ONLY THINK WE WERE TELEPORTED.
TELEPORTED? TO SNOWY MOUNTAINS?
THERE'S NO EXPLANATION FOR A RULE LIKE THIS.
EITHER WAY, WE NEED TO KNOW THE ENEMY'S POSITION...
VUN
?!
SLIP

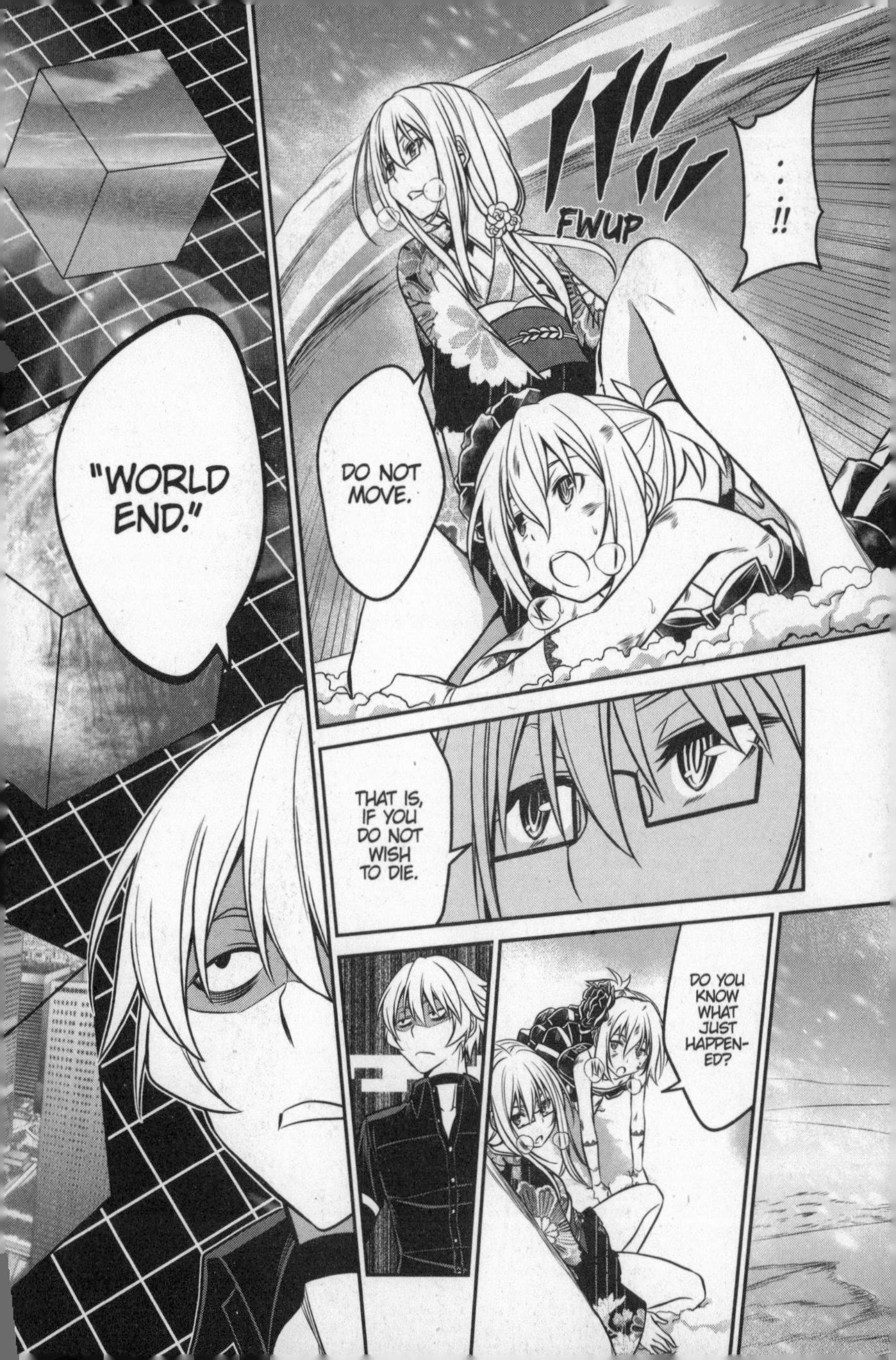
...!!
FWUP
DO NOT MOVE.
"WORLD END."
THAT IS, IF YOU DO NOT WISH TO DIE.
DO YOU KNOW WHAT JUST HAPPEN-ED?

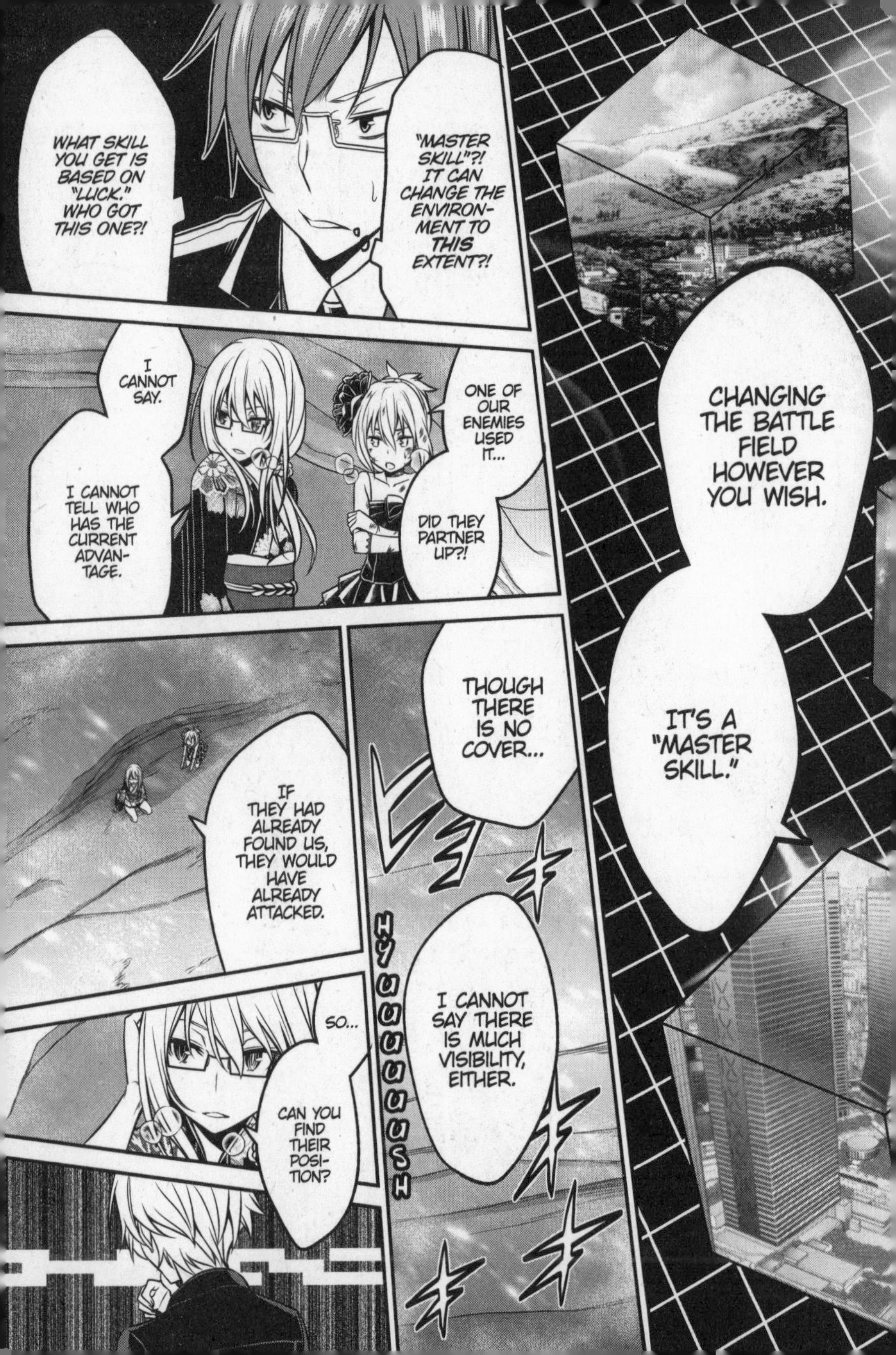
CHANGING THE BATTLE FIELD HOWEVER YOU WISH.
IT'S A "MASTER SKILL."
"MASTER SKILL"?! IT CAN CHANGE THE ENVIRONMENT TO THIS EXTENT?!
WHAT SKILL YOU GET IS BASED ON "LUCK." WHO GOT THIS ONE?!
ONE OF OUR ENEMIES USED IT...
DID THEY PARTNER UP?!
I CANNOT SAY.
I CANNOT TELL WHO HAS THE CURRENT ADVANTAGE.
THOUGH THERE IS NO COVER...
I CANNOT SAY THERE IS MUCH VISIBILITY, EITHER.
HYUUUUUUUUSH
IF THEY HAD ALREADY FOUND US, THEY WOULD HAVE ALREADY ATTACKED.
SO...
CAN YOU FIND THEIR POSITION?

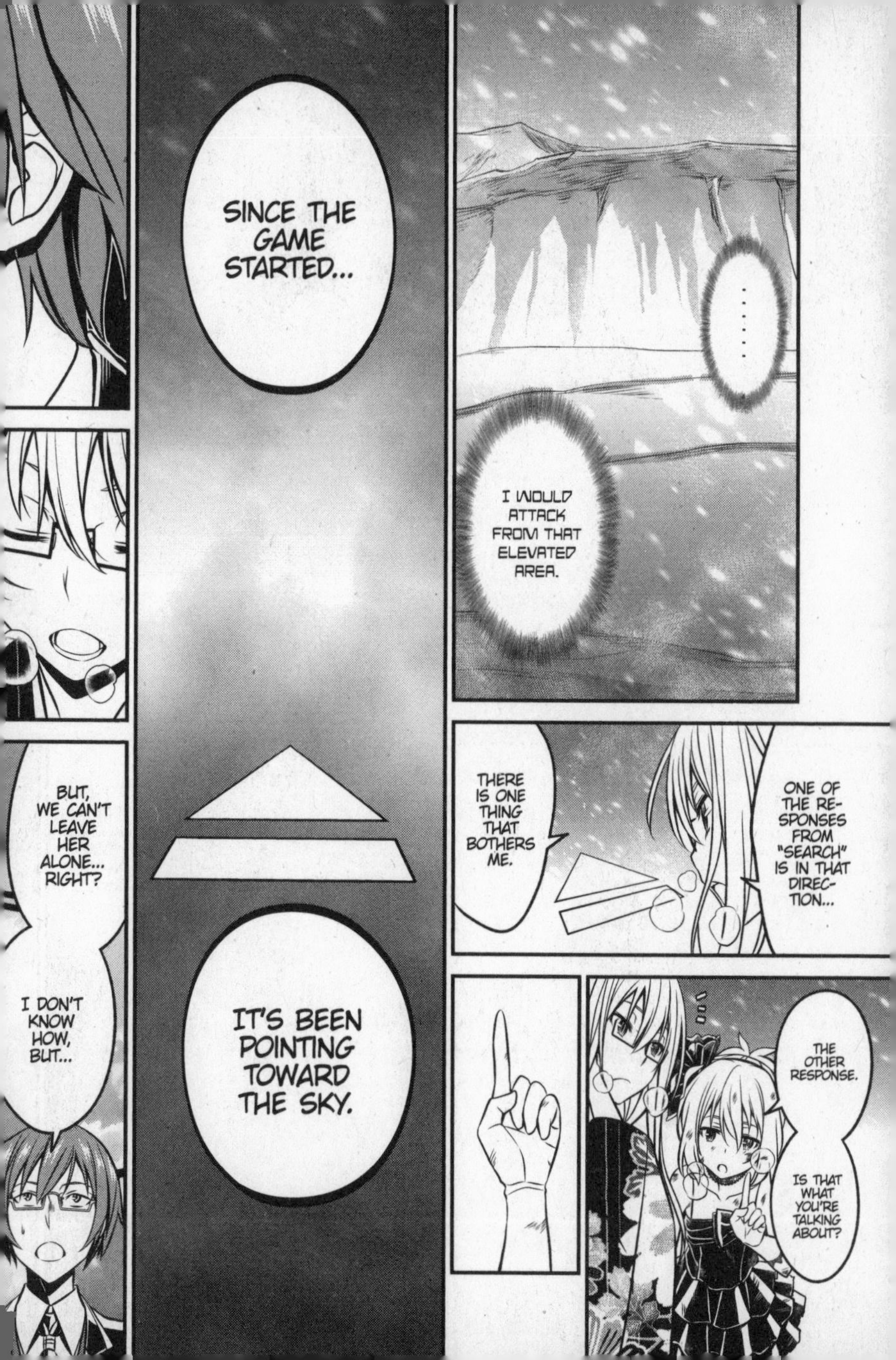
......
I WOULD ATTACK FROM THAT ELEVATED AREA.
ONE OF THE RE-SPONSES FROM "SEARCH" IS IN THAT DIREC-TION...
THERE IS ONE THING THAT BOTHERS ME.
THE OTHER RESPONSE.
IS THAT WHAT YOU'RE TALKING ABOUT?
SINCE THE GAME STARTED...
IT'S BEEN POINTING TOWARD THE SKY.
BUT, WE CAN'T LEAVE HER ALONE... RIGHT?
I DON'T KNOW HOW, BUT...

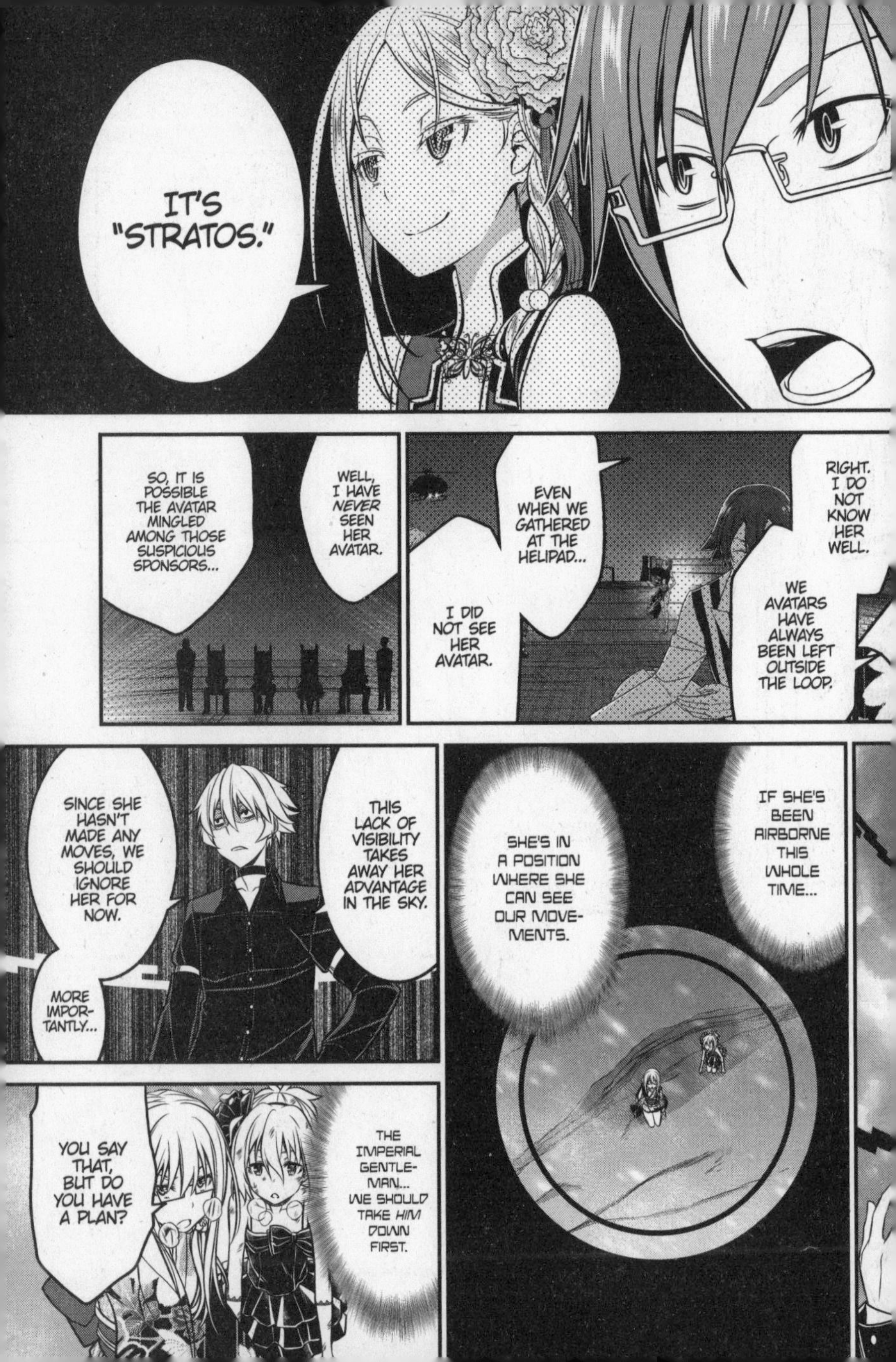
IT'S "STRATOS."
RIGHT. I DO NOT KNOW HER WELL.
WE AVATARS HAVE ALWAYS BEEN LEFT OUTSIDE THE LOOP.
EVEN WHEN WE GATHERED AT THE HELIPAD...
I DID NOT SEE HER AVATAR.
WELL, I HAVE NEVER SEEN HER AVATAR.
SO, IT IS POSSIBLE THE AVATAR MINGLED AMONG THOSE SUSPICIOUS SPONSORS...
IF SHE'S BEEN AIRBORNE THIS WHOLE TIME...
SHE'S IN A POSITION WHERE SHE CAN SEE OUR MOVEMENTS.
THIS LACK OF VISIBILITY TAKES AWAY HER ADVANTAGE IN THE SKY.
SINCE SHE HASN'T MADE ANY MOVES, WE SHOULD IGNORE HER FOR NOW.
MORE IMPORTANTLY...
THE IMPERIAL GENTLEMAN... WE SHOULD TAKE HIM DOWN FIRST.
YOU SAY THAT, BUT DO YOU HAVE A PLAN?

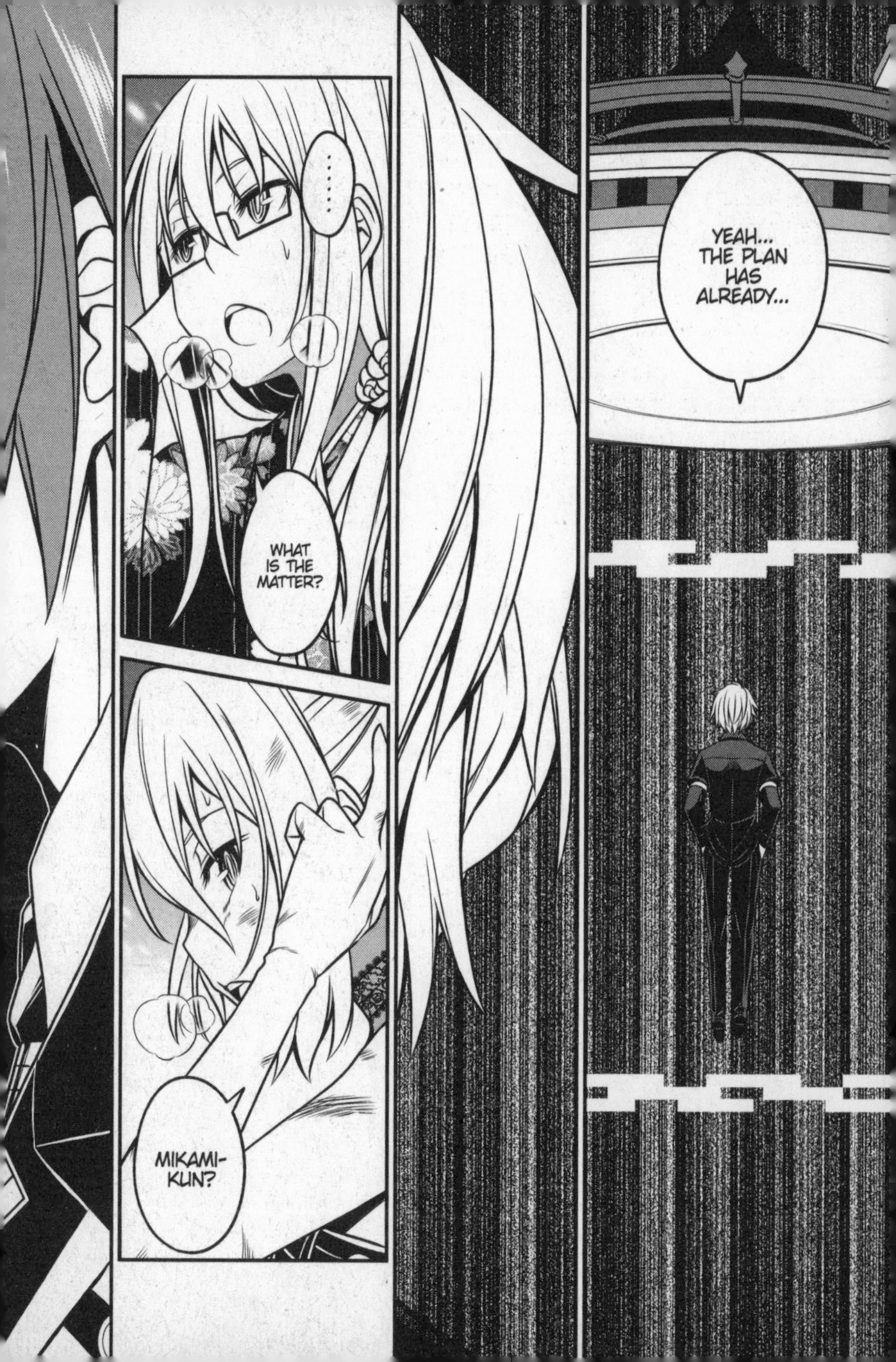
YEAH... THE PLAN HAS ALREADY...
......
WHAT IS THE MATTER?
MIKAMI-KUN?

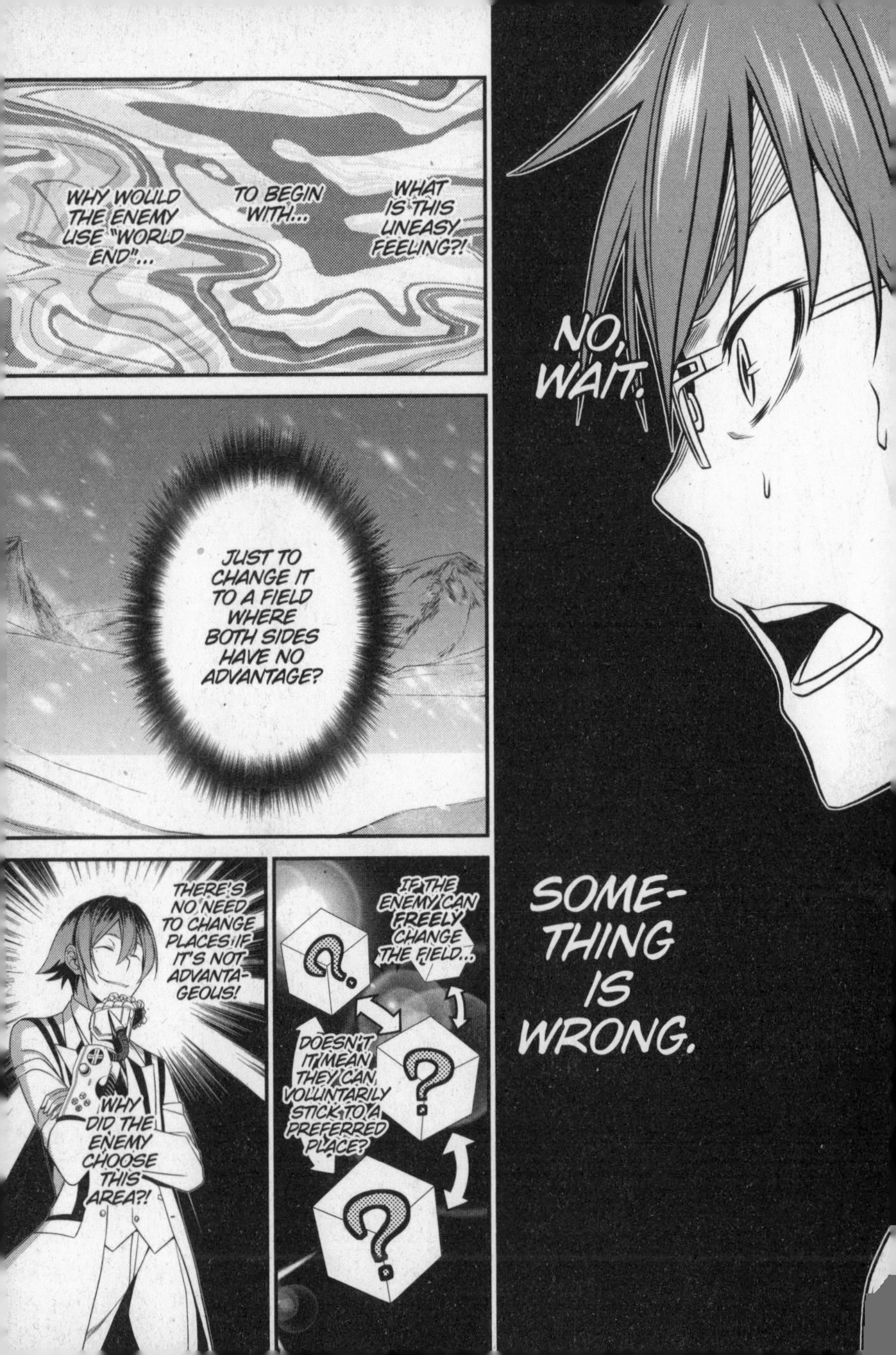
WHY WOULD THE ENEMY USE "WORLD END"...
TO BEGIN WITH...
WHAT IS THIS UNEASY FEELING?!
JUST TO CHANGE IT TO A FIELD WHERE BOTH SIDES HAVE NO ADVANTAGE?
THERE'S NO NEED TO CHANGE PLACES IF IT'S NOT ADVANTAGEOUS!
WHY DID THE ENEMY CHOOSE THIS AREA?!
IF THE ENEMY CAN FREELY CHANGE THE FIELD...
DOESN'T IT MEAN THEY CAN VOLUNTARILY STICK TO A PREFERRED PLACE?
NO, WAIT.
SOMETHING IS WRONG.

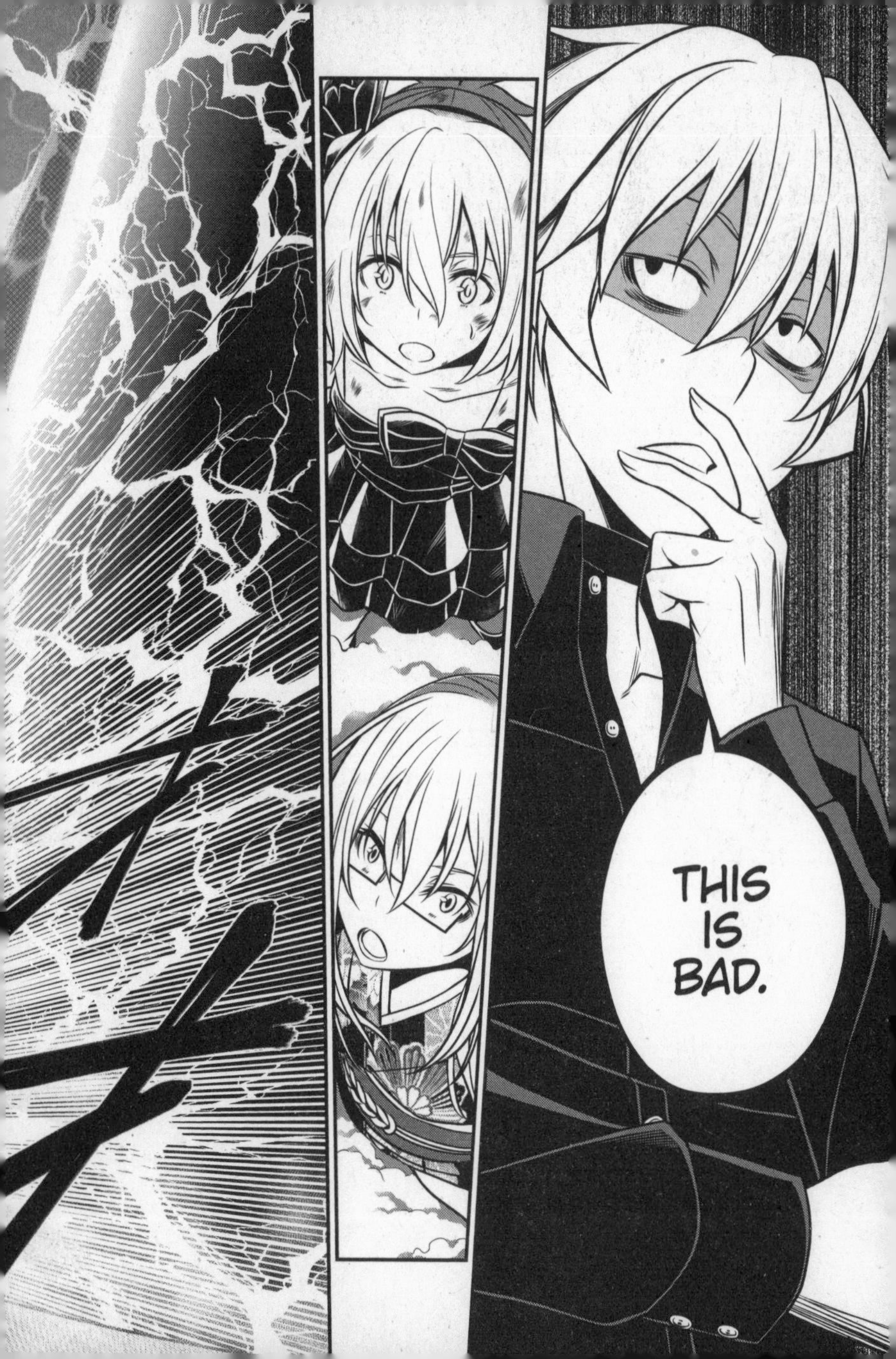
THIS IS BAD.

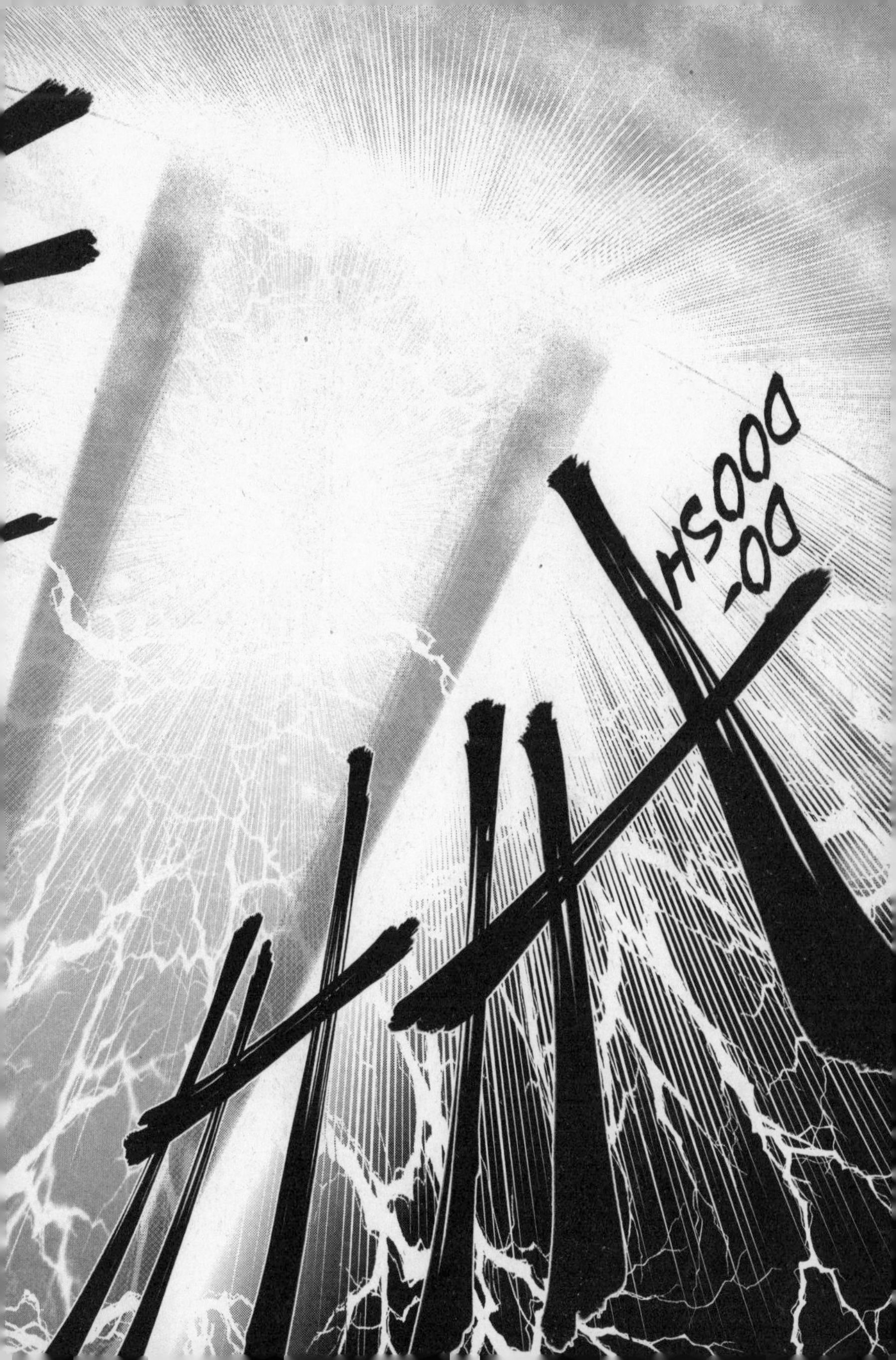
DO-DOOSH

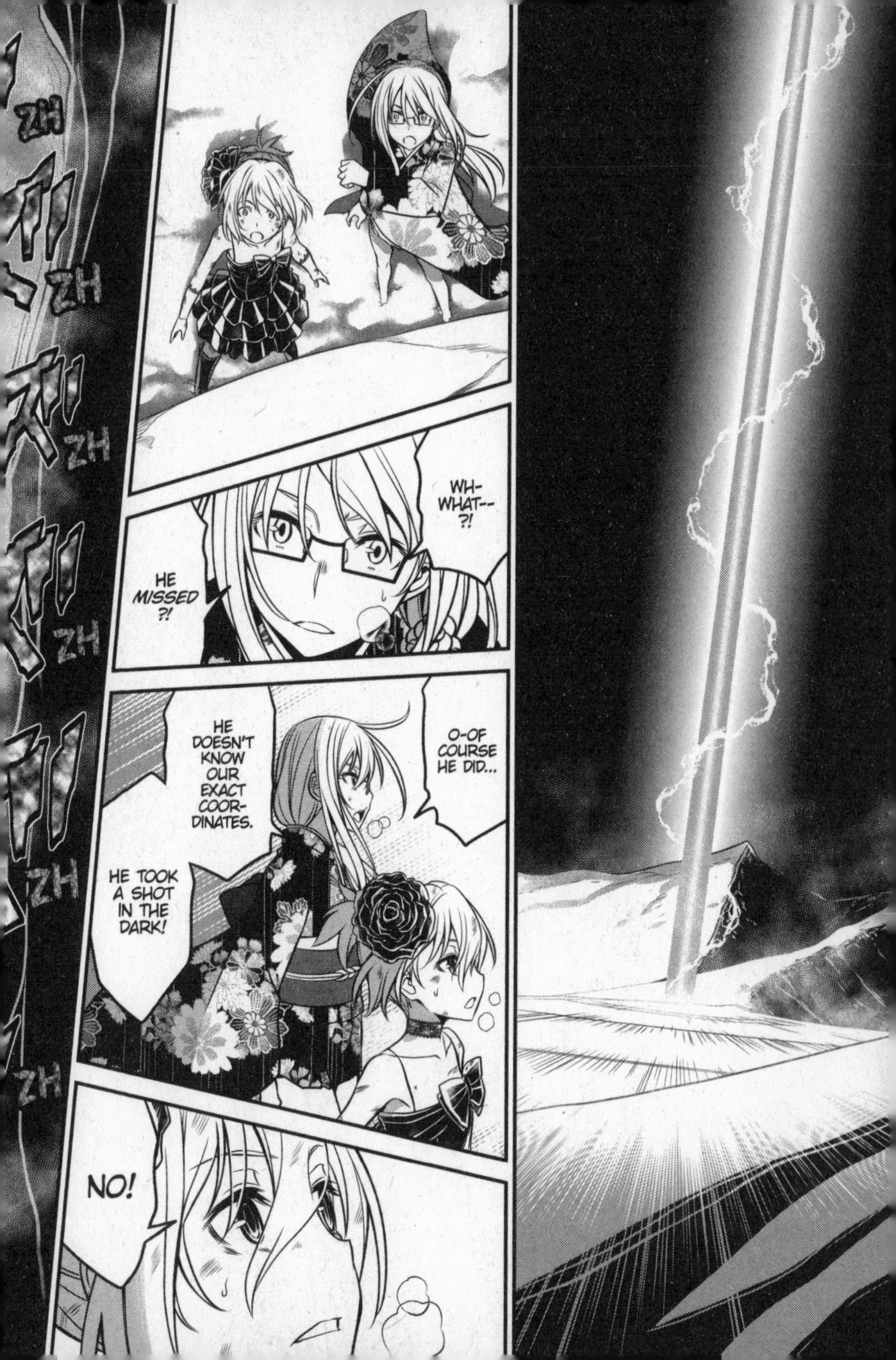
WH- WHAT-- ?!
HE MISSED ?!
O-OF COURSE HE DID...
HE DOESN'T KNOW OUR EXACT COOR- DINATES.
HE TOOK A SHOT IN THE DARK!
NO!
ZH ZH ZH ZH ZH ZH

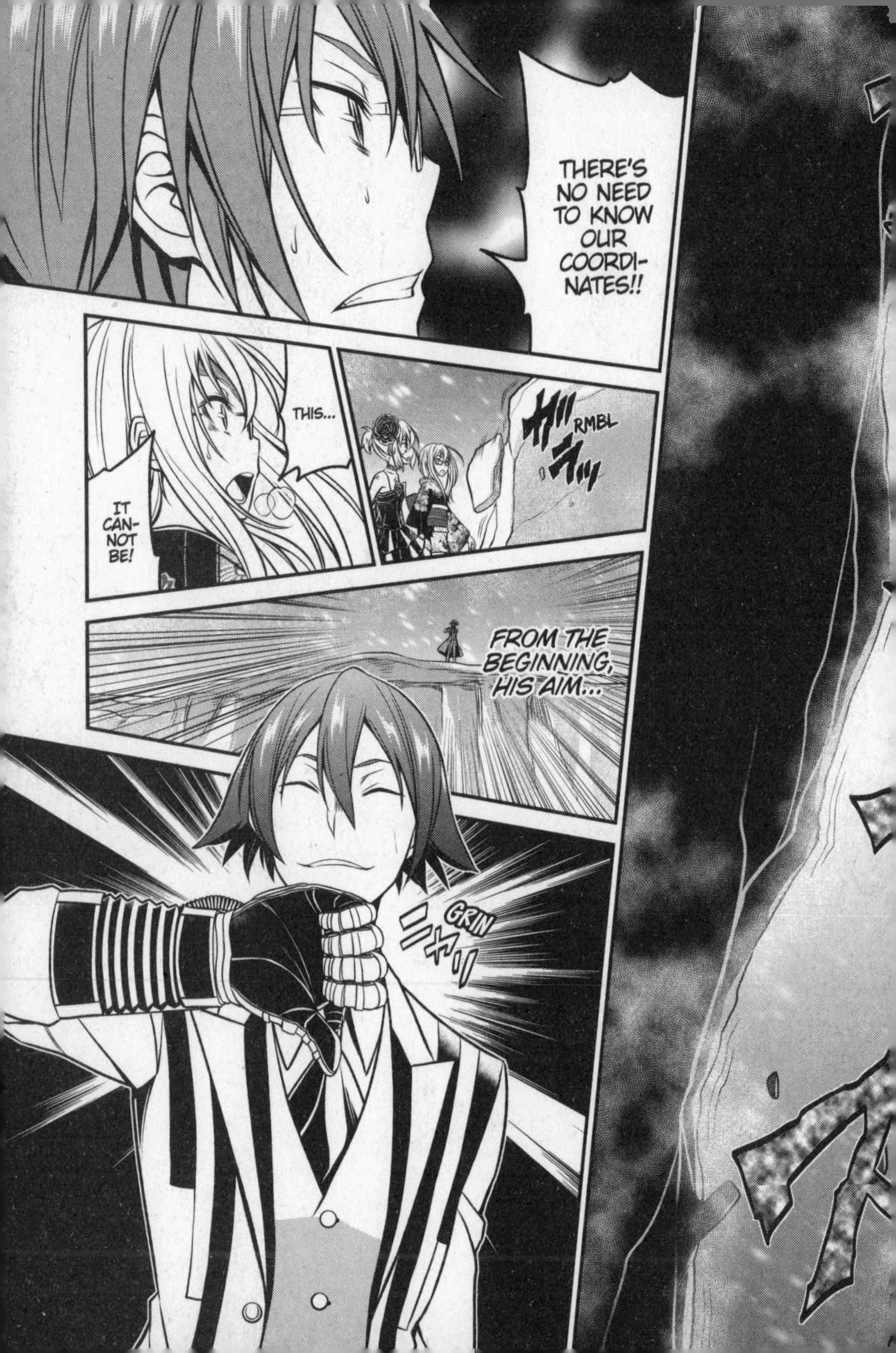
THERE'S NO NEED TO KNOW OUR COORDI-NATES!!
RMBL
THIS...
IT CAN-NOT BE!
FROM THE BEGINNING, HIS AIM...
GRIN

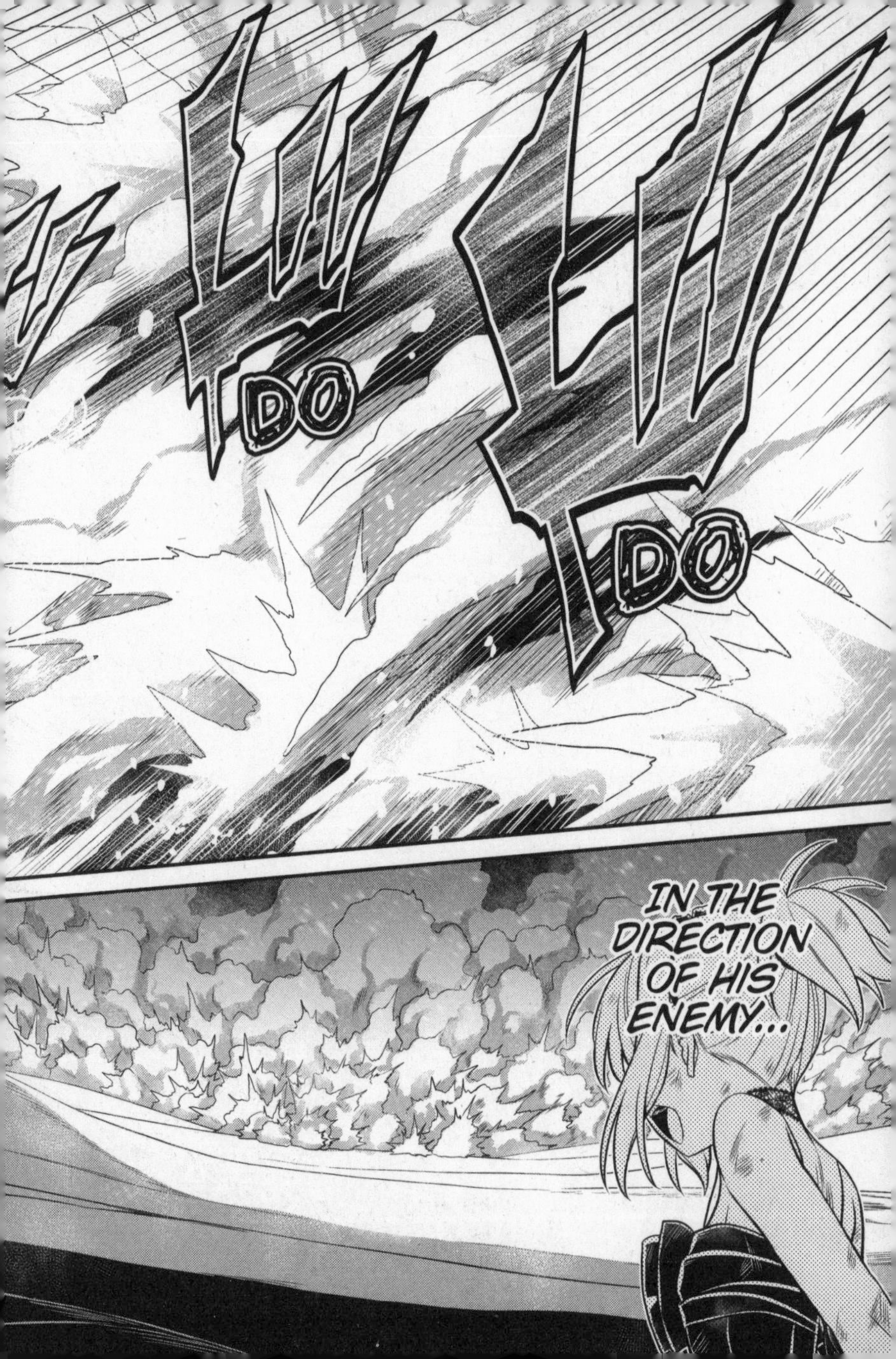
DO
DO
IN THE DIRECTION OF HIS ENEMY...

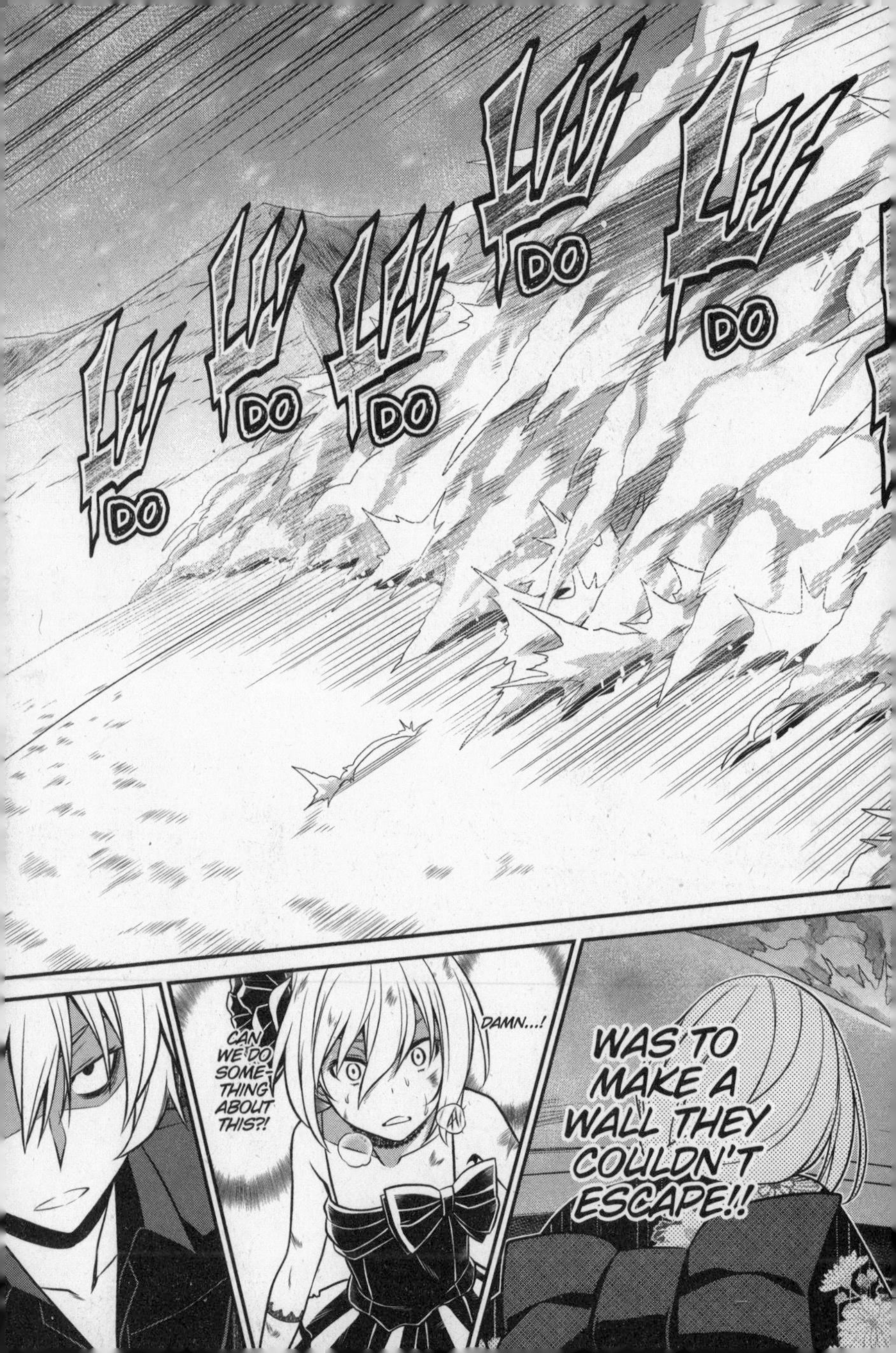
DO
DO
DO
DO
DO
WAS TO MAKE A WALL THEY COULDN'T ESCAPE!!
DAMN...!
CAN WE DO SOME-THING ABOUT THIS?!

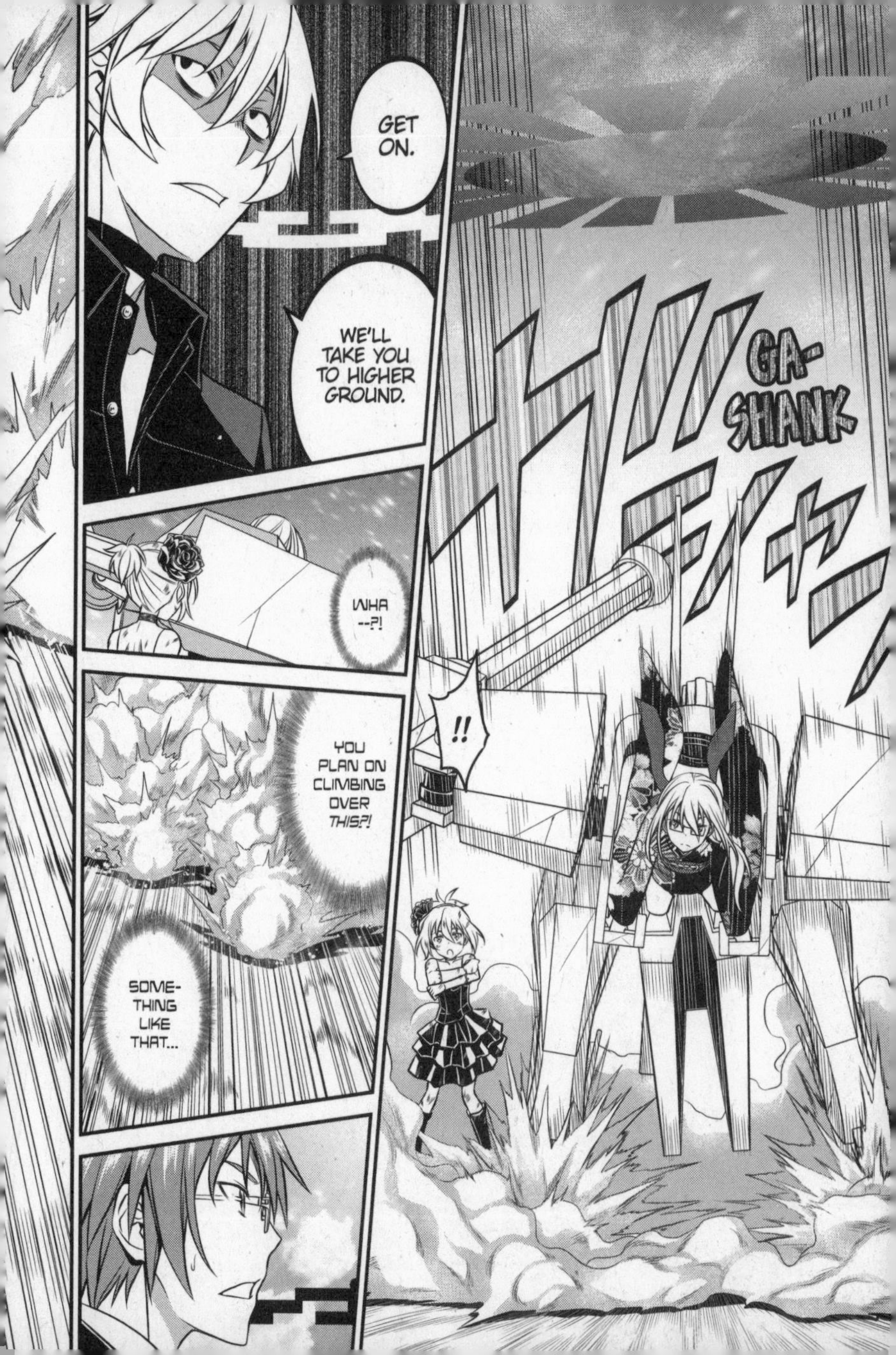
GA-SHANK
!!
GET ON.
WE'LL TAKE YOU TO HIGHER GROUND.
WHA --?!
YOU PLAN ON CLIMBING OVER THIS?!
SOME-THING LIKE THAT...

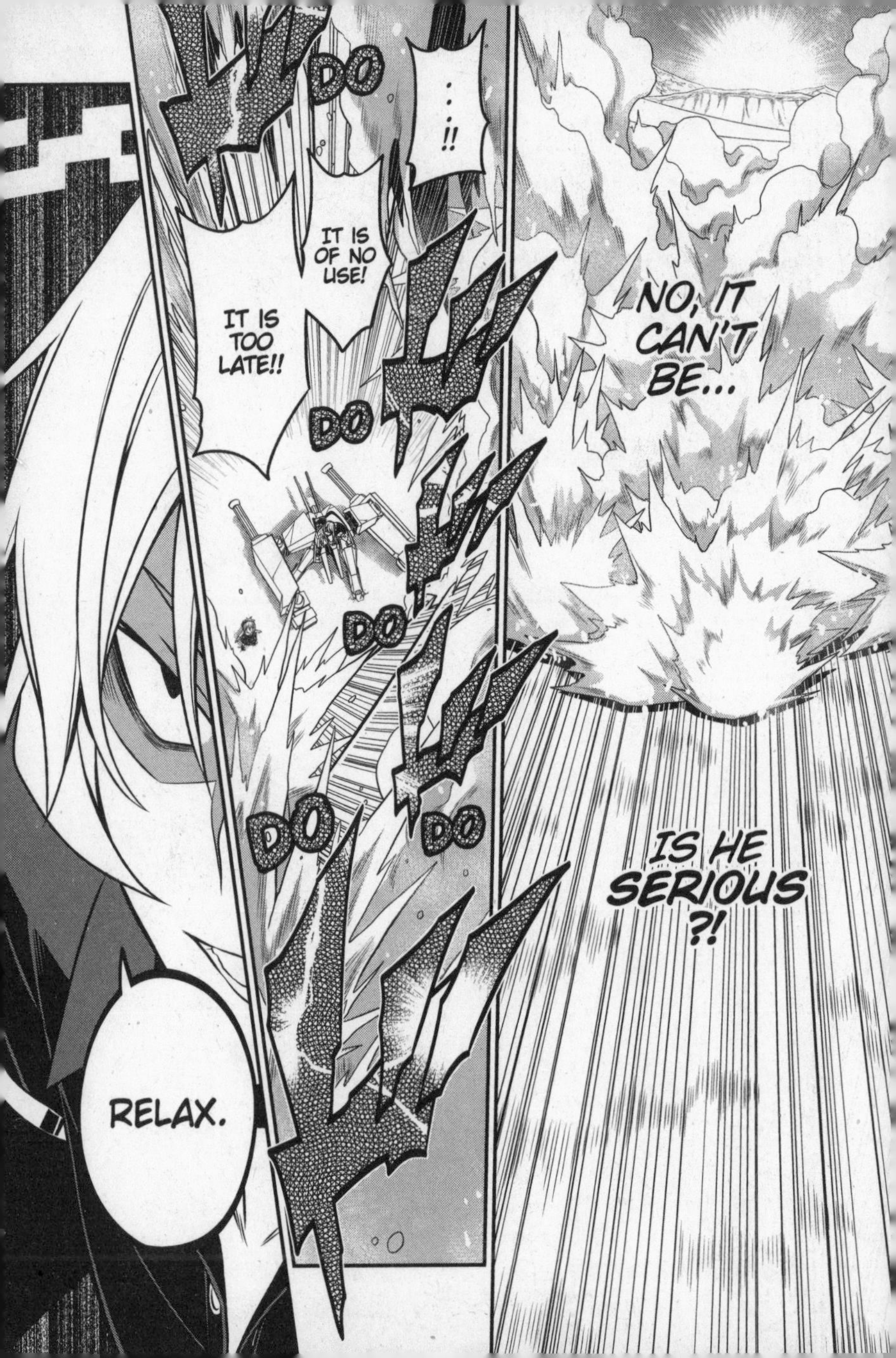
NO, IT CAN'T BE...
IS HE SERIOUS ?!
DO
...!!
IT IS OF NO USE!
IT IS TOO LATE!!
DO
DO
DO
DO
RELAX.

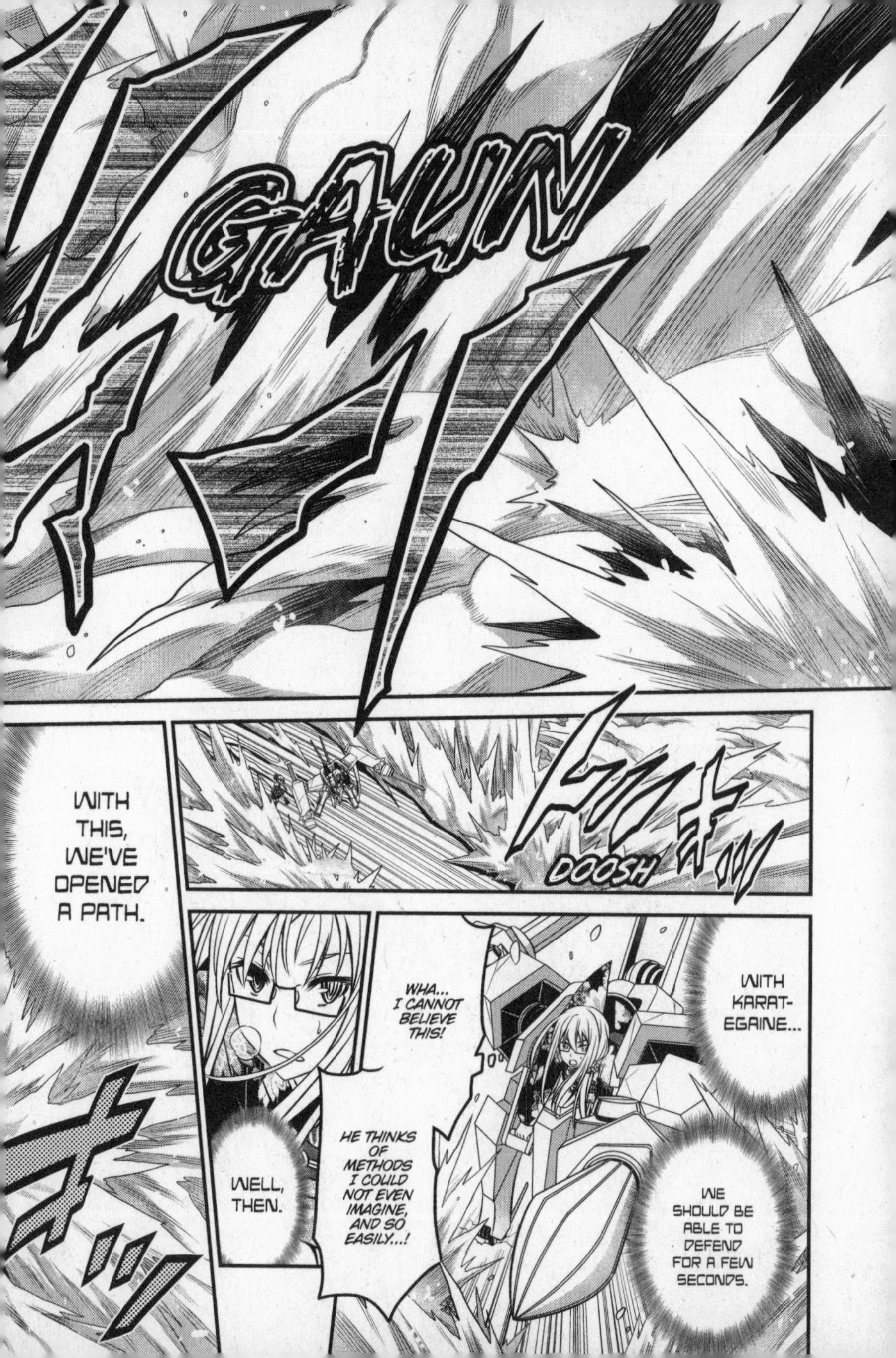
GAUN
DOOSH
WITH KARAT-EGAINE...
WE SHOULD BE ABLE TO DEFEND FOR A FEW SECONDS.
WHA... I CANNOT BELIEVE THIS!
HE THINKS OF METHODS I COULD NOT EVEN IMAGINE, AND SO EASILY...!
WELL, THEN.
WITH THIS, WE'VE OPENED A PATH.

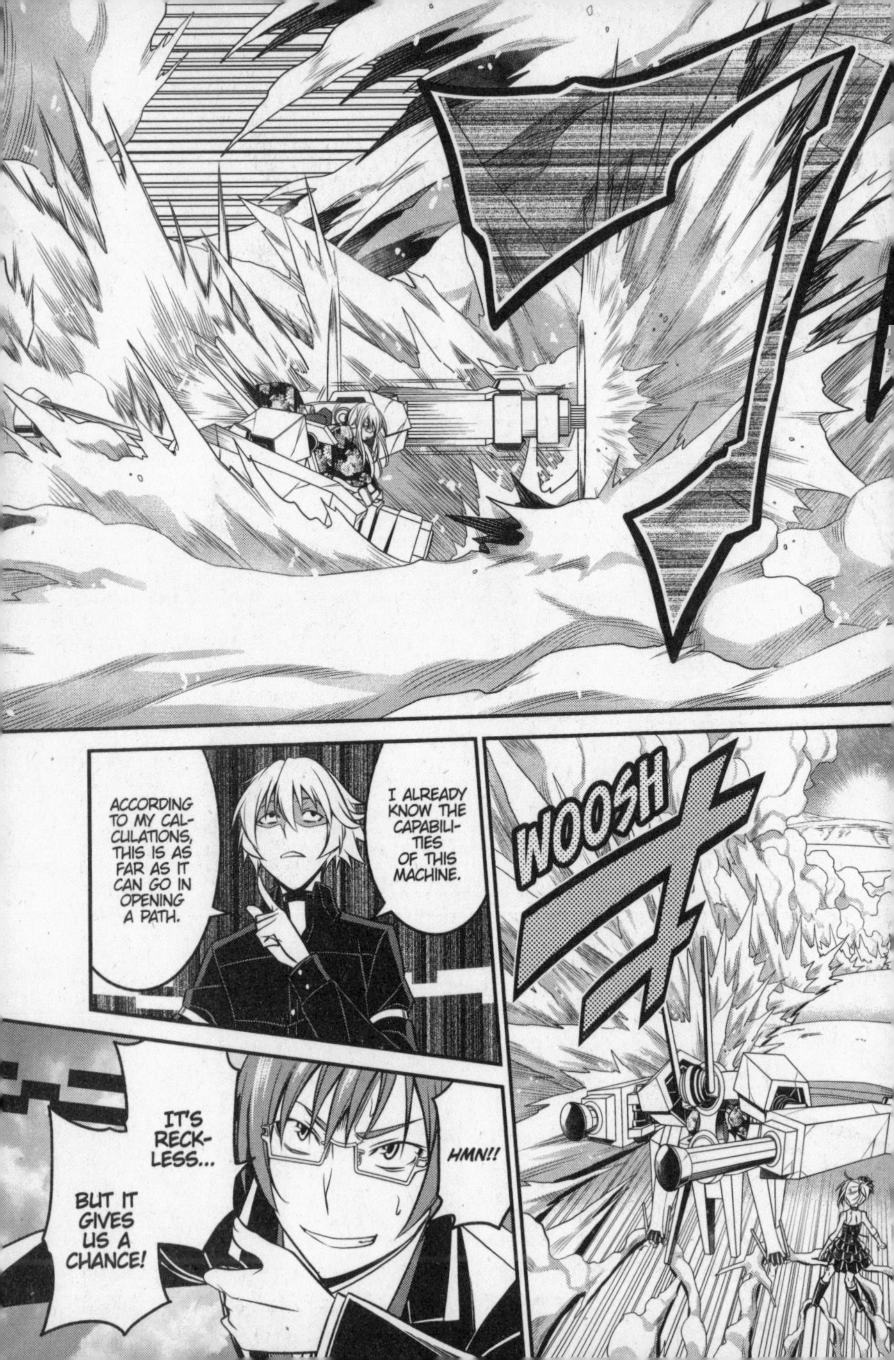
WOOSH
I ALREADY KNOW THE CAPABILI-TIES OF THIS MACHINE.
ACCORDING TO MY CAL-CULATIONS, THIS IS AS FAR AS IT CAN GO IN OPENING A PATH.
HMN!!
IT'S RECK-LESS...
BUT IT GIVES US A CHANCE!

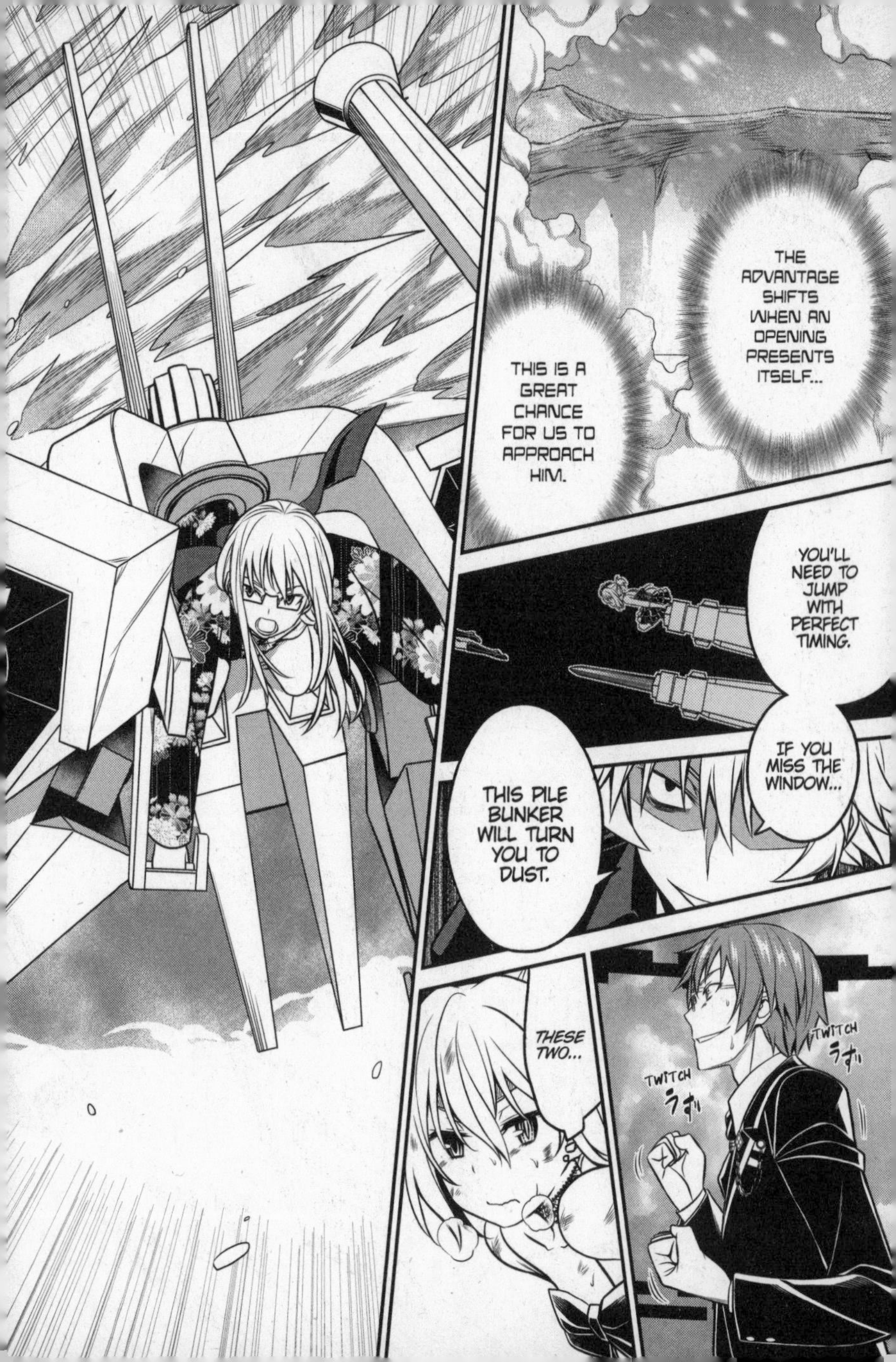
THE ADVANTAGE SHIFTS WHEN AN OPENING PRESENTS ITSELF...
THIS IS A GREAT CHANCE FOR US TO APPROACH HIM.
YOU'LL NEED TO JUMP WITH PERFECT TIMING.
IF YOU MISS THE WINDOW...
THIS PILE BUNKER WILL TURN YOU TO DUST.
TWITCH
TWITCH
THESE TWO...

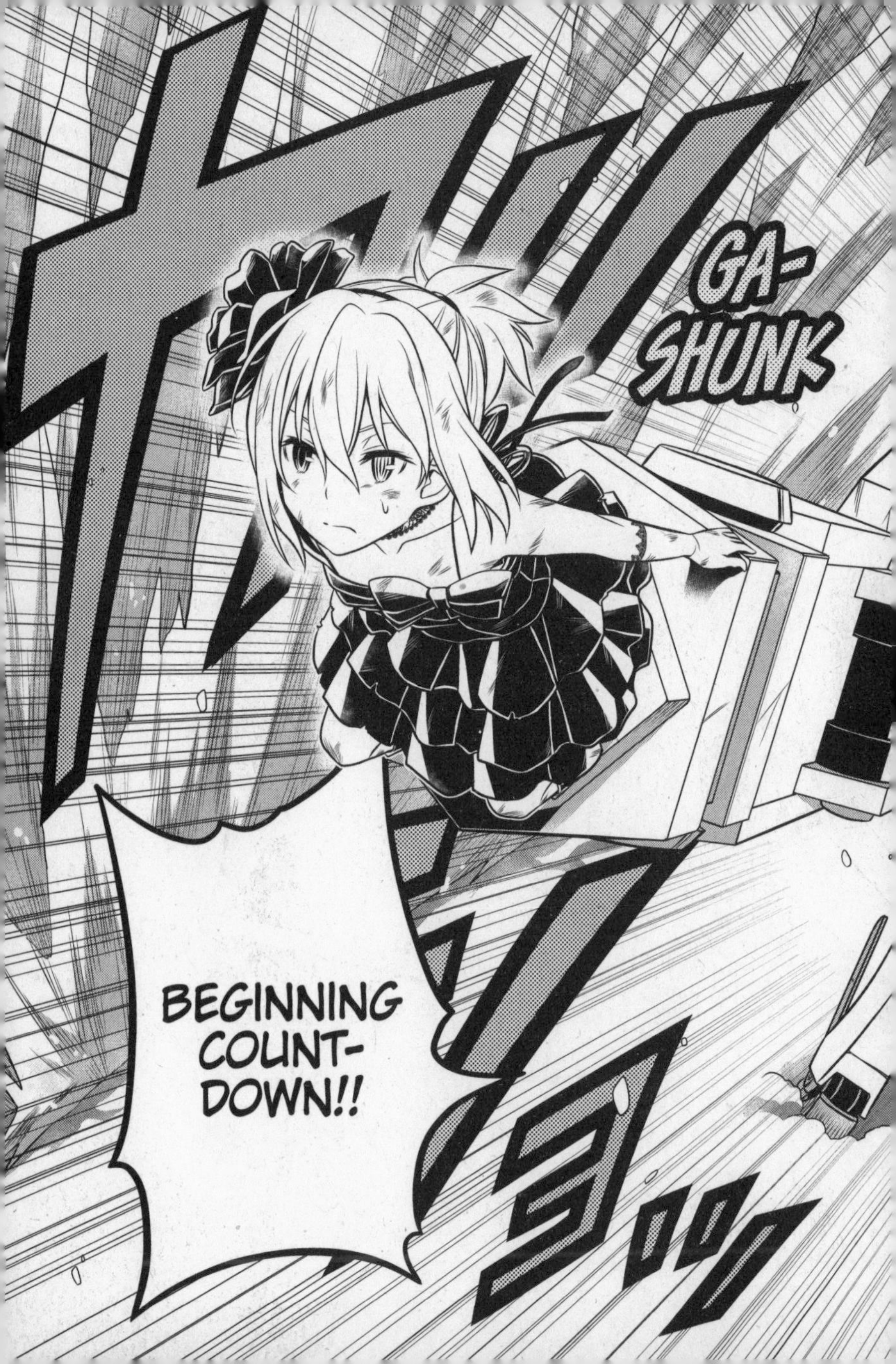
GA-SHUNK
BEGINNING COUNT-DOWN!!

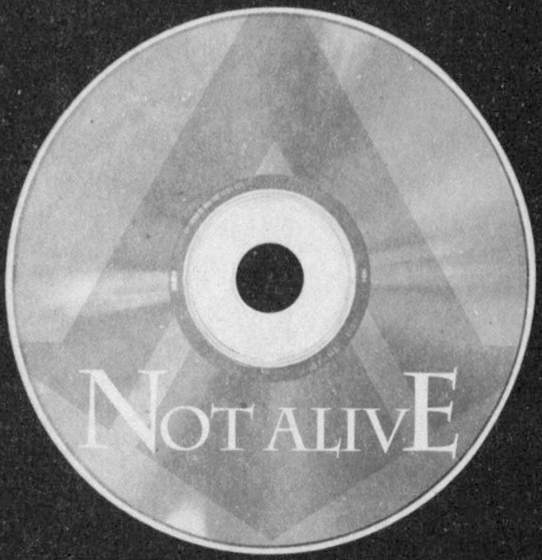
NOT ALIVE

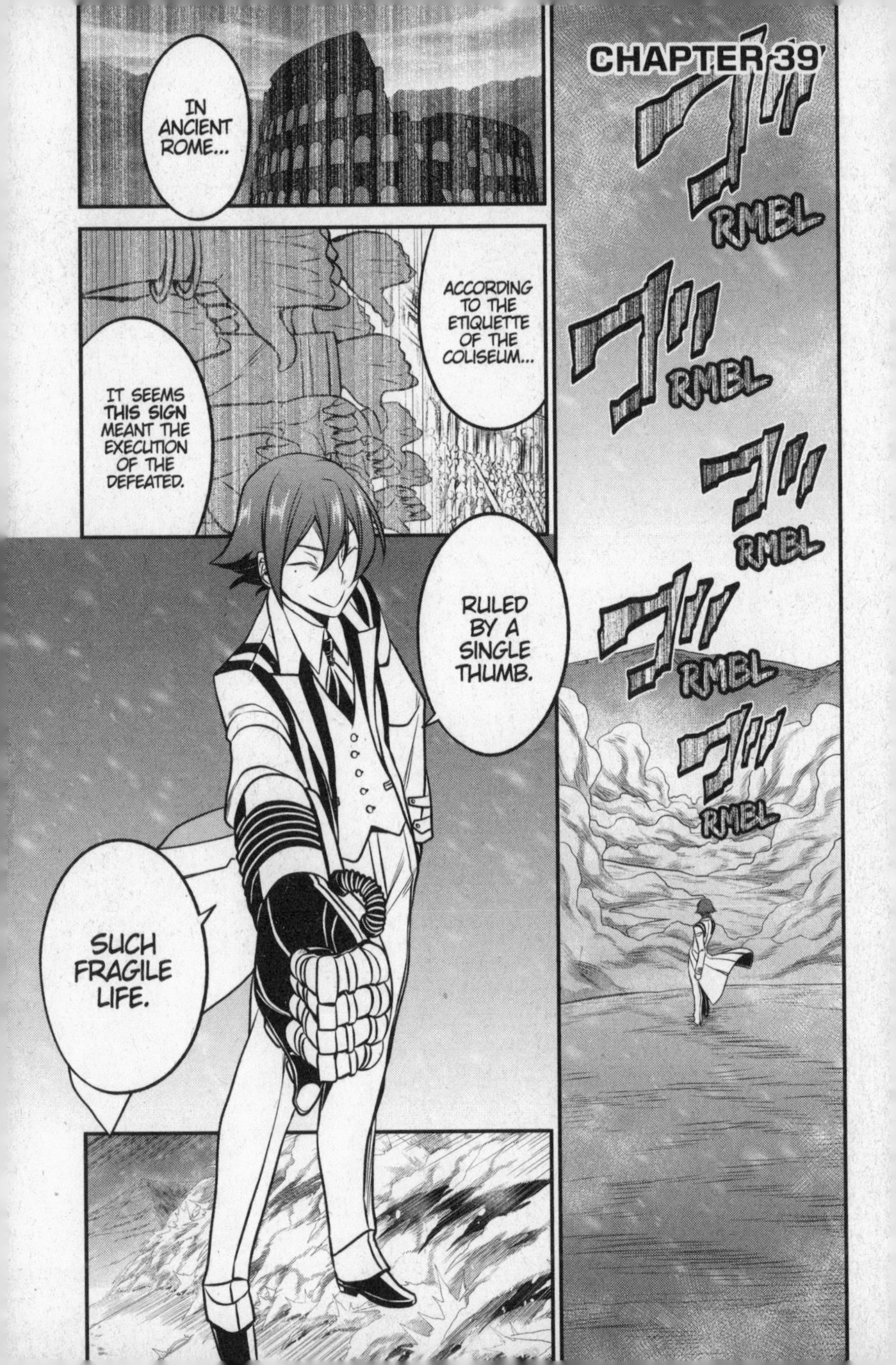
CHAPTER 39
RMBL
RMBL
RMBL
RMBL
RMBL
IN ANCIENT ROME...
ACCORDING TO THE ETIQUETTE OF THE COLISEUM...
IT SEEMS THIS SIGN MEANT THE EXECUTION OF THE DEFEATED.
RULED BY A SINGLE THUMB.
SUCH FRAGILE LIFE.

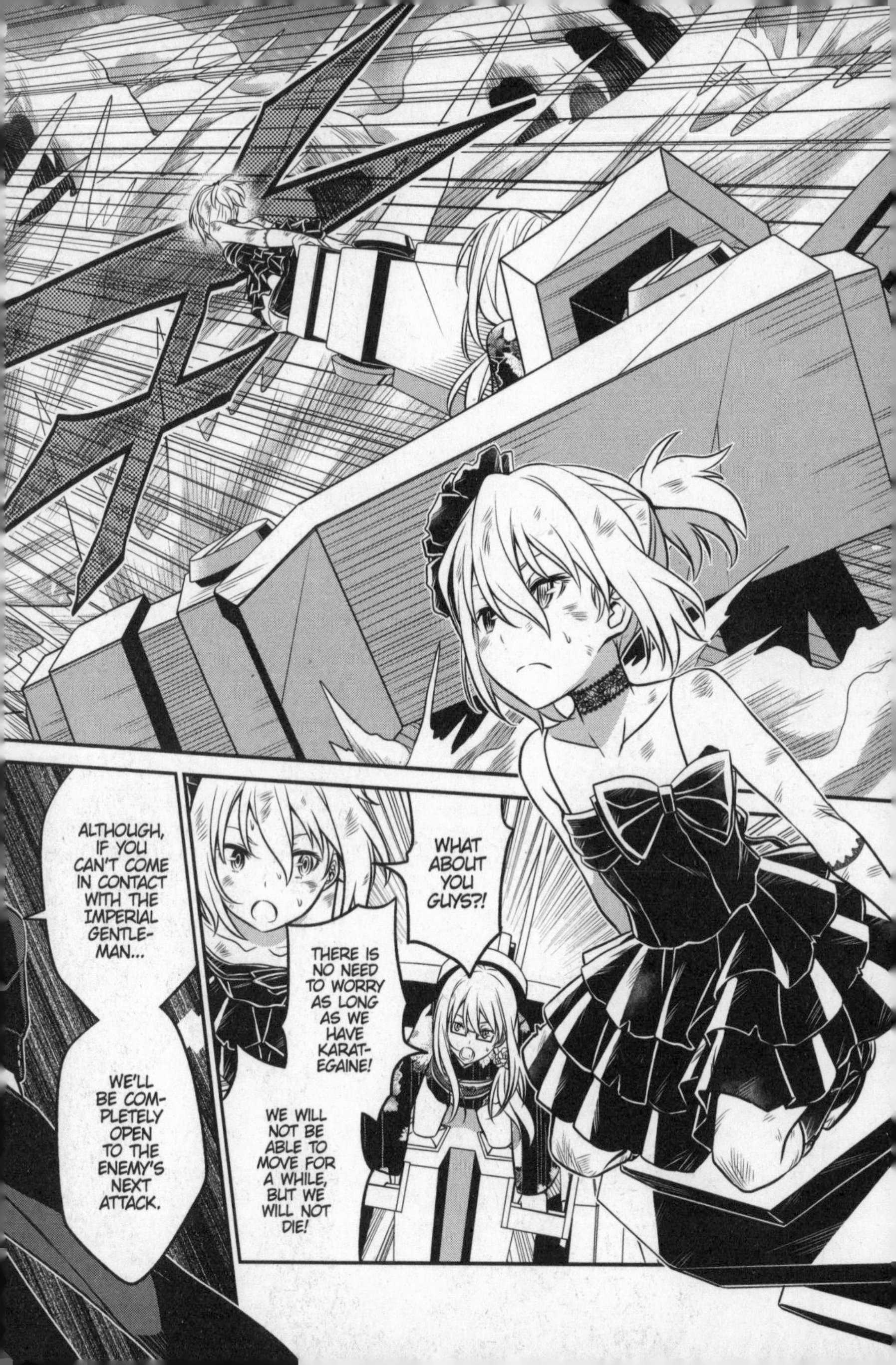
WHAT ABOUT YOU GUYS?!
THERE IS NO NEED TO WORRY AS LONG AS WE HAVE KARAT-EGAINE!
WE WILL NOT BE ABLE TO MOVE FOR A WHILE, BUT WE WILL NOT DIE!
ALTHOUGH, IF YOU CAN'T COME IN CONTACT WITH THE IMPERIAL GENTLE-MAN...
WE'LL BE COM-PLETELY OPEN TO THE ENEMY'S NEXT ATTACK.

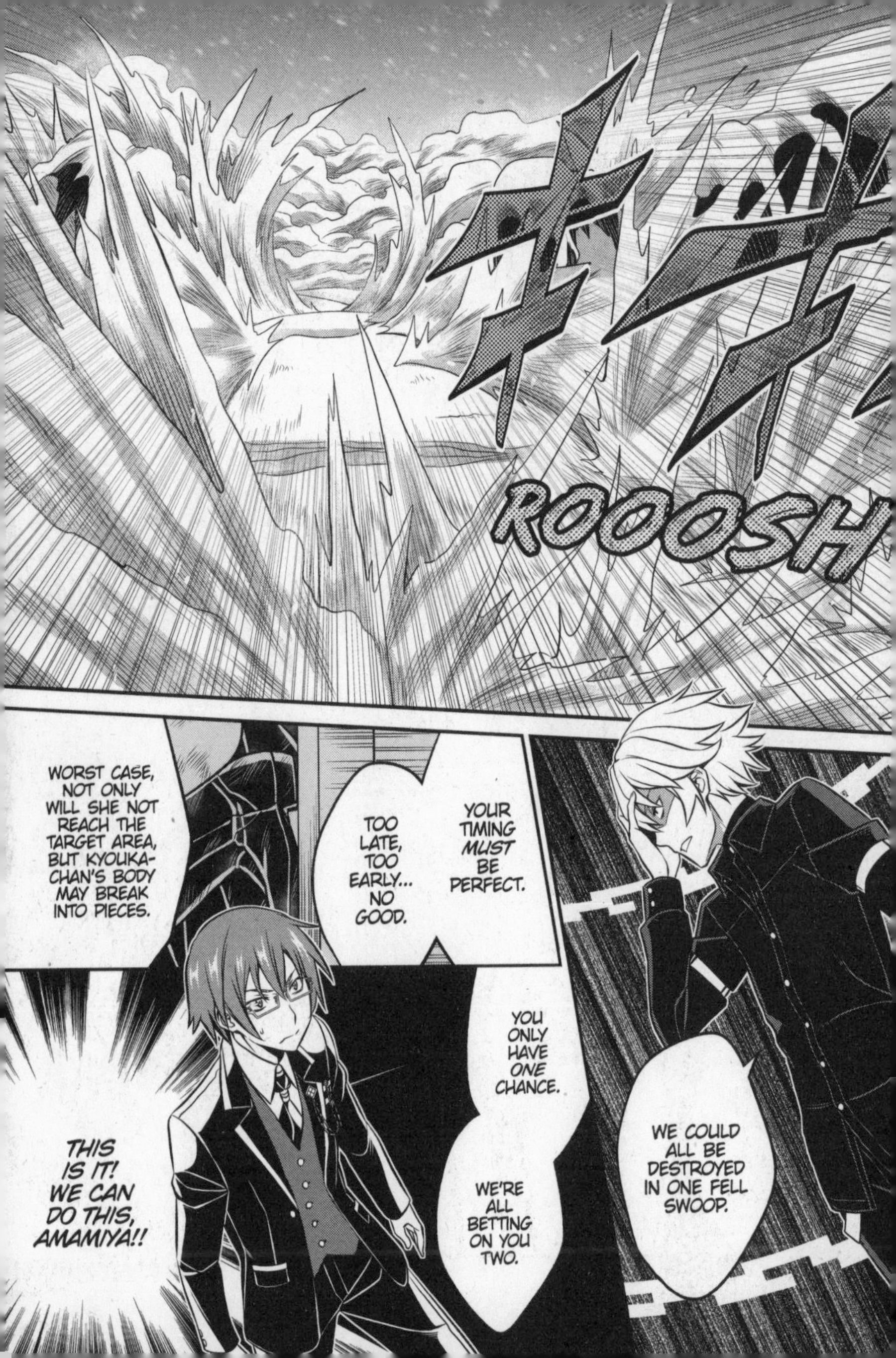
ROOOSH
YOUR TIMING MUST BE PERFECT.
TOO LATE, TOO EARLY... NO GOOD.
WORST CASE, NOT ONLY WILL SHE NOT REACH THE TARGET AREA, BUT KYOUKA-CHAN'S BODY MAY BREAK INTO PIECES.
YOU ONLY HAVE ONE CHANCE.
WE COULD ALL BE DESTROYED IN ONE FELL SWOOP.
WE'RE ALL BETTING ON YOU TWO.
THIS IS IT! WE CAN DO THIS, AMAMIYA!!

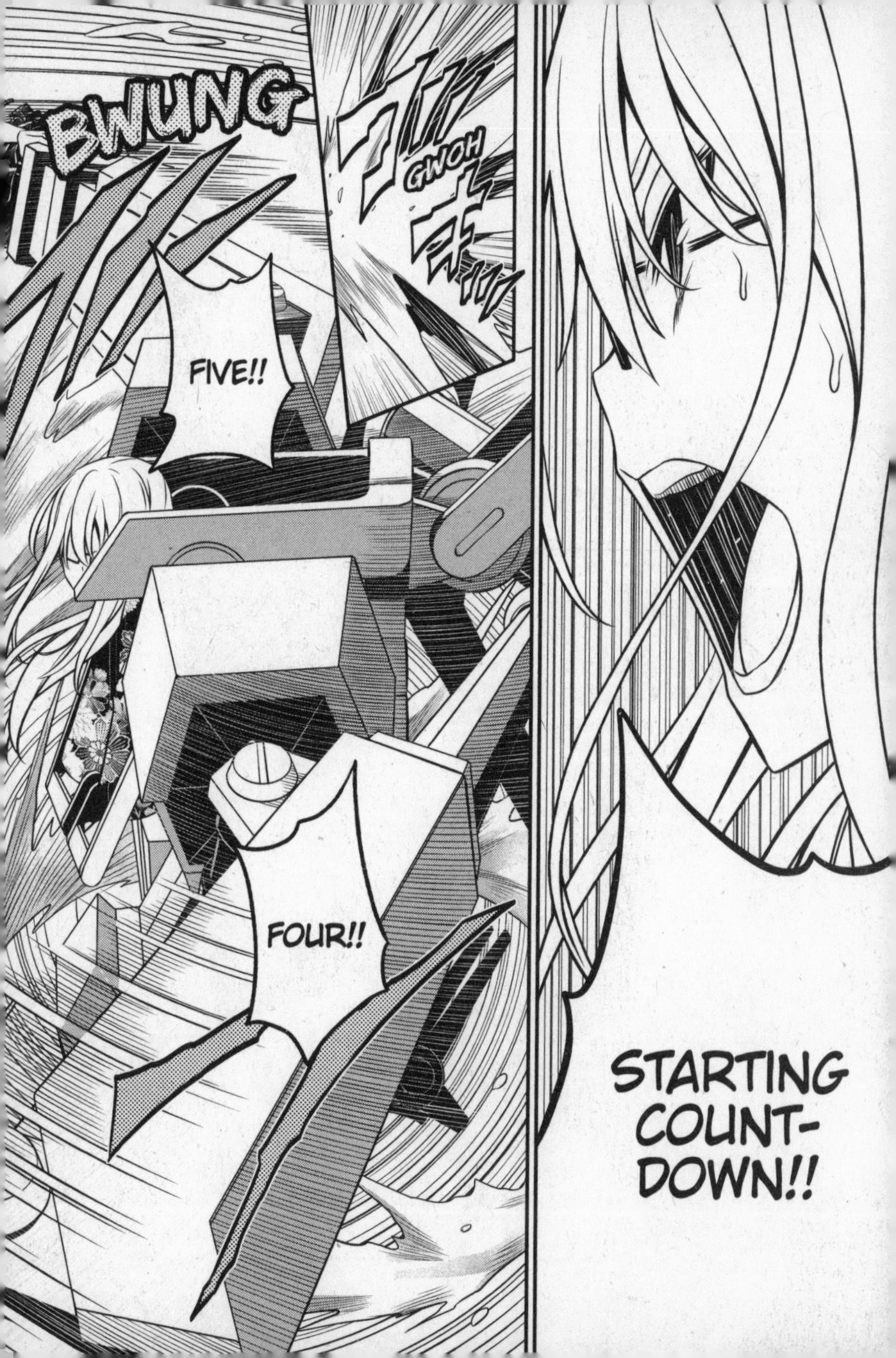
STARTING COUNT-DOWN!!
GWOH
BWUNG
FIVE!!
FOUR!!

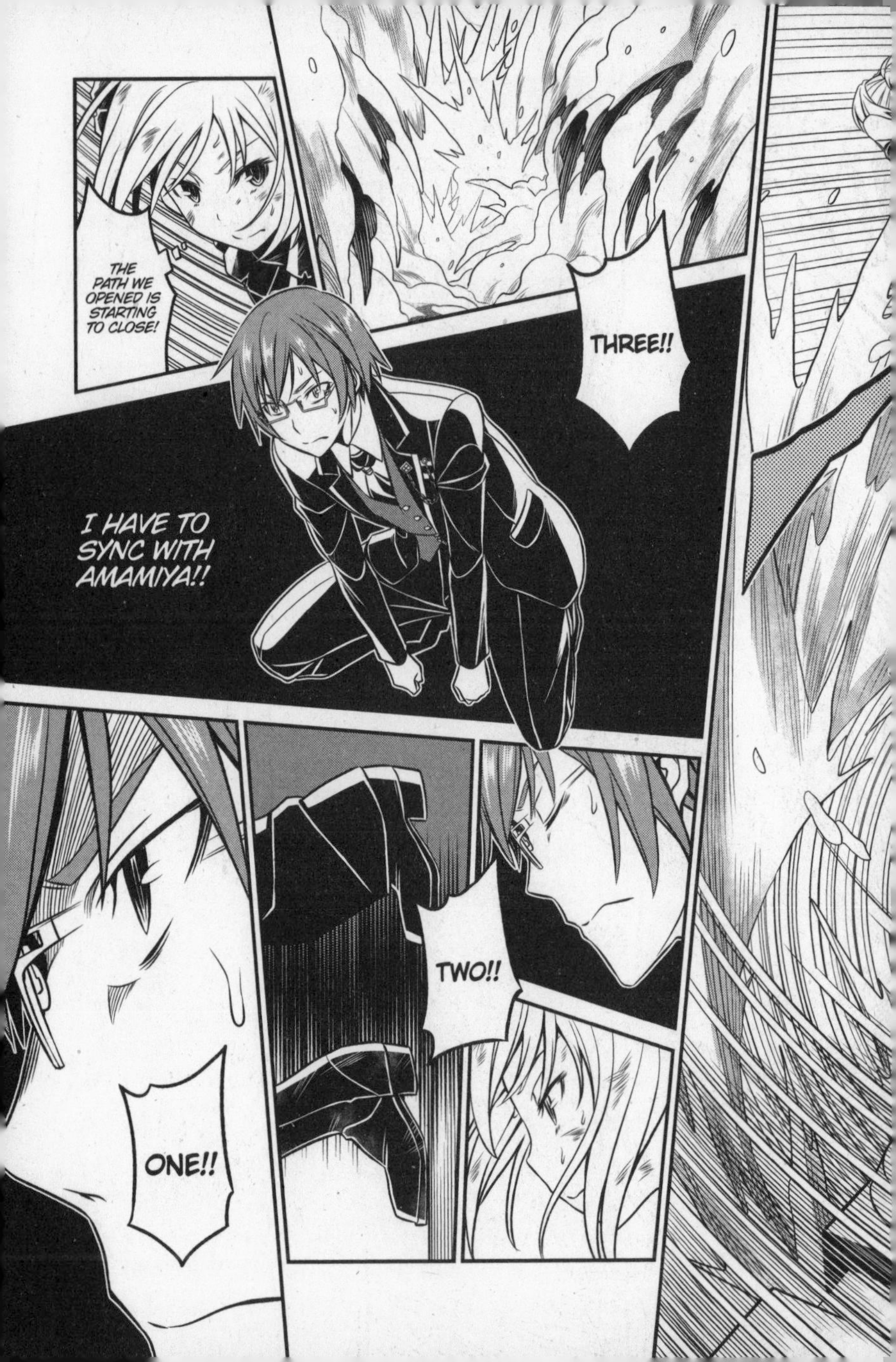
THREE!!
THE PATH WE OPENED IS STARTING TO CLOSE!
I HAVE TO SYNC WITH AMAMIYA!!
TWO!!
ONE!!

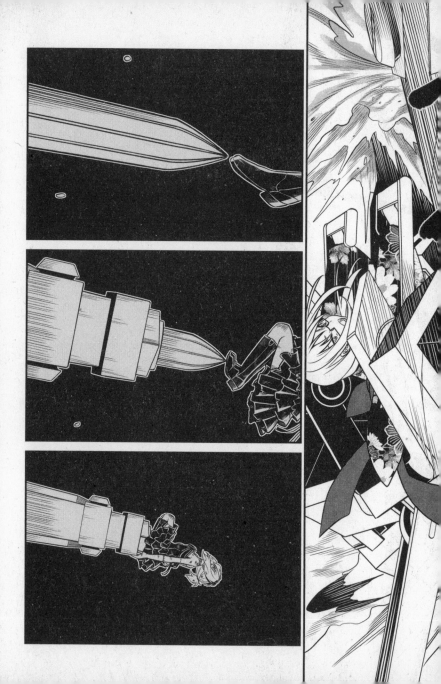

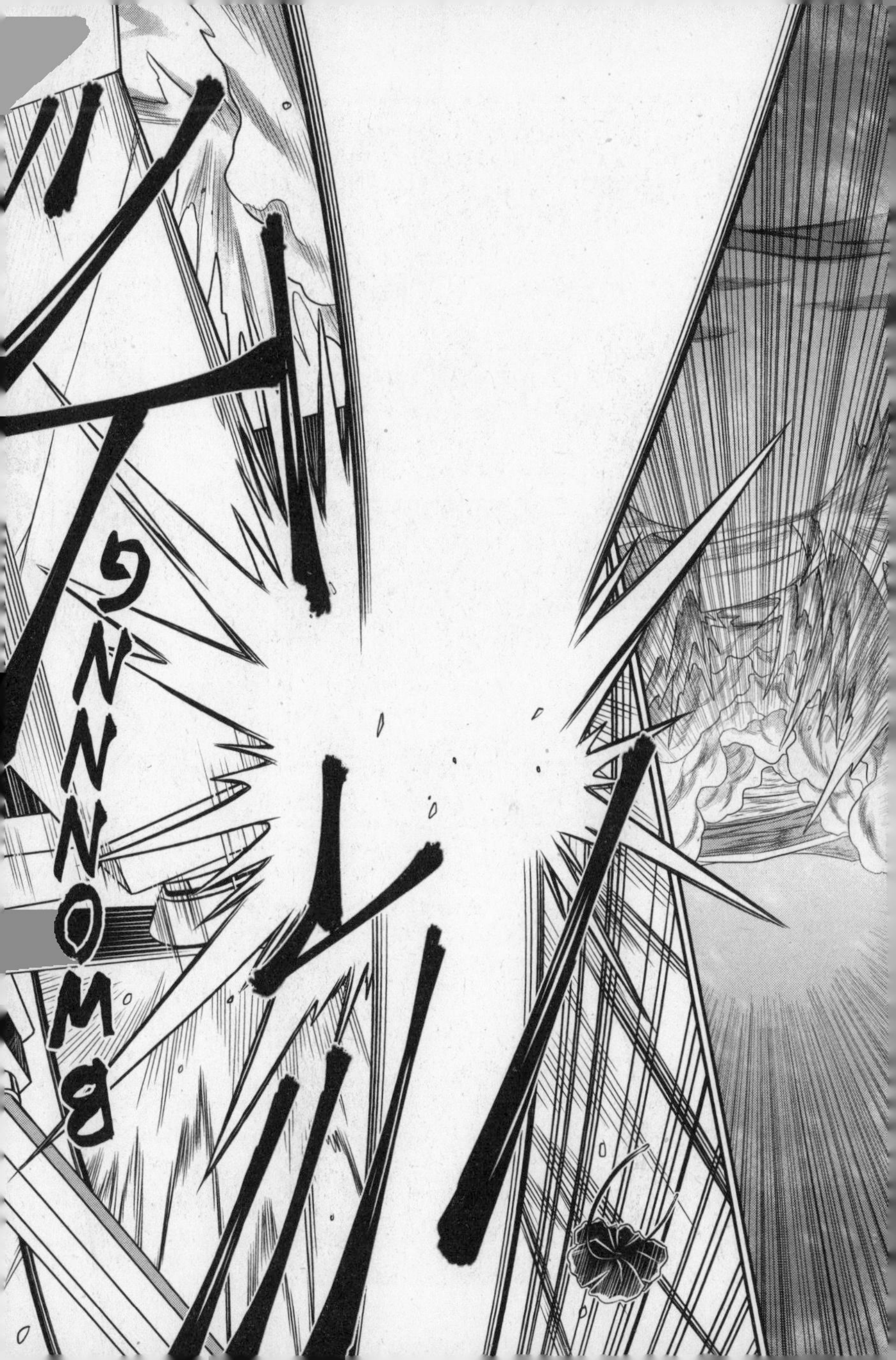
BWONNNG

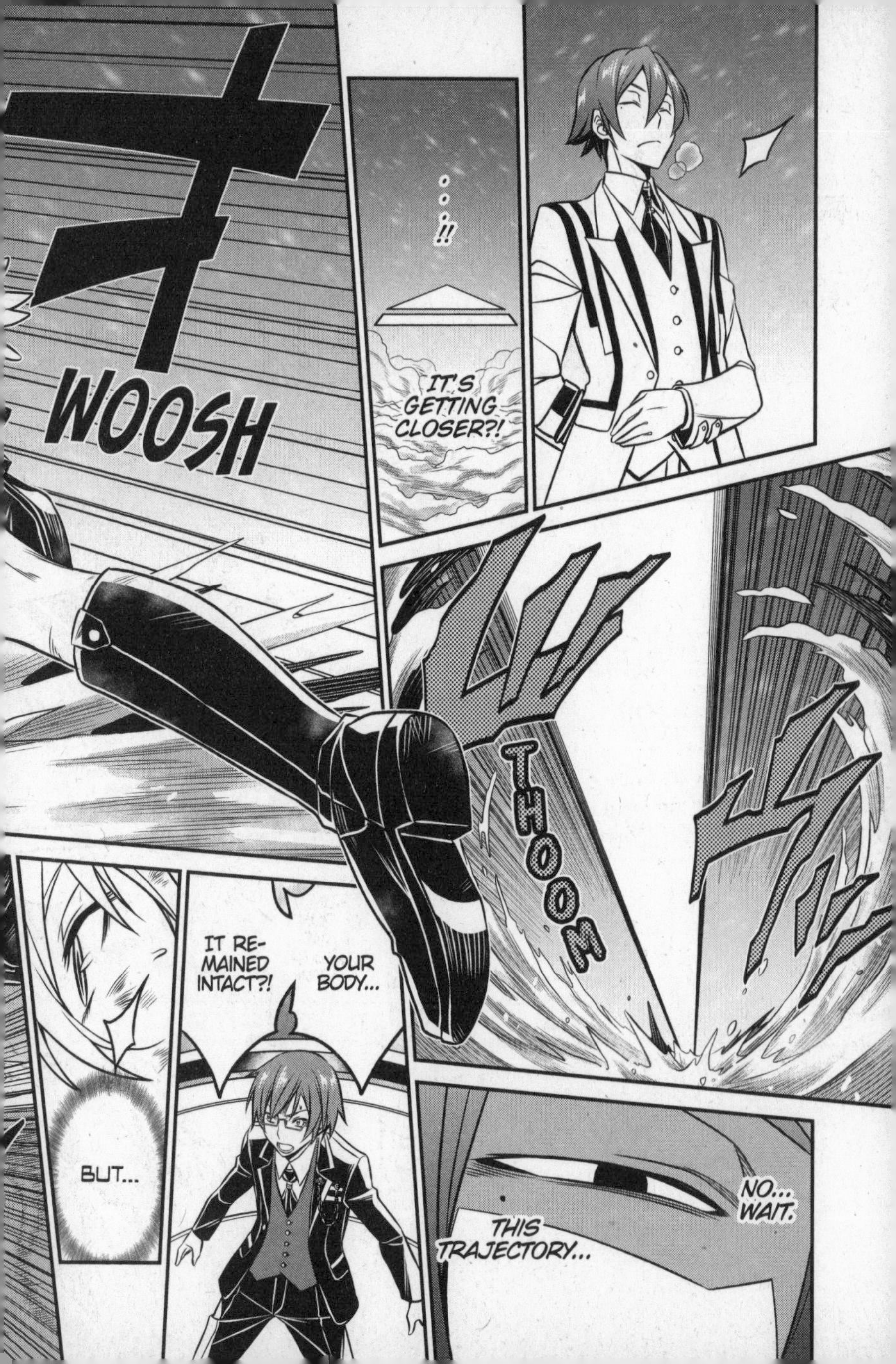

...!!
IT'S GETTING CLOSER?!
WOOSH
THOOOM
NO... WAIT.
THIS TRAJECTORY...
YOUR BODY...
IT RE-MAINED INTACT?!
BUT...

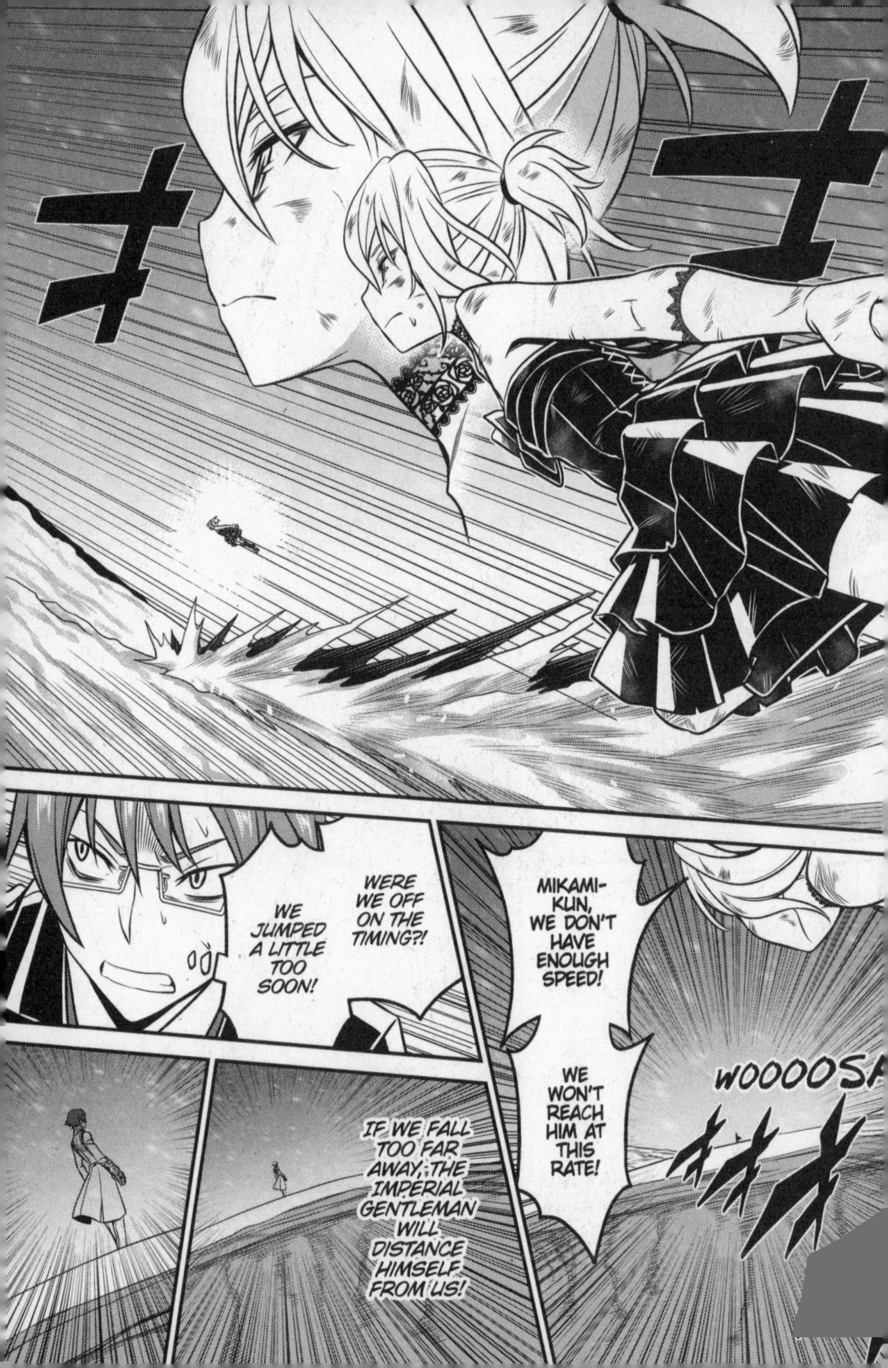
WERE WE OFF ON THE TIMING?!
WE JUMPED A LITTLE TOO SOON!
MIKAMI-KUN, WE DON'T HAVE ENOUGH SPEED!
WE WON'T REACH HIM AT THIS RATE!
WOOOOSH
IF WE FALL TOO FAR AWAY, THE IMPERIAL GENTLEMAN WILL DISTANCE HIMSELF FROM US!

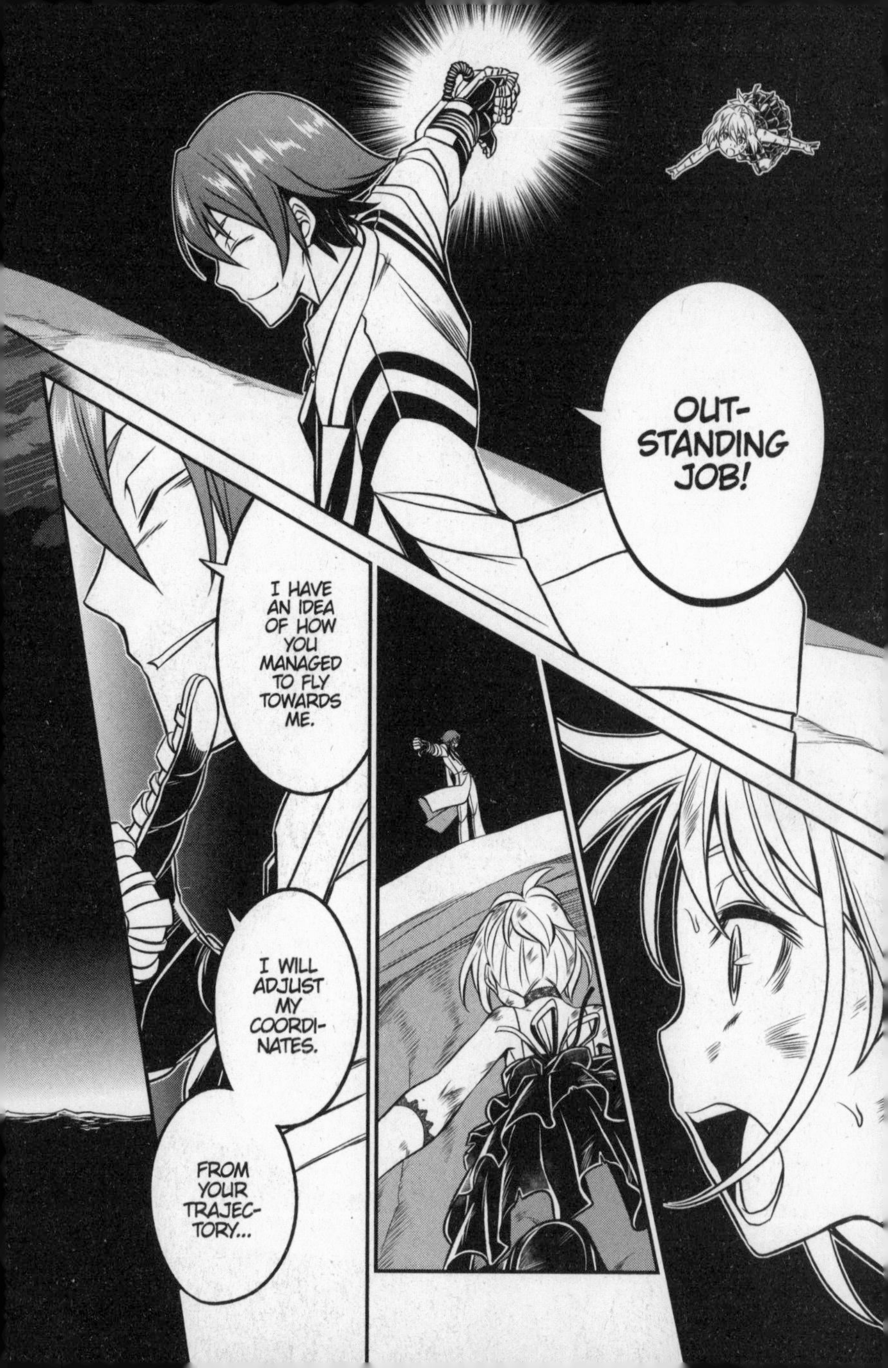
OUT-STANDING JOB!
I HAVE AN IDEA OF HOW YOU MANAGED TO FLY TOWARDS ME.
I WILL ADJUST MY COORDI-NATES.
FROM YOUR TRAJEC-TORY...

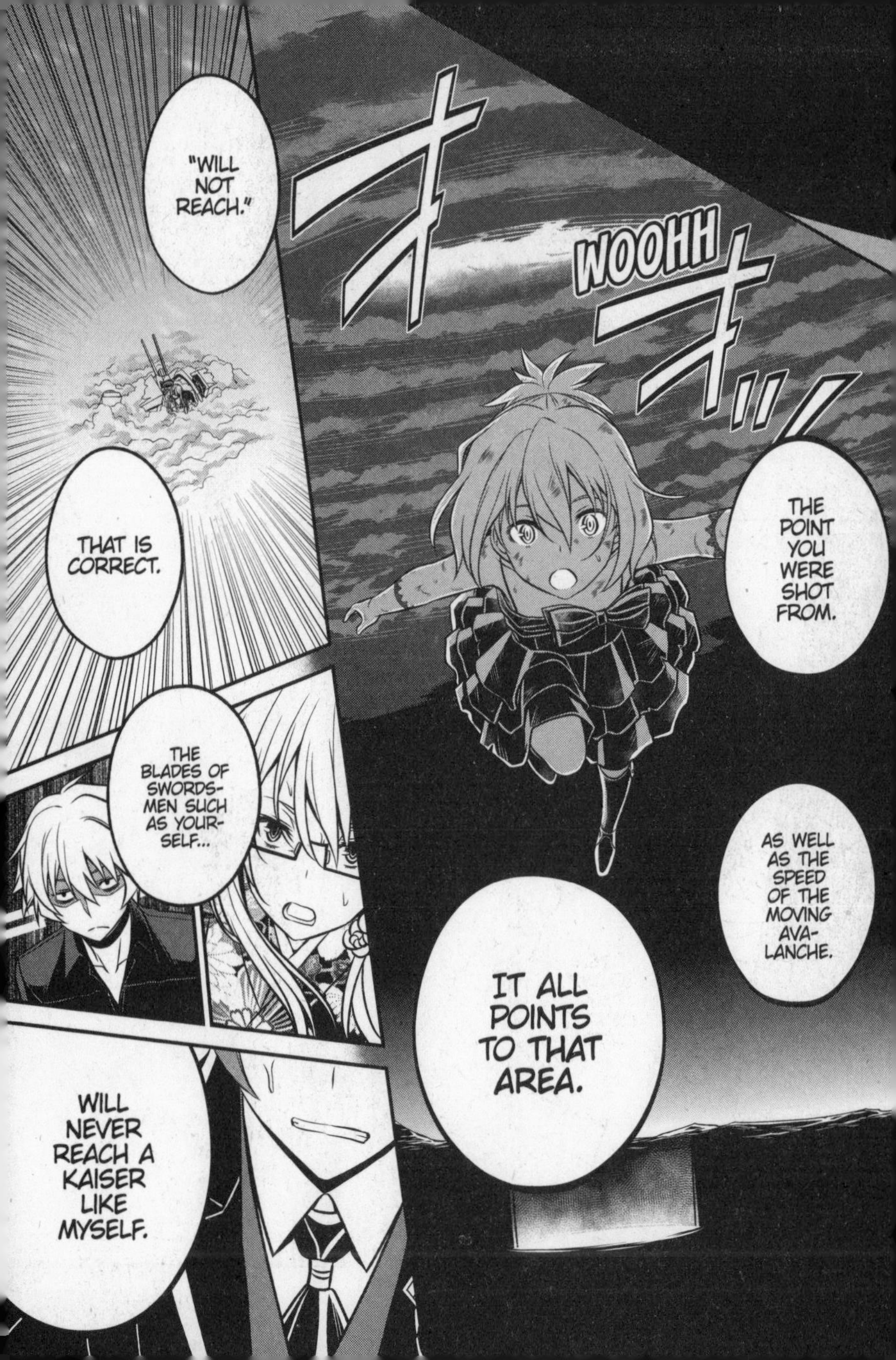
WOOHH
THE POINT YOU WERE SHOT FROM.
AS WELL AS THE SPEED OF THE MOVING AVA-LANCHE.
IT ALL POINTS TO THAT AREA.
"WILL NOT REACH."
THAT IS CORRECT.
THE BLADES OF SWORDS-MEN SUCH AS YOUR-SELF...
WILL NEVER REACH A KAISER LIKE MYSELF.

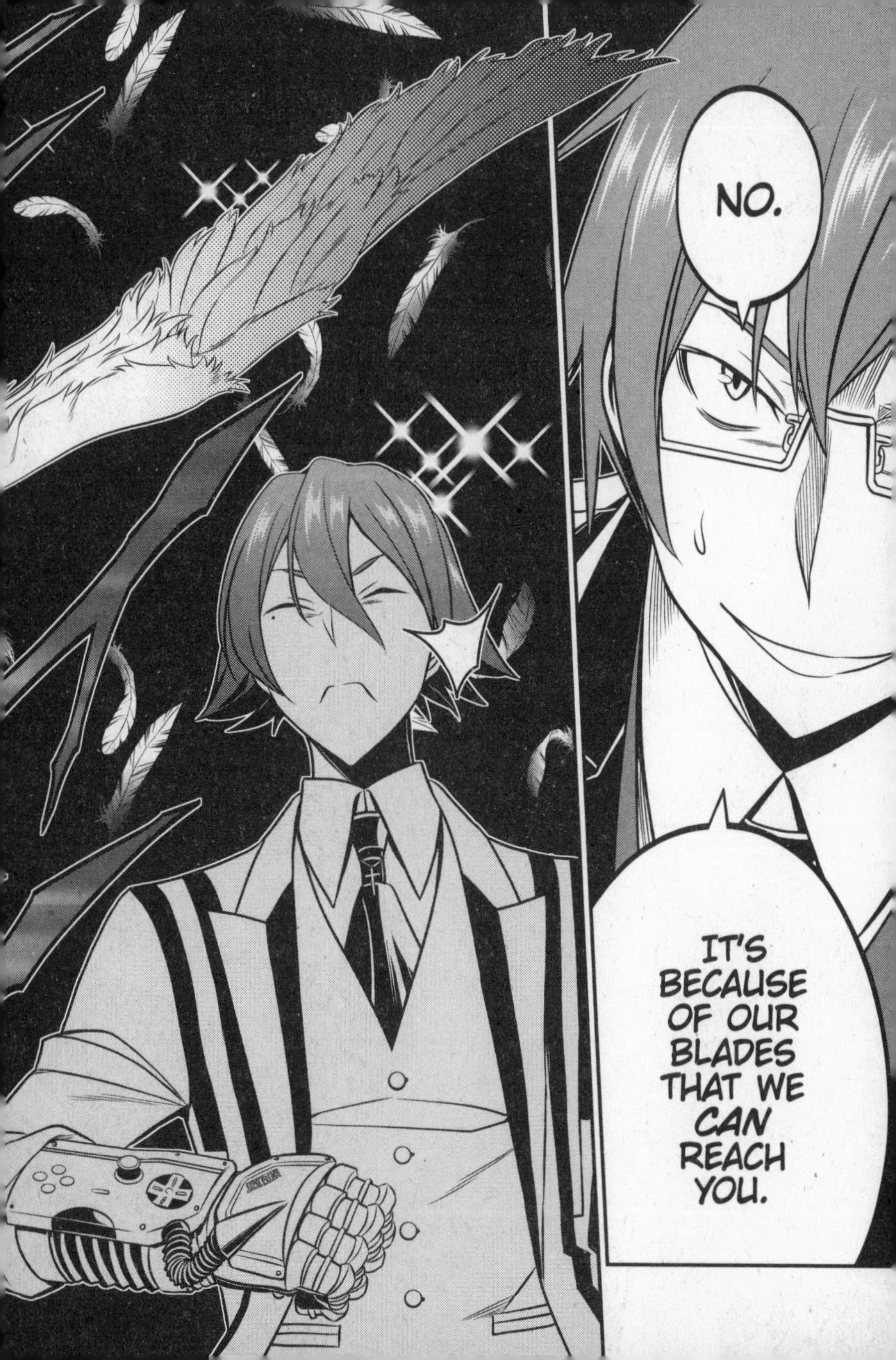
NO.
IT'S BECAUSE OF OUR BLADES THAT WE CAN REACH YOU.

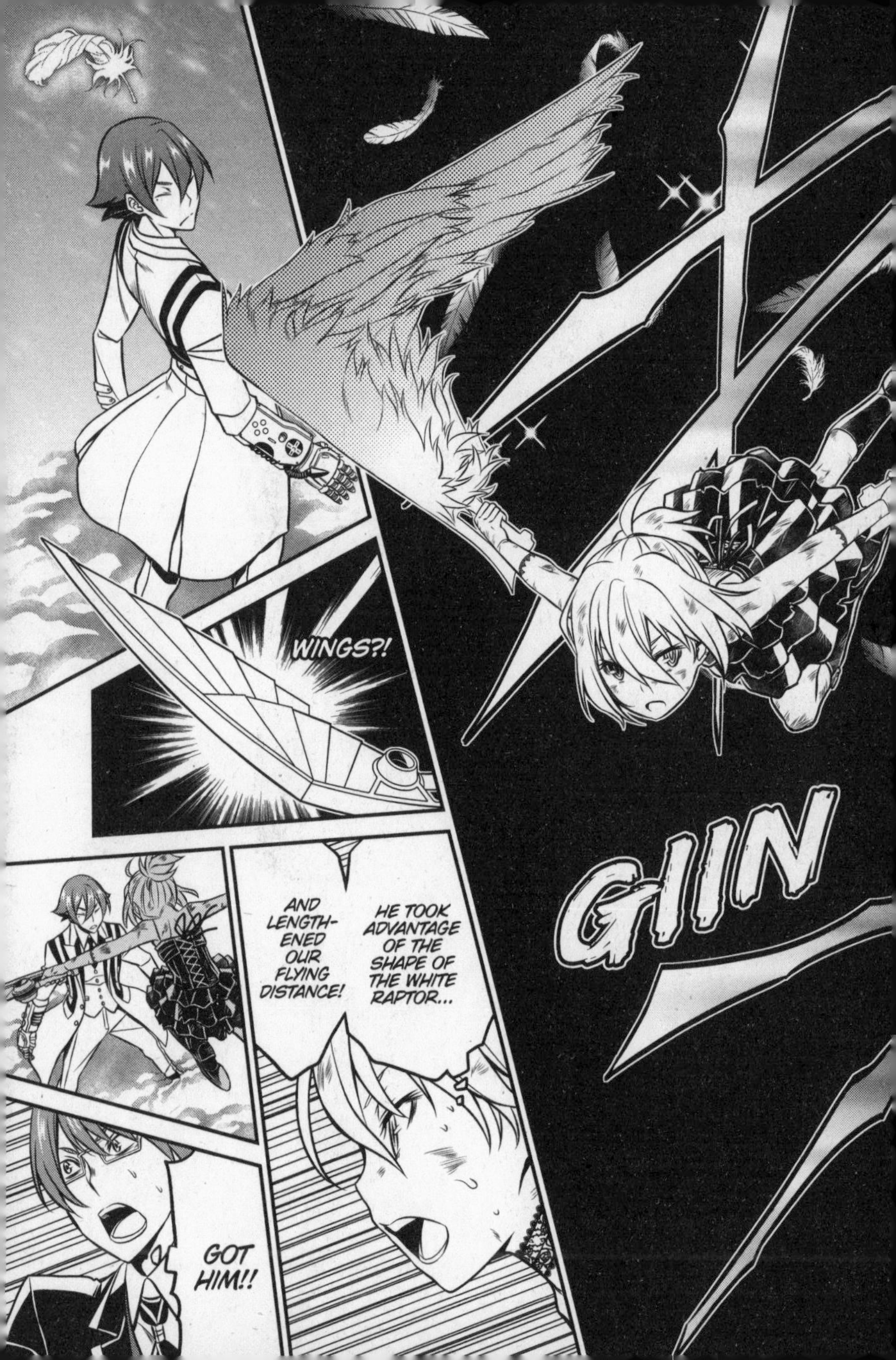
GIIN
WINGS?!
HE TOOK ADVANTAGE OF THE SHAPE OF THE WHITE RAPTOR...
AND LENGTH-ENED OUR FLYING DISTANCE!
GOT HIM!!

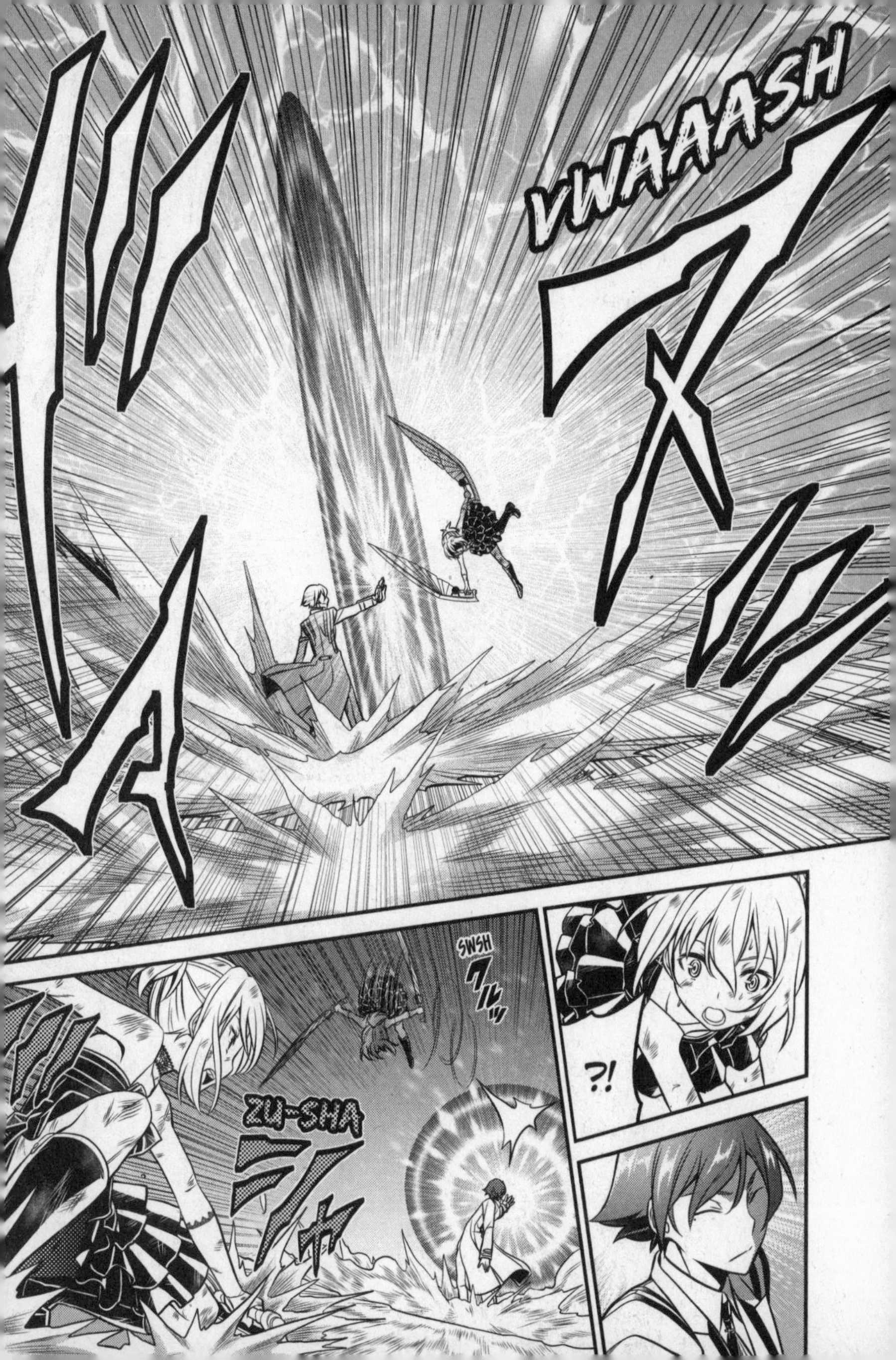
VWAAAASH
?!
SWSH
クルッ
ZU-SHA
ジャ

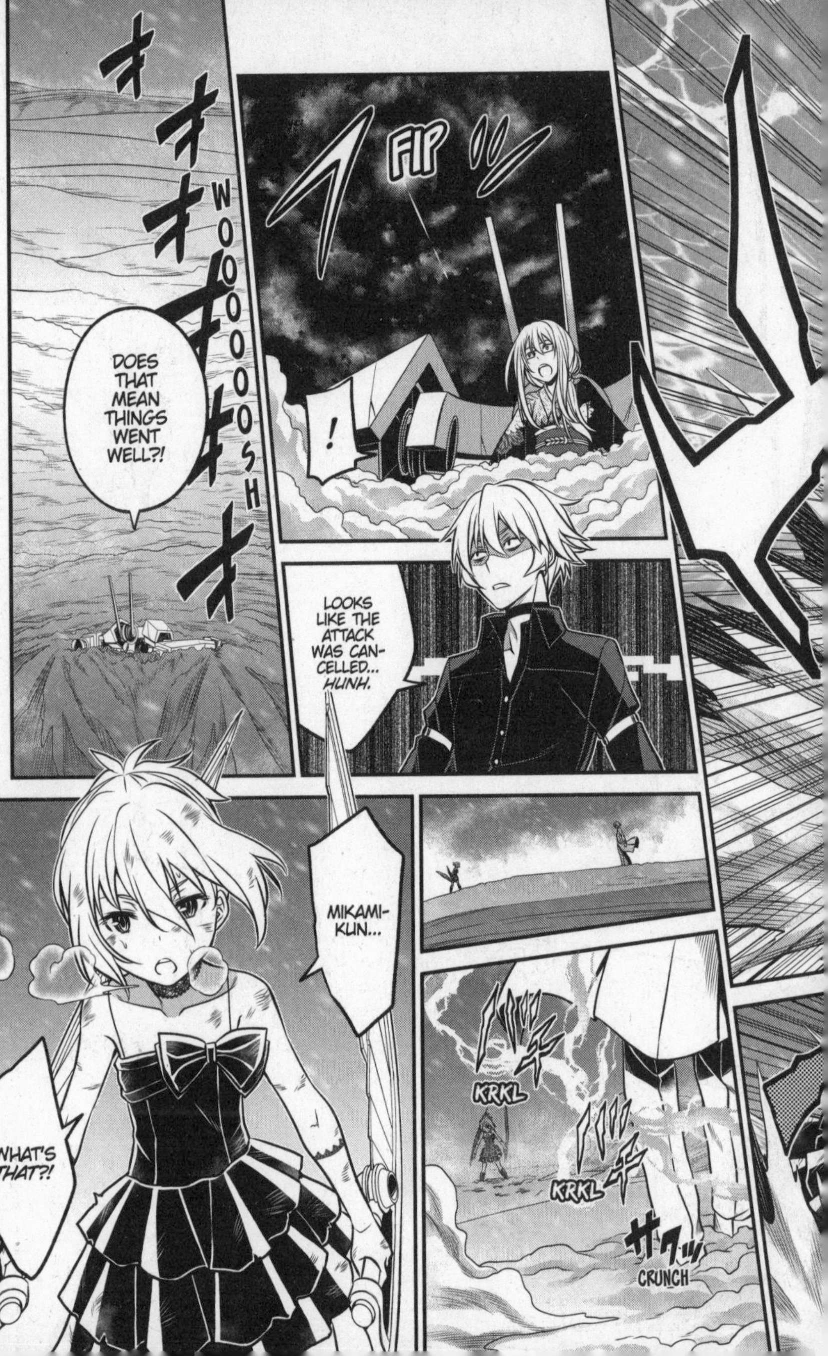
FIP
!
LOOKS LIKE THE ATTACK WAS CAN-CELLED... HUNH.
WOOOOOOOSH
DOES THAT MEAN THINGS WENT WELL?!
KRKL
KRKL
CRUNCH
MIKAMI-KUN...
WHAT'S THAT?!

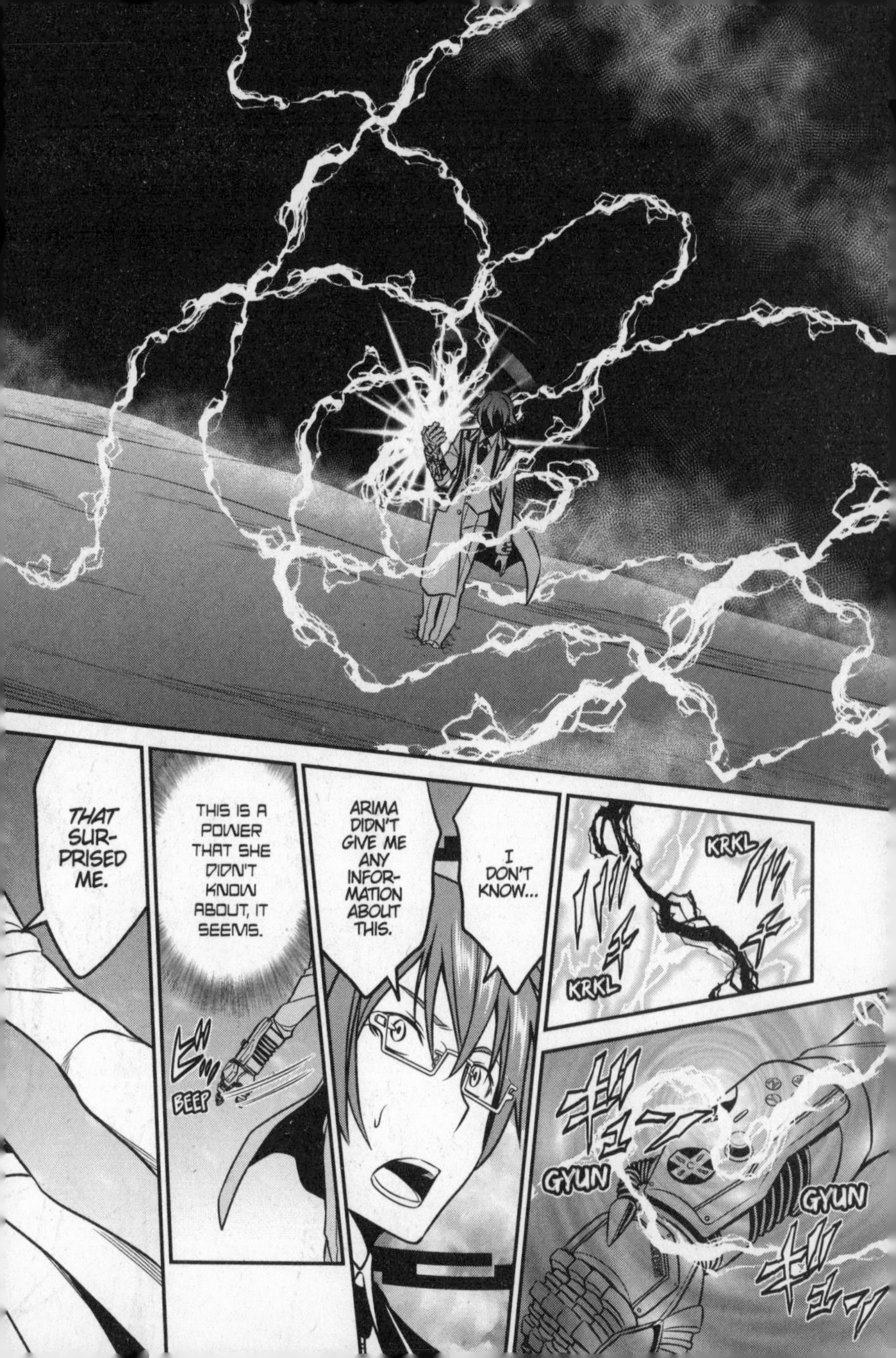
THAT SUR-PRISED ME.
BEEP
THIS IS A POWER THAT SHE DIDN'T KNOW ABOUT, IT SEEMS.
ARIMA DIDN'T GIVE ME ANY INFOR-MATION ABOUT THIS.
I DON'T KNOW...
KRKL
KRKL
GYUN
GYUN

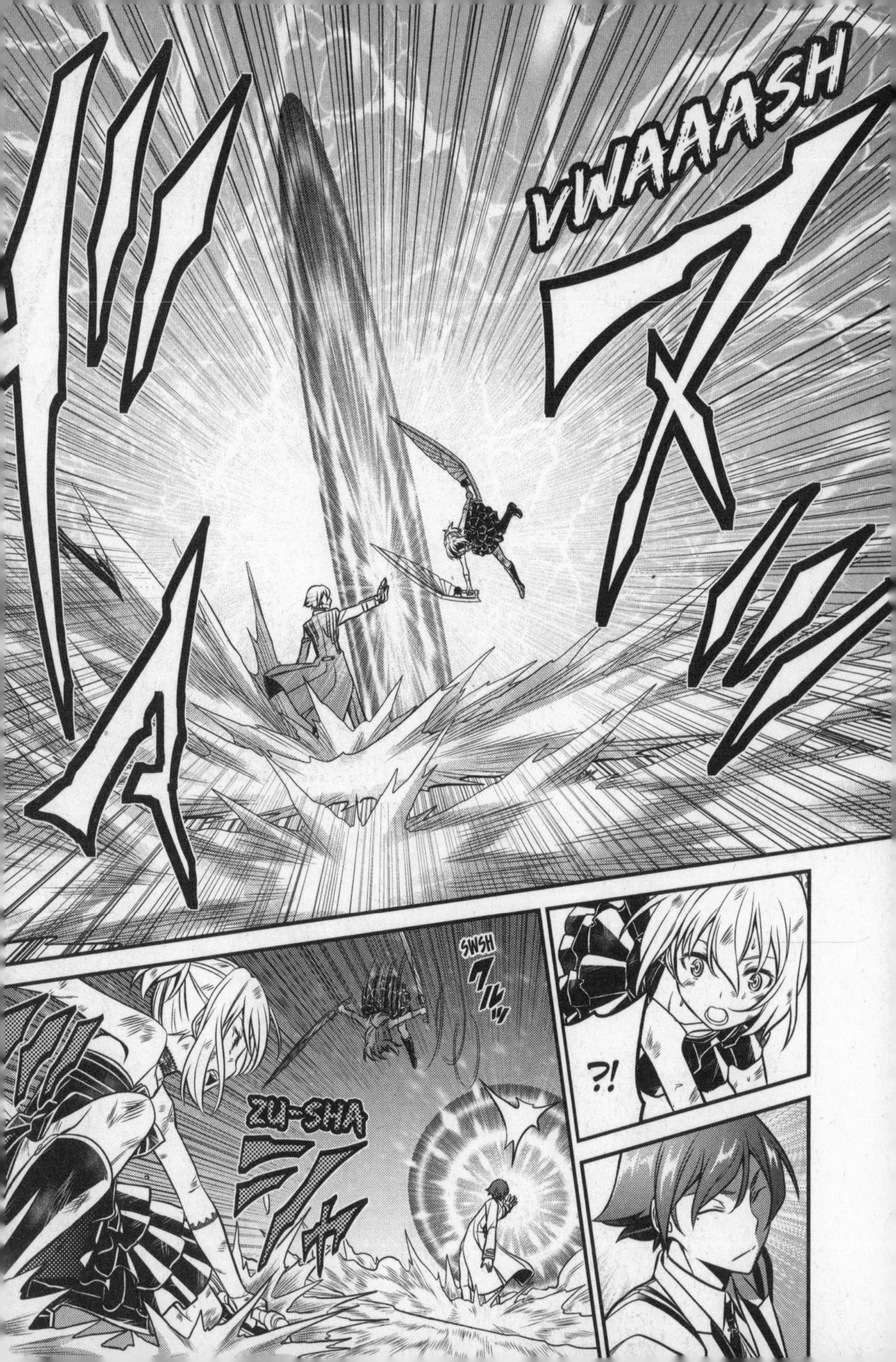
VWAAAASH
?!
SWSH
ZU-SHA

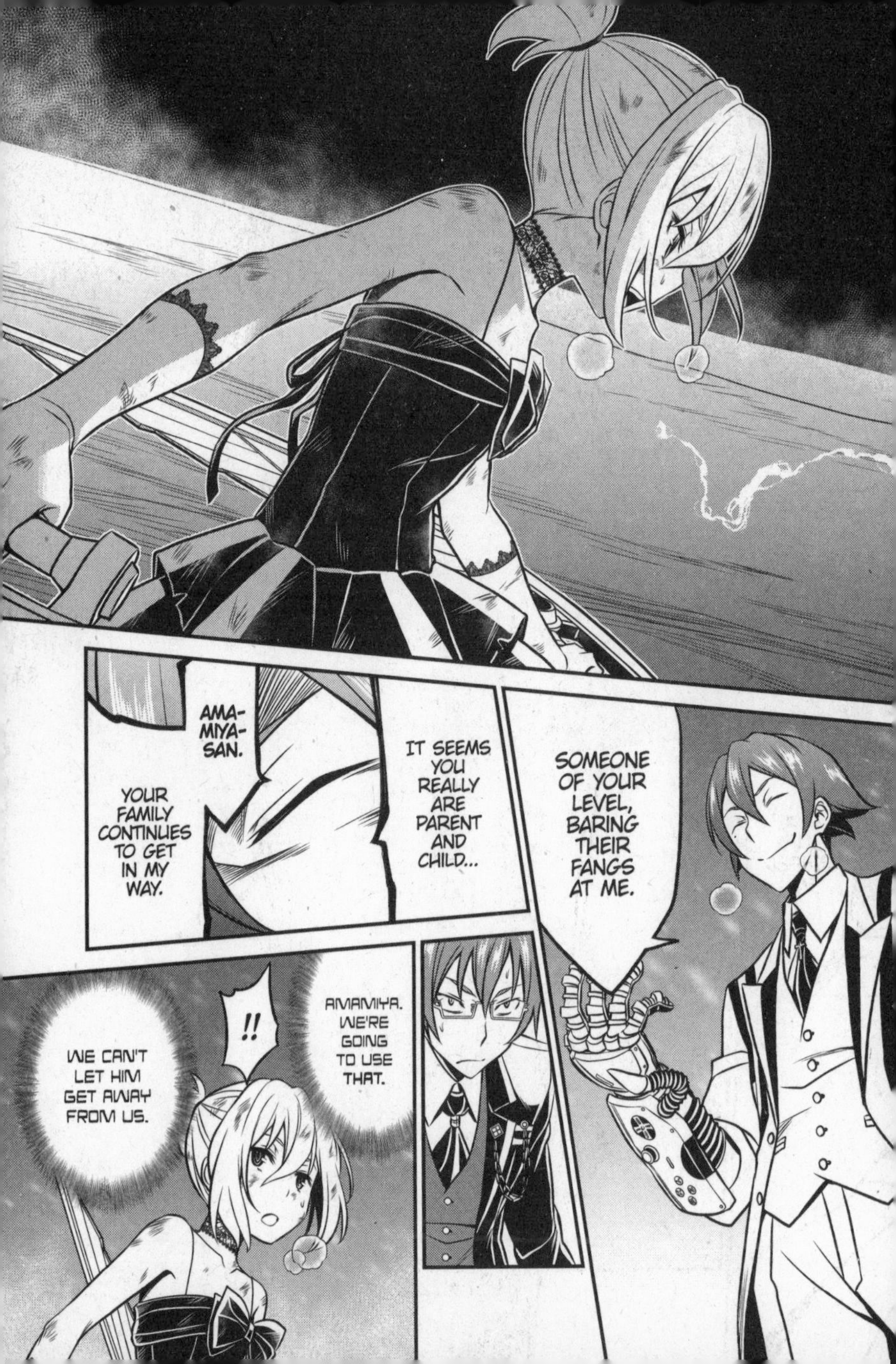
SOMEONE OF YOUR LEVEL, BARING THEIR FANGS AT ME.
IT SEEMS YOU REALLY ARE PARENT AND CHILD...
AMA-MIYA-SAN.
YOUR FAMILY CONTINUES TO GET IN MY WAY.
AMAMIYA. WE'RE GOING TO USE THAT.
!!
WE CAN'T LET HIM GET AWAY FROM US.

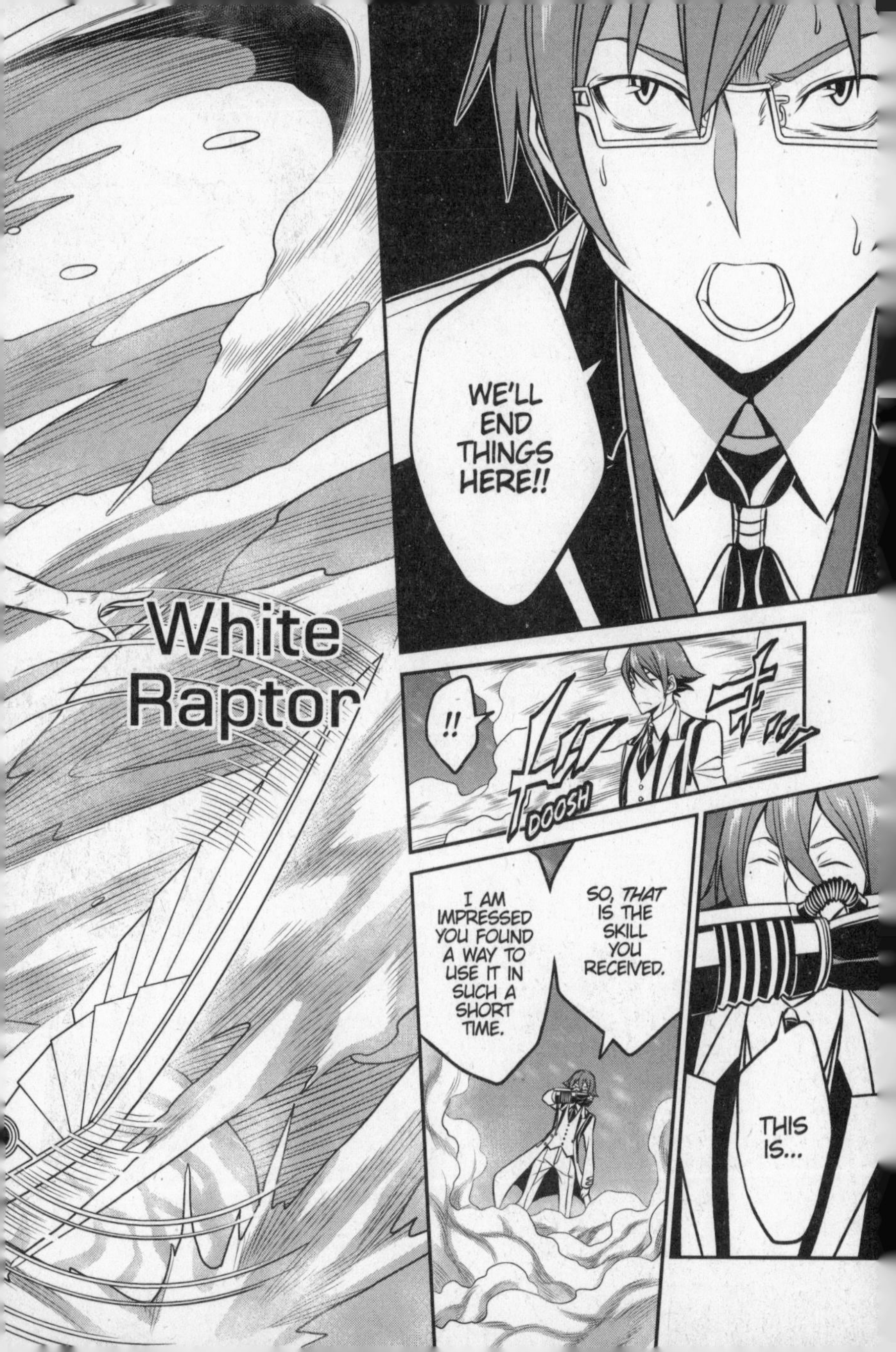
WE'LL END THINGS HERE!!
!!
DOOSH
THIS IS...
SO, THAT IS THE SKILL YOU RECEIVED.
I AM IMPRESSED YOU FOUND A WAY TO USE IT IN SUCH A SHORT TIME.
White Raptor

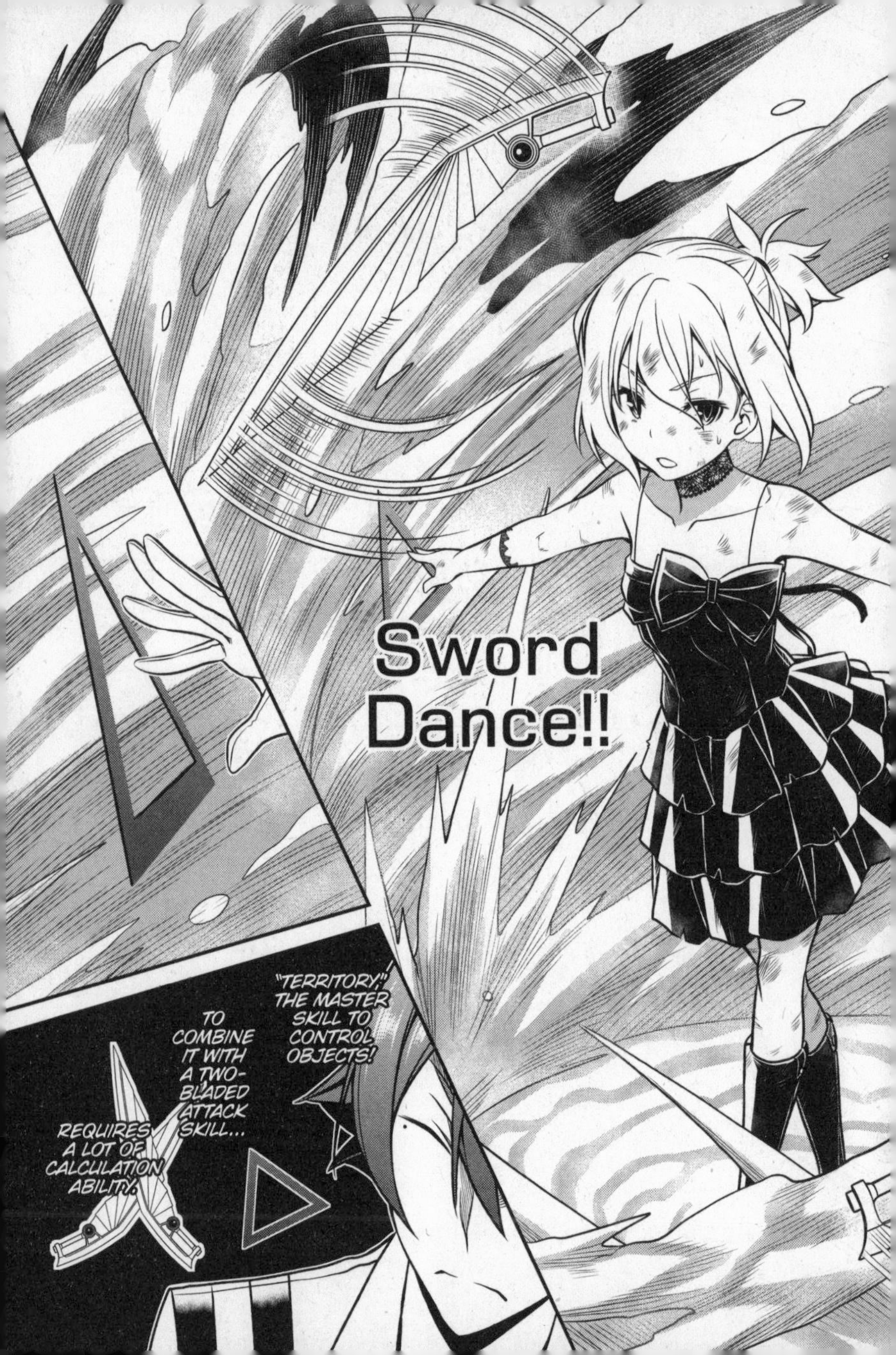
Sword Dance!!
"TERRITORY," THE MASTER SKILL TO CONTROL OBJECTS!
TO COMBINE IT WITH A TWO-BLADED ATTACK SKILL...
REQUIRES A LOT OF CALCULATION ABILITY.

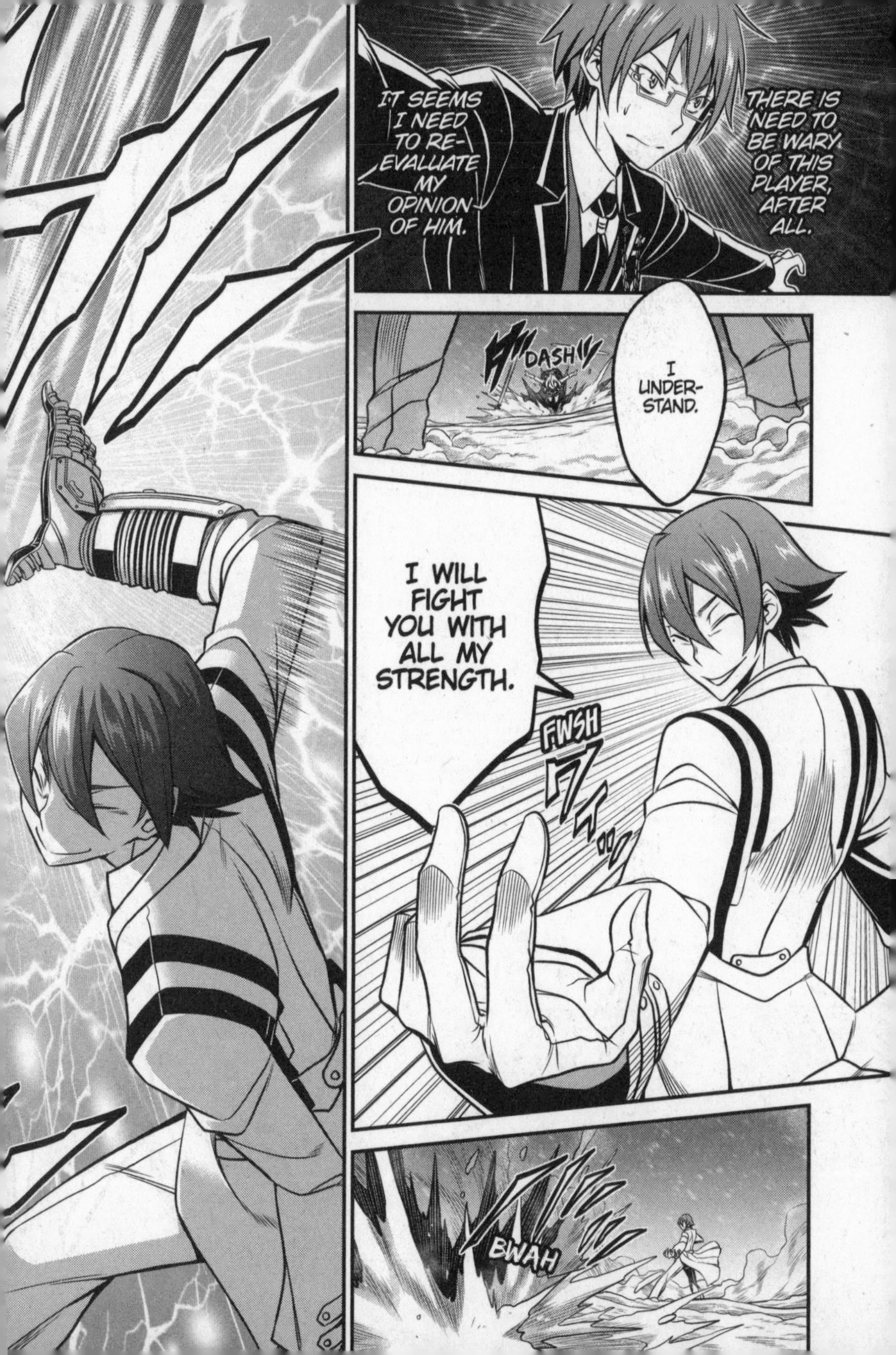
THERE IS NEED TO BE WARY OF THIS PLAYER, AFTER ALL.
IT SEEMS I NEED TO RE-EVALUATE MY OPINION OF HIM.
I UNDER-STAND.
DASH
I WILL FIGHT YOU WITH ALL MY STRENGTH.
FWSH
BWAH

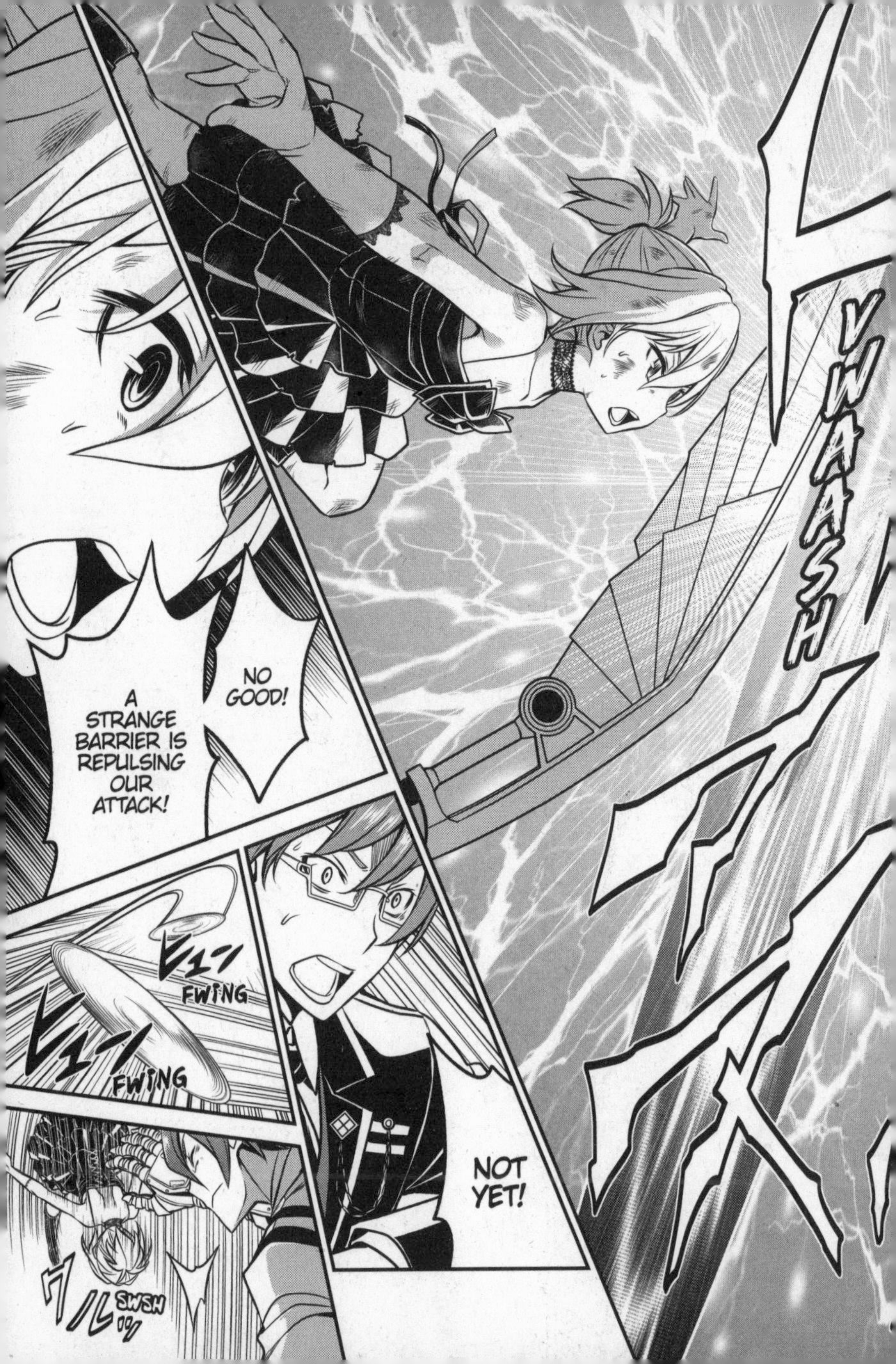
VWAASH
NO GOOD!
A STRANGE BARRIER IS REPULSING OUR ATTACK!
NOT YET!
FWING
FWING
SWSH

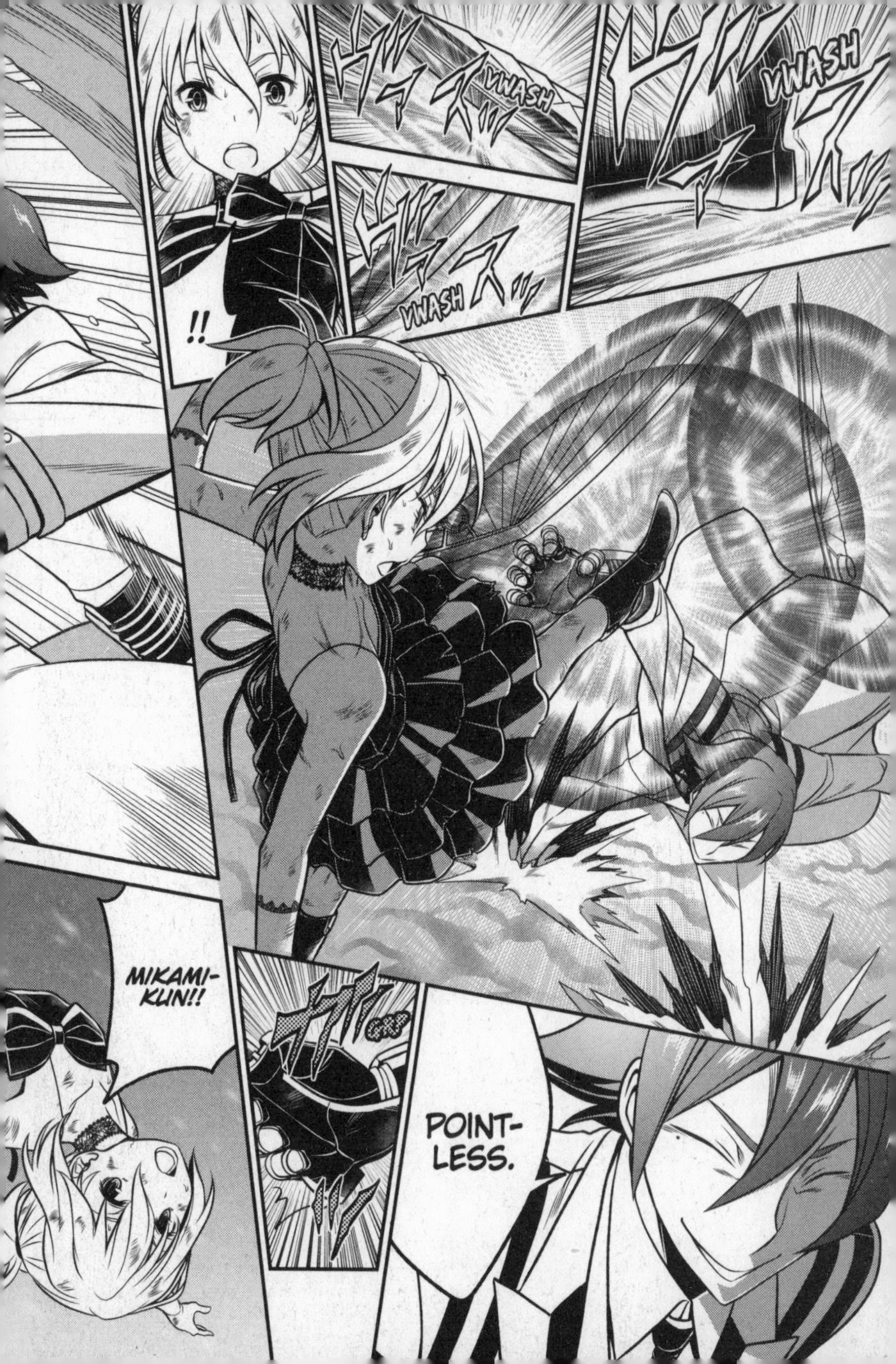
VWASH
VWASH
VWASH
!!
POINT-LESS.
GK
MIKAMI-KUN!!

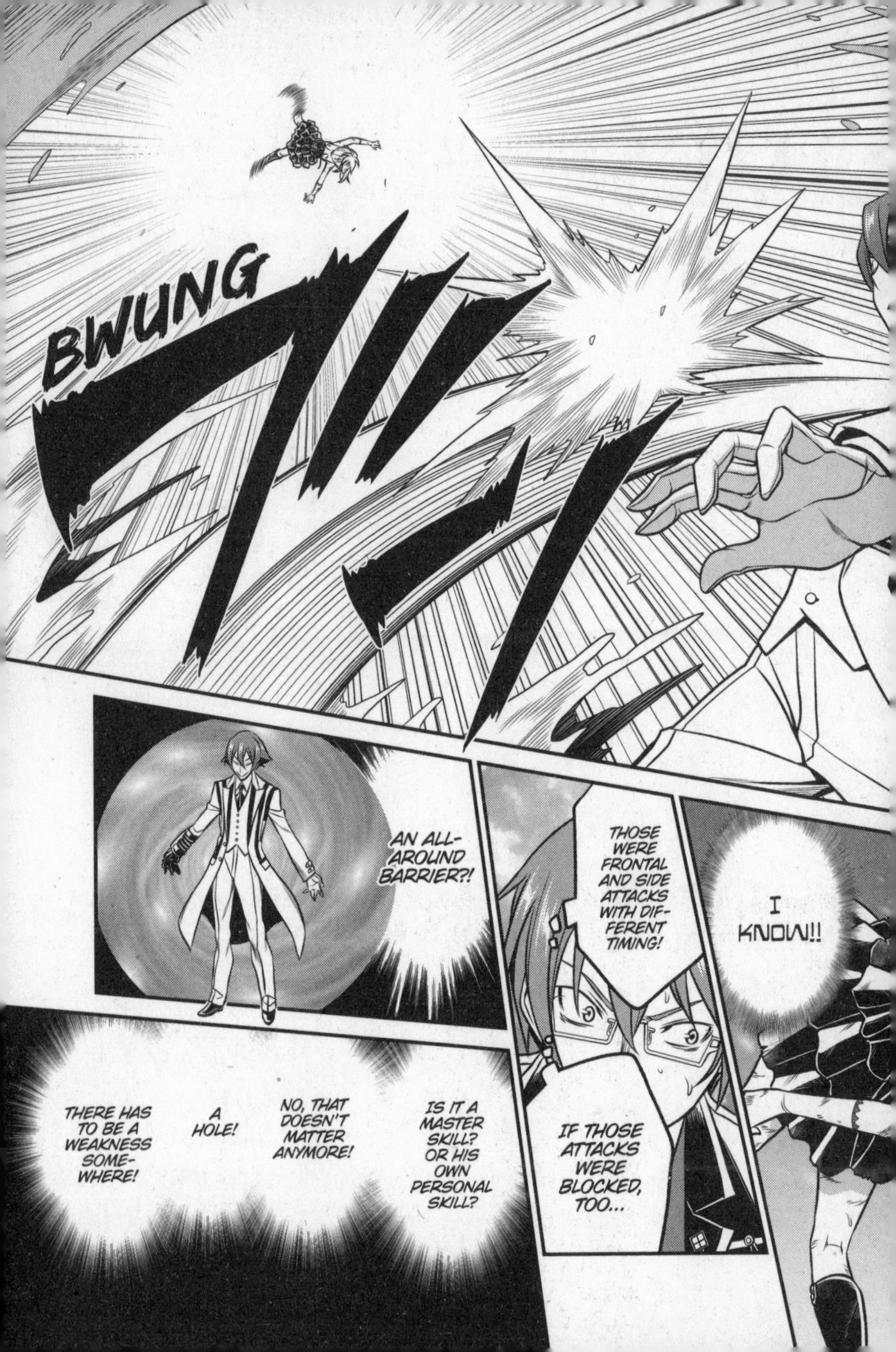
BWUNG
I KNOW!!
THOSE WERE FRONTAL AND SIDE ATTACKS WITH DIF-FERENT TIMING!
IF THOSE ATTACKS WERE BLOCKED, TOO...
AN ALL-AROUND BARRIER?!
IS IT A MASTER SKILL? OR HIS OWN PERSONAL SKILL?
NO, THAT DOESN'T MATTER ANYMORE!
A HOLE!
THERE HAS TO BE A WEAKNESS SOME-WHERE!

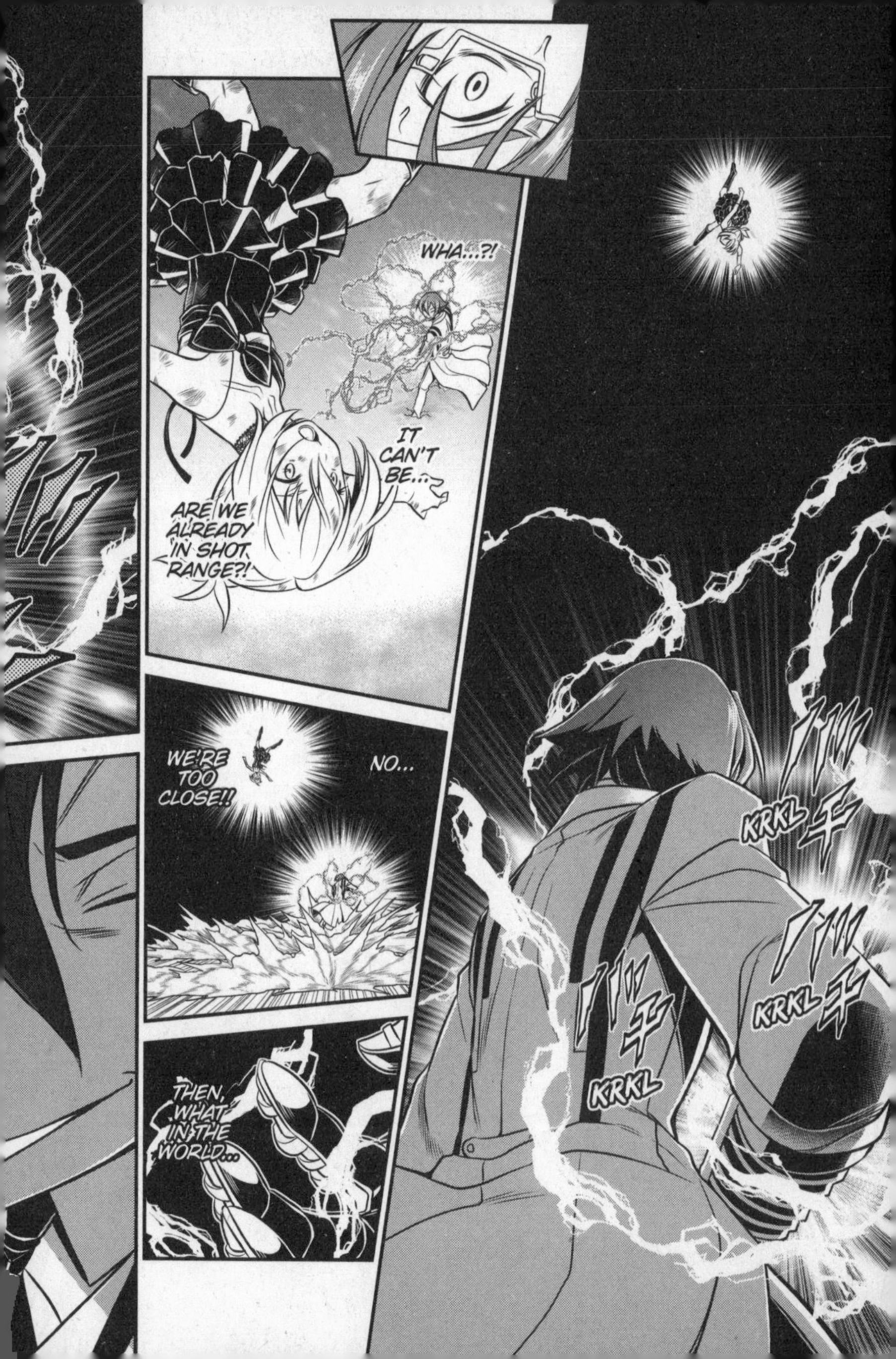
WHA...?!
IT CAN'T BE...
ARE WE ALREADY IN SHOT RANGE?!
NO...
WE'RE TOO CLOSE!!
THEN, WHAT IN THE WORLD...
KRKL
KRKL
KRKL

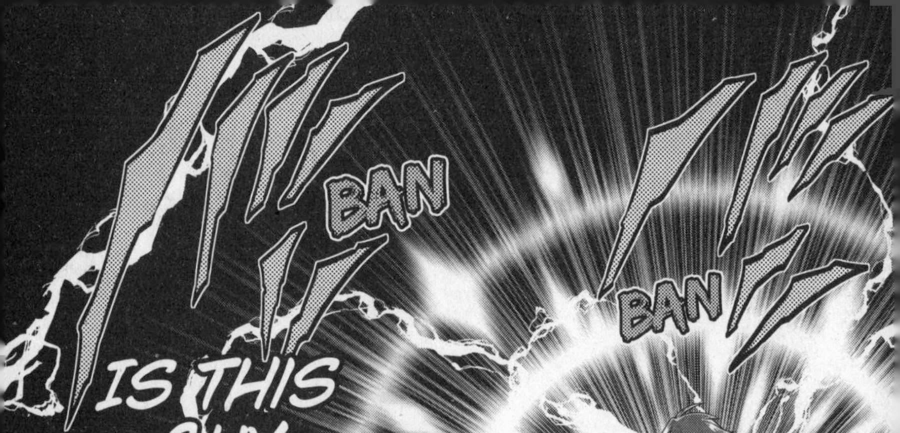
BAN
BAN
IS THIS GUY DOING?!
BAN
BAN

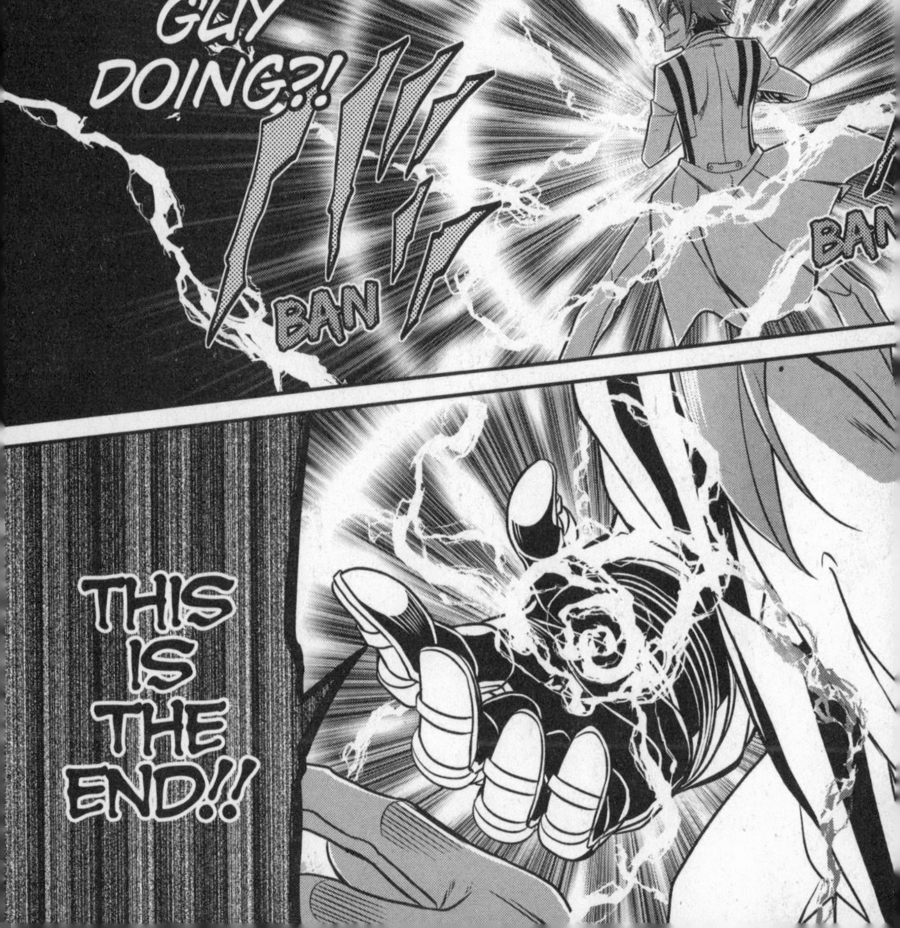
THIS IS THE END!!

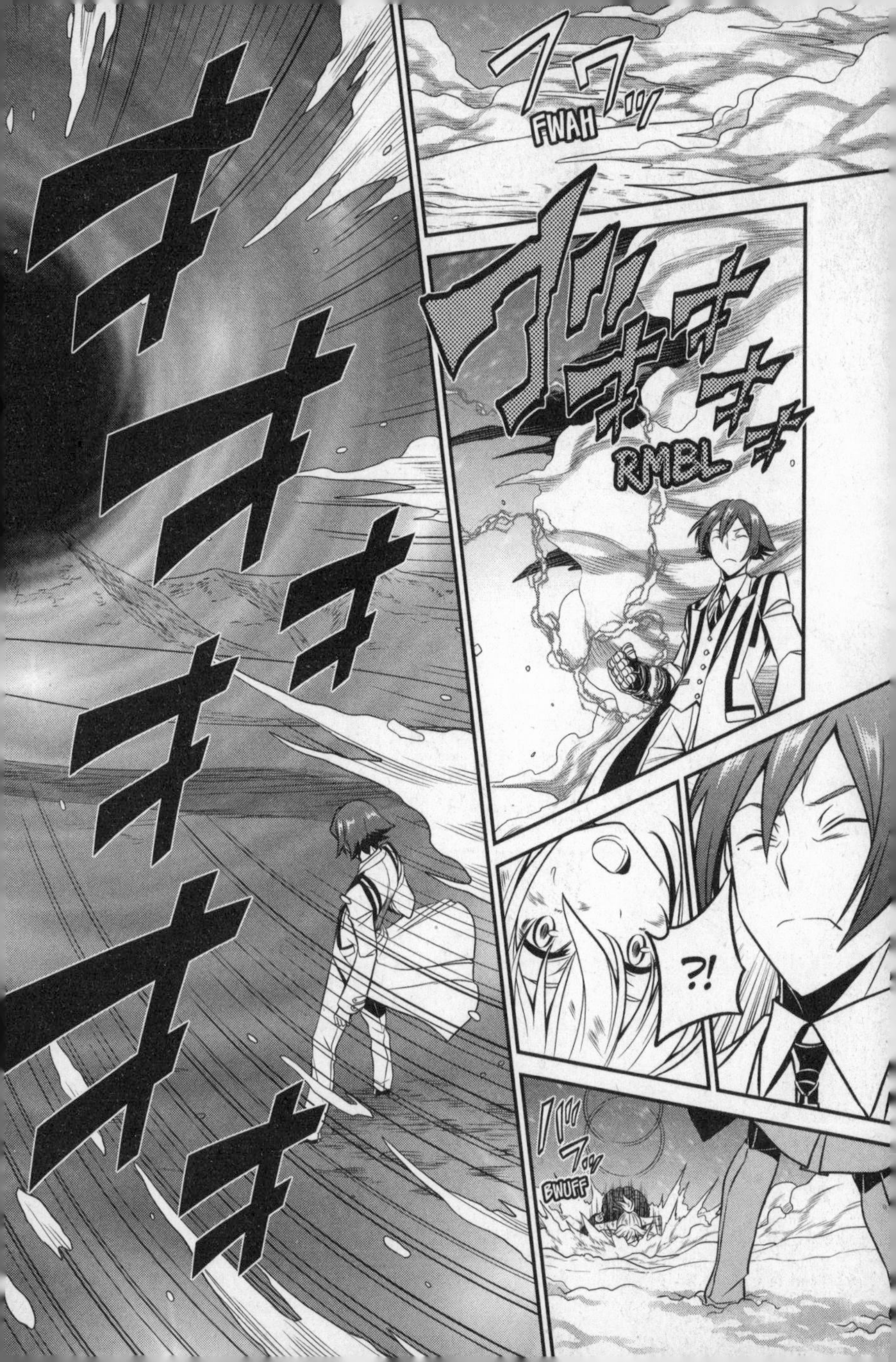
FWAH
RMBL
?!
BWUFF

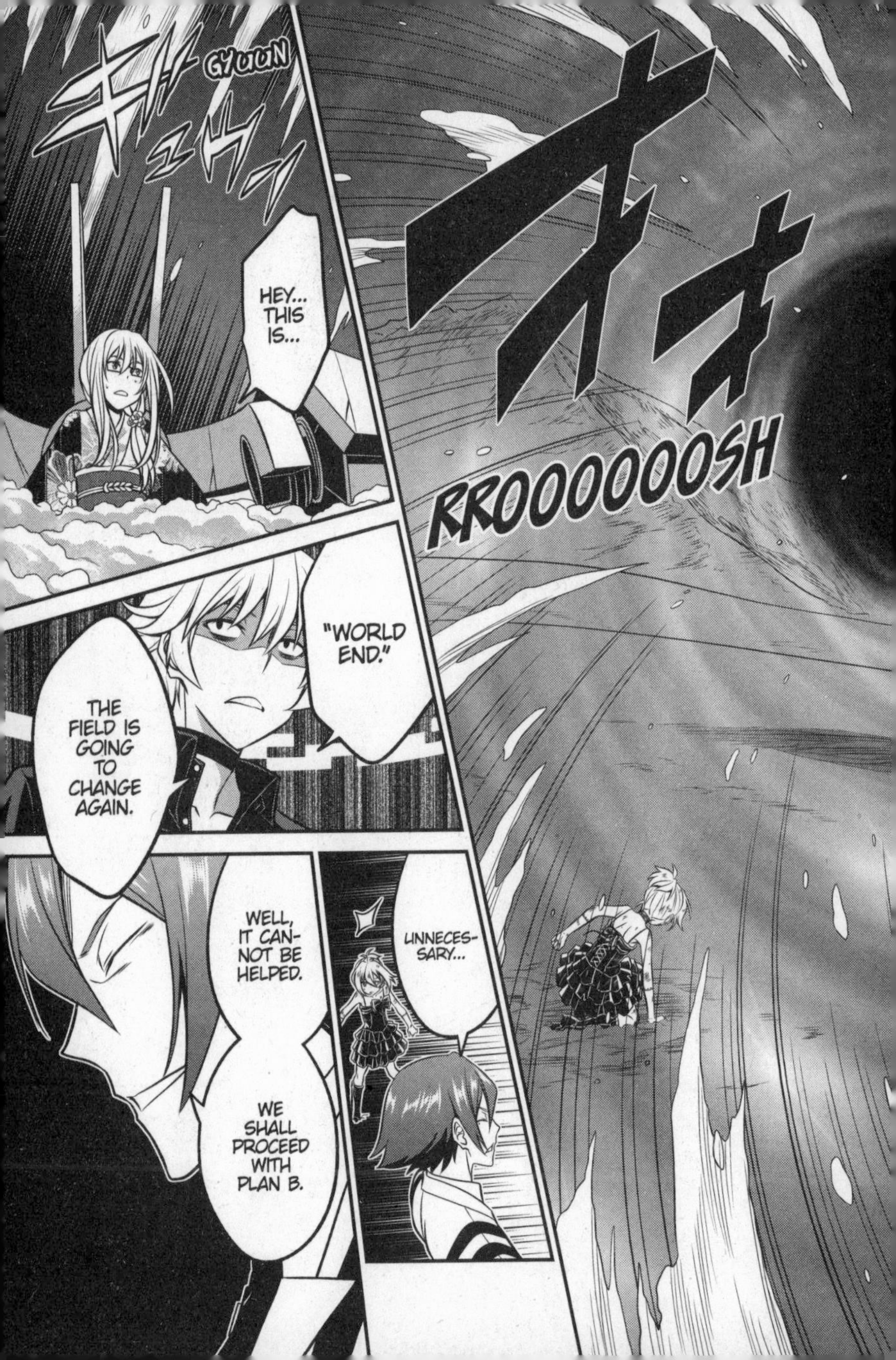
RROOOOOOOSH
GYUUN
HEY... THIS IS...
"WORLD END."
THE FIELD IS GOING TO CHANGE AGAIN.
UNNECES-SARY...
WELL, IT CAN-NOT BE HELPED.
WE SHALL PROCEED WITH PLAN B.

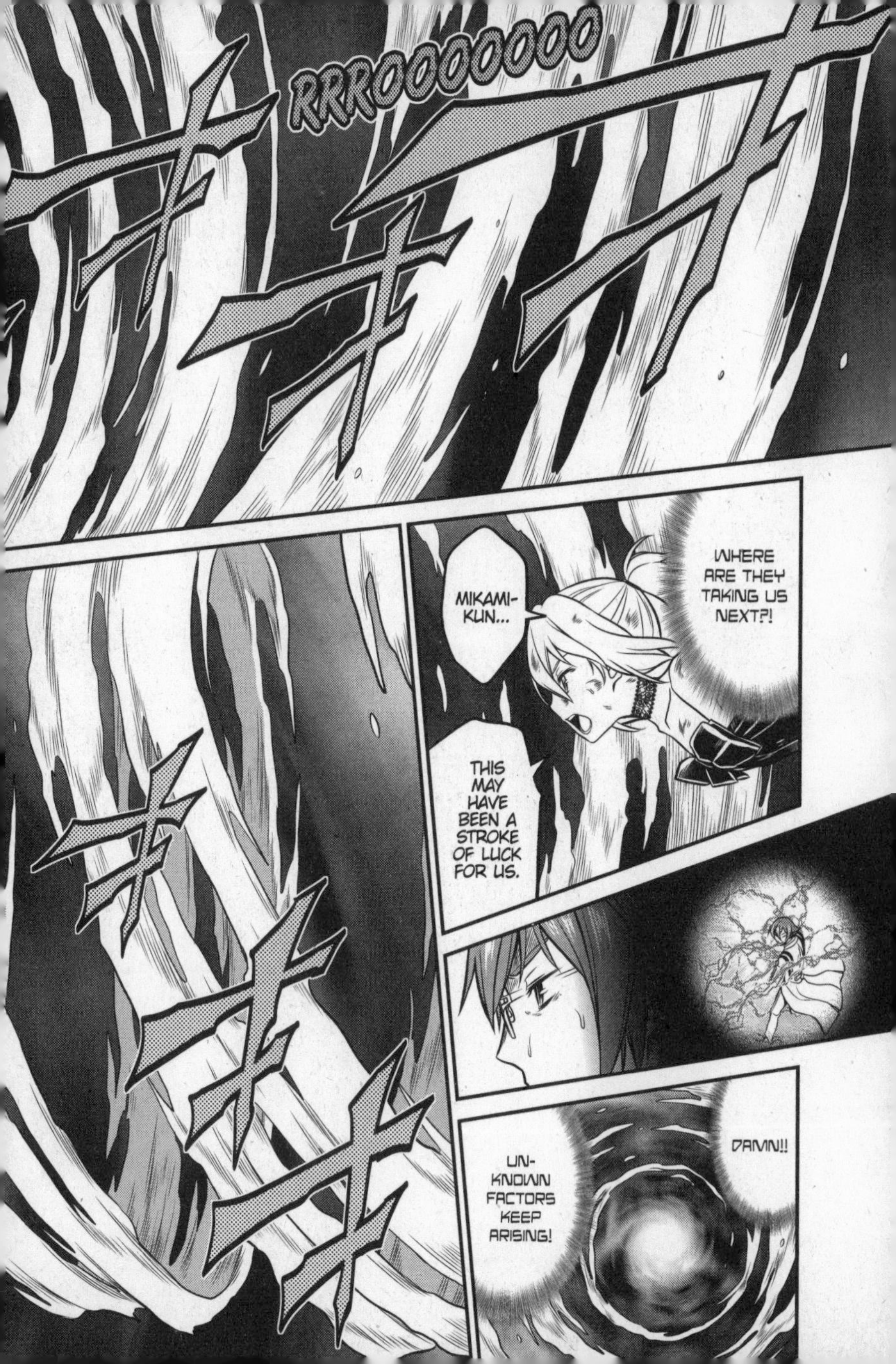
RRROOOOOOO
WHERE ARE THEY TAKING US NEXT?!
MIKAMI-KUN...
THIS MAY HAVE BEEN A STROKE OF LUCK FOR US.
DAMN!!
UN-KNOWN FACTORS KEEP ARISING!

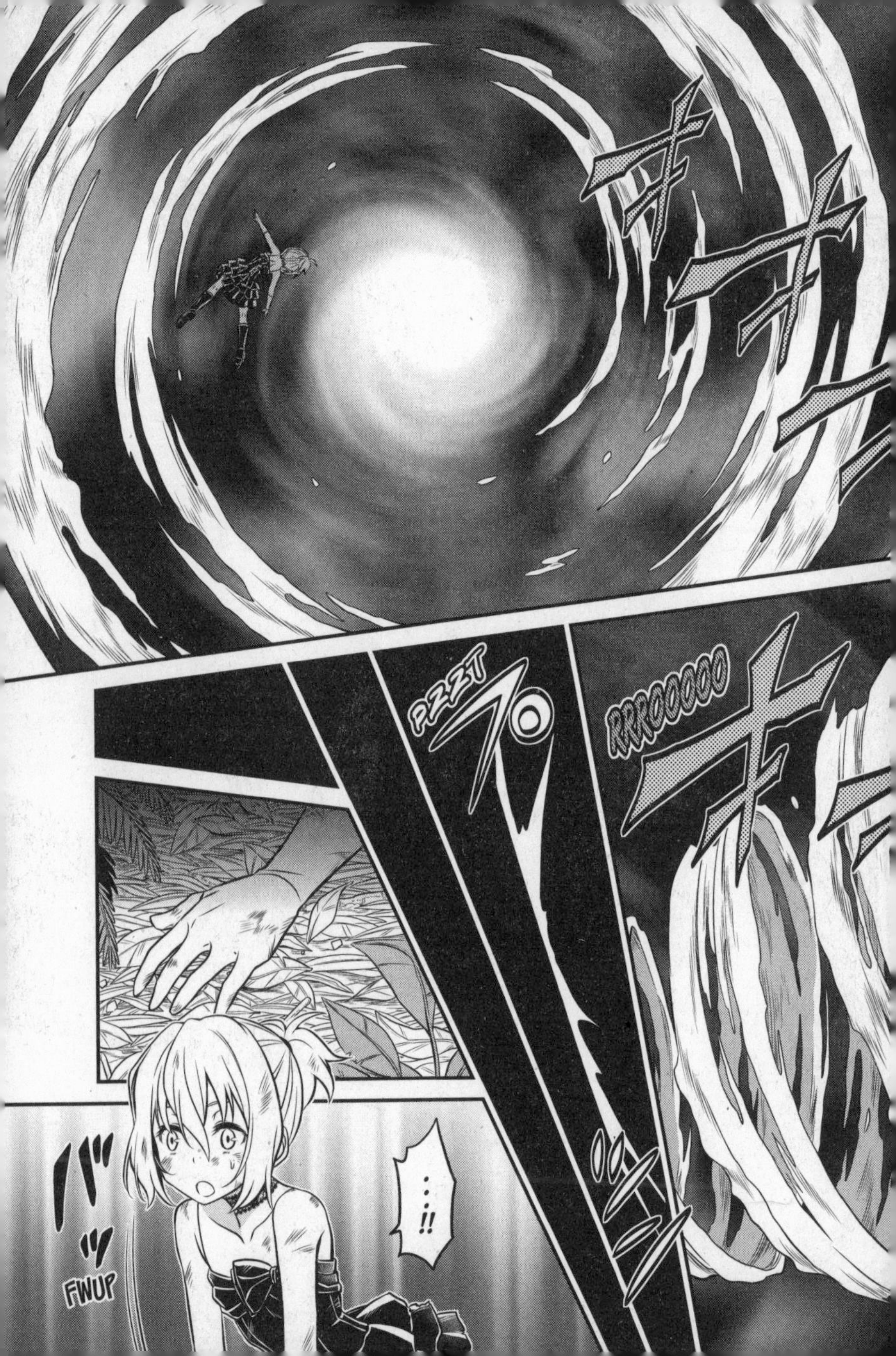
RRROOOOO
PZZT
...!!
FWUP

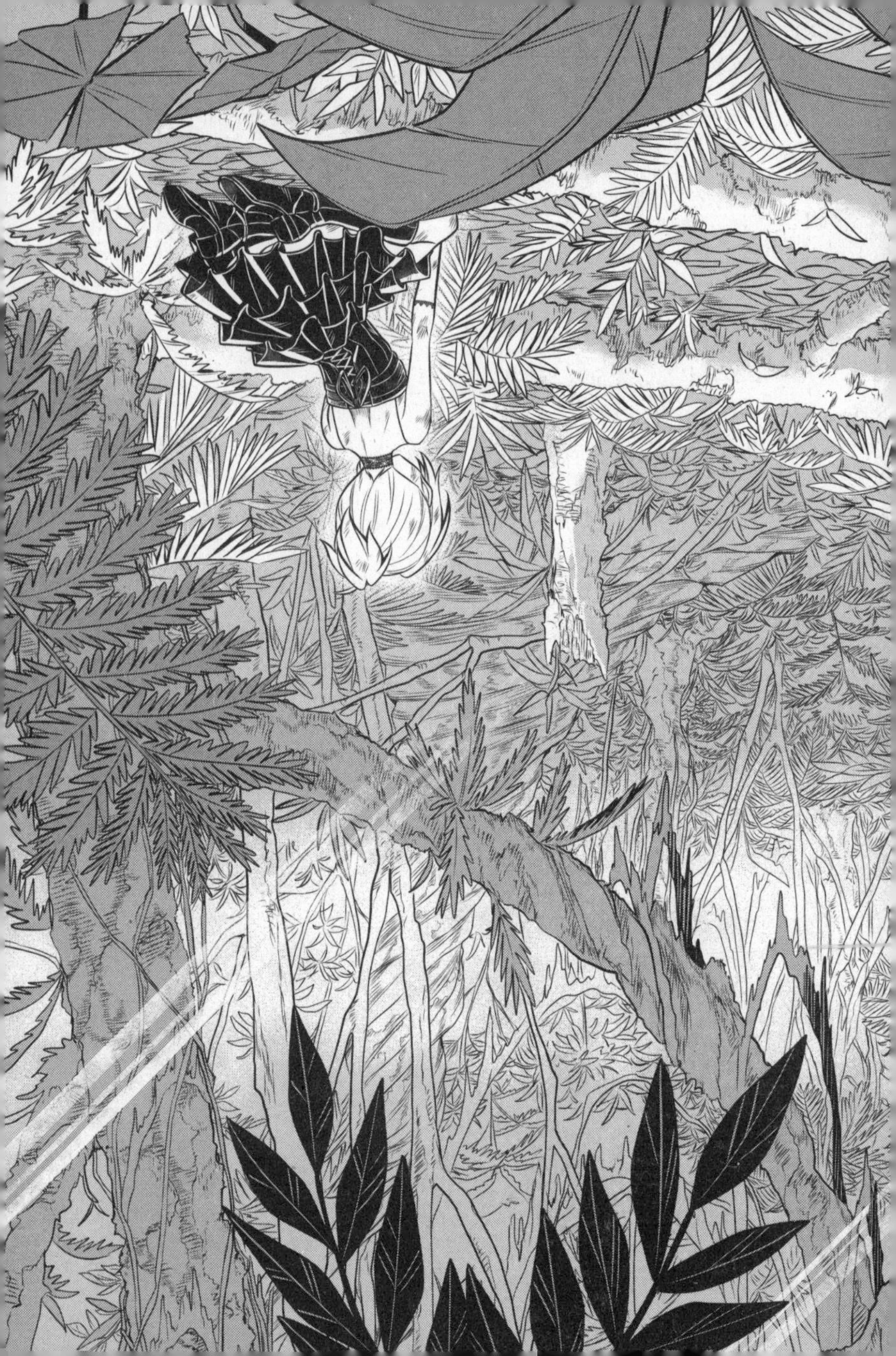

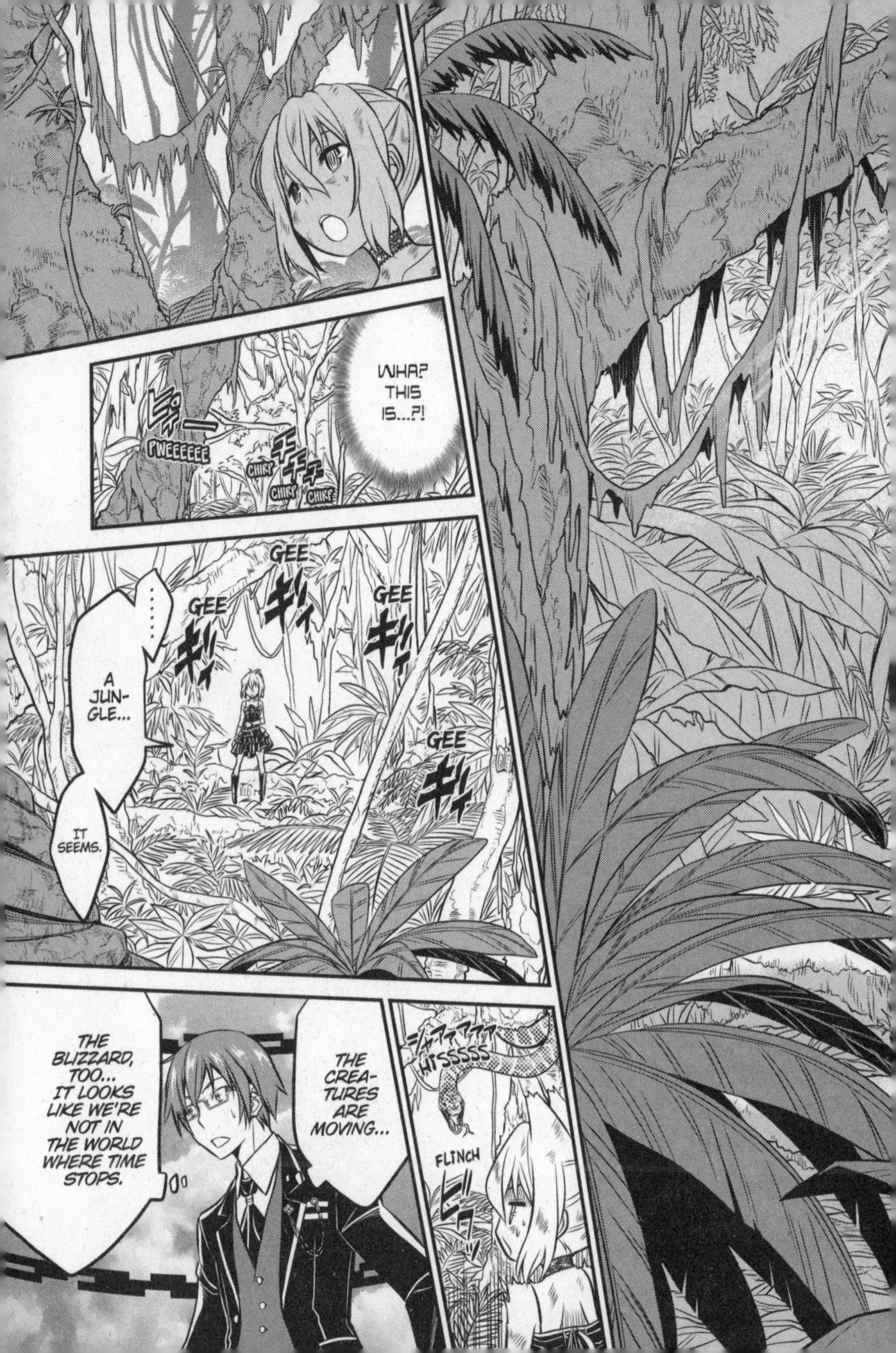
WHA? THIS IS...?!
PWEEEEEE
CHIRP CHIRP CHIRP
GEE
GEE
GEE
GEE
......
A JUNGLE...
IT SEEMS.
HISSSSS
FLINCH
THE CREATURES ARE MOVING...
THE BLIZZARD, TOO... IT LOOKS LIKE WE'RE NOT IN THE WORLD WHERE TIME STOPS.

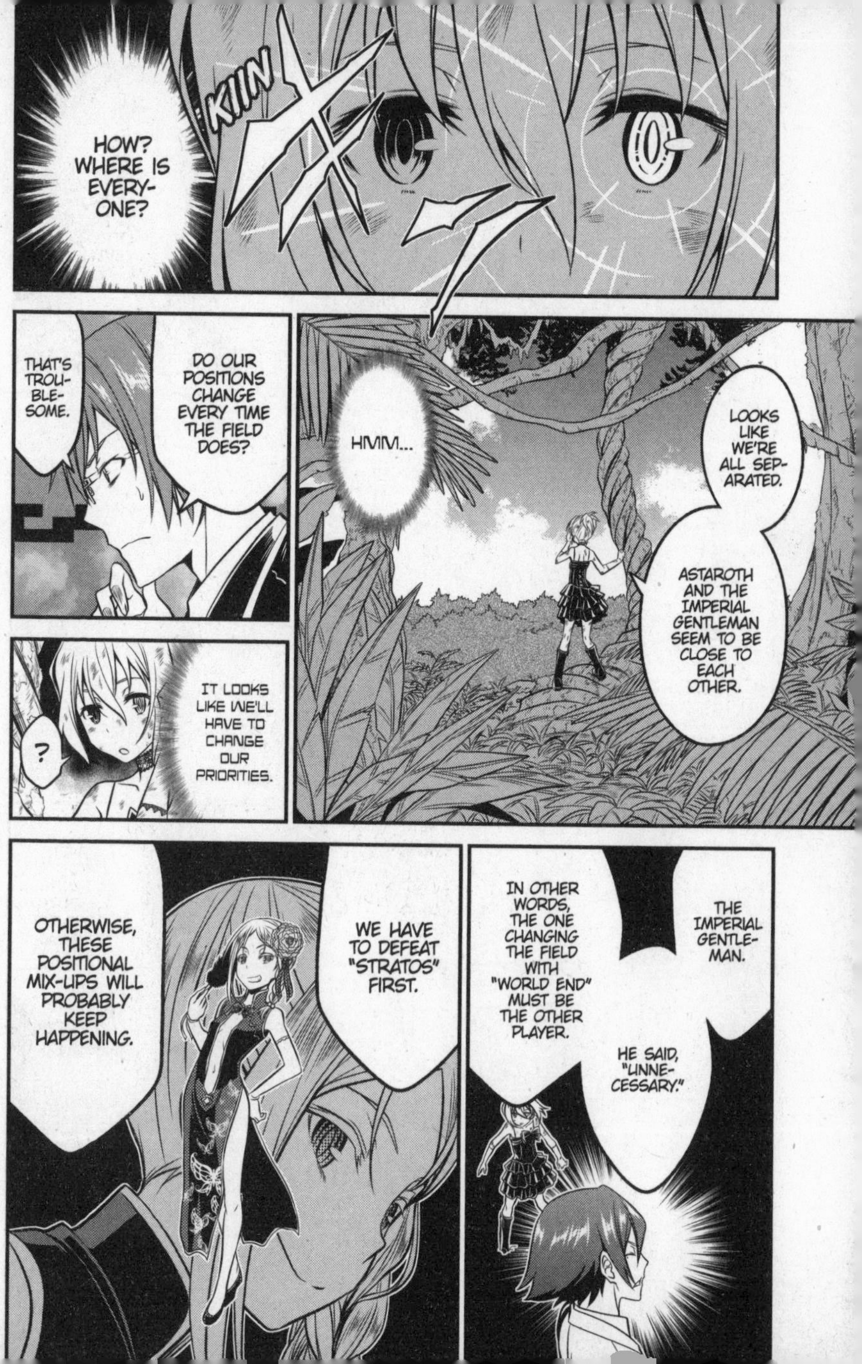
HOW? WHERE IS EVERY-ONE?
KIIN
LOOKS LIKE WE'RE ALL SEP-ARATED.
ASTAROTH AND THE IMPERIAL GENTLEMAN SEEM TO BE CLOSE TO EACH OTHER.
HMM...
DO OUR POSITIONS CHANGE EVERY TIME THE FIELD DOES?
THAT'S TROU-BLE-SOME.
IT LOOKS LIKE WE'LL HAVE TO CHANGE OUR PRIORITIES.
?
THE IMPERIAL GENTLE-MAN.
HE SAID, "UNNE-CESSARY."
IN OTHER WORDS, THE ONE CHANGING THE FIELD WITH "WORLD END" MUST BE THE OTHER PLAYER.
WE HAVE TO DEFEAT "STRATOS" FIRST.
OTHERWISE, THESE POSITIONAL MIX-UPS WILL PROBABLY KEEP HAPPENING.

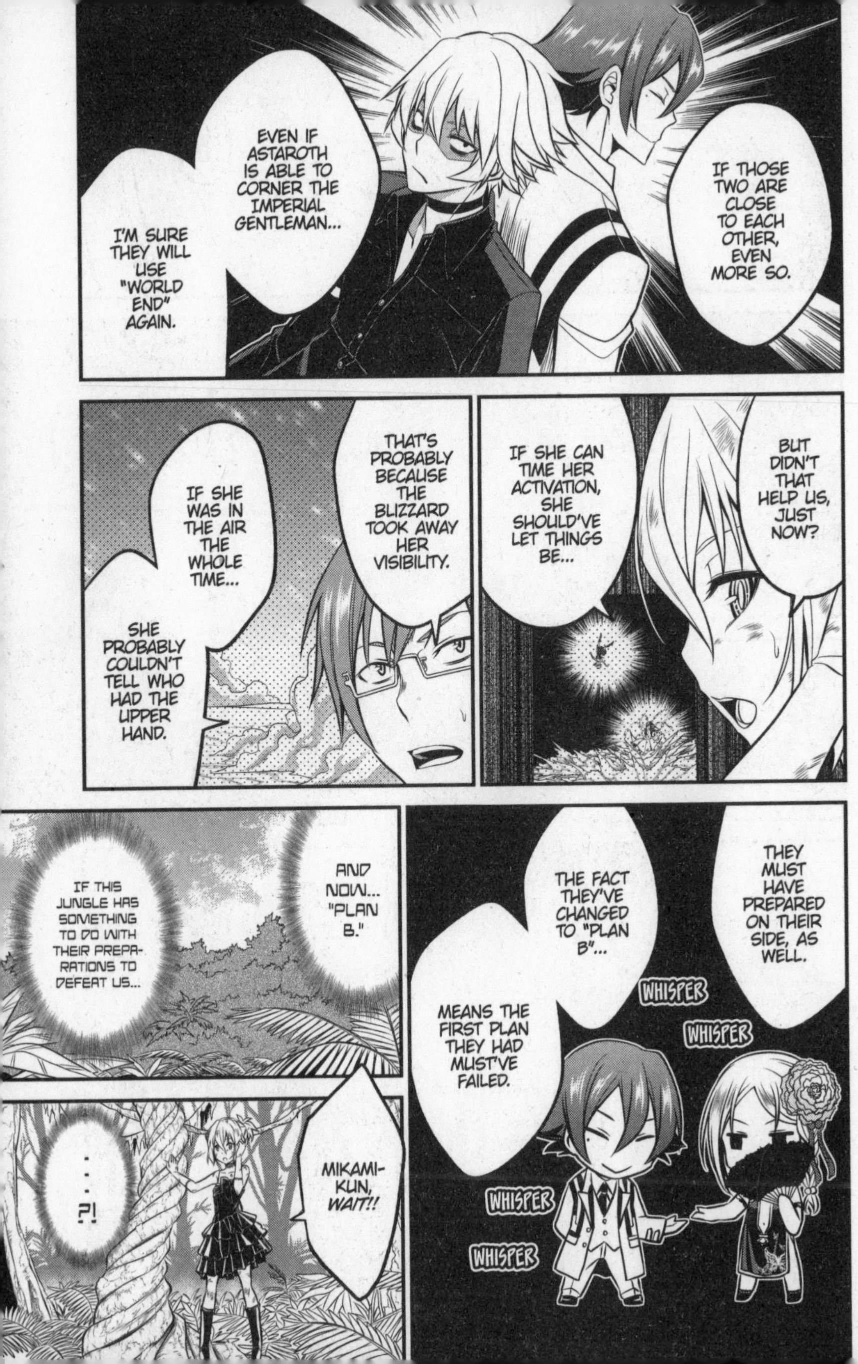
EVEN IF ASTAROTH IS ABLE TO CORNER THE IMPERIAL GENTLEMAN...
I'M SURE THEY WILL USE "WORLD END" AGAIN.
IF THOSE TWO ARE CLOSE TO EACH OTHER, EVEN MORE SO.
BUT DIDN'T THAT HELP US, JUST NOW?
IF SHE CAN TIME HER ACTIVATION, SHE SHOULD'VE LET THINGS BE...
THAT'S PROBABLY BECAUSE THE BLIZZARD TOOK AWAY HER VISIBILITY.
IF SHE WAS IN THE AIR THE WHOLE TIME...
SHE PROBABLY COULDN'T TELL WHO HAD THE UPPER HAND.
THEY MUST HAVE PREPARED ON THEIR SIDE, AS WELL.
THE FACT THEY'VE CHANGED TO "PLAN B"...
MEANS THE FIRST PLAN THEY HAD MUST'VE FAILED.
WHISPER
WHISPER
WHISPER
WHISPER
AND NOW... "PLAN B."
IF THIS JUNGLE HAS SOMETHING TO DO WITH THEIR PREPARATIONS TO DEFEAT US...
MIKAMI-KUN, WAIT!!
...?!

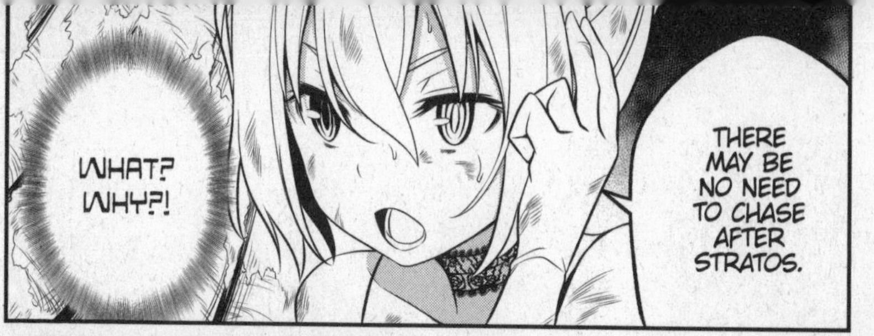
THERE MAY BE NO NEED TO CHASE AFTER STRATOS.
WHAT? WHY?!
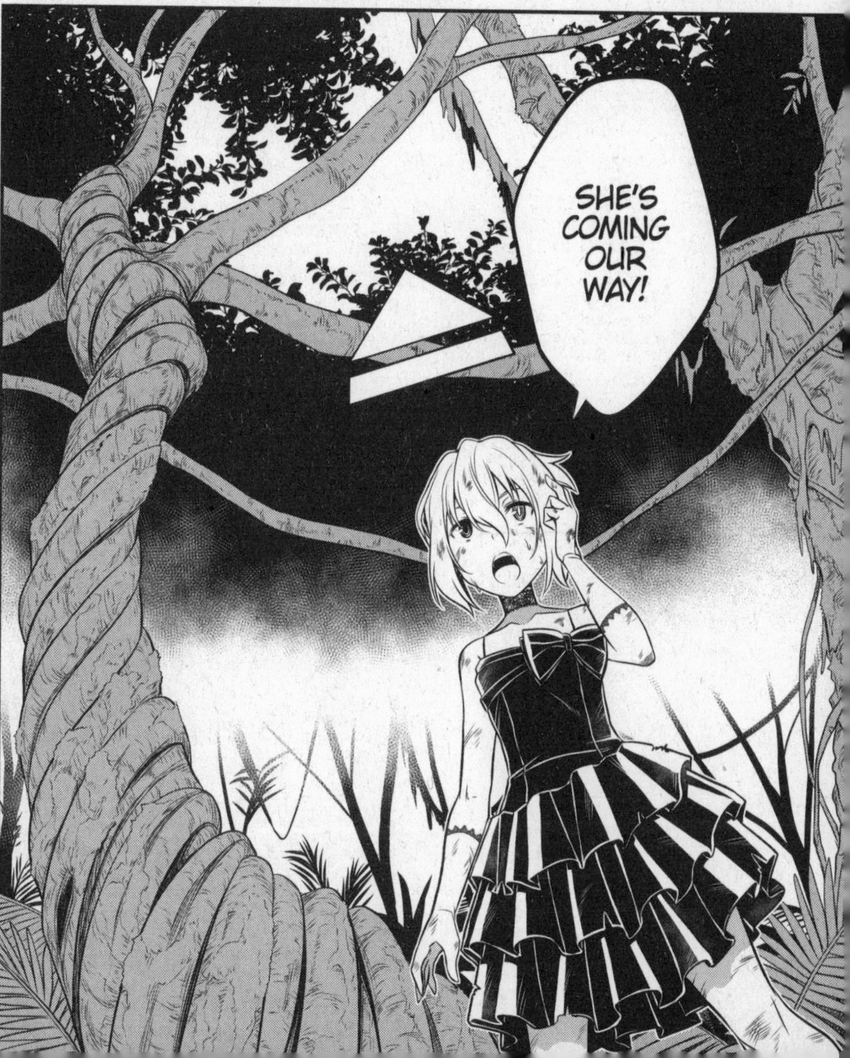
SHE'S COMING OUR WAY!

NOT LIVES
ノットライヴス

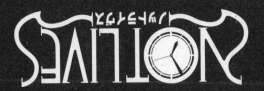

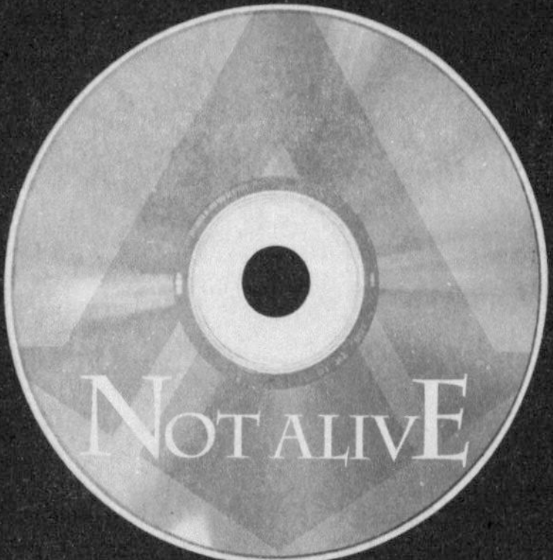
NOT ALIVE

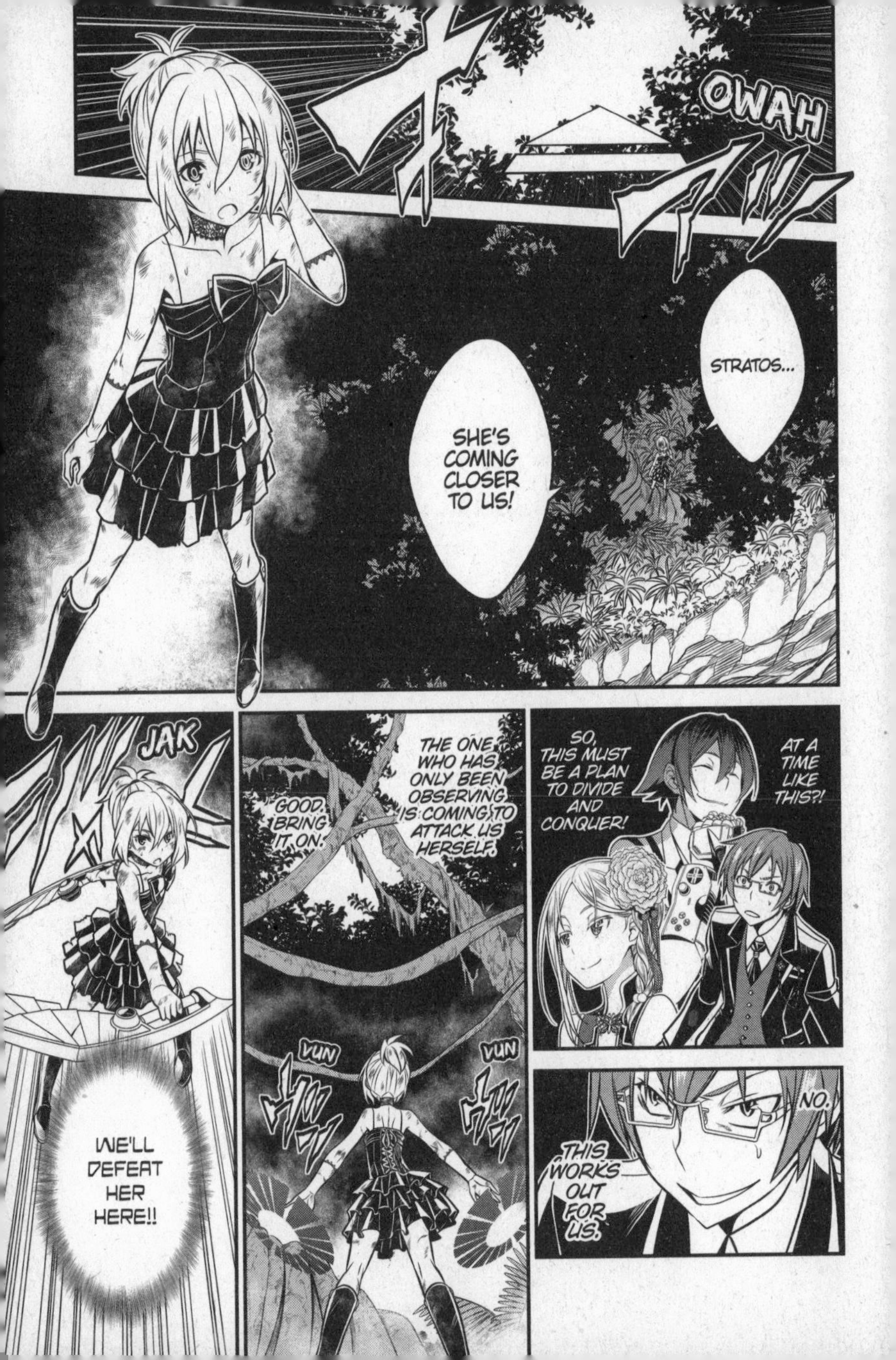
OWAH
STRATOS...
SHE'S COMING CLOSER TO US!
AT A TIME LIKE THIS?!
SO, THIS MUST BE A PLAN TO DIVIDE AND CONQUER!
NO.
THIS WORKS OUT FOR US.
THE ONE WHO HAS ONLY BEEN OBSERVING IS COMING TO ATTACK US HERSELF.
GOOD. BRING IT ON.
VUN
VUN
JAK
WE'LL DEFEAT HER HERE!!

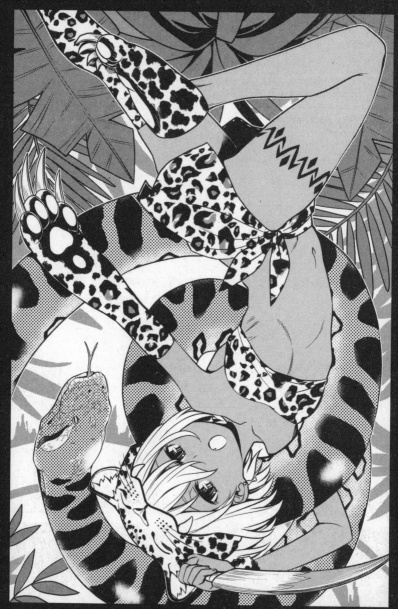

CHAPTER 40

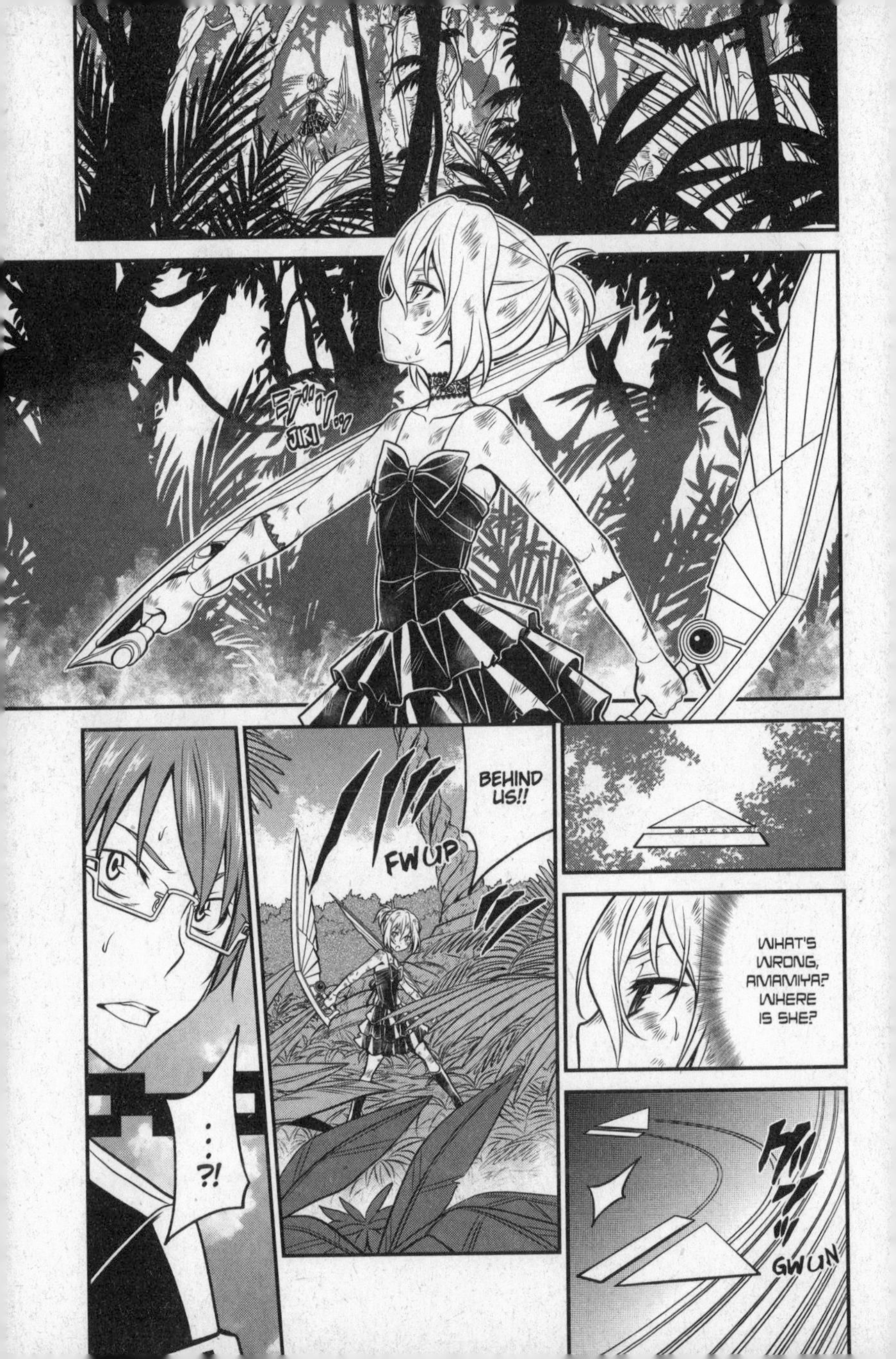
JIRI
WHAT'S WRONG, AMAMIYA? WHERE IS SHE?
GWUN
BEHIND US!!
FWUP
...?!

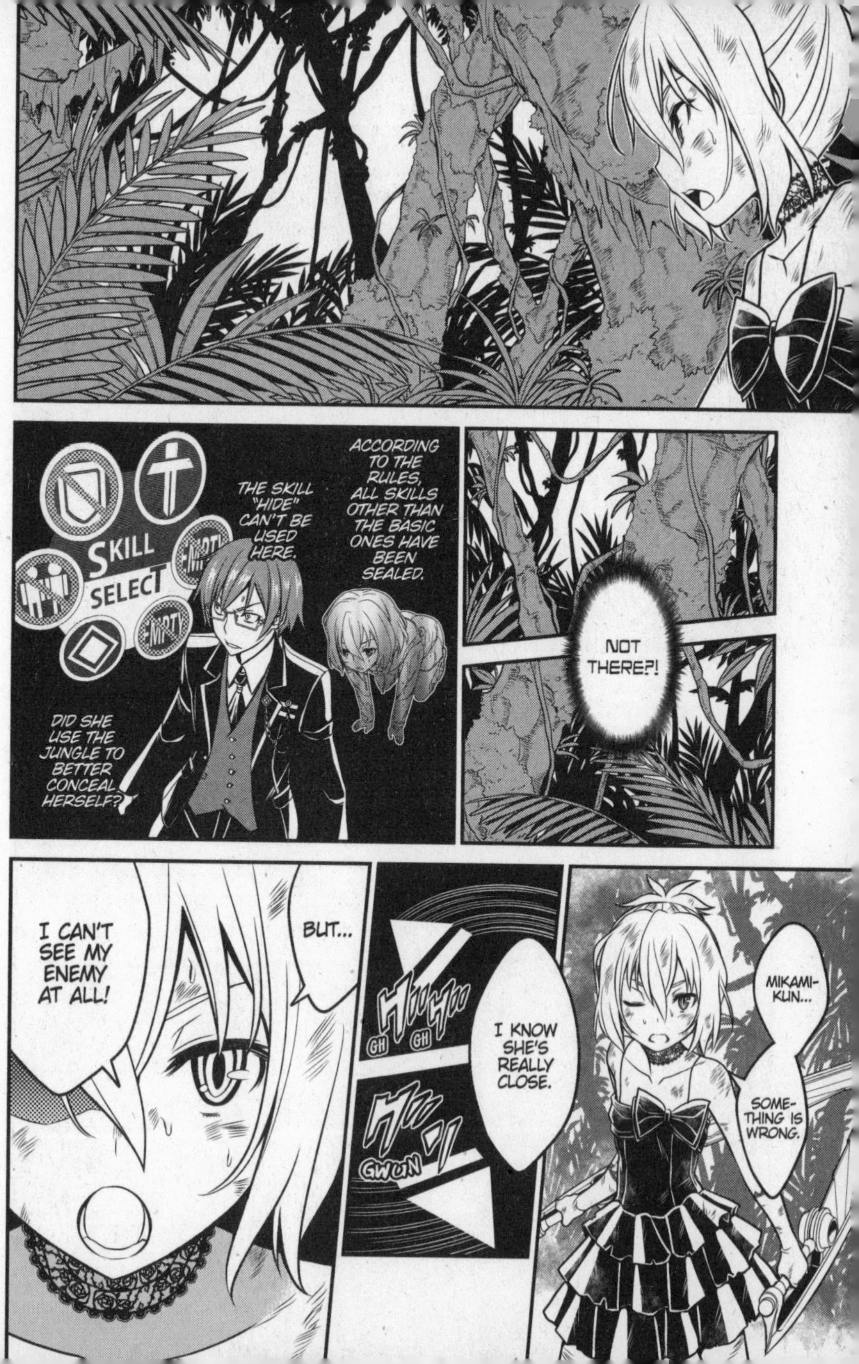
NOT THERE?!
ACCORDING TO THE RULES, ALL SKILLS OTHER THAN THE BASIC ONES HAVE BEEN SEALED.
THE SKILL "HIDE" CAN'T BE USED HERE.
SKILL SELECT
DID SHE USE THE JUNGLE TO BETTER CONCEAL HERSELF?
MIKAMI-KUN...
SOME-THING IS WRONG.
I KNOW SHE'S REALLY CLOSE.
GH GH
GWUN
BUT...
I CAN'T SEE MY ENEMY AT ALL!

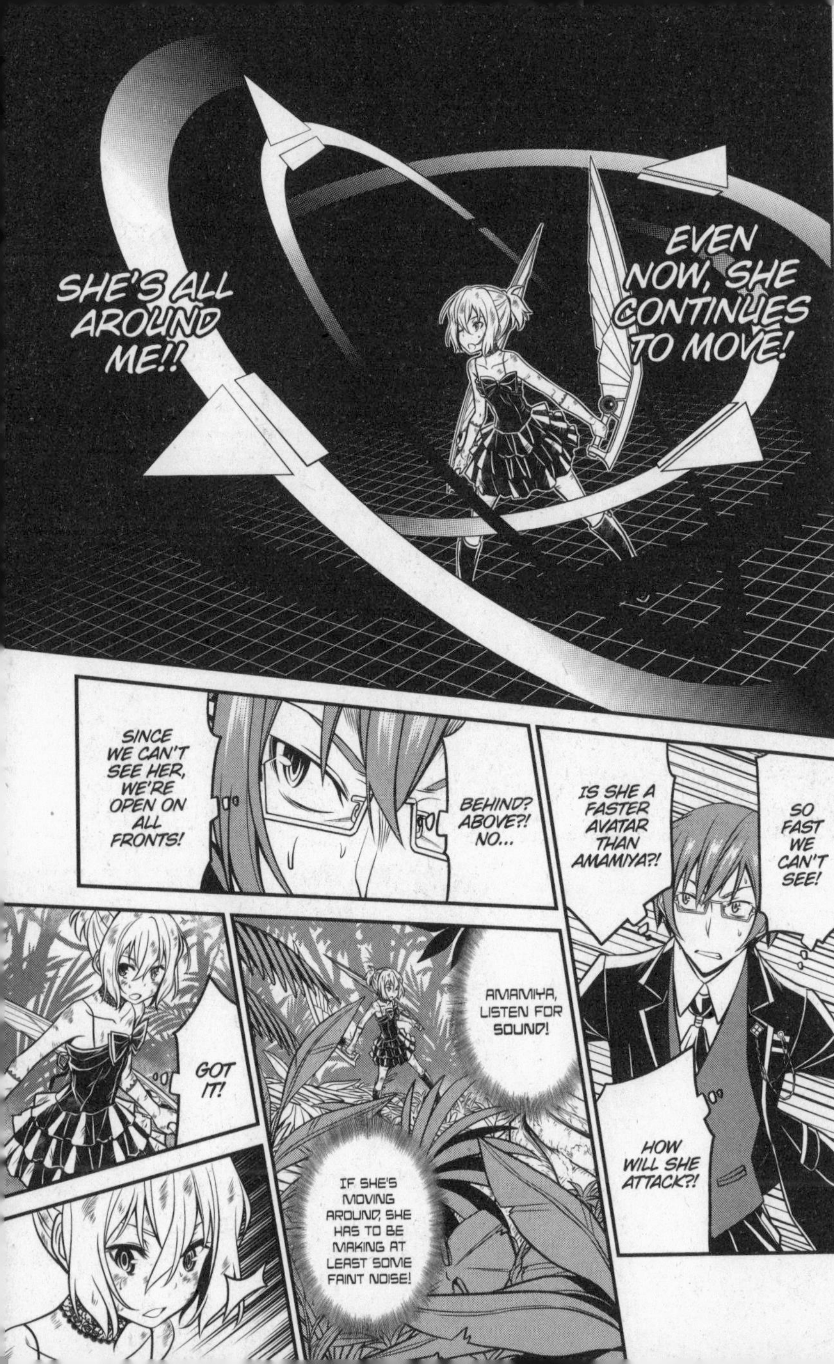
EVEN NOW, SHE CONTINUES TO MOVE!
SHE'S ALL AROUND ME!!
SO FAST WE CAN'T SEE!
IS SHE A FASTER AVATAR THAN AMAMIYA?!
BEHIND? ABOVE?! NO...
SINCE WE CAN'T SEE HER, WE'RE OPEN ON ALL FRONTS!
HOW WILL SHE ATTACK?!
AMAMIYA, LISTEN FOR SOUND!
IF SHE'S MOVING AROUND, SHE HAS TO BE MAKING AT LEAST SOME FAINT NOISE!
GOT IT!

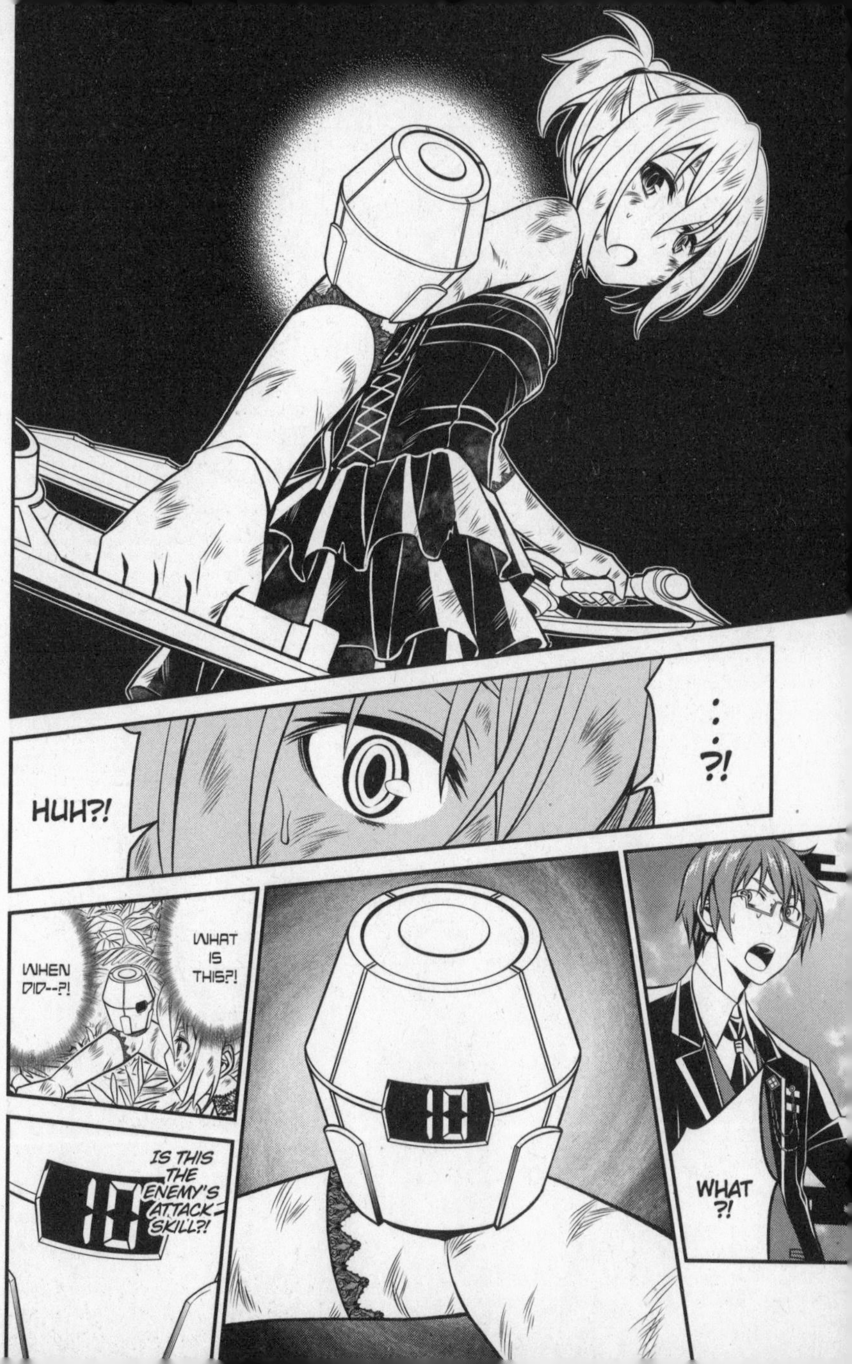
...?!
HUH?!
WHAT ?!
WHAT IS THIS?!
WHEN DID--?!
IS THIS THE ENEMY'S ATTACK SKILL?!

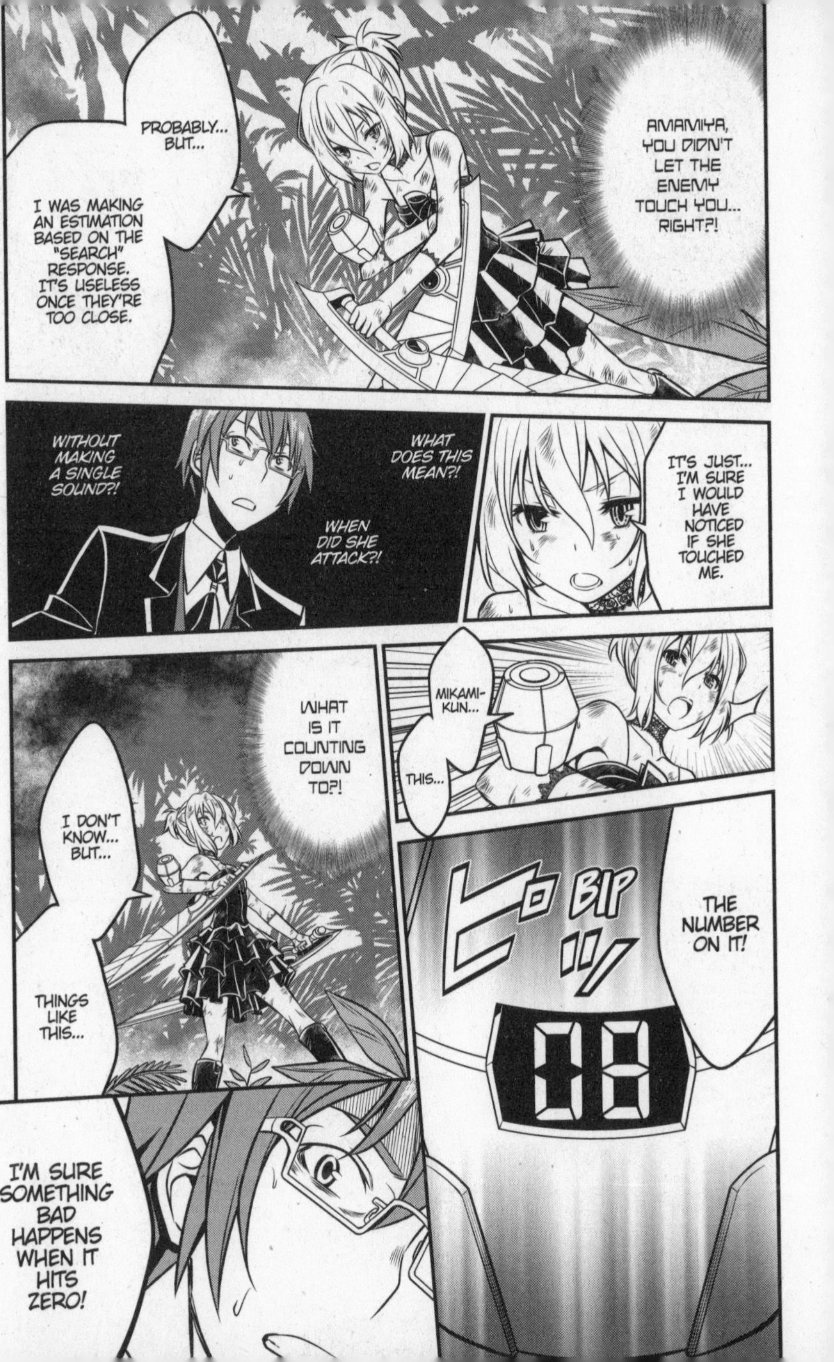
AMAMIYA, YOU DIDN'T LET THE ENEMY TOUCH YOU... RIGHT?!
PROBABLY... BUT...
I WAS MAKING AN ESTIMATION BASED ON THE "SEARCH" RESPONSE. IT'S USELESS ONCE THEY'RE TOO CLOSE.
IT'S JUST... I'M SURE I WOULD HAVE NOTICED IF SHE TOUCHED ME.
WHAT DOES THIS MEAN?!
WHEN DID SHE ATTACK?!
WITHOUT MAKING A SINGLE SOUND?!
MIKAMI-KUN...
THIS...
BIP
THE NUMBER ON IT!
08
WHAT IS IT COUNTING DOWN TO?!
I DON'T KNOW... BUT...
THINGS LIKE THIS...
I'M SURE SOMETHING BAD HAPPENS WHEN IT HITS ZERO!

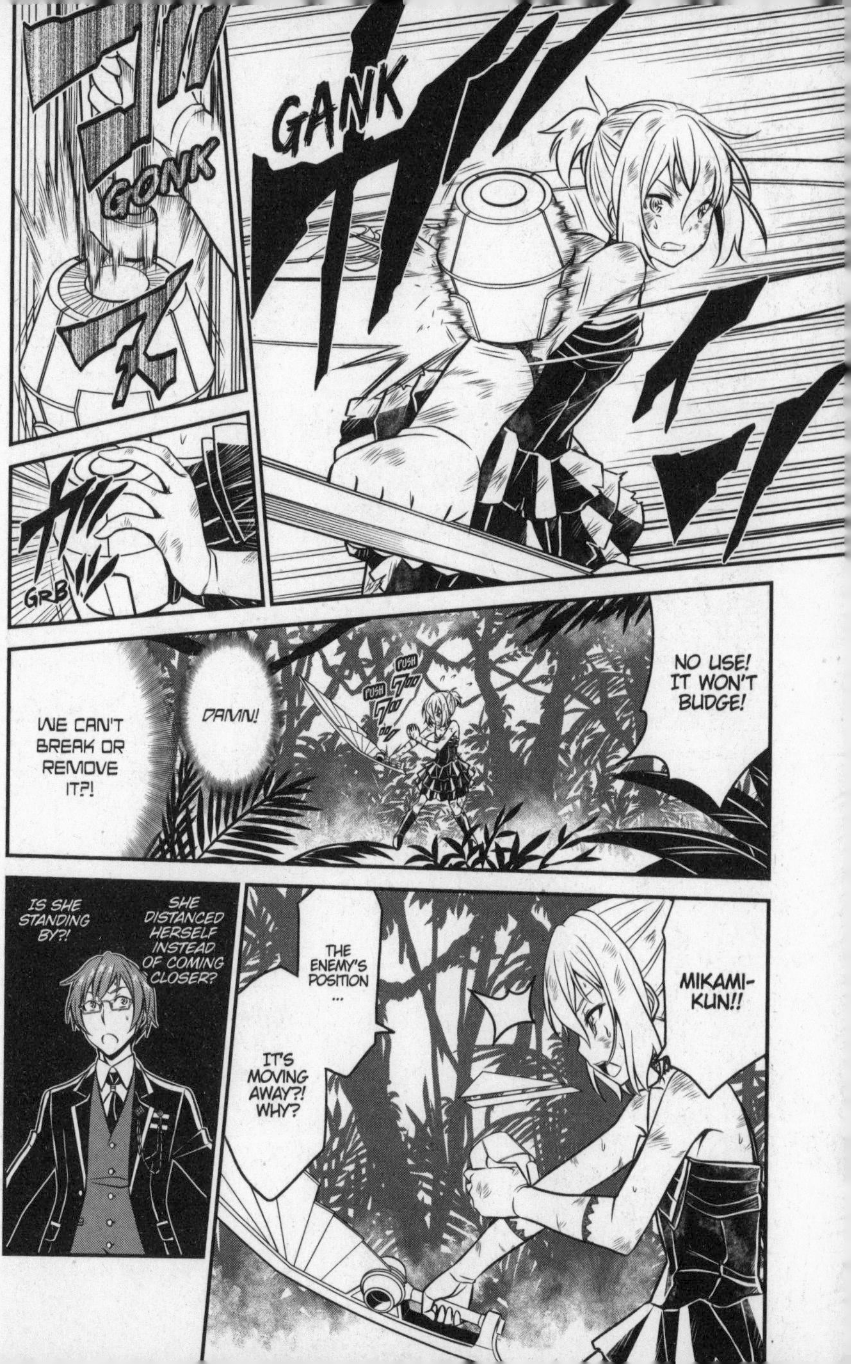
GANK
GONK
GRB
NO USE! IT WON'T BUDGE!
PUSH
PUSH
DAMN!
WE CAN'T BREAK OR REMOVE IT?!
MIKAMI-KUN!!
THE ENEMY'S POSITION ...
IT'S MOVING AWAY?! WHY?
SHE DISTANCED HERSELF INSTEAD OF COMING CLOSER?
IS SHE STANDING BY?!

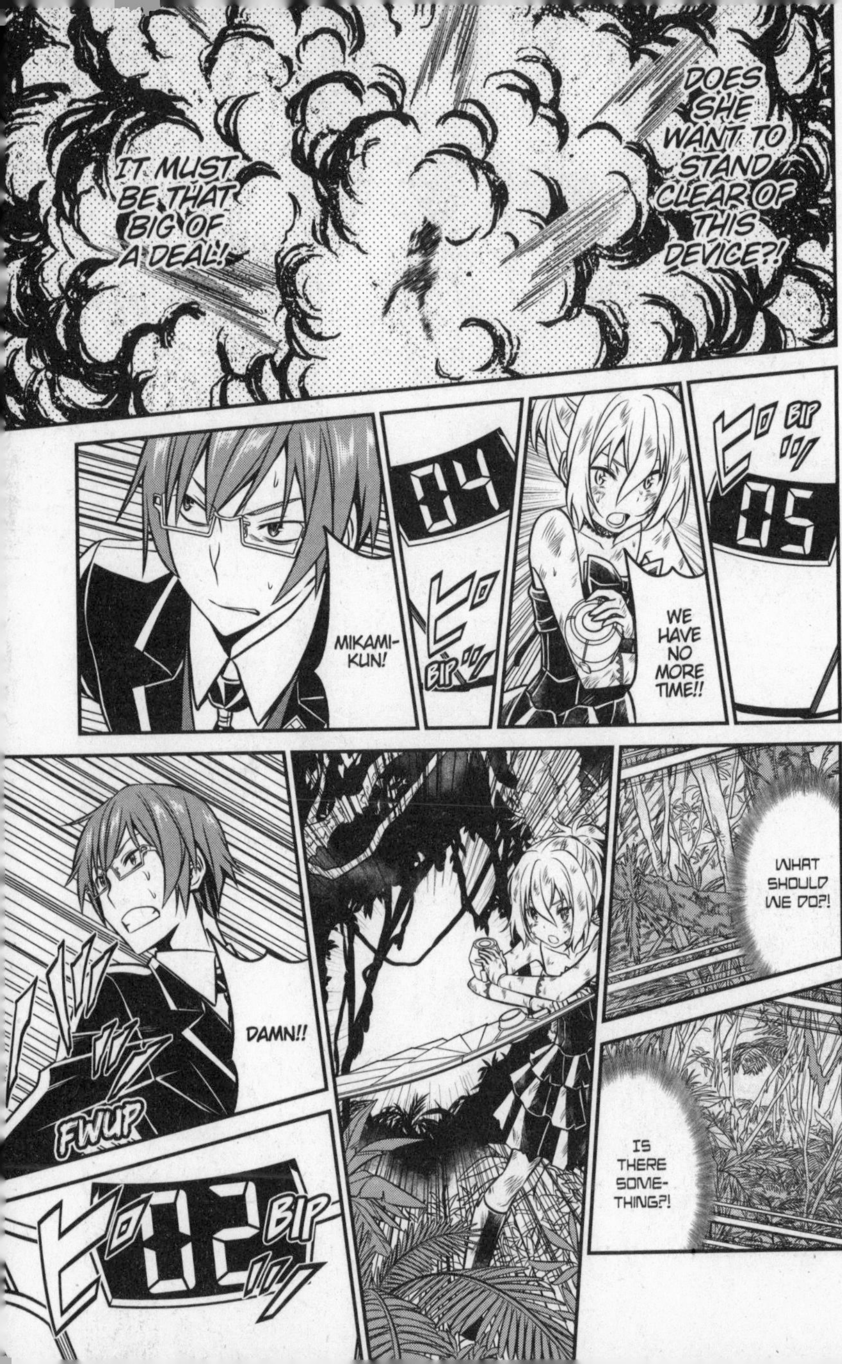
DOES SHE WANT TO STAND CLEAR OF THIS DEVICE?!
IT MUST BE THAT BIG OF A DEAL!
BIP
05
WE HAVE NO MORE TIME!!
04
BIP
MIKAMI-KUN!
WHAT SHOULD WE DO?!
IS THERE SOME-THING?!
DAMN!!
FWUP
02
BIP

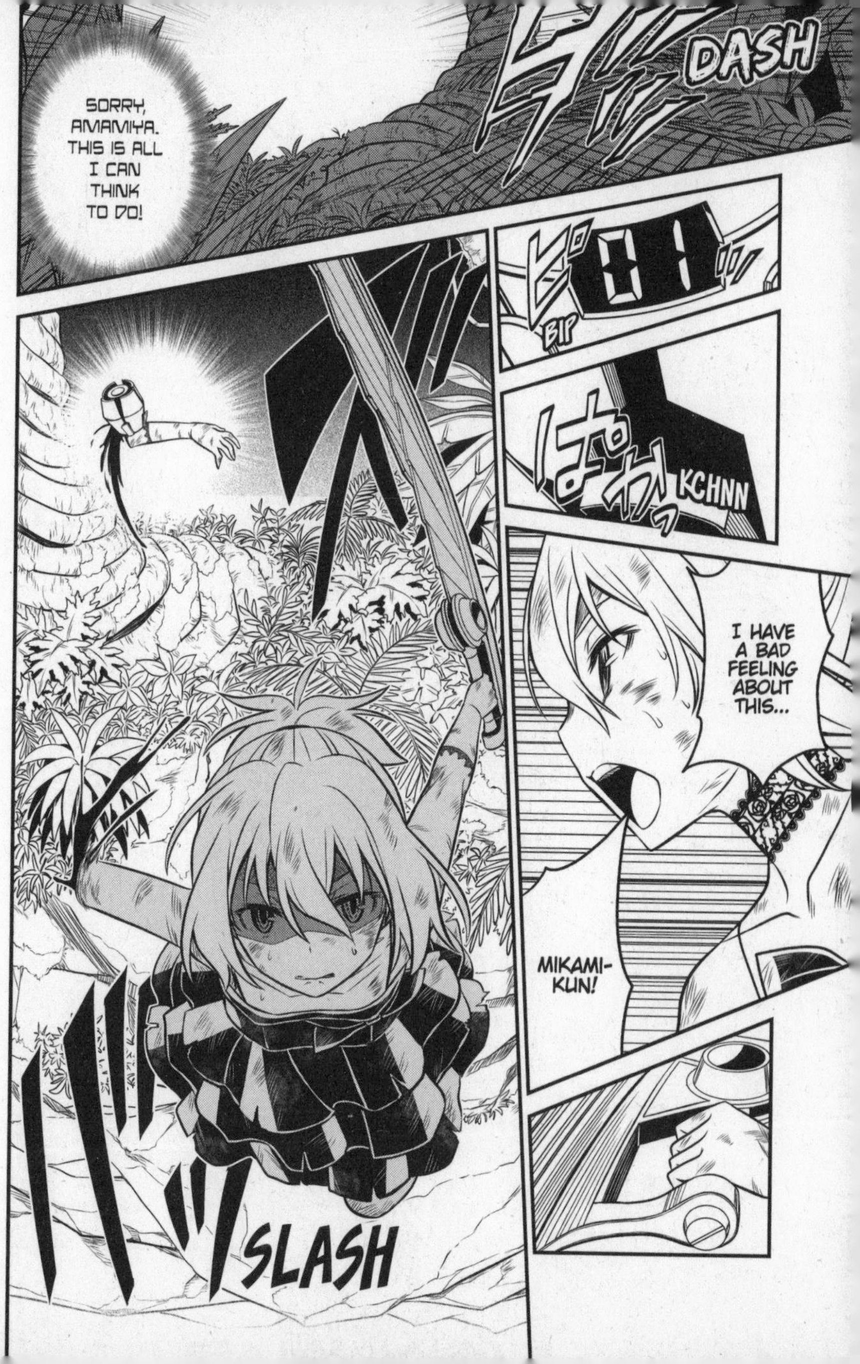
DASH
SORRY, AMAMIYA. THIS IS ALL I CAN THINK TO DO!
01
BIP
KCHNN
I HAVE A BAD FEELING ABOUT THIS...
MIKAMI-KUN!
SLASH

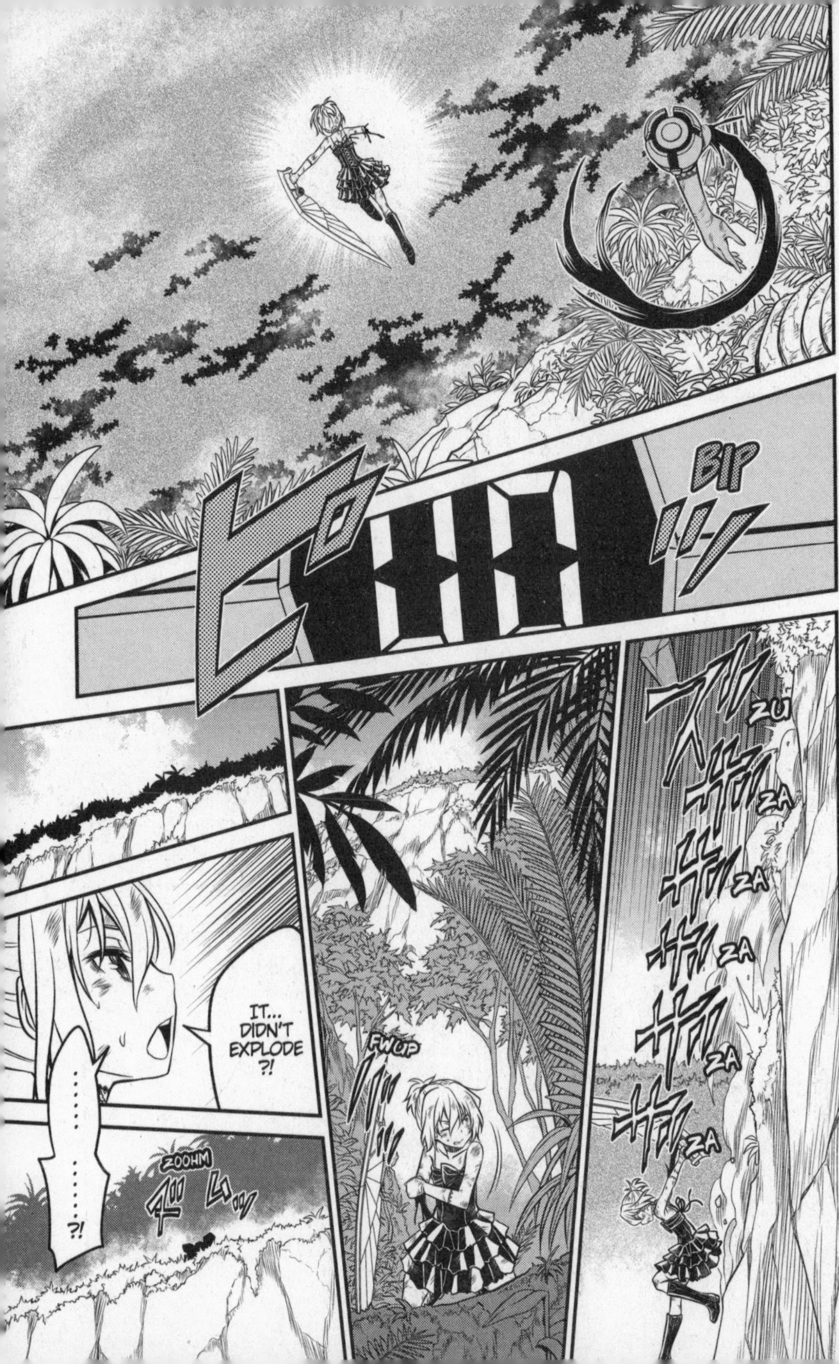
BIP
ZU ZA ZA ZA ZA ZA
FWUP
IT... DIDN'T EXPLODE ?!
......?!
ZOOHM

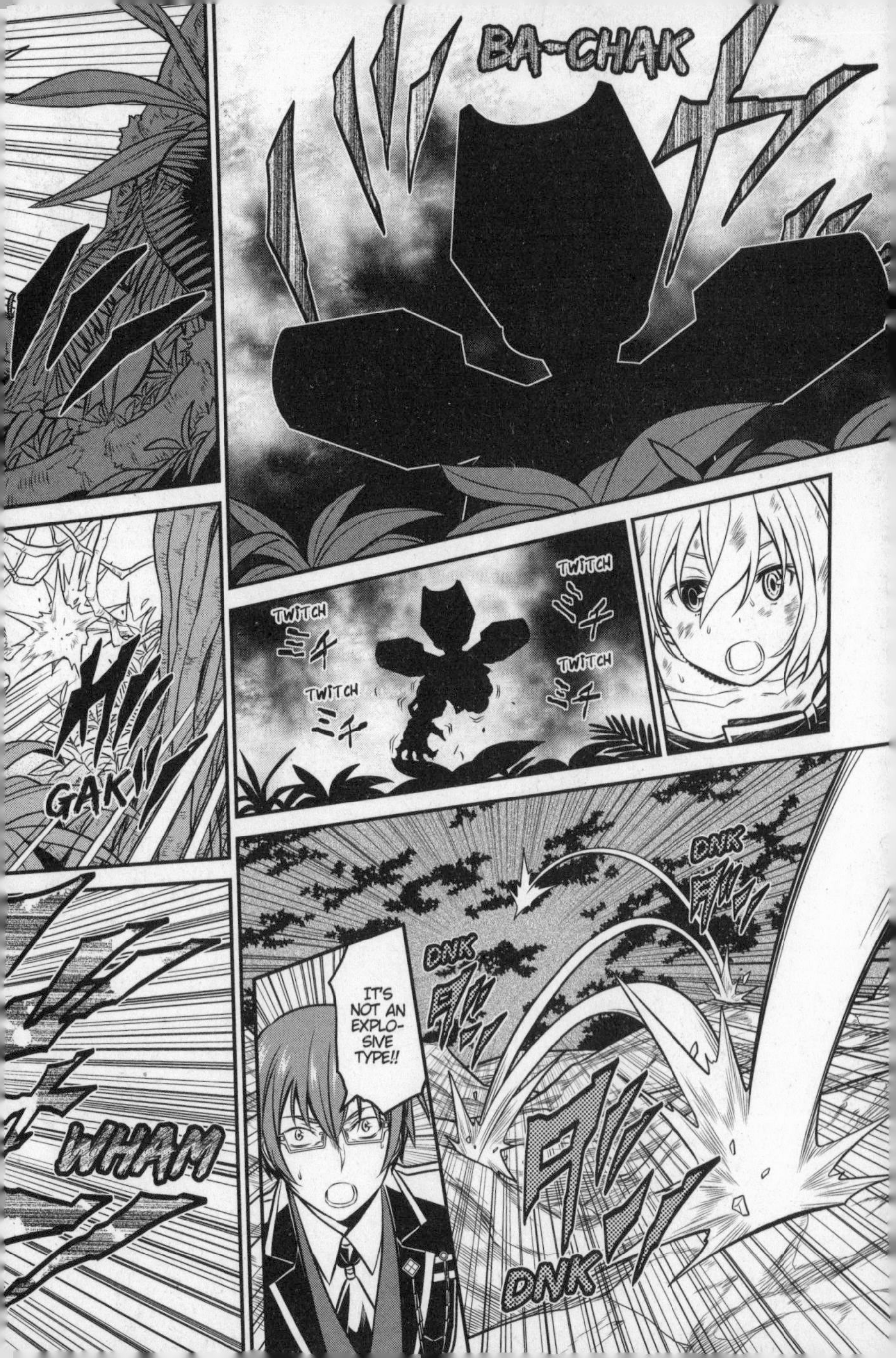
BA-CHAK
TWITCH
TWITCH
TWITCH
GAK!!
DNK
DNK
IT'S NOT AN EXPLO-SIVE TYPE!!
DNK
WHAM

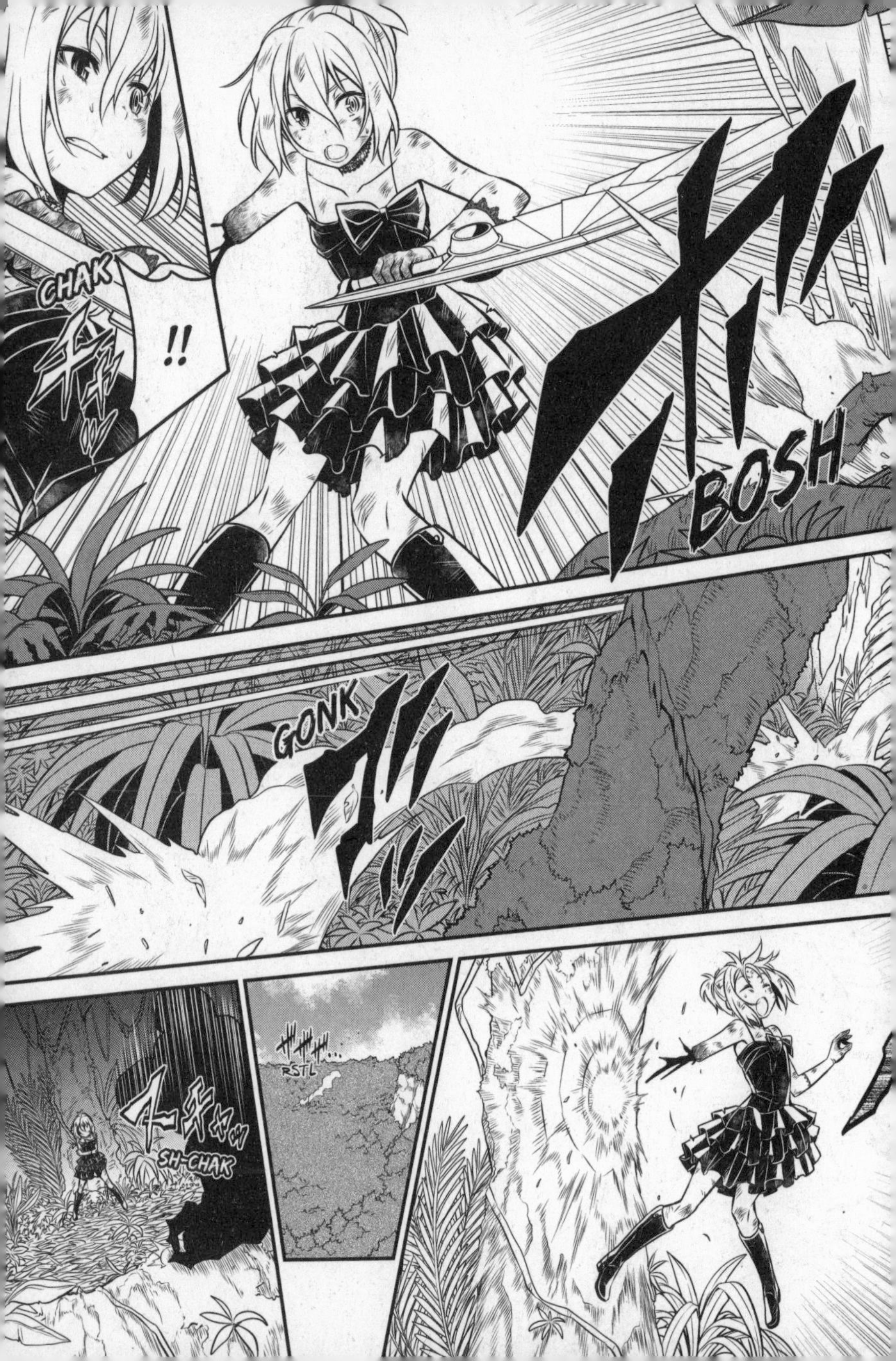
BOSH
CHAK
!!
GONK
RSTL
SH-CHAK

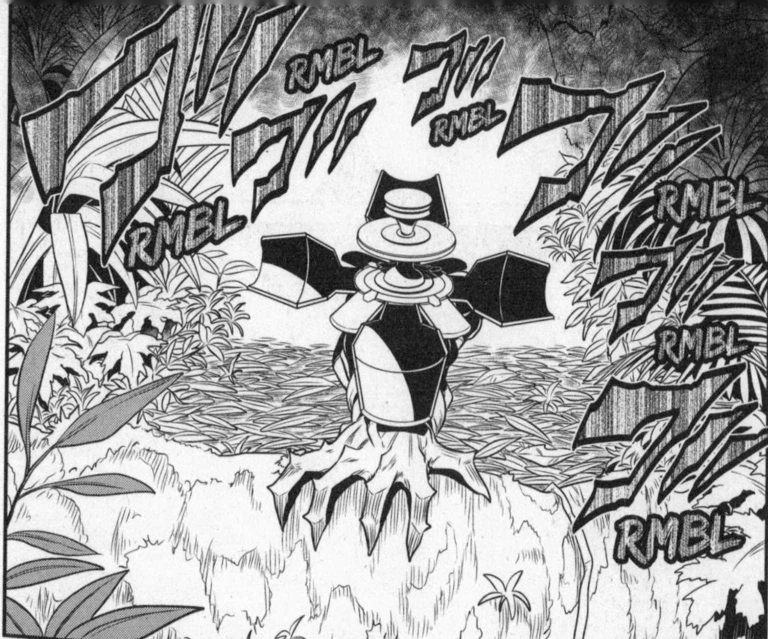
RMBL
RMBL
RMBL
RMBL
RMBL
RMBL

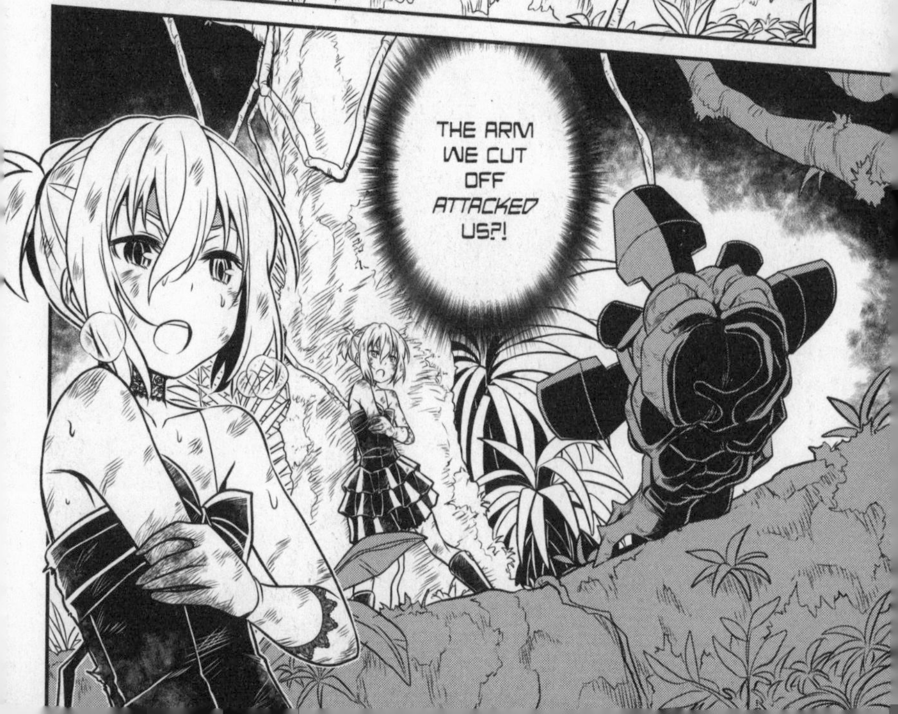
THE ARM WE CUT OFF ATTACKED US?!

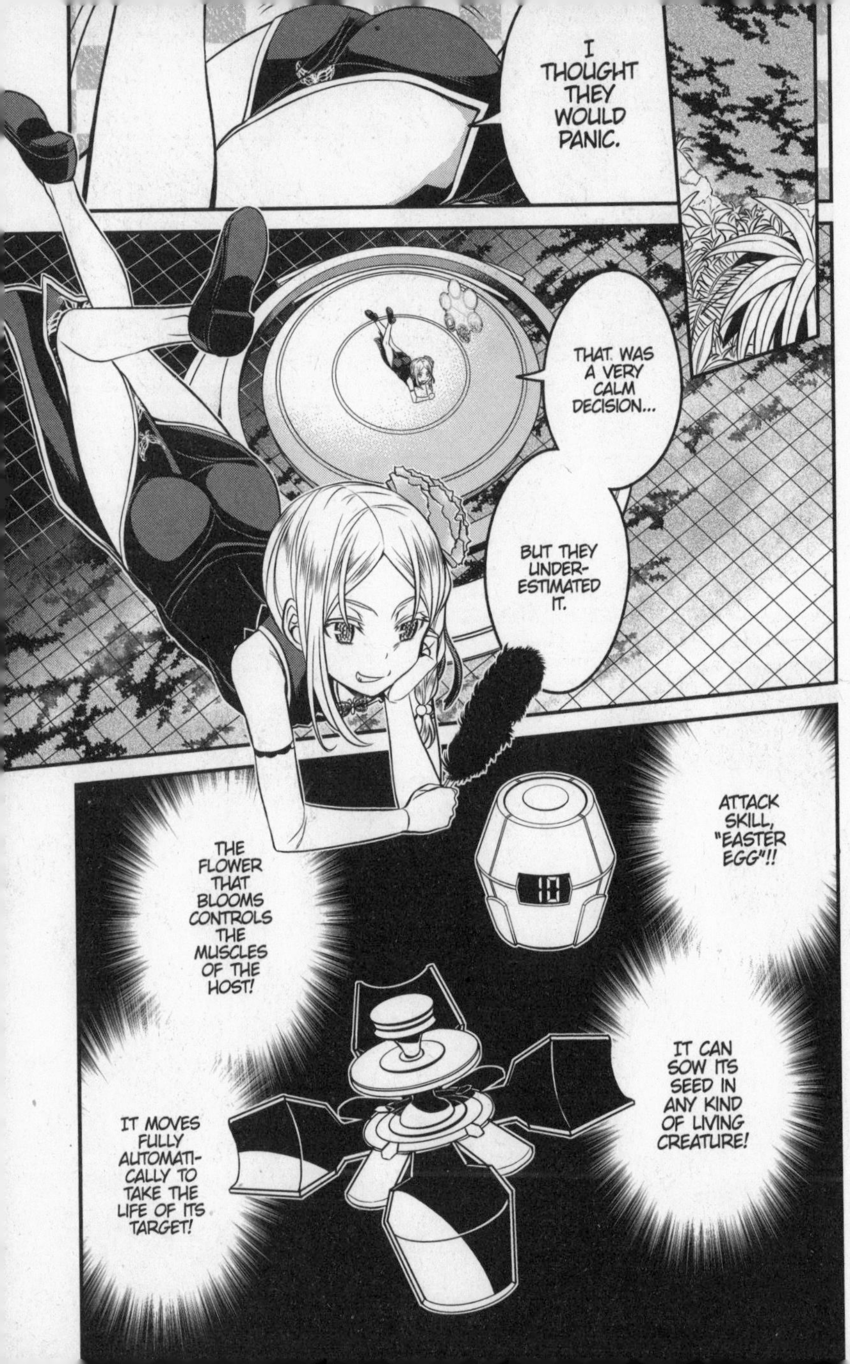
I THOUGHT THEY WOULD PANIC.
THAT. WAS A VERY CALM DECISION...
BUT THEY UNDER-ESTIMATED IT.
ATTACK SKILL, "EASTER EGG"!!
THE FLOWER THAT BLOOMS CONTROLS THE MUSCLES OF THE HOST!
IT CAN SOW ITS SEED IN ANY KIND OF LIVING CREATURE!
IT MOVES FULLY AUTOMATI-CALLY TO TAKE THE LIFE OF ITS TARGET!

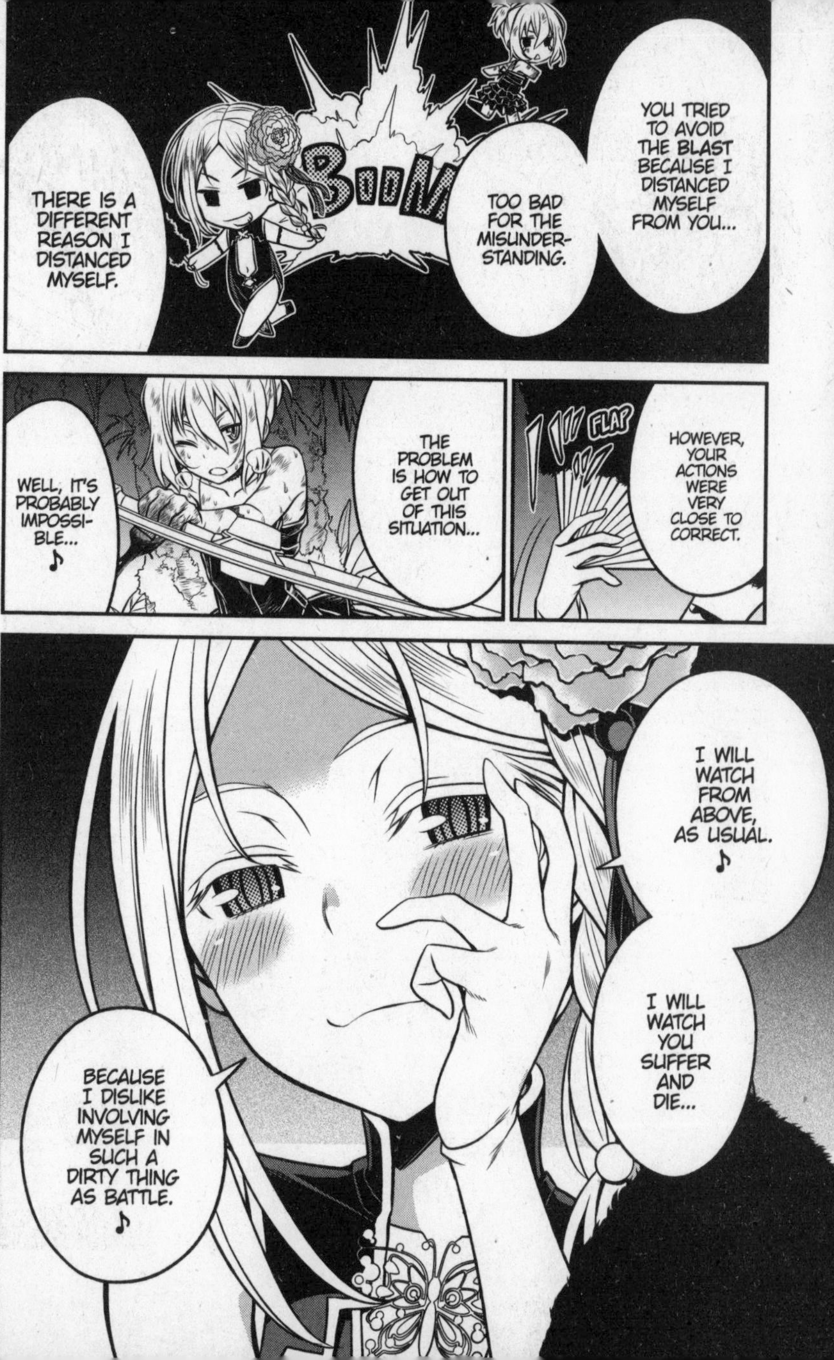
YOU TRIED TO AVOID THE BLAST BECAUSE I DISTANCED MYSELF FROM YOU...
TOO BAD FOR THE MISUNDER-STANDING.
BOOM
THERE IS A DIFFERENT REASON I DISTANCED MYSELF.
HOWEVER, YOUR ACTIONS WERE VERY CLOSE TO CORRECT.
FLAP
THE PROBLEM IS HOW TO GET OUT OF THIS SITUATION...
WELL, IT'S PROBABLY IMPOSSI-BLE... ♪
I WILL WATCH FROM ABOVE, AS USUAL. ♪
I WILL WATCH YOU SUFFER AND DIE...
BECAUSE I DISLIKE INVOLVING MYSELF IN SUCH A DIRTY THING AS BATTLE. ♪

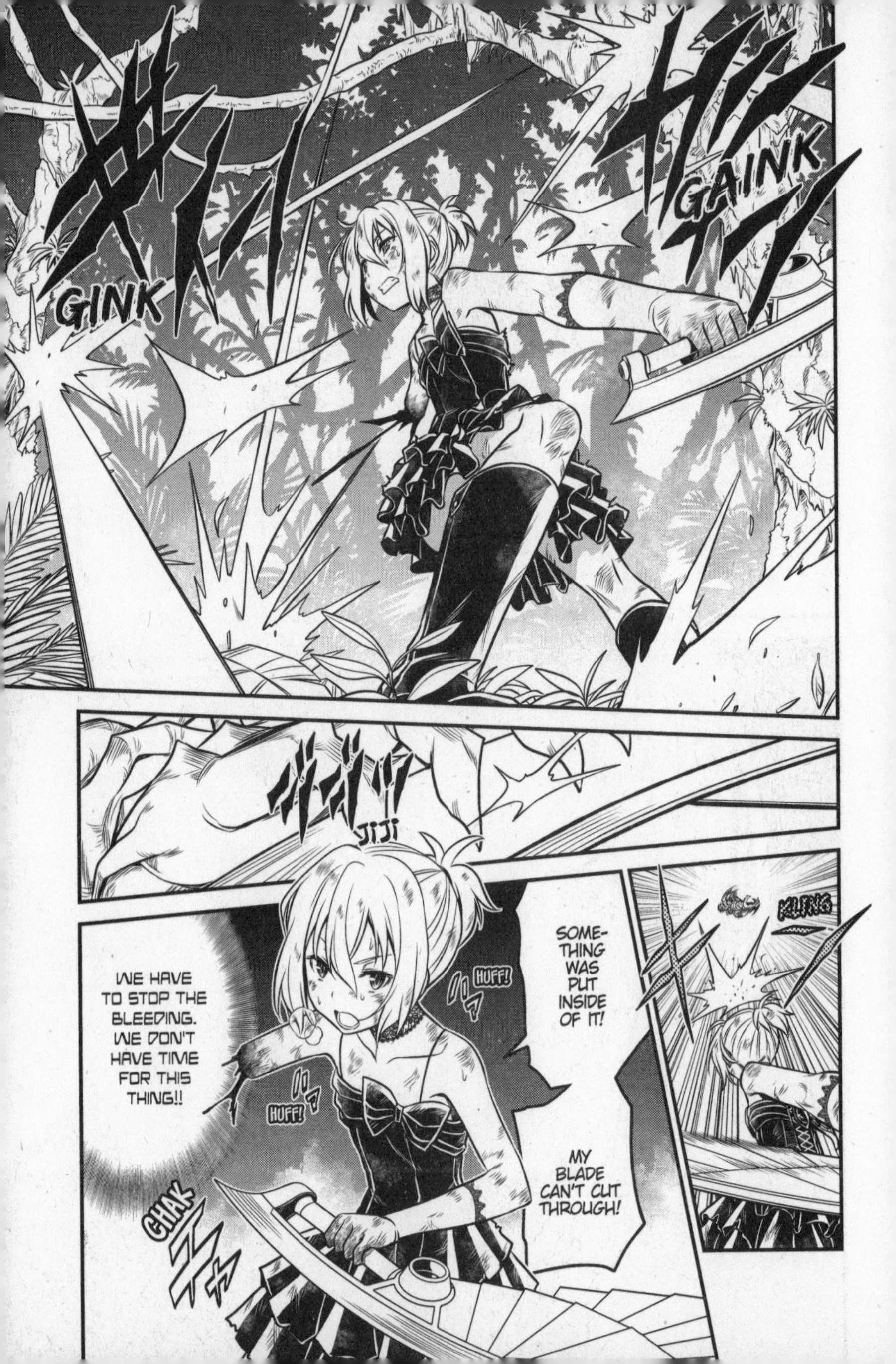
GAINK
GINK
JIJI
KLING
SOMETHING WAS PUT INSIDE OF IT!
MY BLADE CAN'T CUT THROUGH!
HUFF!
WE HAVE TO STOP THE BLEEDING. WE DON'T HAVE TIME FOR THIS THING!!
HUFF!
CHAK

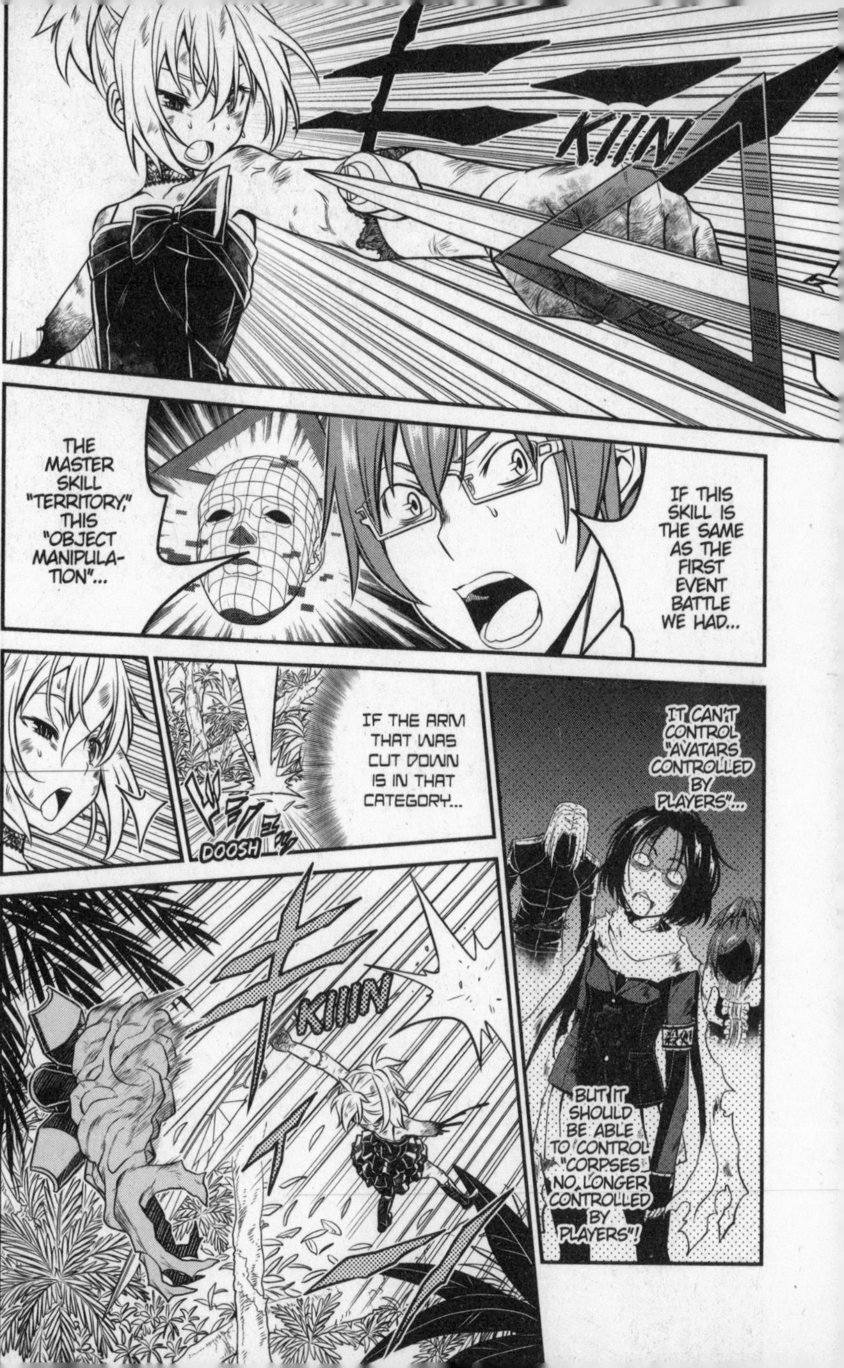
KIIN
IF THIS SKILL IS THE SAME AS THE FIRST EVENT BATTLE WE HAD...
THE MASTER SKILL "TERRITORY," THIS "OBJECT MANIPULA-TION"...
IT CAN'T CONTROL "AVATARS CONTROLLED BY PLAYERS"...
BUT IT SHOULD BE ABLE TO CONTROL "CORPSES NO LONGER CONTROLLED BY PLAYERS"!
IF THE ARM THAT WAS CUT DOWN IS IN THAT CATEGORY...
DOOSH
KIIIN

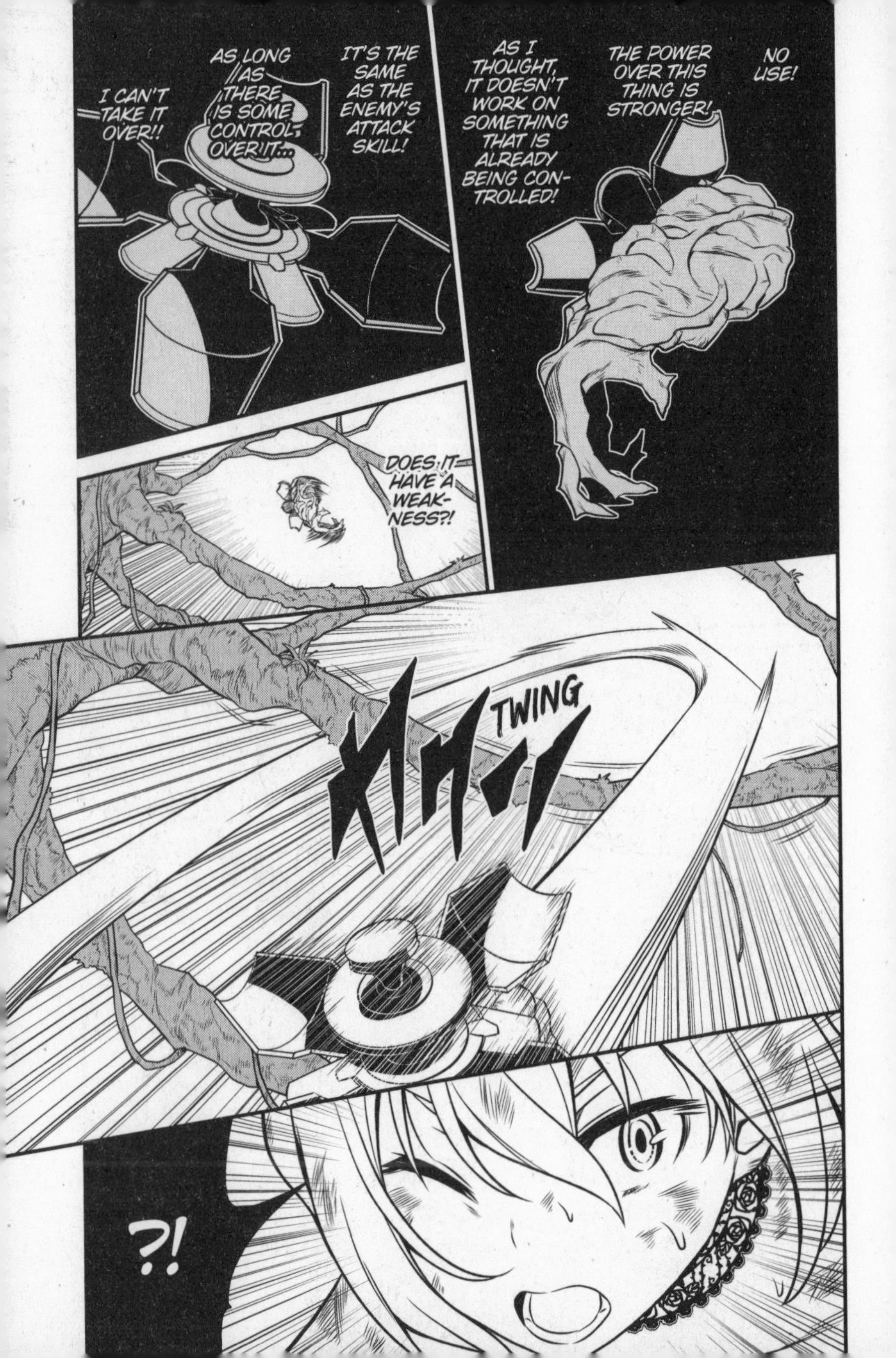
NO USE!
THE POWER OVER THIS THING IS STRONGER!
AS I THOUGHT, IT DOESN'T WORK ON SOMETHING THAT IS ALREADY BEING CONTROLLED!
IT'S THE SAME AS THE ENEMY'S ATTACK SKILL!
AS LONG AS THERE IS SOME CONTROL OVER IT...
I CAN'T TAKE IT OVER!!
DOES IT HAVE A WEAKNESS?!
TWING
?!

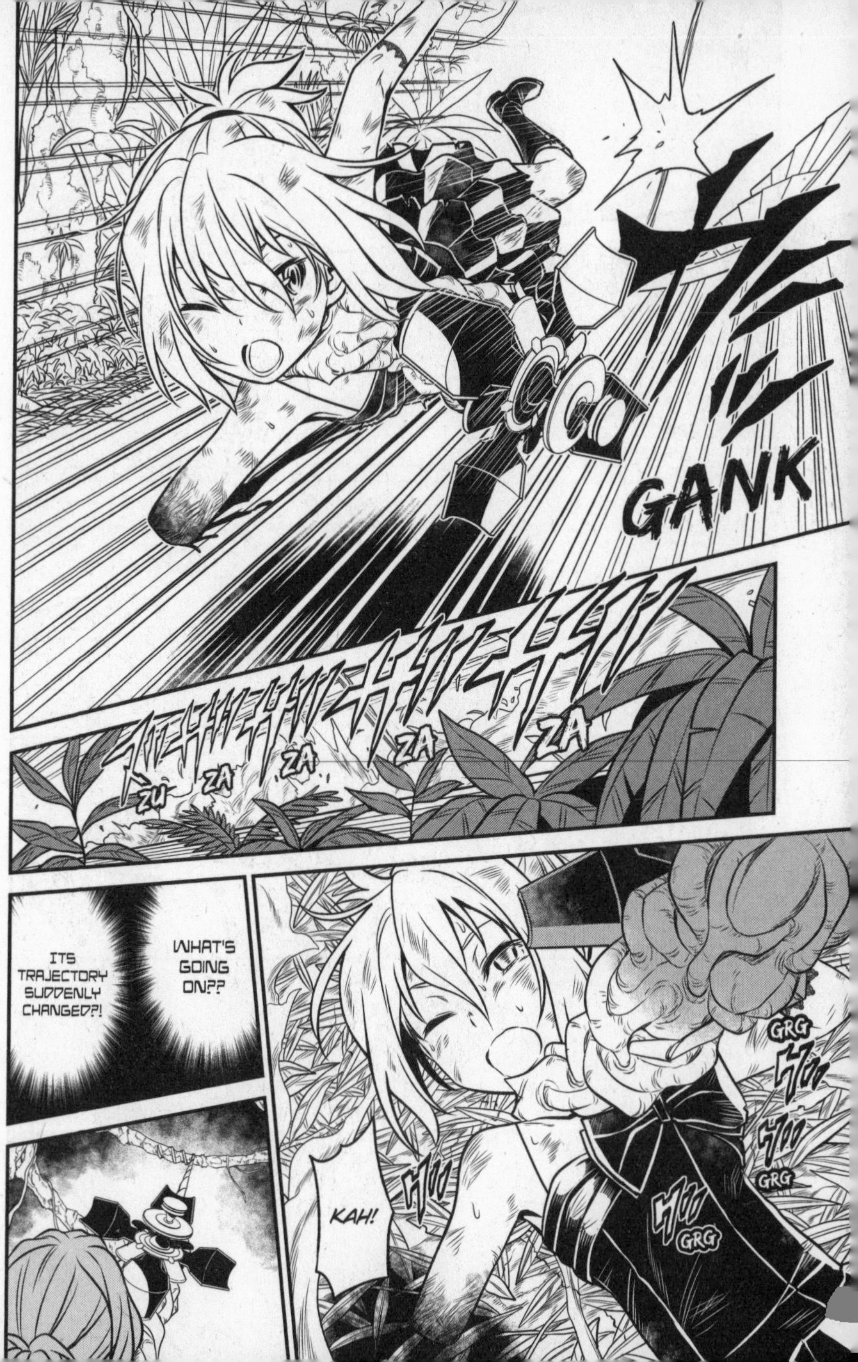
GANK
ZU
ZA
ZA
ZA
ZA
GRG
GRG
GRG
KAH!
WHAT'S GOING ON??
ITS TRAJECTORY SUDDENLY CHANGED?!

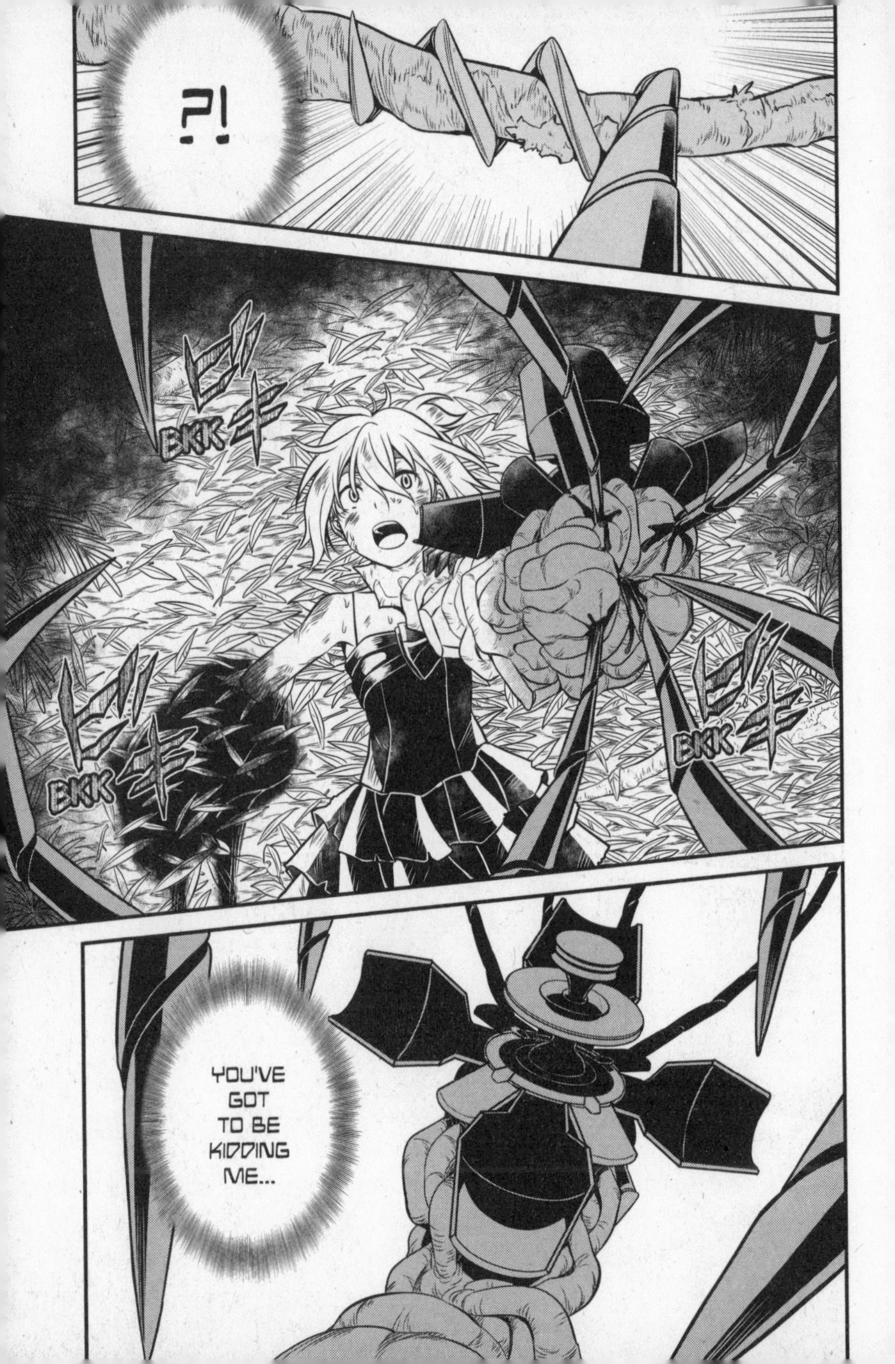
?!
BKK
BKK
BKK
YOU'VE GOT TO BE KIDDING ME...

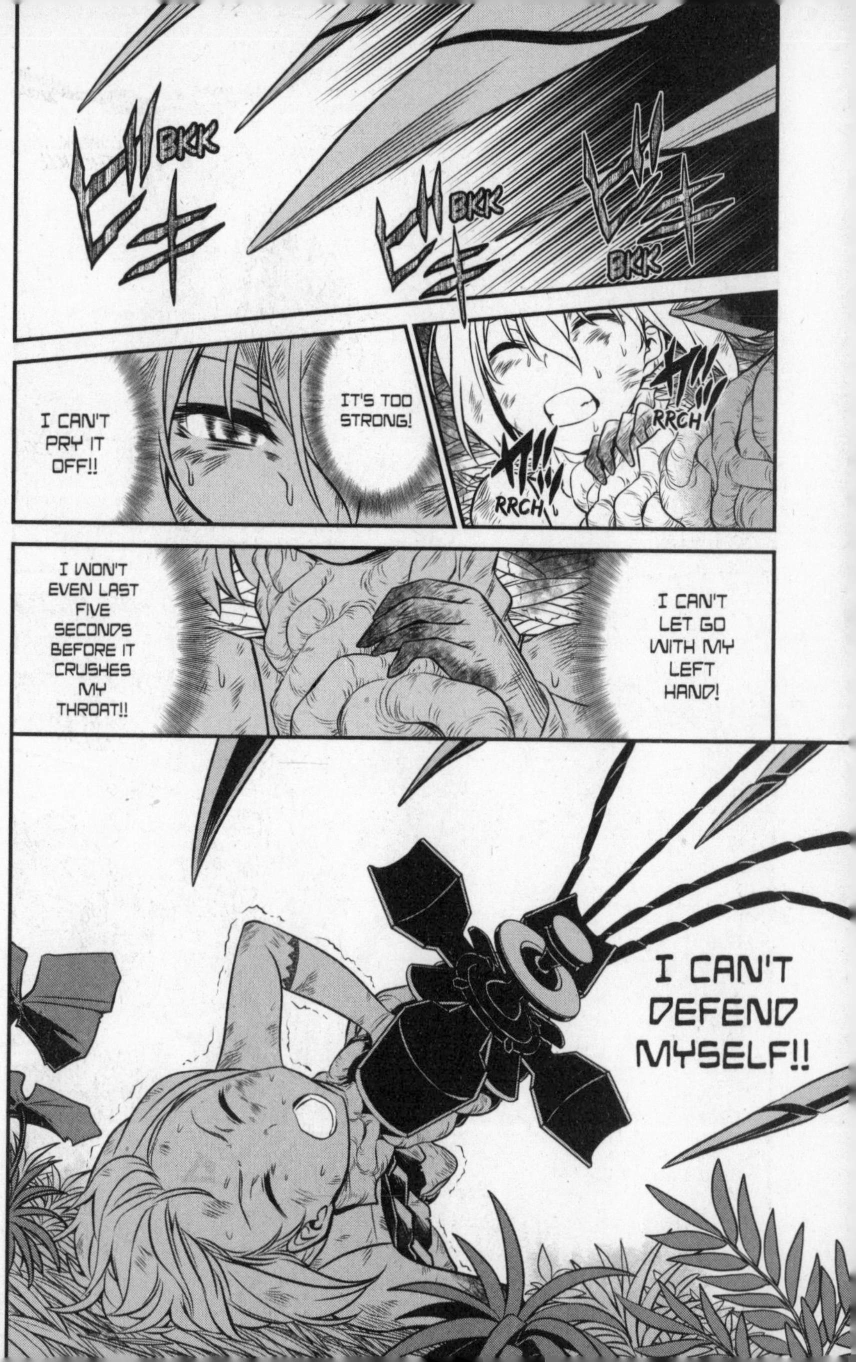
BKK
BKK
BKK
RRCH
RRCH
IT'S TOO STRONG!
I CAN'T PRY IT OFF!!
I CAN'T LET GO WITH MY LEFT HAND!
I WON'T EVEN LAST FIVE SECONDS BEFORE IT CRUSHES MY THROAT!!
I CAN'T DEFEND MYSELF!!

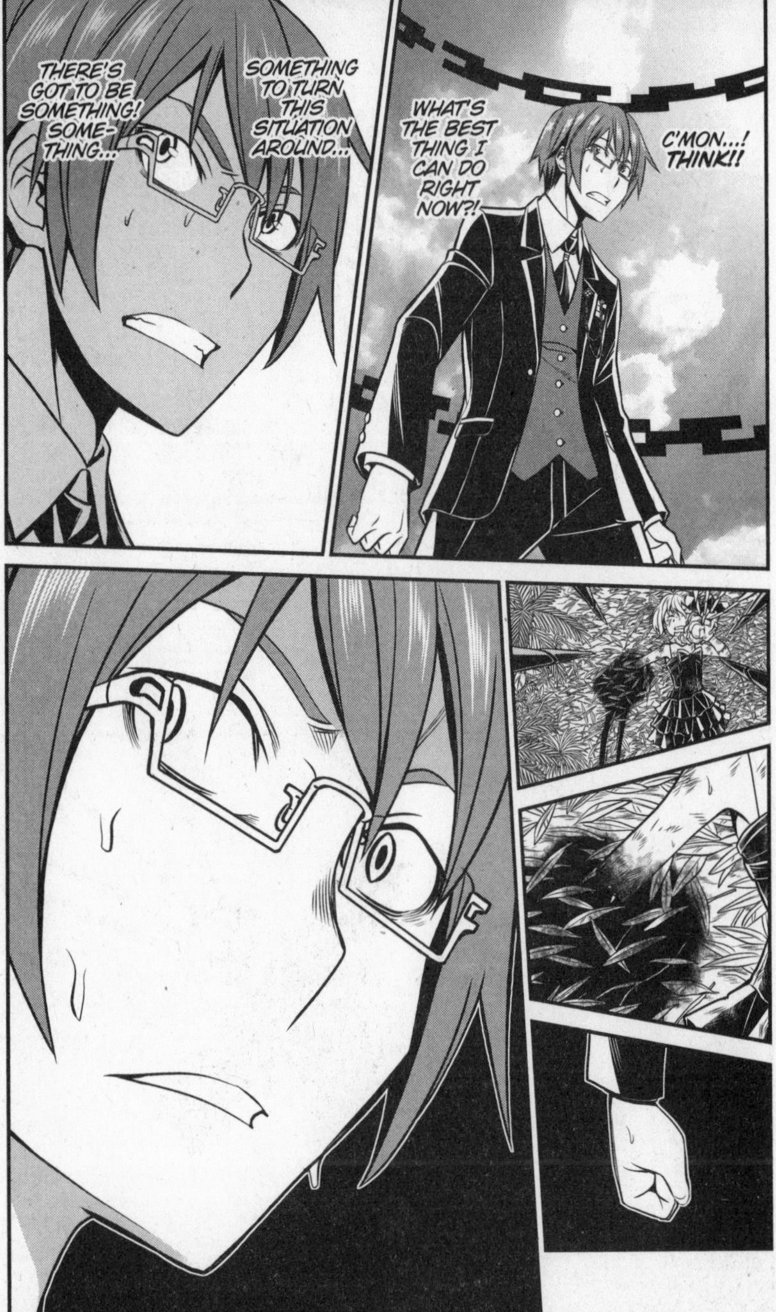
THERE'S GOT TO BE SOMETHING! SOME-THING...
SOMETHING TO TURN THIS SITUATION AROUND...
WHAT'S THE BEST THING I CAN DO RIGHT NOW?!
C'MON...! THINK!!

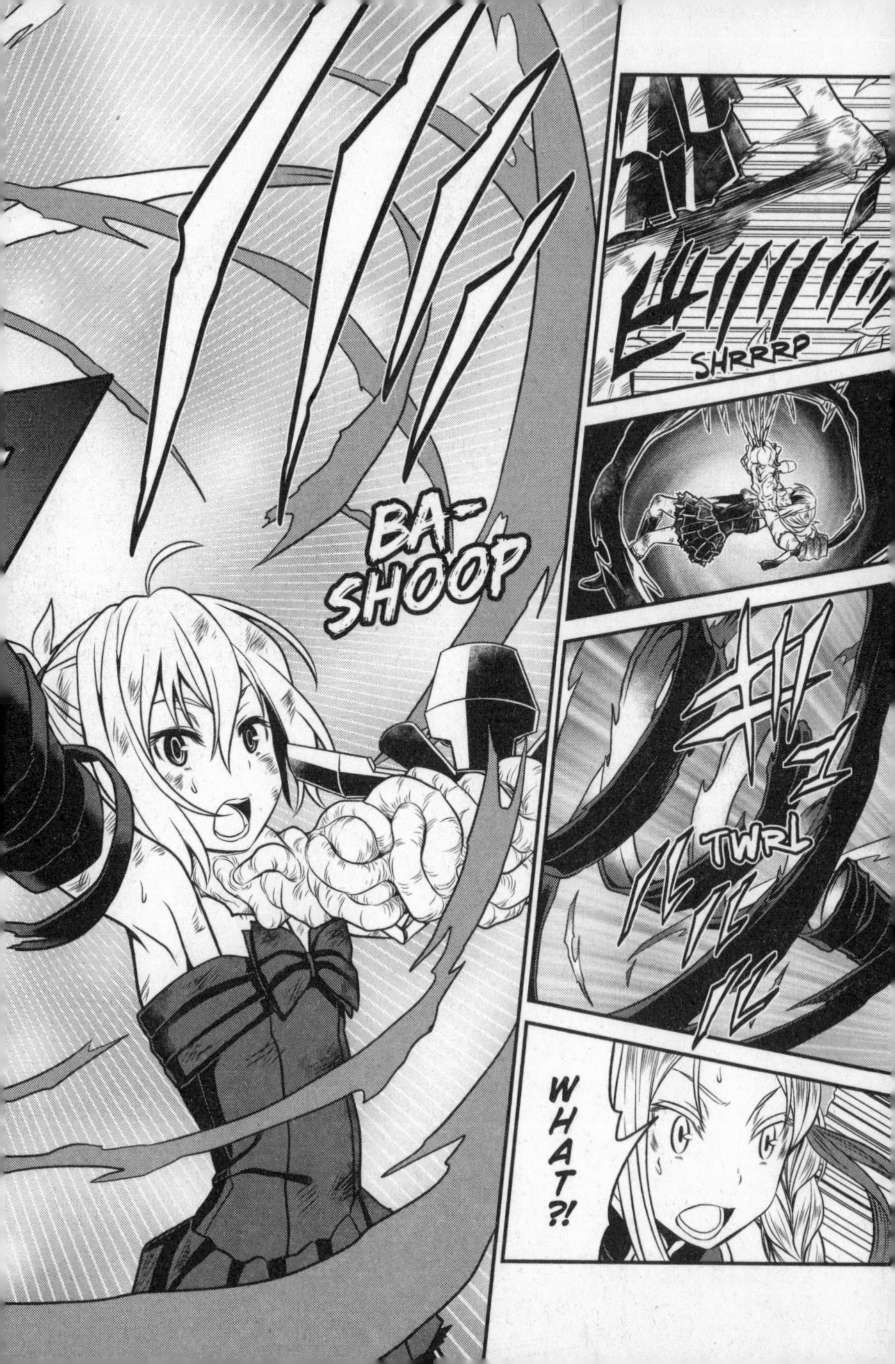
SHRRRP
TWRL
WHAT?!
BA-SHOOP

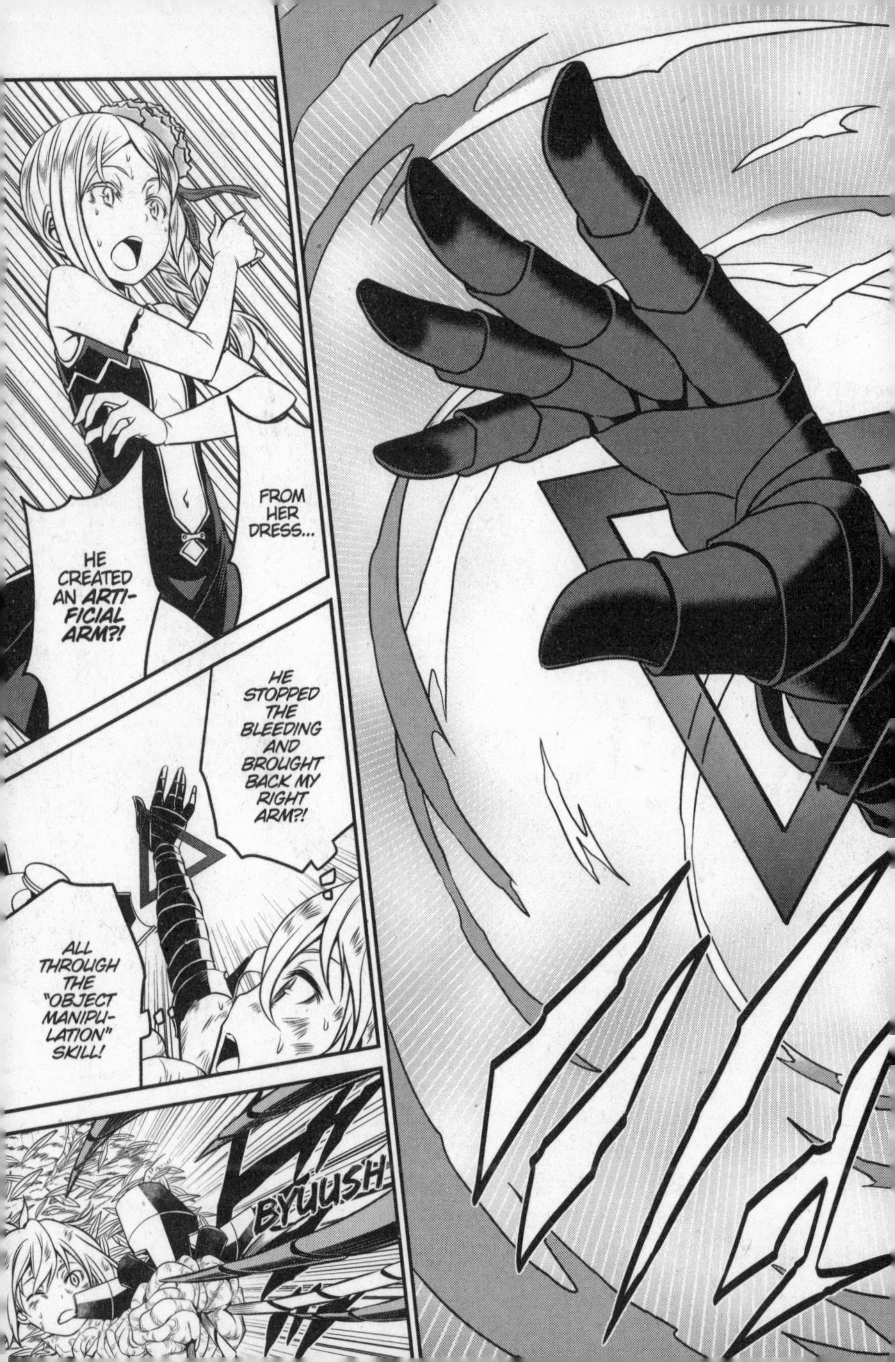
FROM HER DRESS...
HE CREATED AN ARTI-FICIAL ARM?!
HE STOPPED THE BLEEDING AND BROUGHT BACK MY RIGHT ARM?!
ALL THROUGH THE "OBJECT MANIPU-LATION" SKILL!
BYUUSH

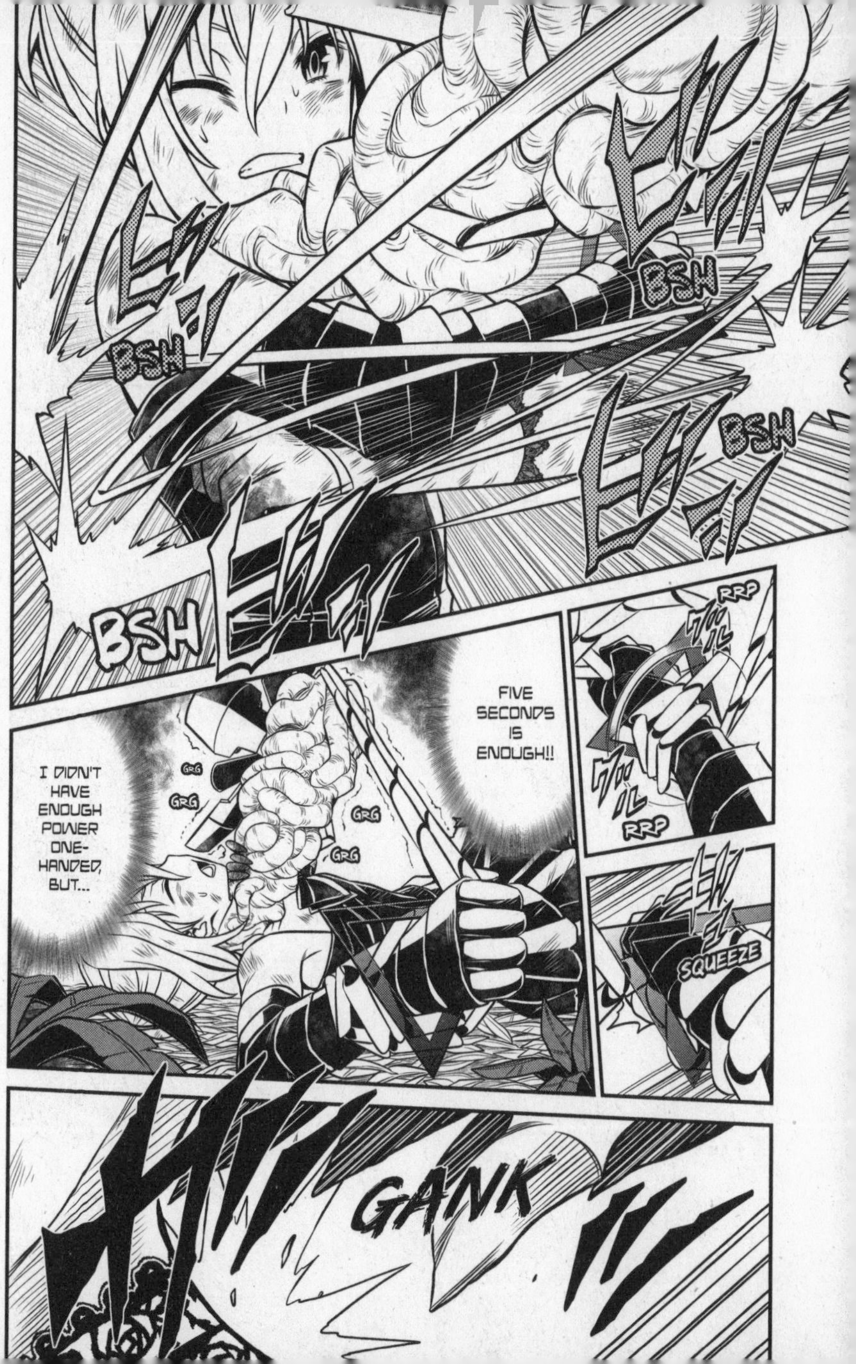
BSH
BSH
BSH
BSH
RRP
RRP
SQUEEZE
FIVE SECONDS IS ENOUGH!!
GRG
GRG
GRG
GRG
I DIDN'T HAVE ENOUGH POWER ONE-HANDED, BUT...
GANK

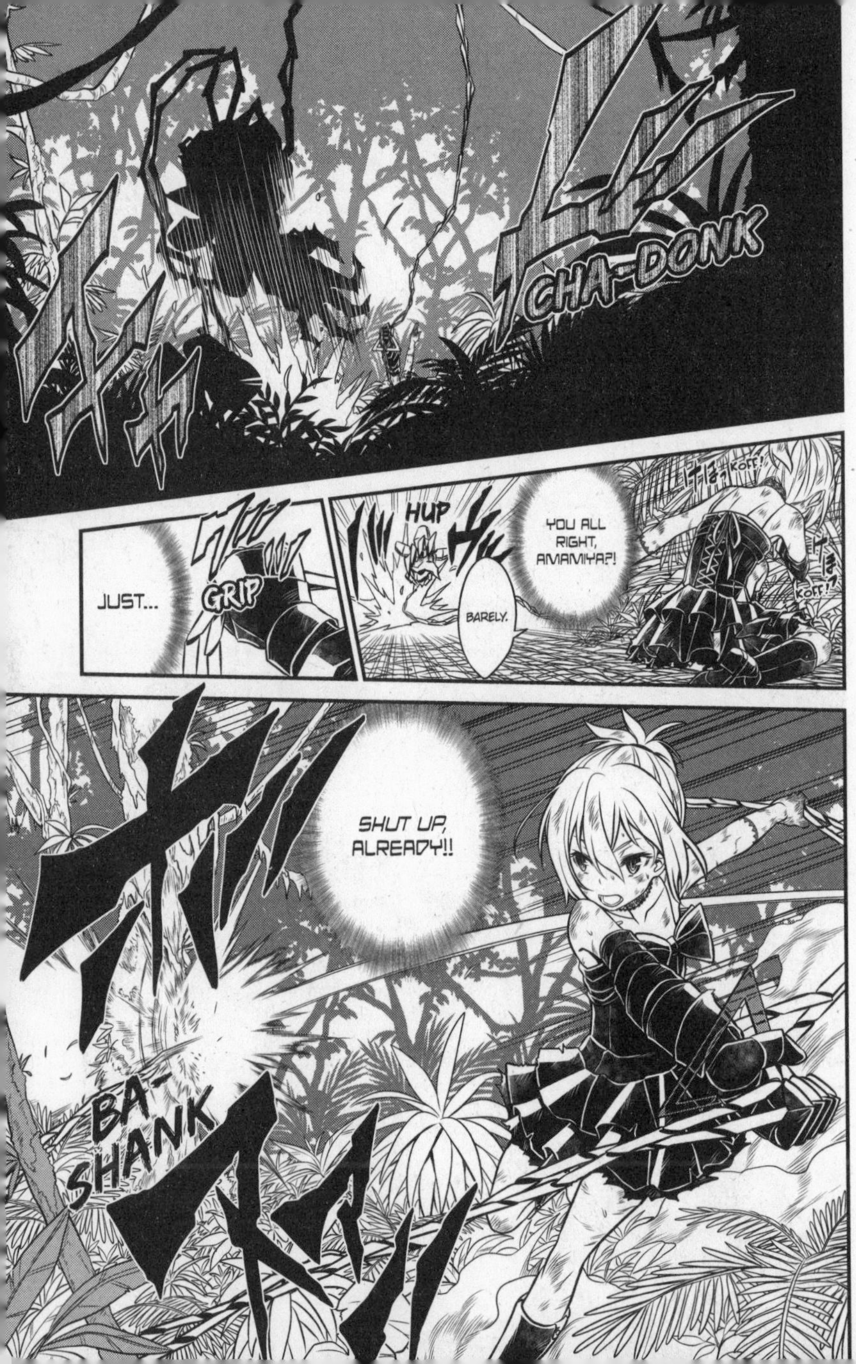
CHA-DONK
KOFF!
KOFF!?
YOU ALL RIGHT, AMAMIYA?!
HUP
BARELY.
GRIP
JUST...
SHUT UP, ALREADY!!
BA-SHANK

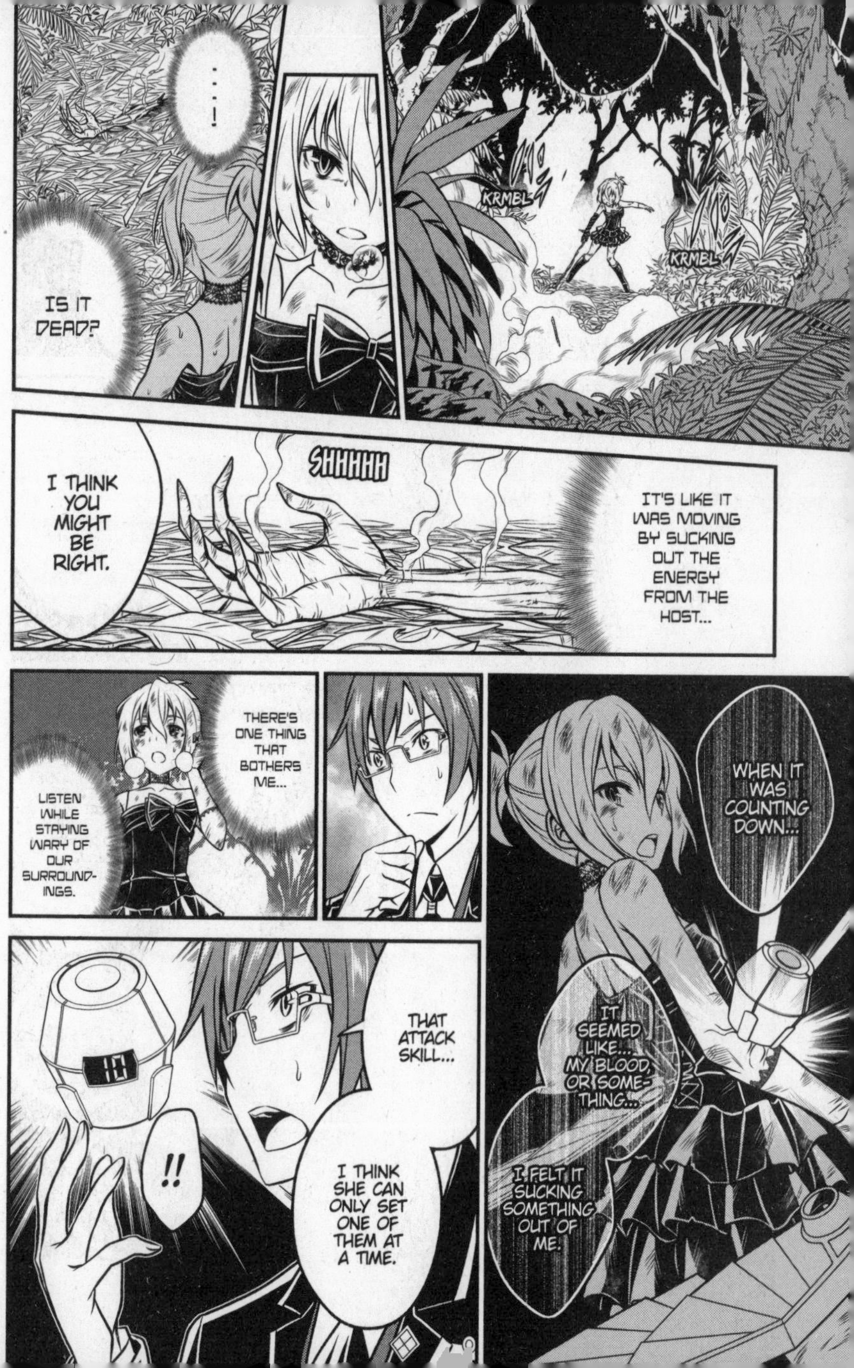
KRMBL
KRMBL
...!
IS IT DEAD?
SHHHHH
IT'S LIKE IT WAS MOVING BY SUCKING OUT THE ENERGY FROM THE HOST...
I THINK YOU MIGHT BE RIGHT.
WHEN IT WAS COUNTING DOWN...
IT SEEMED LIKE... MY BLOOD, OR SOME-THING...
I FELT IT SUCKING SOMETHING OUT OF ME.
THERE'S ONE THING THAT BOTHERS ME...
LISTEN WHILE STAYING WARY OF OUR SURROUND-INGS.
THAT ATTACK SKILL...
I THINK SHE CAN ONLY SET ONE OF THEM AT A TIME.
!!

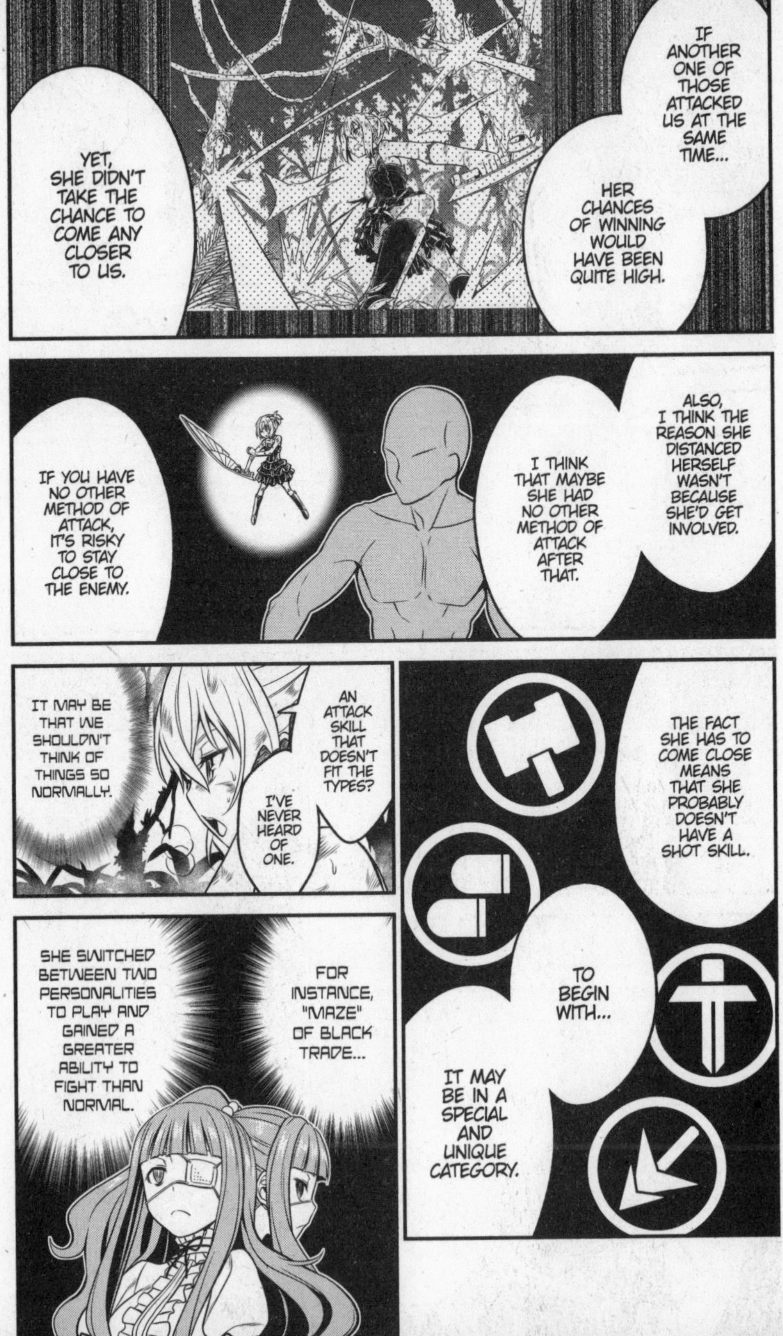
IF ANOTHER ONE OF THOSE ATTACKED US AT THE SAME TIME...
HER CHANCES OF WINNING WOULD HAVE BEEN QUITE HIGH.
YET, SHE DIDN'T TAKE THE CHANCE TO COME ANY CLOSER TO US.
ALSO, I THINK THE REASON SHE DISTANCED HERSELF WASN'T BECAUSE SHE'D GET INVOLVED.
I THINK THAT MAYBE SHE HAD NO OTHER METHOD OF ATTACK AFTER THAT.
IF YOU HAVE NO OTHER METHOD OF ATTACK, IT'S RISKY TO STAY CLOSE TO THE ENEMY.
THE FACT SHE HAS TO COME CLOSE MEANS THAT SHE PROBABLY DOESN'T HAVE A SHOT SKILL.
TO BEGIN WITH...
IT MAY BE IN A SPECIAL AND UNIQUE CATEGORY.
AN ATTACK SKILL THAT DOESN'T FIT THE TYPES?
I'VE NEVER HEARD OF ONE.
IT MAY BE THAT WE SHOULDN'T THINK OF THINGS SO NORMALLY.
FOR INSTANCE, "MAZE" OF BLACK TRADE...
SHE SWITCHED BETWEEN TWO PERSONALITIES TO PLAY AND GAINED A GREATER ABILITY TO FIGHT THAN NORMAL.

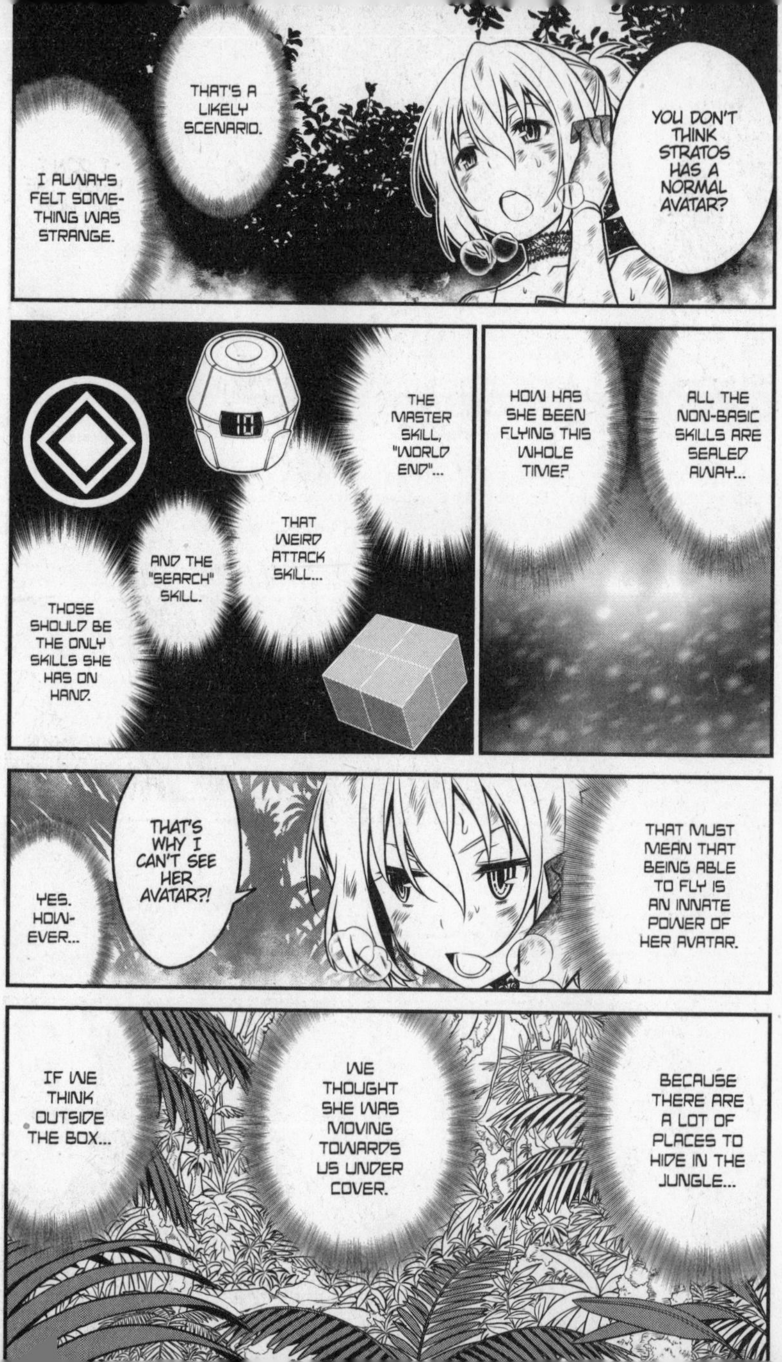
YOU DON'T THINK STRATOS HAS A NORMAL AVATAR?
THAT'S A LIKELY SCENARIO.
I ALWAYS FELT SOME-THING WAS STRANGE.
ALL THE NON-BASIC SKILLS ARE SEALED AWAY...
HOW HAS SHE BEEN FLYING THIS WHOLE TIME?
THE MASTER SKILL, "WORLD END"...
THAT WEIRD ATTACK SKILL...
AND THE "SEARCH" SKILL.
THOSE SHOULD BE THE ONLY SKILLS SHE HAS ON HAND.
THAT MUST MEAN THAT BEING ABLE TO FLY IS AN INNATE POWER OF HER AVATAR.
THAT'S WHY I CAN'T SEE HER AVATAR?!
YES. HOW-EVER...
BECAUSE THERE ARE A LOT OF PLACES TO HIDE IN THE JUNGLE...
WE THOUGHT SHE WAS MOVING TOWARDS US UNDER COVER.
IF WE THINK OUTSIDE THE BOX...

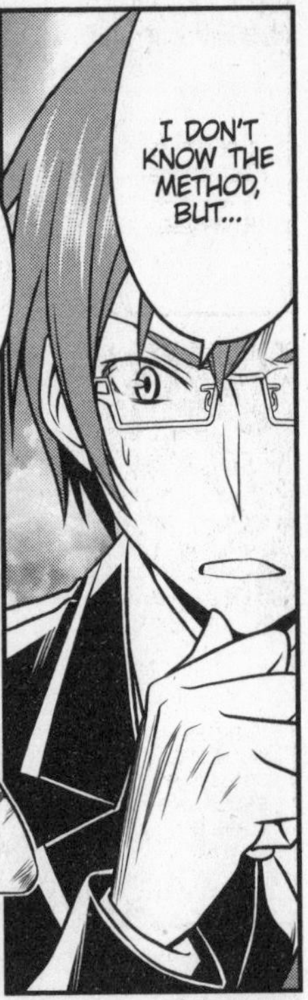
I DON'T KNOW THE METHOD, BUT...
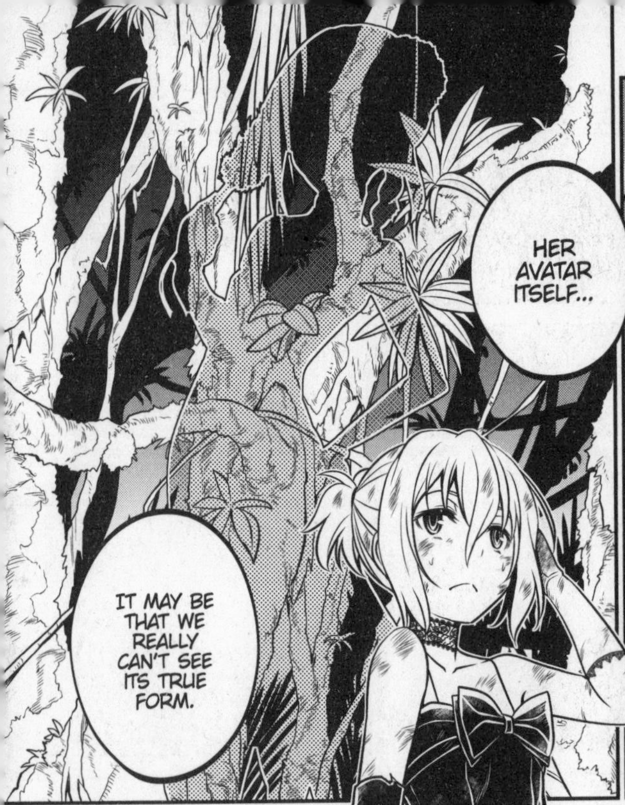
HER AVATAR ITSELF...
IT MAY BE THAT WE REALLY CAN'T SEE ITS TRUE FORM.
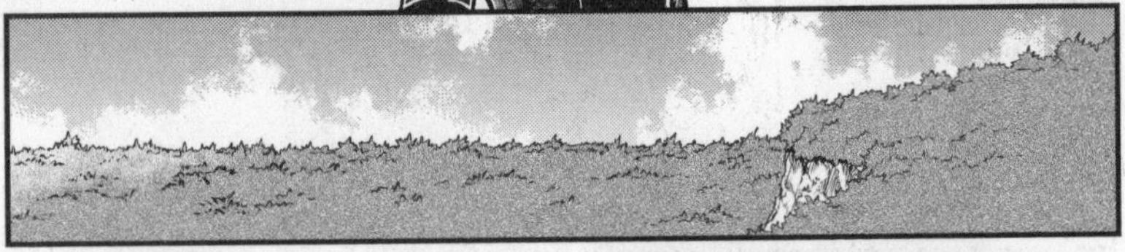
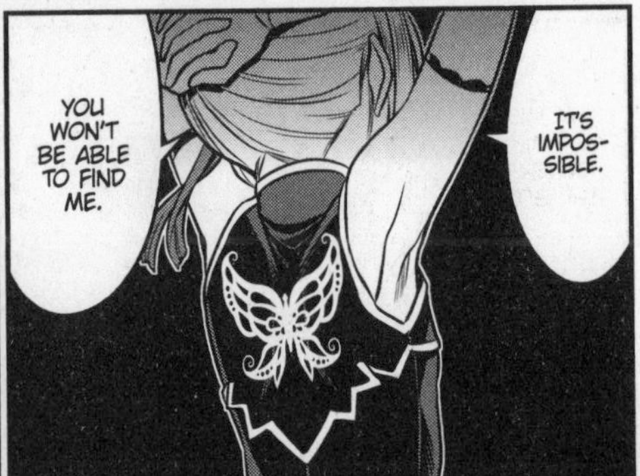
YOU WON'T BE ABLE TO FIND ME.
IT'S IMPOSSIBLE.
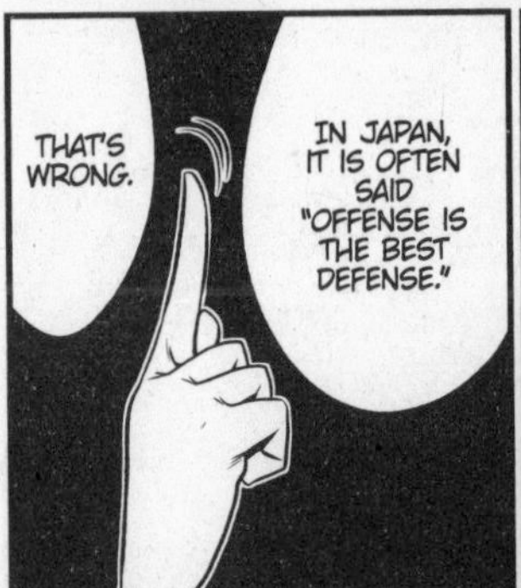
THAT'S WRONG.
IN JAPAN, IT IS OFTEN SAID "OFFENSE IS THE BEST DEFENSE."

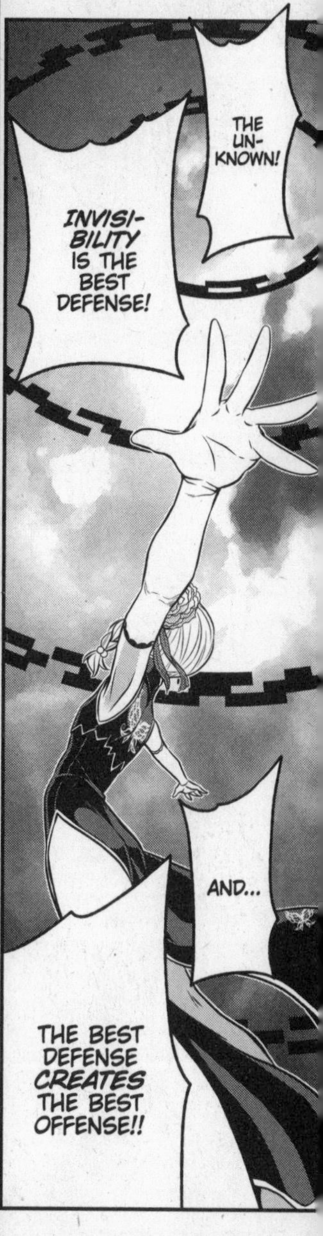
THE UN-KNOWN!
INVISI-BILITY IS THE BEST DEFENSE!
AND...
THE BEST DEFENSE *CREATES* THE BEST OFFENSE!!
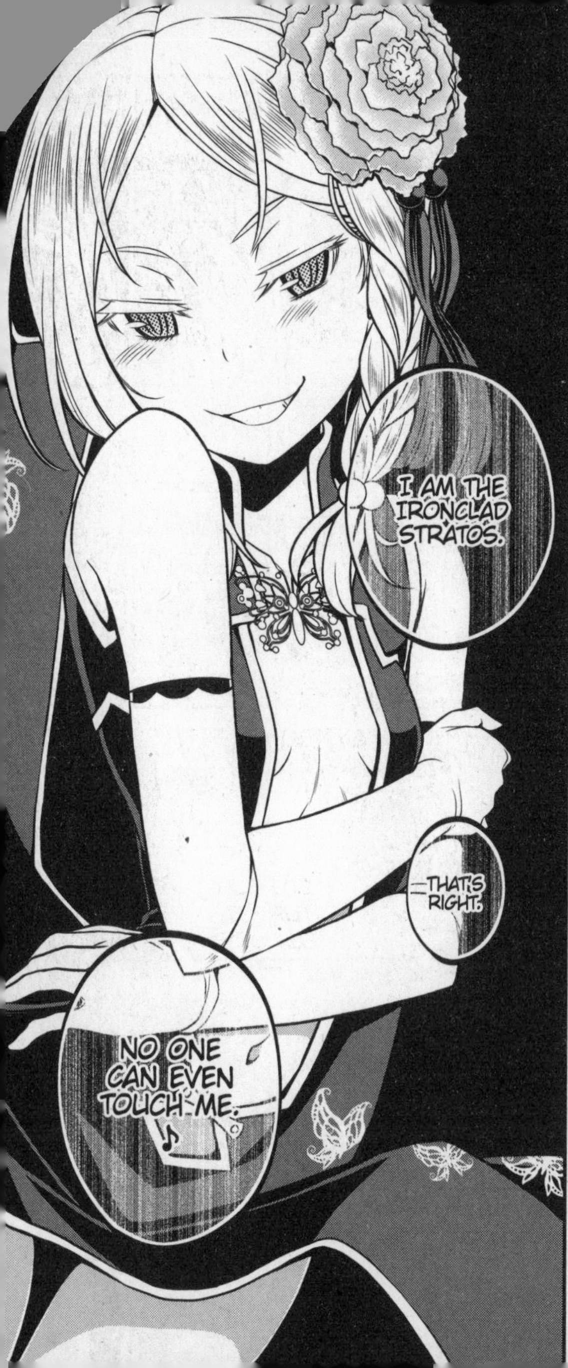
I AM THE IRONCLAD STRATOS.
—THAT'S RIGHT.
NO ONE CAN EVEN TOUCH ME. ♪

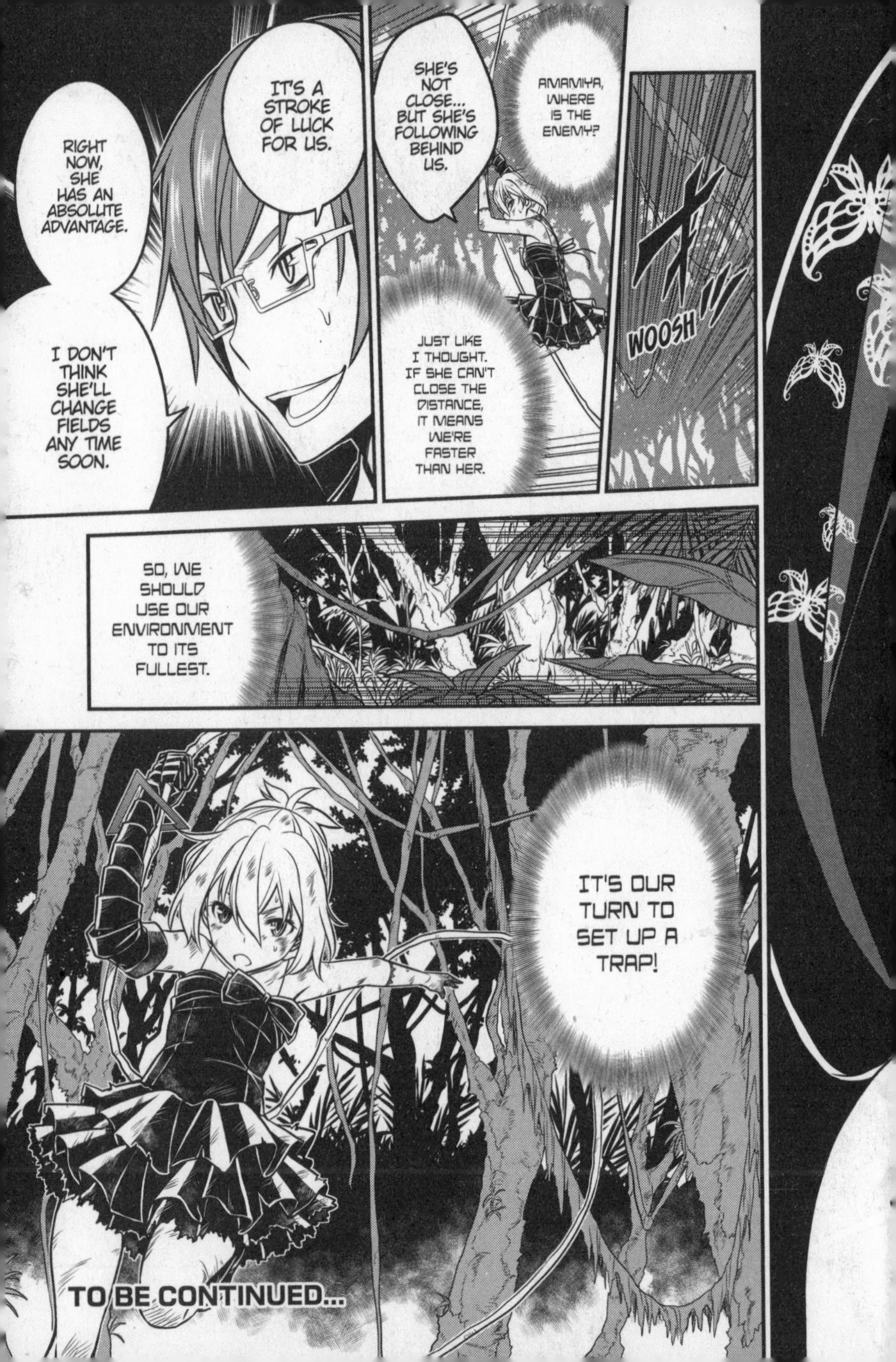
WOOSH
AMAMIYA, WHERE IS THE ENEMY?
SHE'S NOT CLOSE... BUT SHE'S FOLLOWING BEHIND US.
JUST LIKE I THOUGHT. IF SHE CAN'T CLOSE THE DISTANCE, IT MEANS WE'RE FASTER THAN HER.
IT'S A STROKE OF LUCK FOR US.
RIGHT NOW, SHE HAS AN ABSOLUTE ADVANTAGE.
I DON'T THINK SHE'LL CHANGE FIELDS ANY TIME SOON.
SO, WE SHOULD USE OUR ENVIRONMENT TO ITS FULLEST.
IT'S OUR TURN TO SET UP A TRAP!
TO BE CONTINUED...

SEVEN SEAS ENTERTAINMENT PRESENTS

NOT LIVES

story and art by **WATARU KARASUMA**   VOLUME 8

TRANSLATION
Angela Liu

ADAPTATION
Steven Golebiewski

LETTERING AND LAYOUT
James Adams

COVER DESIGN
Nicky Lim

PROOFREADER
Danielle King
Tim Roddy

ASSISTANT EDITOR
J.P. Sullivan

PRODUCTION ASSISTANT
CK Russell

PRODUCTION MANAGER
Lissa Pattillo

EDITOR-IN-CHIEF
Adam Arnold

PUBLISHER
Jason DeAngelis

NOT LIVES VOL. 8
© WATARU KARASUMA 2015
Edited by ASCII MEDIA WORKS.
First published in Japan in 2015 by KADOKAWA CORPORATION, Tokyo.
English translation rights arranged with KADOKAWA CORPORATION, Tokyo.

Seven Seas books may be purchased in bulk for educational, business, or
promotional use. For information on bulk purchases, please contact Macmillan
Corporate & Premium Sales Department at 1-800-221-7945 (ext 5442)
or write specialmarkets@macmillan.com.

Seven Seas and the Seven Seas logo are trademarks of
Seven Seas Entertainment, LLC. All rights reserved.

ISBN: 978-1-626927-25-4

Printed in Canada

First Printing: April 2018

10 9 8 7 6 5 4 3 2 1

FOLLOW US ONLINE: www.sevenseasentertainment.com

READING DIRECTIONS

This book reads from *right to left*, Japanese style.
If this is your first time reading manga, you start
reading from the top right panel on each page and
take it from there. If you get lost, just follow the
numbered diagram here. It may seem backwards at
first, but you'll get the hang of it! Have fun!!

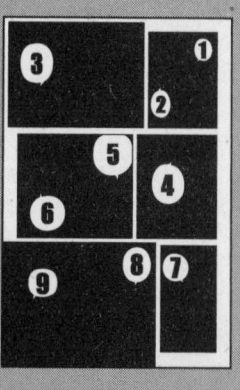